BLACK POWER AND STUDENT REBELLION

The Wadsworth Series in Sociology

General Editors:

Travis Hirschi
University of Washington

Rodney Stark
Survey Research Center
University of California, Berkeley

BLACK POWER AND STUDENT REBELLION

Edited by

James McEvoy & Abraham Miller

Department of Sociology
University of California, Davis

Wadsworth Publishing Company, Inc., Belmont, California

Acknowledgments:

Daniel Bell, "Columbia and the New Left." Reprinted by permission of the author.

Stokeley Carmichael and Charles Hamilton, "Black Power: Its Need and Substance." Chapter 2 from *Black Power*. © Copyright 1967 by Stokeley Carmichael and Charles Hamilton. Reprinted by permission of the publisher, Random House, Inc.

Richard Flacks, "The Liberated Generation: An Exploration of the Roots of Student Protest," from *Journal of Social Issues*, 1967, No. 3. Reprinted by permission of the publisher.

Todd Gitlin, "On the Line at San Francisco State," *Mayday*, February 10-17, 1969, No. 18, pp. 1-4. Copyright 1969 by the The New Weekly Project, Inc.

Nathan Hare, "The Case for Separatism," *Newsweek*, February 10, 1969, pp. 56-57. Copyright Newsweek, Inc., February 10, 1969.

Kenneth Keniston, "The Sources of Student Dissent," from *Journal of Social Issues*, 1967, No. 2. Reprinted by permission of the publisher.

Donald Matthews and James Prothro, "Negro Students and the Protest Movement," from *Negroes and the New Southern Politics* by Donald R. Matthews and James R. Prothro, copyright © 1966 by Harcourt, Brace & World, Inc., and reprinted with their permission.

C. Michael Otten's "Ruling Out Paternalism: Students and Administrators at Berkeley" is reprinted from the *American Behavioral Scientist*, Volume XI, Number 5, (May-June 1968), pages 28-33, by permission of the publisher, Sage Publications, Inc.

Roy Wilkins, "The Case Against Separatism," *Newsweek*, February 10, 1969, pp. 56-57. Copyright Newsweek, Inc., February 10, 1969.

L. C. Cat. Card No.: 70-89502
Printed in the United States of America
3 4 5 6 7 8 9 10 — 74 73 72 71 70

Preface

Recent campus demonstrations have not merely challenged the nature and purpose of academic institutions and the authority of presidents and trustees; they have been directed against the whole of American society. In the eyes of dissident students, the university is a microcosm of a society that is desperately in need of reform. Consequently, the campus is often regarded by militant students as but the first beachhead in the struggle for social conscience, in which what the students regard as the present immoral relationship between the universities and the industrial war machine would be replaced with a new relationship between academic institutions and the socially deprived.

The accuracy of these students' perceptions, the justice of their cause, and the legitimacy of their tactics are among the most serious questions of our time. Yet, these questions have received little serious, scholarly, or objective study. Instead, they have been buried in a clash of polemics and vituperative charges and counter-charges. Much of the blame for this situation must be placed on the sensationalist mass media, which find rioting and violence more newsworthy than the explanation of issues, and which favor simple labels, such as "rioters" and "silent majority," over the complexities of the real-life issues.

This book is an effort to go beyond labels and polemics. It is an attempt to provide students and teachers with material that will help them discuss, analyze, and eventually understand the conflicts which have been occurring on so many campuses in the United States during the past few years. We have included papers that intentionally represent a broad spectrum of opinion on the origins, meaning, and outcomes of student rebellion and the Black Power movement on the campus. The authors include professors, undergraduate and graduate students, radicals, conservatives, and moderates, participants and observers, scholars and pamphleteers, blacks and whites.

We hope that our readers will find the book useful both because of the diversity of opinion that is represented here and because of the empirical and analytical studies which we have included. The book will serve its purpose well if it helps make possible a reasoned and analytical approach to the highly emotional and controversial events with which it is concerned.

A number of persons have made important contributions to this volume. John Finley Scott, Bennett M. Berger, J. Merrill Shanks, and Irving Louis Horowitz have, in various ways, helped us produce a more coherent and complete book. Our publishers, Bob Gormley, Jim McDaniel, and especially Rod Stark, have helped and supported us far beyond the call of ordinary corporate duties. We are most grateful for their patience and advice. Our wives, Betty and Bonnie, helped us in many ways during the preparation of the manuscript, and Jean C. McEvoy and Barbara Dubois were most helpful in the later stages of the project.

We thank all of the authors who worked under severe pressure to meet our publication deadlines; we also thank the journals and publishers who gave us permission to reprint the articles in this book.

J. M.

A. M.

Dedication

To Betty and Bonnie

Contents

Contributors

Bill Barlow is a graduate student in history at San Francisco State College. He is a director of the San Francisco State Community Involvement Program and a political editor of *Open Process*, an "underground" S. F. State newspaper.

Daniel Bell is professor of sociology at Columbia University. Of his many publications, he is perhaps best known for *End of Ideology*.

Stokely Carmichael, active in SNCC and other civil rights groups, is a founder of the Black Power movement.

Robert Chrisman is assistant professor of English at San Francisco State College. He is vice-president of AFT Local 1352, an active member of the Black Faculty Union, and a member of the Black Studies Department at S. F. State.

Richard Flacks is assistant professor of sociology at the University of Chicago. He was active in the formation of Students for a Democratic Society.

William H. Friedland received his Ph.D. in sociology at Berkeley, taught at Stanford, and is now teaching at Cornell. He is co-author of a forthcoming book on student politics.

Todd Gitlin, former president of SDS, has worked as a community organizer in Chicago. He is co-author of *Uptown,* a book on poor whites.

Charles V. Hamilton is a professor of political science. He is the author of a number of publications, among them *Minority Politics in Black-Belt Alabama*.

Nathan Hare is associate professor of sociology at San Francisco State College and was recently removed from the position of Chairman-designate of the Black Studies Department at San Francisco State College.

S. I. Hayakawa is acting President of San Francisco State College. He is the author of *Language in Thought and Action* and a founder of the general semantics movement in the United States.

Irving Louis Horowitz is professor and chairman of the department of sociology at Rutgers University. He is editor-in-chief of

Trans – Action and author of many books, including *Three Worlds of Development.*

Kenneth Keniston   is professor of psychology at Yale University. He is the author of *The Uncommitted.*

Allan Kornberg is associate professor of political science at Duke University. He is the author of *Canadian Legislative Behavior: A Study of the Twenty-Fifth Parliament* and a contributor to many academic journals.

Donald W. Light, Jr., is a graduate student in sociology at Brandeis University and will be moving to Princeton University in the fall of 1969 as an assistant professor.

Donald Matthews is professor of political science at the University of North Carolina. He is the author of *The Social Background of Political Decision Makers.*

James McEvoy is assistant professor of sociology at the University of California, Davis, and assistant professor of political science at the University of California, Berkeley. He served as a special consultant and project director for the National Commission on the Causes and Prevention of Violence. He is the author of *Radicals or Conservatives: A Study of the American Right* and several articles on super-patriotism and conservatism.

Abraham Miller is assistant professor of sociology and assistant systems research analyst with the computer center at the University of California, Davis. He is the author of a recent article on ethnic politics and a consultant to the comparative state election project being conducted by Louis Harris and James Prothro.

C. Michael Otten is assistant professor of sociology at San Jose State College. He is the author of a forth-coming book on the history of campus authority at the University of California.

Melvin H. Posey is a graduate student in sociology at the University of California, Davis, and director of information and education of the Black Students Union at U. C. Davis.

James W. Prothro is professor of political science at the University of North Carolina. He is the author of *The Politics of American Democracy.*

Max Rafferty is Superintendent of Public Instruction in the state of California and a well-known conservative. He is the author of *Suffer, Little Children.*

Peter Shapiro is a junior in creative writing at San Francisco State College. He is an editor of *Open Process.*

Joel Smith is professor of sociology at Duke University. He is co-author of *Social Aspects of Aging* and a contributor to many academic journals.

Robert H. Somers is assistant professor of sociology at the University of California, Berkeley. He is the author of several papers on methodology and statistics, and on adolescence.

Rodney Stark is a research sociologist at the University of California, Berkeley. He is the co-author (with Charles Glock) of a number of books on religious behavior, the most recent being *American Piety.*

Roy Wilkins is Executive Director of the NAACP and a well-known leader in Negro civil rights activities.

BLACK POWER AND STUDENT REBELLION

Introduction

The demands of both black and white students, which are causing controversy and crisis on many American campuses, are specific to their particular colleges only in a minor sense. Even student moderates whom we have interviewed (for our article on San Francisco State) see the college as simply part of a larger set of coercive social institutions and agents—"the System" run by "the Establishment." Student dissatisfactions with the campus are usually expressed in terms of general disapproval of society. In their judgment, society (and their college or university) is racist, corrupt, morally bankrupt and unresponsive and rigid in dealing with the oppressed, whether they be blacks, students, or the poor. Their oppressors are not simply the dean, the college president, or the board of trustees; they include Reagan, Johnson, Nixon, the war machine, and the hordes of complacent middle-class benefactors of a politically cynical, immoral—but affluent—society.

Moreover, these students are not simply indignant, angry, frustrated, or alienated. They share a sense of extremely high political efficacy: they believe not only that they must, but that they *can* do something about the present state of affairs. At the same time, they greatly distrust the national political system.

This is a critical and volatile combination. Theoretical work by William A. Gamson and empirical evidence from Detroit and Newark ghetto rioters, collected and analyzed by Jeffery Paige, suggest that a high sense of political efficacy and low political trust, when they occur together, are major determinants of revolutionary behavior.[1] This model of revolutionary behavior does not seem to be restricted to new left or black nationalist movements alone. Research by McEvoy suggests that this same configuration of attitudes was disproportionately frequent among early supporters of Senator Goldwater in 1964—an affluent, middle to upper class, conservative, activist group.[2]

The students at San Francisco State, Columbia, Berkeley, Wisconsin, and other campuses on which dissent has recently culminated in violence and confrontation, have seen no further need to "work through channels," because campus channels are not relevant to their concerns. Action through these regular channels will not, for example, end the war in Vietnam, correct the abuses and inequalities of the welfare system, or remove racist congressmen and governors from office. Moreover, the students do not believe that by working through campus channels they will be able to restructure academic institutions to put primary emphasis on teaching, promote closer faculty and student relationships, or, ultimately, produce much change either in campus affairs or in American society.

It must be recognized that too often the channels of influence available to students within American colleges and universities have been shams.

In the years when *in loco parentis* held sway, student politics were orderly, low interest, low yield simulations of the procedures of democratic government outlined in the American government textbooks. An enforced norm of status deference, the charismatic authority of the "great teachers," the symbolic integration provided by the football team, the sacredness of the school's tradition, and, as a last resort, the strict but paternal deans with their final control over a student's access to the society's tiny elite stratum at a time when college degrees were granted largely to future elites, were sufficient to control the most difficult of the semi-socialized young primates who were visited upon the administrations and faculties of America's colleges each September.

This pattern of control began to crumble after World War II. Students were no longer exclusively drawn from homogeneous age cohorts with little sophistication. Social mobility brought to the campus students whose parents *encouraged* their radicalism. At the same time, universities and professors began to concern themselves more and more with research. Teaching began to lose its traditional status and to be replaced by research activity. Even at its best, research still took professors out of the classroom and helped to redefine teaching as an unpleasant, but necessary, duty for many research-oriented academicians.

Faculty and administrators in the postwar period were aroused by the same social concerns as the students and, provided with relatively great autonomy from the larger society, encouraged their charges—now increasingly defined as friends and co-equals—in their efforts at social reform. New status hierarchies emerged. College students found that, instead of news of the football team's practice sessions, their daily papers were reporting the political activities of their fellow students. Football players, confronted by smart boys from the Bronx or the South side, found that, in the words of a recent anti-draft poster, girls said "yes" to boys who said "no." More recently, the faculties also supported the boys who said "no"—to Bull Conner, to Wallace, to Goldwater, and then to Johnson. This was a dramatic change, a change which immeasurably increased students' sense of political efficacy. The most visible portion of the Establishment, the American college, was revealed to them as being on their side in a meaningful contest.

During this same general period (1945-1968) American Negroes were experiencing a redefinition of their status in the society. Even though the present economic and social conditions of Negro life are, of course, relatively deprived, a significant number of younger blacks developed an increasing sense of political efficacy. Matthews' and Prothro's studies of Southern Negro students (reprinted in part in this volume) show that political activism among black students was highly approved of by their black peers; they also got support from white liberal students in the North and from the white liberal community; eventually, they heard the President of the United States in his Texas drawl say, "we shall overcome."[3]

Increasingly, as the level of black dissent rose, the American college tried to ameliorate black deprivation. The principal means of this proposed amelioration was (and still is) through the admission, with special supportive training, into regular college degree programs of black students from academically deficient elementary and secondary school backgrounds. At the University of Michigan, McEvoy observed some of the effects of these efforts on the students. The effects may be summarized by saying that everything done to insure the success of these new students was also highly conducive to persuading them that the university was something unlike anything they had ever encountered before: it was responsive, it was protective, and it offered almost unlimited moral, social, and financial support. Again, under these conditions, the expectations of the black students were raised. Their sense of efficacy increased; they began to believe that they had a measure of control over their own destiny.

Until the war in Vietnam emerged, in mid-1965, as the central political issue of the nation, the coalition of faculty, administrators, blacks, and white student activists, while loose and characterized by some mutual suspicion and distrust, was fairly stable; the colleges and universities remained relatively calm. Internally directed dissent, while evident at some campuses such as Berkeley, was not yet general. Trust was high; black students and white radicals, while militant in some cases, were not yet revolutionary. By the end of 1968, however, trust (the most variable component of this attitude cluster) has, on the basis of our observations, nearly disappeared from such colleges as San Francisco State and Berkeley and, we expect, from many other campuses as well.

The change brought to the colleges by the war in Vietnam is perhaps so obvious that it needs little discussion. Viewing the war as a hideous and depraved manifestation of the values they felt were most responsible for the social problems of the sixties, student—and indeed public—opposition to the war rose at an almost linear rate. And the war, unlike the overt racism which had been the focus of student activism in the late 50s and early 60s, made its way into the campus in very tangible ways. Selective Service regulations and revocation of student deferments for dissent, military recruiting and R.O.T.C., corporate recruiting by Dow and other military suppliers, and, of course, the fact that the Pentagon has traditionally drawn upon the academic community, in some cases for assistance in strategic planning and in others for weapons, were all evidence of academic collusion in the eyes of students who opposed the war.

Like the American colonists in their response to the imposition of the Stamp Act, the students began to rebel against the colleges when the old means of obstructionism, co-optation, incrementalism, and "working through channels" were applied by college officials in their efforts to protect the "rights of the university." Of course, these "rights"—to receive war-related research funds, to supply students' grades to the Selective Service System, and to let students have "freedom of choice" in choosing an employer (even if the employer made napalm)—had to be created both to protect important professors and their research funds, with their huge overhead benefits, and to show that colleges and universities were not subversive. The McCarthy era was probably still fresh in the minds of many academic bureaucrats as they pondered the fate of a state or federally supported school openly defying the federal government by yielding to student demands on the war.

It is hardly surprising that students, whose expectations of responsiveness were at a new high, should rebel when confronted with this new (to them) posture of the college. That dissent has increased directly with the expansion of the war is also not surprising. That the level of trust of the whole society by activist students is at a new low should not seem too unusual either, when the assassinations of King and the Kennedys, the events at the Democratic National Convention, the stalling of the peace talks, and the increasing number of students being drafted, are considered. These events, and the changes in the posture of college officials, have activated a revolutionary segment of the society.

The consequences of this small-scale revolution are many and unlikely to be more than partially known for several years. One major effect in California, and perhaps in other states as well, has taken the form of punitive budgetary cuts by the Governor and the State Legislature. The budgets for the state colleges and universities in California (for 1969-70) have been reduced drastically from the amounts requested by the schools' governing bodies. The long-term effect of the cuts will be to reduce the proportion of the population that can be admitted to the colleges, and, if this continues, the colleges may once again become relatively elite institutions—poverty stricken, but exclusive.

The outcome of the present situation on American campuses will also have important consequences for black and white militants and for the movements they represent. For example, S. I. Hayakawa, the acting President of San Francisco State, while acceding to most of the students' demands, has not entirely capitulated and has used increasing police force to control the dissidents. The students' response, so far, has been continued disruption. If this pattern persists, and the administration yields to all the immediate demands, the militants will have won a point tremendously more important than any of the 15 demands sought by them at San Francisco State. This point might be stated as the belief that they can confront the Establishment with persistent disorder and "win," or at least win a series of limited objectives.

Unfortunately, while at one level dissident students may be objectively justified in believing this, and therefore continue and expand the use of these tactics, it is clear that at other levels the use of force by student militants is generating an immensely hostile public response which may well result in the election of public officials committed to the repression of dissent of all types.

If this occurs we look forward (unhappily) to a crisis in the universities and colleges which inevitably will result in the loss of academic freedom, of political autonomy, and even, perhaps, of the constitutional rights of students and faculty in state-controlled institutions of higher education.

This is a brief sketch of the problem and of some possible versions of the future. But, it is obvious that student protest is subject to rapid transformations. The outbreak of demonstrations at Berkeley in 1964 caught both that campus and the nation by surprise. The pattern of this protest, directed at campus rules, was soon repeated on many other campuses and stimulated a number of studies of student protest. However, no one viewing the future from that point in time could foresee Columbia in the Spring of 1968 and the emergence of a new wave of student revolutionaries. Similarly, in the wake of Columbia-like campus outbursts there was little recognition that only a few months later the whole picture would change again, that white revolutionary and radical leadership would give way to that of black and Third World students, and that, consequently, student protest would return to reformist, rather than revolutionary, aims (if not to nonviolent tactics).

Because events have moved so fast, no single definitive account or explanation can be attempted, let alone achieved. Yet, our need to understand is urgent. For this reason we have tried to make available the best of expert opinion and serious analysis of the latest form of campus protest: the merger of black power and student rebellion. This volume is perhaps best characterized as an interim report which presents the best judgments of authors working under the urgency of shifting events. With the luxury of hindsight and the leisure for long reflection, future scholars will probably be able to clarify much that remains murky and contradictory now. But now is when we most need to know. Now is when it's happening. And now is when decisions will be made and actions taken which will shape the future of our society.

The authors of these articles often disagree, both on matters of fact and interpretation. It could hardly be otherwise. Still, on many critical questions there is a unity of findings and predictions in these studies which strongly suggests that there are some basic facts and processes known about student disorders which transcend personal convictions or political commitments. These findings are especially important because they are contrary to popular opinion. Most Americans believe (according to the Gallup Poll) that swift and vigorous use of the police and of strict disciplinary measures is an effective way of dealing with campus protests. But most of the experts, whether or not they support student aims, find that the evidence is to the contrary. Most Americans think student protestors are not serious students, but academic misfits. The evidence is that they are the best students. These two facts alone call into question much of what has been said and done about student protest—a theme around which many of these authors raise serious questions and make provocative suggestions.

Regardless of whether these authors agree or disagree on particular points, their articles present what we think are expert judgments on the origins, meaning, and causes of campus disorder. In addition to expert interpretation, we have tried to include a representative sampling of the spectrum of opinion and aims of the major actors in this crisis, from student militants, both black and white, to academic and political administrators. There is little agreement among them. And that, of course, is why there is a crisis.

It is the mark of the well-edited book of readings that the editors provide lengthy introductions to various sections in which they try to resolve contradictions among various contributors and synthesize the materials into an inclusive conceptual framework. We have not done this because we do not pretend to fully understand current student dissent. Of necessity, we have limited our introductions to some general guidelines for the reader. Neither the editors nor the contributors can offer a complete interpretation. Indeed, some readers may finish knowing less than they thought they did at the start. In our judgment, informed ignorance is preferable to false "understanding."

The volume is divided into three major sections: The Scene, The Spokesmen, and The Sources. The first contains a series of intensive, analytic case studies of recent student rebellions and protests at major campuses across the nation. The second is made up of a series of position papers by such active participants as S. I. Hayakawa, acting President of San Francisco State, and Nathan Hare, a black sociologist who led the strike at S. F. State. Also included are papers by Max Rafferty, Roy Wilkins, Stokeley Carmichael and Charles V. Hamilton, and Todd Gitlin, among others. The third section seeks the roots of campus protests. It examines the participants, the institutional arrangements of universities which lead to protest, and the development of the coalition between black and white student dissidents.

Footnotes

[1]William A. Gamson, *Power and Discontent* (Homewood, Illinois: Dorsey Press, 1968). See especially Chapter 3, pp. 39-58, and Chapter 8, pp. 163-184. See also Jeffrey M. Paige, *Collective Violence and the Culture of Subordination: A Study of Participants in the July 1967 Riots in Newark, New Jersey and Detroit, Michigan*, unpublished doctoral dissertation (Ann Arbor, Michigan: University of Michigan, 1968).

[2]James McEvoy, *Radicals or Conservatives: A Study of the Contemporary American Right* (Chicago: Rand McNally, 1968).

[3]Donald R. Matthews and James W. Prothro, *Negroes and the New Southern Politics* (New York: Harcourt, Brace and World, Inc., 1966), Chapters 14 and 15, pp. 407 ff.

One

The Scene

Analytic Case Studies of
Campus Disorders

Until very recently, student concern with social ills was directed against institutions outside the university. During the early 1960s, students invested their energies in civil rights organizations and made the long journey to a hostile and unfamiliar setting to do witness for their beliefs. If anything, the universities and colleges were benevolent and supportive havens which sanctioned and recognized students' organizations, supplied facilities for meetings, and often served as training and staging areas for the perilous journey south. A common bond of shared ideology between faculty and students on the race problem—which was then seen as mainly a Southern problem—provided additional support for student faith in the university and in what it represented. When demonstrations broke out at Berkeley in 1964 demanding unfettered political expression, the issue involved was a freedom inherent in the conception of academic institutions. Thus, it was a fulfillment of the traditional conception of the nature of the university that was being sought. The basic structure, the role, and the function of the university was not challenged.

But, since 1964, changes have occurred which challenge the relatively high esteem in which students have held the university. The idealism which led middle class white students south was not enough to sustain them through the harassment by local whites and the distrust and humiliation that they sometimes encountered in Southern black communities. White students also became increasingly aware of their own unrecognized prejudice and stereotypical perceptions of black people. Blacks had anticipatory responses to white students based on stereotyped notions of racial differences. Skin color, for both blacks and whites, became a prime determinant of human relations. Distrust became a common sentiment, and under these stressful conditions normal human interaction failed dismally to overcome the color barrier. The ideology of black power sometimes led to the expulsion of whites from civil rights organizations. Idealistic youths felt that they had no outlet for the concern and unexpiated guilt they felt as a result of the nation's continuing repression of blacks. They could find no mission for their almost messianic fervor.

Simultaneously, the war in Vietnam escalated. Resistance to the war and the draft and the abhorrence at the university's complicity with the Selective Service System and Defense Department opened a new channel for the expression of the messianic fervor thwarted within the civil rights movement. The university no longer was viewed as an institution apart from the rest of society. Student militants revised the view of the university as a benevolent oasis of reason in an unreasonable society. A sick society had produced a sick university, and the university, because of its relationship to the rest of society, could be used as a vehicle for moral change.

Militant-led demonstrations no longer sought an expansion of freedom within the existing structure of the university. Rather, the nature and function of the university itself were called into question; demonstrations focused on changing the role of the university from an institution of learning to an institution with a moral and socially conscious purpose. But, to the militants, the nature of the university did not change—only its clients. In their judgment the "traditional role" of the university was a fiction. No such institution ever existed. Instead, they see that the university is the procurer and molder of material for "the system" and, at the moment, for the degenerate industrial war machine. The militants would not change this procurement function of the university; they would change only the benefactors of such procurement. Instead of molding youths to take their places in American business, the university, if changed according to militant ideas, would direct and mold youth to lead minority communities and to mount radical social reforms.

In order to transform the university, the militants must bring into question the very nature and function of the university and must effectively demonstrate to an incredulous mass public that the militants' version of the university's role is accurate, once the fog created by public relations is dispersed. To the militants, the university is a microcosm of the larger society. The degenerate, militaristic, and racist society, so the militants argue, has produced an educational institution that necessarily pursues racist and militaristic policies.

This emphasis on redefinition of the university has often deteriorated into a battle in which the university is contested property. Thus, McEvoy and Miller note, in their paper on San Francisco State, that the "representatives" of the ghetto community made strong appeals before a crowd of black militants and concerned white middle class students, stating that San Francisco State was *their* school and they wanted *their* school to have a curriculum suitable to the educational aspirations of *their* children. Before redefinition of purpose must come transfer of title, and the residents of the black community came to the campus to put forth their claim—recalling a similar situation in New York's Ocean Hill-Brownsville.

The challenge to traditional campus authority is founded on a visionary perception of the university. The dissident student vision seems to be as common at Duke University, in Durham, North Carolina, as at Berkeley, San Francisco State, and Columbia.

The similarity of different campus conflicts is more than just a similarity in underlying perceptions of the linkage between the university and the larger society. The tactics and style of revolt are similar. As Light notes in his article on nonviolence, as Bell observes at Columbia, as McEvoy and Miller report from San Francisco State, and as Stark concludes from the events at Berkeley, students rely heavily on directed resistance. The goal of directed resistance is to provoke the enemy (the administration) to escalate the conflict in the hope that such escalation will win sympathy for the student dissidents.

As the papers in this section suggest, if the dissidents can raise enough havoc to force the administration to bring police on campus in large numbers, the mere presence of police will resurrect a dying cause into a mass movement. McEvoy and Miller observe that at Berkeley and San Francisco State the police have also learned the stratagem of the politics of confrontation. Before the police are used in large numbers, the militants must escalate the confrontation to a point that will result in their own discreditation in the community, even though support could still be garnered on campus. The latest California Poll indicates that the militants have so strongly discredited themselves in the eyes of the community that they have ceded to the campus administration and the governor's office the right to define the situation to the public. One of the basic objectives of directed resistance, as Light notes, is the power to define the situation. But what the militants have overlooked is that directed resistance can only function in this fashion if it is nonviolent.

Another critical aspect of recent student movements, which seems to be virtually universal, is the difference in aims and tactics between black and white student protestors. From San Francisco State to Duke, blacks tend both to be more tactically militant and less concerned with abstract questions of political philosophy than are whites. Black demands are tangible. They require tangible and immediate responses. Blacks care deeply about the specific demands they raise, whereas, for white radicals, demands are often "merely" issues. On the other hand, blacks are casual about tactical questions which agonize white radicals. Perhaps the violence of the ghetto streets makes blacks relatively casual about violence as a means for gaining a response. Whatever the case, as Melvin Posey argues in a later section, nonviolence as a tactical commitment of the black community died with Martin Luther King.

In the following section these themes, and others, are developed within the specific context of student movements from San Francisco State to Duke, from Brandeis to Berkeley. Despite geographical and institutional differences, significant similarities run through these episodes like a continuous filament through a seemingly varied brocade.

San Francisco State

"On Strike... Shut It Down"

James Mc Evoy and Abraham Miller

On Monday, December 2, we traveled from the placid setting of the Davis Campus of the University of California to San Francisco State College, where student strikers and the administration had been battling for control of the campus for over a month. Our intention in undertaking this trip was to interview (and record the opinions of) students and faculty about the disorders there and to try to get some sense of the reasons for the intense level of conflict which was occurring on a campus marked, only a few years ago, by a generally pragmatic student body with only a handful of radicals. Furthermore, the new acting President S. I. Hayakawa's introduction of a "hard-line" policy on the student demonstrations and strike would, we thought, give us a chance to evaluate the success of authoritarian methods of dealing with dissident students.

Under the circumstances, it was impossible for us to collect our data from State with anything like systematic sampling methods. Accordingly, we simply interviewed about 100 students and faculty we selected by their access, responses to speakers, physical location, and participation in various demonstrating groups. It was our intention to contact as many students and faculty as possible while at the same time trying to include as wide a range of opinion and attitude as we could. We tape recorded each interview and undertook an exhaustive analysis of the protocols. These are the data upon which this analysis is based.

We begin our discussion of the strike at San Francisco State with an account of the activities on the campus which we observed during the two days we conducted our interviews. What we saw was fairly representative of the pattern of confrontations which occurred on the campus at State during much of December and January.

During this period, the AFT faculty members struck, with San Francisco Labor Council approval, over the working conditions at the college. The settlement of that strike at State on March 1 and the simultaneous, rapidly escalating conflict between students, the police, and the administration at Berkeley, over a set of almost identical issues, are the events which surround the writing of this paper. Although it is too early to make any definite statement, we believe that support for the student strikes at State and Berkeley is now diminishing and that, as a result, violence, in the form of arson, bombing, and the like, will probably increase on both campuses. This is likely to happen, we believe, in spite of the unprecedented use of police, the California Highway Patrol, and the National Guard at Berkeley (where Ronald Reagan declared a state of emergency and took direct control of the police from the administration).

We complete our discussion of the conflict at State with a consideration of a number of underlying issues which we believe are important components of the basis of the conflict. Of primary importance to our discussion is our observation that the administration at State has almost no legitimacy among even the moderate students we interviewed; we discuss, at some length, the role that the Governor and the Trustees have had in undermining the authority of the school's administrators. We see this as the central problem of the strike.

We then discuss the role of the police in the crisis, the reaction of white militants to the black students' demands, the role of the community in the strike, and, finally, the students' conceptions of the nature and importance of the press and public opinion. Our introduction to this volume makes several suggestions concerning the causes of the revolutionary behavior of students in the United States at this period of time. The introduction should be considered generally applicable to the events and actors at State and should be consulted for a better understanding of the events which have occurred there during the past year.

Late in 1967, severe disruption of State's campus occurred. Members of the Black Students Union, enraged at what they felt were racist implications in an article published in the Daily *Gater* (the school's paper), invaded the editorial offices and assaulted the editors. One of these invaders was George Murray, whose suspension (on the direct orders of Chancellor Glenn Dumke) after a controversial black power speech in November, precipitated the present conflict at State. At the time of the *Gater* invasion, John Summerskill, who was then president of State, faced a situation in which left-liberal support for the BSU's actions was strong enough to mount a sizeable demonstration in their favor. Marching to the administration building on December 6, 1967, students and at least one faculty member broke into the building; other buildings were also attacked. Summerskill closed the campus in the midst of the Trustees' calls for police to restore order.

By the end of the third week in February, Summerskill's authority was shaky at best. Faced both with increasingly hostile and violent incidents on the campus and more and more pressure from the Trustees, he chose a course which satisfied neither side. On February 22, he offered his resignation, effective the following September. By the end of May, however, Glenn Dumke, the Chancellor of the State College system, and the conservative Trustees were enraged at the continuing disorders; on May 24, Summerskill therefore resigned, in the belief that if he did not he would be fired. He had not taken a hard enough line.

His successor, Robert Smith, fared little better. Although the level of campus disruption had declined, Smith still faced a Board of Trustees, now openly led by Reagan, which was determined to clamp down on radicals at any cost. The clamp-down came when Reagan was informed that George Murray, the recently appointed Minister of Education of the Black Panthers, had not only been hired as an instructor in the English Department, but had given a speech advocating that minority students arm themselves for self-protection. Prior to that point, on September 26, Dumke "requested" that Smith transfer Murray to a non-teaching job. Smith demurred. A month later (after the speech in which Murray advocated arming for self-protection), on October 31, Dumke ordered the suspension of Murray both as student and instructor; on November 1, Smith complied. Within a week the campus was in serious disorder. A strike was called by the BSU and by various white radical groups. Within two weeks, the campus had been closed on the orders of the new acting President, S. I. Hayakawa, who replaced Smith on November 26. Smith found, as had his predecessor Summerskill, that the Trustees simply would not let him make the decisions.

They had ordered Murray suspended against Smith's wishes and had insisted on keeping the campus open in the face of Smith's desire to close it.

On December 2, the morning we arrived on campus, we were greeted by a student representing the Committee for an Academic Environment, an ad hoc student group committed to keeping the campus open. He was dispensing blue ribbons to be worn as armbands by students supporting the new president's decision to open the campus (with police force, if necessary). He told us that he thought people had a right to strike but that others, like himself, "had a right to learn." He also stated that students like himself had no objection to most of the demands (a series of 15 conditions for discontinuing the strike put forward by the BSU, including the establishment of a "Black Studies" Department and the reinstatement of Murray) of the strikers; his primary objection was to the tactics of the strike. His opinions on this point were, as far as we could tell, representative. Most of the students we talked with also supported these demands, but we found that many, while disturbed and angry about the strikers' tactics, believed that they were justified or inevitable in the face of what they perceived as unnecessarily authoritarian controls imposed on the administration, faculty, and students by Dumke, Reagan, and the Trustees. Characteristically, students saw the State officials as unresponsive to their needs or desires, as rigid and uncompromising with regard to the issues at the college.

We questioned this student, and many others, about the tactics of the strikers and found, as might be expected, that the reports in the local press of classroom violence and intimidation, while not simply fantasies, were hardly congruent with the experiences of most students whose classes were disrupted. Typically, in the first stage of the strike (about November 6-15), members of the "Strike Committee" (a white radical umbrella group including SDS, Experimental College Students, Peace & Freedom Party members, etc.) or the BSU would knock on the door of a classroom and request that they be given "five minutes" to present their position to the students. Usually they were admitted after a vote of the class and were allowed to give their side of the issues. This was, we found, the modal experience of the non-striking students we talked with who had been in a class entered by the Strike Committee. However, as an active member of the committee told us, ". . . we simply asked for five or ten minutes to discuss . . . most of the time . . . we were allowed to speak. A couple of times they went on longer, took up the whole period. Occasionally, though, fist fights did break out in classes . . . then, later the tactics were changed. After the convocation (a meeting to discuss the BSU demands) broke down for the first time, it was the policy of all the groups . . . to, simply, go into classes and try to dismiss the classes. Then, naturally, (more) fist fights occurred. Individual encounters set the tone for the violence."* Probably more classes would have been disrupted in this way had not President Smith closed the campus on November 13.

Much of our morning's discussion centered on Hayakawa's probable future and on whether or not students felt that he could resolve the problems at State. In line with a general refusal to assign legitimate authority to Hayakawa (which we discuss later in the essay), most of the students we encountered did not see him as an effective crisis manager. One student said, "The Trustees will use him [Hayakawa] as long as they can and then get somebody else, it really doesn't matter." The crisis, most students felt, was not going to be resolved—at least not from their side of it. Generally supporting the demands of the BSU, most white students believed that there would be no compromise, that the crises would continue, that police would remain on campus, and that Hayakawa only shortened the fuse on an already explosive situation.

On Monday the pattern of activity for the next two months was established; major changes took place in the size of the crowds and in the number of police brought in to control them. Beginning at noon, an "illegal" rally (under Section III of the "Declaration of Emergency" issued by Hayakawa that morning) began on the speakers' platform, an area in the middle of the large quadrangle around which the campus buildings are spaced. About 500 people assembled at first, but gradually their numbers increased to at least 2000. The speeches on this first day were highly emotional and slightly incoherent. Allusions to First-Amendment freedoms were mixed with the moral imperatives of the Nuremburg judgment by various black and white militants. In their view, the strikers represented absolute good; the non-strikers, the President, Reagan, Rafferty, the Trustees, and the Establishment represented absolute evil. The implications of the militants' speeches were nicely symbolized by a poster tacked on a nearby bulletin board in which babyfat lettering of a line from the Beatles song "Back in the USSR" was used to produce an outline map of the United States: "Back in the US . . . back in the US . . . back in the USSR."

At approximately 1:30, the crowd of about 500 hard-core supporters moved across the quad to the administration building and were addressed from its steps by BSU members, including Murray, and by members of the Third World Liberation Front. They screamed for an appearance by Hayakawa. This call went un-

*(Other instances of student violence occurring at this time included five bombings of classrooms, attacks on non-striking students outside classrooms, and widespread window breaking. College officials were also threatened and one had a bomb explode in his driveway.)

answered, and a move developed to occupy the building. At this point the San Francisco Police Department's Tactical Squad was summoned from seclusion on a nearby street. The Tac Squad (we were observing from the roof of the Administration Building), marching in formation, occupied the lobby of the building. The students retreated from the doors. After about twenty minutes of additional speechmaking by BSU leaders, the Tac Squad withdrew.

Within a few minutes the militant portion of the crowd grew intensely hostile; shouting again began, and six or eight bricks, some hidden in lunch bags, were thrown at or through the windows. The squad returned and the strikers, now numbering about 400, moved to a classroom building to disrupt classes by making noise outside. The police inside prevented their entry. The Tac Squad moved into the area in front of the building; the strikers scattered but returned to pelt the police with broken flower pots, rocks, and sod, and then moved on to another building to repeat the performance. Within fifteen minutes about 250 additional policemen were on the commons, and by 3:00 the strikers had been dispersed across 19th Avenue. We did not observe a single instance of police violence' during this series of incidents.

This same general series of events occurred on Tuesday, with the difference that this time the police were violent—chasing students into the cafeteria and indiscriminately beating some innocent bystanders. By Wednesday the force of police had grown to nearly a thousand. After a rally in which "members of the community" spoke for over an hour, a march of student strikers, now numbering about 1500, was dispersed simply by the presence of corps after corps of police, who assembled in a line six deep stretching across the entire Commons and who were directed from two helicopters flying overhead with spotters aboard.

We returned to State on Wednesday, partly to get more information and partly to assess the effects of the police violence the day before. Student after student told us they felt the police were only "making things worse." At noon, instead of the 300-500 hard-core supporters of the strike present on Monday, there were, as we said, closer to 1500. Evidently, the students were correct.

The speeches at the rally which preceded the march were especially interesting to us, in view of the role that many persons have assigned to the spill-over of various minority groups in San Francisco into the present crisis. Much of what was said at this rally, by "members of the black community," Orientals, Mexicans, Filipinos, a State Legislator, representatives of CORE, Urban League members, and self-styled black moderates will sound very familiar to those who have followed the recent school crises in New York. "This is our school and these [the students and BSU members] are our kids and we are not going to let Reagan or Hayakawa tell us how to run our school," said one nearly hysterical speaker. To this speaker, and to the hundreds who applauded her, the college had evidently become contested personal property.

Again, the parallels between the position of this speaker and that of the Trustees and Reagan should be made explicit. Representing what one student termed the "divine right of taxpayers," the Governor and the Trustees have, from the point of view of the dissidents, systematically undermined the authority of the previous administrations at State in their efforts to run *their* campus in *their* own way. Presumably they were also acting as instructed delegates for the legions of outraged citizens who, as taxpayers, are defined as entitled to *their* say about how *their* campus is run. The concept of autonomous educational institutions is no longer even mentioned in the debates which surround the situation at State.

The Underlying Issues

The events immediately precipitating the crisis are well known, although, as we have noted, somewhat distorted in the popular media. Some portion of almost every daily television newscast in and around the Bay Area was devoted to the latest incidents at San Francisco State. The details of the almost-daily encounter between police and students, from December 2 to the premature dismissal of classes for the holidays on December 13, made front page news in almost every Northern California daily. While the public was saturated with detail, description, and moving pictures of confrontations, broken glass, and bloodied heads, comparatively little was done in the early days of the strike to acquaint the public with the full dimensions of the issues at San Francisco State.

However, as the strike continued, press coverage, particularly in the *Chronicle* and on KPFA (an educational radio station), began to provide extended analyses of the situation without overt editorializing. Indeed, we noticed that as the crisis developed, the press began to serve the role that one might hope it would through its analytical presentation of the issues, its documentation of assertions by participants concerning police behavior, and its printing of accounts of the development of the crisis at State. Up to the time of this writing, press coverage has been thorough and reasonably fair, although at the time of our interviews the students responded negatively to what was then somewhat biased coverage.

As we have noted, the crisis was precipitated by the suspension of George Murray. Fully aware that Murray's suspension without a hearing would provide a catalyst for bringing both black militants and white liberals together in opposition to the administration, S.F. State President Robert Smith attempted to forestall any action against Murray until the normal academic procedural mechanisms could be implemented. Hardly prepared to indulge Murray with procedural formalities, Chancellor Dumke and the Trustees decided to intervene directly. Smith was ordered summarily to suspend Murray.

Murray has gone on record saying that he himself is not an issue. The issue to most students and faculty, partly represented by Murray's case, is what they see as continual and arbitrary misuse of power by the Chancellor and the Trustees. As one instructor told us, "The students are responding with physical violence to the ideological violence of a capricious authority that has no concern for fundamental liberties or basic human rights."

The hasty suspension of Murray stood out in clear contrast to the lethargic response of the Trustees to the requests of black and other minority students over the past three years. Murray's suspension crystallized support for a set of issues as yet unresponded to by the Trustees. Student and faculty dissidents not only demanded Murray's reinstatement but resurrected long-standing grievances as worthy of equal and immediate attention.

In an era when the academic community has been responsive to the educational demands of a broad and sometimes questionable clientele, resulting in the development of training programs for policemen, the granting of Ph.Ds in the field of mobile homes, and the creation of weapons for warfare, the black militants view the refusal of S.F. State's administrators to respond to their needs as a further extension of pervasive white racism.

Even the majority of students we interviewed from the Committee for an Academic Environment (the group supporting the "get tough" policies of interim President Hayakawa) felt that the Trustees had brought the crisis upon themselves by their refusal to consider student demands that had been brought repeatedly to their attention over the past three years. The CAE members, however, felt that no demand or set of demands was important enough to bring about the closing of the school; here lay their fundamental difference with the strikers.

Hayakawa himself gave public notice on several occasions that the demands were justified and shortly acceded to most of them, including the formation of a "Black Studies" program and the appointment of Professor Nathan Hare as its head, with power equal to that of any other department chairman. (Hare, however, was, in effect, fired when he was notified early in March that he would not be granted an appointment for the academic year 1969–70. This action was taken by Hayakawa after Hare and other black faculty and students disrupted Hayakawa's welcoming speech to the State faculty at the opening of the Spring semester.) Although the veracity of Hayakawa's public statements was questioned, one black faculty member informed us that many of the blacks believed in Hayakawa's sincerity but felt that his sentiments, like those of his pre-decessors, were worthless, because the role he had been called upon to play was simply one of a puppet. With Reagan and Rafferty pulling the strings, he said, the blacks felt there was little value in the public pronouncements of the "Governor's marionette."

Some of the issues at State mentioned by our respondents were: the preservation of accepted procedures of due process, the right of political dissent, academic freedom, the right of the students to have a voice in their education, and the continued intrusion of the Chancellor and the Trustees into affairs that, they felt, were in the jurisdiction of the campus administration. Students and faculty of almost all shades of opinion, including a substantial majority of the CAE members we interviewed, saw these issues as the underlying causes of the current crisis. In interesting contrast to the positions of the whites, black students tended to ignore the "larger issues," emphasizing instead the current demands being made by the BSU and the Third World Liberation Front. Unlike the concerns of the whites that found root in matters of precedent and somewhat abstract ideology, the blacks spoke of very pragmatic and visible goals whose attain-ment required not rhetoric, but a tangible response on the part of the administration.

When we pressed white students and faculty for specific illustrations of their more general concerns, we found that we inevitably were presented with lengthy lists of long-standing griev-ances. Among these were: the resignation last winter of President John Summerskill, the intervention of Chancellor Dumke in forcing Smith to suspend George Murray, the subsequent resigna-tion of Smith in the face of what students saw as the "get tough" policy of the Trustees, the dismissal of Professors Martinez and Gerassi for their political views and actions, the recent denial of tenure to Professor William Stanton for his role in the strike and to Professor Patrick Gleason for no apparent reason other than his initial responsibility in hiring George Murray, and the lack of action on programs that a majority of students and faculty felt should have been implemented— including the Trustees rejection of the design (by Moshe Safdie, Habitat, Montreal Expo '68) of the proposed Student Union, although the building would be completely paid for and operated by students. These were a few of the items cited as specific illustrations to support the dissident students' more general charges.

Hayakawa, Dumke, and Reagan (in a special telecast dealing with the problems at S.F. State) charged that the "silent majority" of students and faculty did not support the strikers and wanted the college to return to a state of normality. But if the majority stood against the strikers, why did it stand silently? In a December 17 letter to the editor of the San Francisco *Chronicle*, Frederic W. Terrien, Professor of Sociology at San Francisco State, raised this very issue: "What keeps the majority silent is this very disenchantment [a reference to the Reagan administration's lack of support for the State College system], together with the sharp awareness that some of the militants' demands should long since have been college policy." Terrien went on to say that even if Hayakawa—whom Terrien, incidentally, supports—succeeds in keeping the College open, ". . . the Chancellor, most of the Trustees, and the Governor will back off and sell him short on what is really required for change and growth. Save for the company of Mayor Alioto and a few Trustees, Dr. Hayakawa stands alone."

The general feeling that the Chancellor and the Trustees are *unwarranted intruders* into the affairs of the College and basically unconcerned with the real needs of the College was repeatedly echoed through the course of our inquiries.

In the midst of the strike, the Trustees proposed to revise Title V of the California Administrative Code, thus shifting control of student money and affairs to the Trustees. Under a more recent court order, student government officials were removed from their posts, stripped of their power to disburse funds, and charged with various felonies and misdemeanors relating to their alleged misuse of student funds during the past year. One effect of this order was to stop publication of the *Gater* (an anti-Hayakawa paper), although Hayakawa made a special exception which allowed continued publication of an anti-strike paper. Needless to say, this further widened the gap between students and administrators at the College. Another obvious implication of this development was that black programs currently supported by student funds would be directly controlled by the Trustees. The Academic Senate was strongly opposed to this reduction of local autonomy.

In short, the Trustees were viewed by the students as pre-emptors of power, as dictators without concern for precedent or procedure. The result of their repeated intrusions, we believe, was a total breakdown in the clear chain of command.

*The Erosion of Local Autonomy and
the Decline of Perceived Legitimacy*

One of our major interests when we began interviewing was how students and faculty would react, not only to the appointment of Hayakawa but to the manner in which he was appointed. Prior to the opening of school during the Thanksgiving recess, Professor McClatchy, head of the Academic Senate, disclosed, in a televised interview, his displeasure with the hurried procedure used to appoint Hayakawa. To many, it was another case of the Trustees disregarding the autonomy of the institution and the opinions of its faculty. What McClatchy did not point out in his interview was that the five most probable candidates for Robert Smith's position had agreed amongst themselves not to accept the office without prior consultation with each other. Apparently, this strategy was to have been used to gain some bargaining power with the Trustees. Although Hayakawa and McClatchy were among the five, Hayakawa did not consult with the other members.

In contrast to the resentment of both students and faculty over what they considered a long history of unwarranted intervention by the Trustees into matters of local concern, no particular anger was expressed over the manner of Hayakawa's appointment. This was not due to acceptance of the procedure used to appoint him, but rather seemed to be the result of a complete disenchantment with the nature of the office. The Trustees had so often intervened in the affairs of the College that it appeared to the students that the powers of the president were at best ambiguous and that in all probability he operated solely at the whim of the Trustees. Both the nature of his appointment and the public announcements that Hayakawa was in constant contact with Governor Reagan reinforced this rather general opinion of the office. The students and faculty members we spoke with were generally unconcerned with the procedural characteristics of Hayakawa's appointment because, as they told us, the manner of making an appointment to an office that is already illegitimate is completely irrelevant. When the students rallied outside Hayakawa's office Monday afternoon (December 2), prior to the outbreak of violence, their rallying cry was, "We want the puppet. . . .We want the puppet."

Any explanation of the strike—we are distinguishing firmly between explanation and justification—must consider the strikers' perception of the breakdown of legitimate authority. By responding, on an ad hoc basis, with the pragmatism of a nineteenth-century vigilante committee to the problems of both the University of California system and the State College system, the respective governing bodies have, among other things: removed a few radicals from the campus, forced the resignation of unresponsive and unsubmissive presidents (including Clark Kerr), restricted the academic role of Eldridge Cleaver on the Berkeley campus, and rescinded credit for Sociology 139X (the course Cleaver was participating in). The price they paid for these and similar victories was higher than they had imagined or have yet realized. In winning the battles, they have in effect lost the war. Subsequent violence at Berkeley was supported by students of our acquaintance because they no longer saw any sense in "working through the system;" they cite these events as reasons why such attempts would be foolish.

Adherence to procedural requirements sometimes results in what appear to be arbitrary and senseless decisions. Yet because the procedures are maintained, continuity, stability, and legitimacy are preserved. For this very reason, the Supreme Court will unflinchingly turn loose a "confessed killer" in order to preserve a procedural system whose value and legitimacy far outweighs the social costs of turning loose even a hundred "confessed criminals." Nineteenth-century pragmatism, however, dictates ad hoc reactions to every new situation. Concern for precedent and procedural continuity may worry academicians, but right is right and wrong is wrong, as any man with "common sense" can plainly see! The Trustees (and the Regents) had, along with the Governor, adopted and pursued policies which emphasized pragmatic rather than procedural solutions; this, we believe, greatly exacerbated the crises at both State and Berkeley.

Admittedly one could think of a procedural requirement that might have resulted in the decision restricting Eldridge Cleaver to one lecture at the University of California, Berkeley, and restricting no other lecturers. Had this occurred, the proponents of Cleaver's right to speak could have sought justice through changing a procedure that produced an unjust decision. But when the authorities impose arbitrary and capricious decisions clearly directed at specific individuals, then not only the legitimacy of the decision, but the nature of the authority itself (and, consequently, all future decisions that emanate from that authority) is called into question. Physician-publisher Carlton Goodlett, in his speech at State on December 4, compared the authority of the Trustees to that of the Georgia State Police; from his perspective, the authority of the former was no more legitimate or binding than that of the latter.

Merely having traditional authority or achieving authority through legal means does not legitimate authority on a campus; the manner in which authority is exercised also affects its legitimacy. Hayakawa is President of State solely because the Trustees, without consulting the faculty, have appointed him. Such an appointment is clearly within the powers delegated to the Trustees, but since the powers of the president's office have been constrained by the

Trustees in their quest to stifle disruption, dissent and opposition, the office itself is perceived as illegitimate. But not only has the president's office been compromised by the actions of the Trustees, these actions have called the authority of the entire educational structure into serious question.

The Erosion of Authority and Police Power

The final enforcement of the decisions of authorities is generally the responsibility of the police. When authorities are viewed as illegitimate, the police are viewed by the students as nothing more than armed mercenaries. From the perspective of the dissidents, the police, in the final analysis, are free men. As free men they are—naively—presumed by the students to have a right to choose whether they will implement the whims of a capricious and illegitimate authority or refuse. The logic of this argument is often based on the Nuremburg judgment. The practical concerns of job, pay, promotion, etc., are irrelevant to the dissidents' perception of the police. The issues the students are fighting for are, in their minds, larger than the mundane concerns of day to day existence. After all, the students are prepared to get their heads bashed in for what they believe. Shouldn't the police possess equal courage to preserve freedom and refuse to cooperate with the Establishment?

The attitudes of the students toward the police may have been exacerbated by the coincidental announcement late Sunday night (December 1) of the report of the special commission investigating the actions of the Chicago Police at the Democratic National Convention (The Walker Report) and by the replay of some of those violent scenes of police brutality on national television. The full extent to which the students hated the police was not demonstrated until the start of the noon rally, Monday.

In defiance of Hayakawa's suspension of various civil liberties under the emergency declaration, black militants and their white supporters held a rally on the Commons. Shortly after the beginning of the rally, the head of the campus police, in plain clothes and surrounded by three uniformed members of the San Francisco Tactical Squad, approached the platform in an effort to inform the group that they were in defiance of the emergency order. The sight of the police turned the rather casual crowd into a potentially violent mob. One attractive, neatly dressed girl standing next to us distorted her face in anger at the sight of the uniformed police, raised her hand in a clenched fist, and shouted, "Up against the wall, you mother . . . . ." Similar and sometimes more creative obscenities erupted from the crowd.

A chant developed, "Get their guns, get their guns." The police then rapidly withdrew.

There is no doubt in our minds that one of the results of Mayor Richard J. Daley's actions during the 1968 Democratic Convention was to hamper the effective use of the police against students for generations to come. The reaction of students to police is completely emotional. Both sides recognized this. The militants were frustrated by the lack of a response from Hayakawa to their defiance of the emergency order and to their shouting rally in front of the administration building. It is to Hayakawa's credit that he used the Tactical Squad judiciously—bringing them in and having them depart as soon as some temporary order was restored. This initially restrained and calculated use of the police further frustrated the militants. Finally, angry at being ignored, they escalated the use of force to compel Hayakawa to call in the police in large numbers and to keep them on campus. The militant blacks called for action, and a few persons in the crowd threw rocks at and through the windows of the administration building. When the police appeared on the scene to disperse them, the crowd once again grew vicious and shouted obscenities. It was obvious that one of the prime reasons for the militants' desire to bring the police on campus was to capitalize on the students' blind hatred of the police.

Despite the restrained attitude of the police Monday afternoon, students responded to the scene by seeing what they thought they should see rather than what did in fact occur. Almost every student we talked to thought the police had provoked violence by "charging into the crowd" despite the fact that the police did not come into physical contact with the crowd or charge into it during the confrontation on the Commons Monday. Feigning ignorance of what had occurred, we asked respondents on the scene, "What happened?" The students we talked with responded that the police provoked violence by "charging the crowd." The fact that Hayakawa held the police off campus, calling them only after the windows in the administration building were broken, was not mentioned; nor did they mention the fact that at that point the police had not laid a hand (or a club) on a single student, although they had been pelted with everything from a twenty-four inch pipe to broken flower pots.

A group of girls who had been in a modern dance class came rushing out onto the Commons, completely ignorant of the events which had just occurred, shouting, "Get those mother . . . pigs off campus." One of the girls, looking at the dispersion of forces, volunteered to us that the ". . . pigs" caused all the violence; she had, though, just emerged from a basement gymnasium that provided no view of the Commons, long after all the incidents between police and students had taken place.

The reaction of the students to the police violence on Tuesday, December 3, 1968, increased support for the strikers. This fact was recognized by strikers and CAE members alike. Many of the students who had been vacillating on the fringe of the movement swelled into the ranks of the strikers after Tuesday's violence. One girl stated that, up until the incidents Tuesday, her main concern was getting back into class, but that after witnessing the beating of SDS co-chairman Howie Forman by police in the Commons dining area, she felt she had to side with the strikers.

We found it especially interesting that the brutality of the police increased support for the strikers, although the corresponding brutality of the strikers toward the police did not diminish the students' support for the strikers. This was true even for the large majority of the strikers who disagreed rather vehemently with the use of violence. Consequently, the administration was caught in the unfortunate situation of either turning over the buildings to the students or calling in the police, thereby swelling the strikers' ranks with sympathizers.

One of the primary objectives of the strikers was to bring police on campus. It was only when the strikers saw the police return from the administration building to their staging area that they employed violence. The presence of the police was clearly to be used to increase support for the strikers by playing on the hostile attitudes of the students toward the police. The police, an ostensible tool of authority, had been manipulated into a tool of the forces opposing authority.

Voluntary Servitude: The White
Militant Response to the Black
Demands

We repeatedly asked white students and faculty why, if the larger issues were of such major concern, they were not more actively involved themselves in the leadership positions of the movement. White student activists responded by pointing out that the authorities (usually white) were repressive in their encounters with blacks. As soon as the reactionaries move against the blacks, the white liberals move in and take over. The whites, we were told, were worried about precedents of intrusion being set and the larger abstract implications of the crisis, but the blacks were viewed by whites as having more immediate concerns. The needs of the blacks, we were told, get swallowed up in the whites' rush to embrace abstractions. The whites forget the blacks' needs. The continuation of the plantation mentality in both blacks and whites, the white student activists told us, has got to stop. A white student summed up the feelings of the white militants as follows: "We support the blacks despite the fact that we disagree with some of their demands and some of their tactics. What is really important is for the black students to create their own sense of identity. By supporting them and not imposing ourselves into the leadership positions, we foster the creation of that identity, the fulfillment of their immediate needs, and our own concerns with the larger issues at stake."

The same self-effacing response was heard when we asked white students how they felt about supporting a black studies program that would be open only to black students and staffed exclusively with black faculty. Overwhelmingly, the white militants felt that it logically made no sense, but psychologically the blacks needed it because the white, culture-bound curriculum had little meaning for them. Blacks encounter a side of America few whites can imagine, let alone comprehend, we were told. The white, culture-bound curriculum is designed to perpetuate the myths, symbols, and rhetoric of a degenerate racist society. Blacks or, for that matter, white militants have no stomach for that. Whites talk about the glories of a Constitution that legalized enslavement of black men and once formally tallied them as three-fifths of a human being. Whites talk about law and order, the white militants said, but in America law and order does not have the same meaning or consequences for whites that it does for blacks. The black heritage, perspective, and experience is different, they said. Blacks want their point of view expressed. They want their children to be exposed to the truth about this degenerate racist society rather than to be socialized as cogs in "whitey's machine." A segregated black studies program was, in the face of these beliefs, a demand acceptable to most white students.

When we asked white militants if the tactics of the black militants and their justifications of violence were in fact valid, we were told that physical violence, if not justified in the face of ideological violence, was understandable. They also believed that much of the rhetoric of violence, like the fifteen demands, served to promote a black identity that white racism had denied, rather than promote any real disorder.

None of the white militants appeared to recognize the incongruity of their position. On the one hand the blacks must be indulged in order to promote the creation of a black identity; on the other hand blacks already possess an identity and cultural heritage that makes it difficult, if not impossible, for them to function in the white culture-bound curriculum. The white militants, when echoing the need for a black identity, speak in the voice of E. Franklin Frazer: The blacks in America were systematically stripped of every vestige of their African heritage to the point where the primary culture of blacks is an American one. When supporting the foundation of a black studies program, they speak in the voice of Nathan Hale: In becoming Anglo-Saxons, blacks deny their unique cultural heritage, a heritage that clouds their view of the white, culture-bound curriculum.

These sentiments confirm the long-known principle of attitude theory that strict logical incongruity of cognitive material is no guarantee that attitudinal consistency will be present in any given individual. White militants at State were no exception to this rule and manifested severe compartmentalization and rigidity of expression when discussing these issues.

Charles Hamilton, noted black political scientist, has said that white student movements differ markedly from black student movements in that the former are largely directed at abstract and symbolic goals while the latter are channeled through more instrumental designs toward realistic ends. To some extent, our own observations confirm those of Hamilton. The immediate, tangible demands of the blacks were in themselves of little interest to the white militants. In many cases the white militants disagreed with the black demands and simply indulged the blacks. The whites tended to see black demands as either symbolic or real stepping stones toward larger issues. For the blacks, on the other hand, the issues were to a large extent present in their demands. Whatever concern they had for abstraction and precedent was hidden beneath very real issues whose resolution required implementation, not rhetoric.

If the blacks were concerned with precedent, their concern centered around tactics, not issues. Would revolutionary militant tactics work and convince the "black laggards" (i.e. black non-supporters) that these are truly revolutionary times? Would "whitey" back down in the face of violence, or would he reveal his own capability for violence and seek to demonstrate that students would capitulate by increasing the level of force in the contest?

No observer could refuse to recognize that San Francisco State was a testing ground for both sides to determine the necessary costs of victory. The "get tough" policy of interim President Hayakawa found its roots in a dozen pronouncements by Governor Reagan and State Superintendent of Public Instruction Max Rafferty. Similarly, the actions of the hard-core militants had firm foundation in the rhetoric of Black Panthers Eldridge Cleaver and George Murray and of militants like Stokeley Carmichael.

Whatever else might be said of the black leadership of the movement, they did not become simple tools of their own rhetoric. Their aims were specific. Victory required a visible response on the part of the Trustees, and precedent and tactics were tested with bricks, pipes, and clubs. Ghetto life, perhaps, does not encourage the luxury of abstraction. As Carlton Goodlett said in his speech before the dissidents, "Man can dream but the time comes in a man's life when he has to get out of the dream and live." The luxury of dreaming was only for the white militants.

The Community

There may have been some ironic delight on the part of the Trustees in their appointment of Hayakawa as President of San Francisco State. Black militants would now have to confront an Oriental "white racist." Hayakawa, in addition to his race and his impeccable academic credentials, had served as a newspaperman for Chicago's *Defender*, a Negro newspaper, before embarking on his academic career. Hayakawa took the position that the militants did not speak for the Negro community or for other minority groups. They were a noisy rabble, hell-bent on destruction. Decent black men, like decent white men, had no use for them This stance challenged the claims of the movement's leaders that they were spokesmen for their respective communities. It also provided a safety mechanism to dissipate what was increasingly portrayed as a racial conflict into a conflict between decent people and rabble-rousers.

The militants were not to be so readily categorized nor so quickly decimated. Capitalizing on the deterioration of the office of President at San Francisco State, it was easy for the militants to characterize Hayakawa as a puppet of the administration. To the strikers Hayakawa was a "Tom," a "Tojo Tom." But it was not only necessary for the strikers to portray Hayakawa as a puppet; they had also to disprove his characterization of the masses of blacks and minority groups as disaffected from their movement. On Tuesday, December 3, and Wednesday, December 4, the militants paraded onto the speaker's platform "representatives" of the black and minority communities in a show of solidarity for the strikers. Among the community leaders were Rev. Cecil Williams of Glide Methodist Church, Assemblyman Willie Brown, Carlton Goodlett, Berkeley School Board member Ron Dellums, and representatives from the Mexican, Chinese, Japanese, and Filipino communities. CORE, the Urban League, and the NAACP were also officially represented.

The strongest blow to Hayakawa as a spokesman for the silent majority of the minority ethnic groups came from a "representative" of the Japanese community, who attempted to make it unequivocally clear that Hayakawa was not and had never been a member of the Japanese ethnic community in the Bay Area. Hayakawa's newly claimed role of spokesman for San Francisco's minority communities was, they insisted, entirely incongruent with his past behavior.

There were also, we noted, indications of the Ocean Hill-Brownsville issue in the strike at San Francisco State. Black mothers "representing" the community spoke of the strike as an effort to develop a black studies program of which the community could be proud. The school, they said, had not been responsive to the needs of the black community and, as black parents and black taxpayers, they were concerned about the context and quality of the education their children were receiving. They also demanded that, for the safety of their "innocent children," the police be removed from the campus— an idea that received wild acclaim from the audience, which shouted in enthusiasm, "Pigs off campus, pigs off campus."

The Press: Agent of the
"Power Structure"

The press was at this time another target of the students. We repeatedly found that many students who refused to talk to us when they perceived us to be members of the press would talk to us only when they learned we were sociologists. One respondent said, "The press is hovering around the administration building like a bunch of vultures waiting for some poor kid or some cop to get his head bashed in so they can film the blood and gore in living color." Almost all the students we talked to, from strikers to CAE members, claimed that they could recognize neither the incidents they had witnessed nor the issues at stake from reading the newspapers, watching t.v., or reading weekly newsmagazines. One student, who also worked with a national t.v. technical crew, stated that, while the press had created a picture which played up the sensational at the expense of the issues, the fault was not with the reporters on the scene. The fault was rather with the editors who, he said, had a greater stake in boosting circulation and Nielsen ratings than in informing the public. (On Saturday, December 7, strikers paraded around downtown San Francisco and made a point of demonstrating in front of the San Francisco newspapers.)

The Huntley-Brinkley Report's film coverage came under specific attack a number of times; the San Francisco *Chronicle* was often praised for some of its attempts to get beyond the superficial aspects of the strike, but condemned by one student for following a story of George Murray's inflammatory comments about the need for students to bring guns to campus with a story about a Black Panther shoot-out with police.

For many of the students, the incidents at San Francisco State have provided a first-hand opportunity to test the veracity and competence of the press. The daily incidents the students observe on campus and their understanding of the surrounding issues can be compared to the mass media's depiction (whether accurate, representative, or not) of the same incidents. Like so many other facets of the society that students are examining critically, the press has often been found wanting. While we have noted that the press coverage changed rather dramatically in early December, we do not know what the effect of the more objective and detailed reporting has been on the general sentiment. We doubt if it has changed greatly, however.

The implications of this mean far more than just the apparent loss of faith by the students in another important aspect of their society. To the students, the adult population only knows what it reads in the press and sees on t.v. Public opinion, which has tightly congealed behind Hayakawa's "get tough" policy, has little, if any, relevance for the students. The strike is fundamentally a moral issue, they say, and counting heads was never an adequate mechanism for resolving moral problems. In addition, the public has insufficient information for arriving at valid conclusions. Hayakawa may be impressed with his fan mail, but the students are not. On the basis of what the students have observed, a letter of praise to Hayakawa is a fatuous conclusion drawn from a distorted premise.

Columbia

Columbia and the New Left

Daniel Bell

The "siege," "insurrection," "rebellion" at Columbia—all these terms are extravagant, yet it is hard to find one which is apt—has been characterized by the Students for a Democratic Society (SDS) as a spontaneous protest by the student body, or a substantial portion of it, against the "complicity" of the university in the war, and against the "institutional racism" of the university in the neighborhood; they explain the scope and intensity of the events by the extent to which the university was guilty of these charges. The administration itself attributes these events to the organized efforts of a small cadre of the SDS that was able, successfully, to manipulate a larger body of students who had been politically disoriented by the war in Vietnam. Some observers, noting that the events at Columbia were almost simultaneous with student agitation in Berlin and Paris and Milan, have talked of a "world-wide" movement of students against "bureaucratic" society.

The first interpretation I regard as an untruth, the second as a half truth, and the third I regard as possibly true, but too gross an explanation to account for the particularities. What is striking about any social situation that is examined in detail is how complex all the circumstances are, and while one risks losing an over-all configuration in the patient effort to sort out the details, the effort to find meaning—in sociology as in language—has to begin with the simplest description of what happened. This is especially true in the case of Columbia, for if one looks at the background—the years, say, from 1966 to 1968—the events which exploded in April and May are, at first glance, largely inexplicable. It is easy, of course, since history is always written after the fact, to give some apparently plausible account of "the causes" and "the determining factors," and these tend to give an air of inevitability to the sequences. But as I have studied this history, and reflected on my own participation in it, I find the "outbreak," "uprising," "revolution"—none of these words is adequate—extremely puzzling. In this essay, I have attempted an answer, but even now I am not entirely sure it is adequate. I have tried to reconstruct the salient events—and the reader will have to be patient with the many details if he wants to follow "history"—and then to provide a commentary and some personal judgments. Even so, I have restricted myself to a single dimension, the relation between students and the administration, in order to highlight, and necessarily in chiaroscuro, the extraordinary change in moral temper that took place on campus in the seven days at the end of April. To this extent, the account neglects many important secondary factors, particularly in the actions of the faculty and the trustees, in this effort to follow the thread of student behavior. On another occasion, I hope to relate the Columbia events—more specifically the phenomenon of the New Left—to some broader historical and sociological contexts.

Microcosm I—The Events

On April 19, 1968, Columbia College—or, at least, the Committee on Instruction, which is the policy-making body of the college—had cause for self-congratulation. The end of the term was little more than three weeks away and seemingly Columbia had escaped the "confrontations" that had wracked so many other schools during the year. The "big issue" of the year at Columbia—each school year had a single major issue—had been campus recruitment by representatives of the Dow Chemical Company and the military, and Columbia had been prudent if not sure-footed on the question. For example, when military recruiters were due to appear on campus at the end of October, the Committee on Instruction had voted to postpone all such activities until a college-wide policy had been worked out by the faculty. A poll was conducted by the *Spectator*, the student newspaper, in which 2,750 students voted; it showed 67.6 per cent in favor of completely open recruitment, 14.3 per cent opposed to all recruitment, and 18.1 per cent selectively opposed, most of them singling out the military as the group to be barred. Finally, a faculty committee headed by Professor Allan Silver wrote a long, thoughtful report that reaffirmed the principle of "institutional neutrality," and called for open recruitment on campus.[1] Yet when General Hershey recommended to draft boards that they induct young men obstructing recruitment, the Committee on Instruction voted to postpone all military recruitment visits until this procedure could be clarified; and such visits were duly postponed until White House Assistant Joseph Califano, in response to a letter from President Kirk and several other university presidents, disavowed the Hershey statement.

The demonstrations had gone without incident. Military recruiters arrived on campus, and although they were picketed, and a pie was thrown, not many students had turned out. The Dow Chemical recruiting had come to nothing—only a few students signed up for an interview, then withdrew their names—and the Dow recruiter, though he made one appearance on campus, came and went quietly.

In short, the college was being sensitive to and responsive to possibly inflammatory situations. The year before, again on the initiative of the faculty, the college had voted—it was the first major school in the country to do so—to discontinue both the ranking of

---

[1]Anticipating the possibility of student obstruction, despite the faculty recommendations, the Silver Committee stated: "We have, as a practical matter, inquired into administrative arrangements at the University in connection with the prospect of obstruction, disorder or violence among students in these contexts. Your committee believes these arrangements to be eminently sensible, reasonable and prudent. They call for the invoking of disciplinary sanctions—such as warning, probation and suspension—in the case of students who deliberately obstruct University activities or who physically attack other students. We recognize that penalties such as these are not trivial. . . . We agree, however, that in view of the gravity of these offenses, such sanctions are appropriate and should be applied."

students and the release of student grades to draft boards. There were moves to widen student participation in the college and reduce some of the academic pressures on students. On the initiative of David Truman, when he was still dean of the college, two students were invited, for the first time, to sit in as consultative members of the Committee on Instruction. Truman himself had spent considerable time appearing at free-for-all "bull sessions" in the dormitories and had acquired an enormous popularity in the college for his responsiveness to students. A "pass-fail" option had been introduced so that students could take one course a term without a letter grade, thus encouraging them to attend classes that interested them without the risk of receiving a low grade because the subject was far from their major area of competence. During the spring term of this year, a full day was set aside, with the agreement of the college, for seminars and talks by various authorities about the impact of the new draft regulations, and there was a full and honest discussion of the consequences of resistance, and even of exiling oneself to Canada.

There was also the issue of the gymnasium. Columbia University was planning to build an $11 million gymnasium on two acres of Morningside Park, a project first proposed by the city in 1959, but which had been delayed for lack of funds. In the past year some people had expressed doubts about unilateral control of the gymnasium by Columbia, and there had been negotiations in an attempt to widen the area of community facilities in the gym. But the public—and the college—remained apathetic. A poll of the neighborhood by the Columbia *Spectator* on November 21, 1967, revealed that almost half of "the community" bordering the eastern part of Morningside Park (i.e., in Harlem) had not even heard about the gym, and among those who had, 56 per cent favored its construction. At a faculty meeting, a motion to discuss the gymnasium aroused so little interest that it was not even seconded, and a report in the spring by a faculty committee on civil rights, which had raised some questions about the propriety of the gymnasium, received scant attention. The Columbia faculty, by and large, was little concerned with neighborhood issues, except for those living on Morningside Drive facing Morningside Park. This group felt a strong apprehension, often discussed in the meeting of the Committee on Instruction, about the fact that muggings and thefts, largely unreported, increased alarmingly when the gates of the park were opened to Harlem, after being closed for years. It was hoped that the presence of the new gymnasium, with many students moving back and forth, would reduce crime in the area. When the first construction cranes appeared on the park site in March 1967, some Harlem groups called for sit-downs and the blocking of construction.

Yet only one or two demonstrations materialized, and only a handful of opponents of the gymnasium turned up.

In sum, the situation at Columbia had *not* been going from bad to worse, and it is this record of seeming progress which makes the subsequent events of April and May all the more incomprehensible.

Enter Mark Rudd

Toward the end of term, one new factor did appear. Traditionally, about three-quarters of the way through the spring term, student organizations elect new officers for the coming year. The *Spectator* had changed editors. The student radio station, WKCR, had changed officers. So had the Students for a Democratic Society. In the SDS elections, the old administration of Ted Kaptchuk had been attacked violently by a group of young Turks—or, rather, young Maos and young Che Guevaras—for having conducted only peaceful demonstrations and for having limited its activity to "building a base" on campus. What was now needed, the group opposing Kaptchuk claimed, was the thrust of guerrilla fighters who would see to it that the campus seethed with continual confrontations. On this platform, in early April, the SDS elected a hitherto unknown student, Mark Rudd, as president.

Mark Rudd, a junior, is a tall, hulking, slack-faced young man with a prognathic jaw and blue-gray eyes so translucent that his gaze seems hypnotic. Rudd's father, born Rudnitzky, had mild left-wing sympathies before World War II, then joined the army, found it a place for a congenial career, served long enough to become a lieutenant colonel and to retire on a pension, and subsequently became a real-estate agent in New Jersey. The first stirrings of radicalism in Mark Rudd himself, according to his mother, occurred during his boyhood visits to his grandmother's candy store in the Newark slums. His high-school record was good, and he applied to Harvard, which rejected him. Columbia, which accepted him, was his second choice. At Columbia he was virtually unknown on campus until he was elected president of SDS and, at about the same time, published a series of articles in the student newspaper entitled "The Cuba I saw," reporting on a youth convention he attended in Havana earlier that term. In the articles Rudd acclaimed the progress he had observed in Cuba; as an example of the new spirit under Castro, he quoted an aging bellboy at his hotel who told Rudd that he felt he "owned" the hotel. What bellboy in an American hotel, Rudd wrote, would ever make such a remark? As part of his platform for election, Rudd wrote a "Position Paper on Strategy for the Rest of the School Year—Complicity," in which he said that the goals of SDS now had to be: "The radicalization of students . . . showing them how our

lives really are unfree in this society and at Columbia, getting them
to act . . . and striking a blow at the Federal Government's war
effort." He concluded: "Let us clearly state that our goal is to end
the university complicity with the war."

On Monday, April 22, SDS called for a demonstration the next
day at the sundial, which is at the center of the university campus, on
the issues of the universities' ties with the Institute of Defense
Analysis (IDA) and the suspension of six students who had
conducted an indoor demonstration on March 27 in Low Library,
the administration building, in violation of a published university
rule. That same day, SDS issued an eight-page newspaper, as a
rallying call for the demonstration, called *Up Against the Wall*, and
the dateline read: "April 22, 1968—The Year of the Heroic Guerrilla." One entire page was devoted to two woodcuts of Che Guevara
speaking at mass meetings, with the caption: "The Duty of Every
Revolutionary Is to Make the Revolution." The lead article was an
open letter to President Kirk from Rudd, headlined "Reply to Uncle
Grayson." It was a reply to a speech Kirk made in Charlottesville,
Virginia, on April 12, 1968, in which Kirk expressed concern about
the "turbulent and inchoate nihilism whose sole objectives are
destruction," which had seized young people "in disturbing
number." (In this same speech, though SDS did not mention it, Kirk
said he wanted to reduce the American involvement in Vietnam.)
Rudd threw down the gauntlet to "Uncle Grayson": "Your cry of
nihilism represents your inability to understand our positive values,"
and Rudd concluded: "There is only one thing left to say. It may
sound nihilistic to you, since it is the opening shot in a war of
liberation. I'll use the words of Leroi Jones, whom I'm sure you
don't like a whole lot: 'Up Against the Wall, mother . . . , this is a
stick-up.' Yours for freedom, Mark."

Two Issues and Their Background

In all eight pages of the SDS newspaper there was not a word
about the gymnasium. The agitational cry was "Protest the IDA and
University Repression," and those two issues alone, being quite
complicated, seemed to offer little promise for rousing the students;
certainly they did not seem to carry the emotional appeal of Dow
Chemical. Nor were these new issues. Behind each of them there was
a long, involved history of discussion on campus.

On September 27, 1967, at the beginning of the fall term,
President Kirk had unilaterally issued a policy statement forbidding
demonstrations within any university building. The reason for the
ban was not ideological but utilitarian. In the previous year, members
of SDS has clashed with athletes and other students during a

demonstration inside a student hall, and it was pure luck that there had been no injuries. The university placement office is on the sixth floor of Dodge Hall, which has narrow corridors, and the administration was afraid that any picketing or demonstration against outside recruiters using those offices would lead to violence. Hence the ban. On three occasions during the year, SDS groups had nevertheless held small demonstrations inside some buildings, mostly against recruiting; but the administration prudently chose to ignore them. On March 27, Rudd, as the new head of SDS, announced that an indoor demonstration would be held in Low Library to present a petition to the administration against the university's affiliation with IDA. Using bullhorns, which had also been forbidden, Rudd and about a hundred SDS members rampaged through the corridors, but both President Kirk and Vice President Truman refused to meet with them.[2]

Some weeks after this demonstration, five students in the college were asked to report to the dean's office on April 22 on the charge of violating the ban on indoor demonstrating; they were told that they could request a formal hearing or respond in any other way. All five chose not to respond at all, and they were placed on disciplinary probation for the remainder of the spring term. (The sixth student was a graduate student.) Instead, the SDS called for a demonstration in Low Library for April 23 to protest these suspensions. Why the administration waited so long to take this action is unclear. Most likely it hoped that the issue could in some way be avoided. On April 12, for example, Dean Platt, the dean of students, proposed a meeting of three SDS leaders with President Kirk to discuss the ban on demonstrations and the IDA connection. The SDS leaders flatly refused to meet with President Kirk. Later, student groups accused the administration of "entrapment" by not acting on the earlier infractions and thus giving the students the illusion that any violation of the ban would go unpunished. In actual fact, the administration had been indecisive and unwilling to be punitive. This was the extent of "university repression."

[2]A characteristic distortion of the incident was presented by *Ramparts,* whose account was widely distributed on the campus: "Grayson Kirk's ban on student demonstrations inside campus buildings was so sweeping that it prevented candidates for student office from collecting signatures in their dormitories. It was assumed that the rule, hastily enacted a few months ago, would only be used to outlaw unruly demonstrations. Therefore, Columbia students were amazed when Kirk employed the ban to put on probation six students out of a group of 200 who showed up at his office one day with a petition bearing the names of ten percent of the student body."

The IDA

The Institute of Defense Analysis had been picked by SDS, at its national convention, as a symbol of the universities' complicity in the Vietnam War, and a national campaign had been underway all year. IDA was formed in 1955 as an effort of the Defense Department's Weapons System Evaluating Group, to enlist the help of scientists in weapons evaluation. Like many government agencies, defense had been unable to build an adequate "in-house" staff because of the reluctance of independent-minded scientists to work either in uniform or in government laboratories. The RAND Corporation, which was set up originally by the Air Force, was a successful demonstration of the possibility of recruiting top-flight brains for work on defense projects, under appropriate conditions. IDA was a similar effort on the part of the Pentagon's research arm to set up a nonprofit corporation. At first five, and subsequently twelve, universities were invited to become members of the consortium to administer IDA, as a means of guaranteeing academic independence for researchers. Columbia was an institutional affiliate, along with MIT, Chicago, Princeton, Stanford, Berkeley, Case, and others. Grayson Kirk, as president of Columbia, and William Burden, a trustee, sat on the board.

At Columbia, the ties with IDA had stirred no interest on campus. Nor was there any significant participation by the university in IDA projects. Yet the SDS sought to imply otherwise. A year earlier, a number of students and faculty met with Ralph Halford, then the dean of the graduate faculties, to question him about the university's contract obligations to defense agencies. The meeting, a public one, was held in the rotunda of Low Library. Halford stated that the university had no contract obligations with IDA. He was asked about Kirk's status on the board of IDA, and he answered that Kirk was present as an individual but that Columbia had no institutional affiliation with IDA. Halford had in mind his own status as a trustee of Associated Universities, Inc. (the Atomic Energy Commission laboratory at Brookhaven), and he assumed that Kirk's status at IDA was the same. When he learned that this was not so, he soon corrected himself. But the following year SDS repeatedly asserted that "University officials had lied" to the students about the university's tie with IDA.

There was also the Electronics Research Laboratory that had conducted defense research. This unit was set up by Professor Lawrence O'Neill, of the Engineering School; under contract with the Defense Department, it had expanded considerably. The ERL conducted research for the Advanced Projects Research Agency of the Defense Department on classified radar design, not weapons, called "Project Defender." But the university had become unhappy about the scope of ERL. In the previous decade and a half, much of the nation's defense systems planning had been tied into university research laboratories, such as the Jet Propulsion Lab at Cal Tech, or the Lincoln Lab and MITRE (MIT Research and Engineering). Increasingly, too, universities were discovering that the administration of laboratories not connected with basic research was becoming more of a liability than a help to a campus. (For one thing, researchers at these labs often demanded faculty status, and this created conflicts with established departments.) As a consequence, MIT had divested itself of MITRE, which had then been set up as an independent nonprofit corporation. For the same reason, Columbia in 1967-1968 decided to divest itself of the Electronics Research Lab, which was reorganized as the Riverside Research Institute, an independent nonprofit corporation. Because IDA also did some research work on "Project Defender," SDS tried to tie the Electronics Research Lab to the symbol it had created of IDA.

As for IDA itself, a number of individual faculty members—principally four physicists, Henry Foley, Leon Lederman, I.I. Rabi, and adjunct professor Richard Garwin—maintained membership in the IDA's "Jason Division," an effort by IDA to acquaint the nation's outstanding physicists with advanced research problems in order to solicit their advice. The university was originally affiliated institutionally, but after the issue was raised by the students, Columbia, as a corporation, severed its ties with IDA. Kirk and Burden retained their seats on the IDA board as individuals—a move later attacked by SDS as a sneaky device. In a sense it was: since the institutional affiliation of Columbia was largely symbolic, Kirk's membership retained something of the symbolism. But a different change was in the offing. In its report on military recruitment and university policy, the Silver Committee had proposed that the university set up a committee to investigate all institutional ties of the university with the defense agencies. President Kirk then named Louis Henkin, Hamilton Fish Professor of Constitutional Law and a respected faculty member, to head such a committee, which would formulate university policy on all such affiliations, including IDA.

To this extent the university, in its slow and lumbering way, was beginning to scrutinize all these issues. But this fact was almost entirely ignored by the SDS, which repeatedly demanded that the university "end" its ties with IDA. And this became the chief substantive issue of the demonstration which erupted into the Columbia insurrection.

Storming "The Bastille"

The Students for a Democratic Society had called a rally at the sundial for noon on Tuesday, April 23. There had been a desultory meeting the night before, attended by about 100 students, in which the main theme had to do with breaking the ban on indoor demonstrations by going into Low Library. It was also announced that the question of the gymnasium, even though construction had already begun, was being added to the list of grievances in order to indict Columbia's policy of "institutional racism."

At noon, on Tuesday, the rally began. Various speakers denounced the university for "complicity" in the war. They demanded the reinstatement of the six students who had been put on probation. To the delight of the crowd, a representative of the Students' Afro-American Society mounted the sundial and denounced the university for proceeding with the construction of the gym against the wishes of the "Harlem community." At this point a letter from Vice President Truman was read to the crowd, which by now numbered about 500 demonstrators and listeners. In the letter, Truman declared that, since it was the intention of SDS to conduct a demonstration inside Low Library, and a large crowd of students would constitute a hazard, Low Library was being locked. He offered to meet with the students "immediately" in the McMillin theater on campus, if they wished to do so. The *Spectator* reported the ensuing events thus:

At first, SDS and SAS leaders were divided over how they should respond to Dr. Truman's offer. However, after an extended debate behind the sundial, Rudd informed Dean Platt that he would agree to move the demonstration into McMillin only if Dr. Truman would allow the protestors to set the ground rules of the meeting.

Rudd asked that Dr. Truman permit a student to chair the meeting and to allow the student audience to decide the case of the six disciplined students as a "popular tribunal."

Dean Platt stated that he could not commit Dr. Truman to any ground rules prior to the meeting, but the dean suggested to Rudd that he ask Dr. Truman to allow the students to set down certain conditions once the demonstrators are inside McMillin.

"Dr. Truman gives us this alternative because he is a very liberal man," Rudd told the crowd. "After we've gone up to the son-of-a-bitch a million times before with our demands, he has refused to discuss them, and now he decided to meet with us," Rudd added.

At this, the crowd howled down the invitation and began marching up the steps of Low Library. At Low, a group of about 100 counterdemonstrators were massed to block entry. After a slight scuffle, the crowd tried to storm a side entrance that was maintained by security guards, and they were again repulsed. The SDS crowd marched back to the sundial and, after some debate among the leaders, marched off to hold a demonstration at the gym site on Morningside Drive and 112th Street, about a quarter of a mile away. At the gym, a chain fence was torn down, some policemen were assaulted, and finally the crowd fell back, though one of the protestors was seized by the police and arrested. Back at the dial—it was now two and a half hours after the start of the demonstration—the crowd again milled around, and various suggestions were shouted. Clearly, neither Rudd nor any of the SDS leaders had a specific tactical plan; at that point the demonstration could just as easily have dispersed as gone forward. At that moment, someone in the crowd shouted that since the original intention was to hold a demonstration *inside* a building, the crowd ought to go inside Hamilton Hall, the college building. Someone else shouted that since the police had seized one of the students, the crowd itself ought to take a hostage. They surged toward Hamilton Hall. Within a few minutes, the acting dean of the college, Henry Coleman, who had just entered the building, was pinioned by some students and told that he could not leave until the administration met their demands. Coleman said that he would not negotiate under coercion, and walked into his office. The students sat down and the siege was underway.

At that point, and well into the evening, the students' aim was simply to sit in. Classes had not been disturbed. Professors went to their offices. The building was still open. In the early hours of the morning, the first fateful steps that transformed the demonstration from a sit-in to a siege and from a siege to an insurrection were taken—not by the SDS, but by the blacks.

Enter the Blacks

During the early evening, a prolonged debate about their next tactical moves had taken place among the demonstrators. Some students wanted to barricade the building, others felt that such tactics would merely alienate the rest of the student body. A vote was taken, and the barricade resolution lost. At that point, the black caucus stepped in. Only about half of these blacks were connected with Columbia. Some came from other colleges, quite a few were from the Harlem branch of CORE, and others came from SNCC and from Charles Kenyatta's "Mau Mau" group. They stated that they were going to barricade Hamilton Hall and keep it that way until construction of the gym was halted. If the white students wanted to stay they could, but only by accepting the leadership of the blacks. Many of the white students were outraged. Rudd himself was shocked and open-mouthed. Again there was a debate, this time involving Tom Hayden, one of the founders of SDS, who had come to Hamilton Hall in the early part of the evening and was acting as a "counselor" to SDS. Hayden advised them to accept the leadership of the blacks. But now the black caucus had made its own ultimatum: The whites would have to get out. One black leader was quoted as saying: "The whites would vacillate and panic, and we felt they could not be depended upon."

The action by the blacks was the *first turning point* of the Columbia insurrection, and its effect was threefold. First, it made the gymnasium—and the cry of "institutional racism"—the central issue on campus. Now the issue of the gym was "legitimate." As one of the black student leaders remarked afterward:

We didn't care if the majority of Harlem wanted the gym; they were wrong. We have to build a sense of black community and we didn't want Columbia crossing the line, even if it was providing some facilities for the community. Harlem has to control its own actions.

Second, the black stand on the gym embarrassed the administration. For the past two years, Columbia had energetically sought to attract black students to the university. A black man had been named assistant director of admissions. The college itself now had about eighty black students, as against five only a few years ago. A large number of them were on scholarship and special aid. Now, in their first organized political action, they were separating themselves, symbolically and literally, from Columbia, and declaring themselves to be, primarily, the representatives of the "community" *to* Columbia. And, in addition, there was the ominous threat, whose magnitude nobody knew, that if any police action were taken against the blacks in Hamilton, "Harlem" might march onto the campus and, as the idea was repeatedly expressed, "burn it down."

Third, there was the tangible fact that by their determination and discipline the blacks had provided a model of action for the white students, many of whom were still playing in the doll's house of revolution. ("Some of those black guys were willing to die," one white boy said. "That really frightened me. It made me wonder how far I'd go. They certainly have more guts than we do.") The fact that the blacks were interested in the larger political issues underlying the original SDS demands, and more importantly (as became clear only later) that they differed sharply with SDS about their attitudes to Columbia ("The SDS seized a building in order to wreck the university," a black leader remarked later. "We retained a building in order to gain some power in the university"), did not become apparent at the start. What mattered at the time was that the blacks had "acted." Given, the touchiness, fear, sensitivity, and guilt about the blacks that is so predominant in liberal society, their action provided a guise of legitimacy for the extreme tactic of uncivil disobedience.[3]

Into Kirk's Office

The white students were now perplexed. "They got out and congregated around the sundial, waiting for somebody to decide what to do," Jon Shils recalled to an interviewer from *The Washington Post.*

I remember telling Mark that if he didn't pick the demonstration up somewhere else, he was through at Columbia. . . . Somebody suggested that we go around pulling fire alarms; somebody else said we should take Low Library. Somebody got a bullhorn, so they went up to Low Library, broke through the door, rushed the security people and went into Kirk's office. There must have been 130 people.

The students entered the outer rooms of the President's four-room suite early Wednesday morning. One of the participants, writing in *New York* magazine under the pseudonym Simon James, recreated the subsequent events thus:

We expect the cops to come any moment. . . . At about 8:30 a.m. we heard that the cops are coming. One hundred and seventy-three people jump out of the window. . . . That leaves 27 of us sitting on the floor, waiting to be arrested. In stroll an inspector and two cops. We link arms and grit our teeth. After about five minutes of gritting our teeth it dawns on us that the cops aren't doing anything . . . they tell us they have neither the desire nor the orders to arrest us.

The police entered Grayson Kirk's inner office to remove a Rembrandt, valued at $450,000, and a television set.

Even then the students did not have a long occupation in mind. As Simon James tells it:

[3]An added factor, revealed initially by SDS students who had been in Hamilton, was the rumor that a number of the blacks had guns and were prepared to use them.

Enter Mark Rudd, through the window. He says that 27 people cannot exert any pressure, and the best thing we could do is leave and join a big sit-in in front of Hamilton. We say no, we're not leaving. . . . Rudd goes out and comes back again and asks us to leave again, and we say no again. He leaves to get reinforcements.

Buoyed up by the decision to stay, a number of students decided to search Kirk's files for material about IDA and on the gymnasium. As an account in *Ramparts* tells it:

They knew that the fourth room, Kirk's personal office, was likely to harbor documents elucidating these matters. And after some debate, a small group—which called itself "the radical caucus" and did not put its action to a vote—broke into it. They did indeed find evidence. . . .

All day Wednesday, the campus seethed with rumors of impending police action and of Harlem militants marching onto the campus. In a special session of the college faculty early that afternoon, the right to protest was overwhelmingly endorsed, but the use of coercion was condemned. The faculty also voted against giving amnesty to the protestors, proposed the creation of a tripartite faculty-student-administration body to deal with disciplinary affairs, and recommended immediate suspension of work at the gymnasium site. It also declared that "we believe that any differences have to be settled peacefully and we trust that police action will not be used to clear university buildings." The purpose of that resolution was to begin negotiation and to encourage the students to leave the buildings.[4]

Because of the fear of outside intervention—by Harlem residents and by radical groups in the city who were mobilizing that week for a city-wide peace march—the university called on the police to seal off the campus and thus close all the buildings. Early Wednesday evening, students of the School of Architecture refused to leave their building, Avery Hall, and later that night fifty graduate students decided to occupy Fayerweather, the social-science graduate building. When a large group of counterdemonstrators tried to oust them, they set up barricades at the two front doors. Thursday morning, a group from Low Library, largely Maoist in their political stand, decided to seize a building for their very own and moved over to Mathematics, where, according to the ubiquitous Simon James, "We are joined by 20 radicals who couldn't stand establishment liberal

---

[4]The writer of this article was the author of the faculty resolution.

Fayerweather any longer. We get inside and immediately pile up around 2000 pounds of furniture at the front door."

Thus, within three days, in a series of unplanned and often accidental events, five buildings were occupied and Columbia was on the historical map of student revolutions. The significance of all this was not in the number of demonstrators involved—in the first three days there were not more than 250 people in the buildings, about 50 of whom were outsiders—but in the *double* nature of the actions: tactically, the student actions had "leaped" five years, by adopting the latest methods of the civil-rights and peace movement, which had passed, in "five hot summers," from protest to confrontation to resistance and to outright obstruction; even more startling, the university as a general institution, itself, was now regarded as *the enemy*, the target for disruption.

This attitude was all the more paradoxical in that, over the past eight years, universities provided an arena for radical action, and in some instances even a sanctuary. The universities in the previous five years had been the initiating center for the peace movement: the teach-ins had begun in the universities, most of the antiwar pressure had come from the universities (at Columbia, Vice President Truman was one of a small group of distinguished professors who, for more than a year, had tried to influence the White House against the escalation of the war and to halt the bombings), and most of the draft resistance found its source in the university. But now the radical students sought to identify the university as the "intersect" of the corporate and military worlds; to ignore all other aspects of university life, particularly scholarship and learning; in fact, to tear it down. However accidentally the events occurred, the intentions to disrupt and the continual efforts to exploit situations that would lead to extreme action, were there. If not in April 1968 at Columbia, it might have happened the following year; if not at Columbia, then at some other university. The point is that little in the Columbia situation per se provided the basis for the "rebellion." The decisive fact lay in the changed character of left-wing student intentions and tactics, and in the responsiveness in the substantial minority they were able to influence.[5]

---

[5]At this point it is useful to cite the testimony given to the Cox Committee, which has been inquiring into the events at Columbia, by Christopher Friedrichs, editor of the *Spectator* from March 1967 to March 1968 and one of the most thoughtful observers on campus. In his testimony, Mr. Friedrichs stated that prior to April 23, the Columbia campus was *not* on the brink of revolution; large numbers of students, although they had grievances, were essentially satisfied with the existing institution (or satisfied to the extent that they never would have contemplated becoming involved in the extreme disruptions that occurred).

A Moment Suspended in Time

For the next five days, the world shrank to the dimensions of Columbia. Time seemed suspended, and for the students inside the buildings, cut off from the campus and living in a siege atmosphere, "reality" took on an intensity they had never known before. There was the shared sense of danger as rumors about police action spread, and each demonstrator wondered whether he would be man enough to "take it" when the time came. Emancipated from many of the psychological restraints and taboos of customary life, the students began to poke around freely within previously closed-off premises.[6] There was the intense, frenetic discussion of ideas, strategies, and tactics, in which words become all-important, for the right words would magically transform the situation into victory. Negotiations with famous professors were conducted on the level of equality and, in some cases, of triumphant insult (as when Mark Rudd told an audience of two hundred faculty members that their conciliatory efforts were just "bull . . . "). Emotions were lifted high by songfests and films from Cuba and Vietnam. Red flags were raised from the roofs of two buildings. As national and international attention

---

Mr. Friedrichs argued that the events that occurred between the afternoon of Tuesday, April 23, and Wednesday, April 24, were the critical elements that turned the situation into a full-scale crisis. He further argued that had decisive action been taken by the administration any time in this period, the entire crisis would have been averted. In his view, the administration's failure to call the police was crucial. He stressed his belief that police action, at least against students in Kirk's office, would have been widely viewed as "appropriate, if not inevitable," and that the Hamilton Hall situation could have been dealt with separately because it was, in fact, a totally different situation in which no actual criminal actions had been committed.

When the administration failed to call the police immediately, it lent a sense of "legitimacy" to the actions of the students. This factor, he felt, led other students to occupy buildings because it was "acceptable" and resulted in their later anger that the university did not live up to this theory of its sentiments and intentions.

[6]An account in *The Village Voice*, entitled "The Groovy Revolution," stated: "Don't underestimate the relationship between litter and liberty at Columbia. Until last Tuesday, April 23, the university was a clean dorm, where students paid rent, kept house rules, and took exams. Then the rebels arrived, in an uneasy coalition of hip, black and leftist militants. They wanted to make Columbia more like home. So they ransacked files, shoved furniture around, plastered walls with paint and placards. They scrawled on blackboards and doodled on desks. They raided the administration's offices (the psychological equivalent of robbing your mother's purse) and they claim to have found cigars, sherry, and a dirty book (the psychological equivalent of finding condoms in your father's wallet)."

mounted, famous journalists and poets thrilled to the adventure of being hauled up onto ledges and entering the barricaded buildings through the window, to be told by the embattled students about the inequities of Columbia. (Neither the journalists nor the poets bothered to go to the administration later to find out if these stories were true.) It is little wonder that, for most of the students, those five defiant days were a transfigured moment which made them feel that the prosaic routine of study and classes was empty and hollow.

The single problem, of course, was how the defiance would end. Ever-present was the threat of the police—though as the days passed and the police still did not come, many students began to have a deceptively safe feeling that they never would. When they were warned later by faculty emissaries that the danger was acute and the consequences might be savage, they half refused to believe it would ever happen. As the days moved on, the substantive issues too began to recede. It became clear early on that the gymnasium was stymied and would have to be reconsidered; IDA itself was being studied, but in fact it had always been a vague and ambiguous issue to most of the students, few of whom ever knew what IDA actually did. The primary issue now was the students' demand for "amnesty."

The meaning of the demand was singularly clear to the SDS. As one student put it, quite precisely, in the *West Side News*, a local community newspaper, just before the police action:

SDS members are holding out for total amnesty because less than that would put them in the position of admitting the administration's right to punish them. Such an admission would be tantamount to repudiating their guerrilla tactics and agreeing with the logic of the administration, which is: we don't dispute your right to criticize, but we disagree with your tactics—i.e., subverting our authority. For this reason SDS members cannot settle for less than total amnesty. *The fact is their tactics are their ends*—that is, to show that the students could take over the university and bring that consciousness to the whole student body.... The unspoken politics of the battle are that the student rebels are afraid that they will lose popular support by asking what they really want, which is student control of the university, and the administration, consciously or unconsciously aware of this, can avoid the heart of the matter by pretending to take the rebels' demands at face value. (Italics added.)

In actual fact, there was a double complication. While SDS was basically uninterested in the specific demands being made—they *were* simply tactical maneuvers—a large number of students who followed them, including many in the buildings, were sincere about the limited aims. They were uneasy about the morality of such extreme tactics for specific ends, and they sought to justify these tactics on the ground that the administration would not listen and that there was

"no other way." On the other hand, the administration, well aware
of the true aims of SDS, refused to take the demands at face value,
and was waiting for a propitious moment to call in the police to clear
the buildings. What tied the hands of the administration was the
attitude of an active group of faculty.

A Third Force?

On Wednesday morning, April 24, the day after Hamilton was
taken over, a group of college faculty, dispossessed from their
offices, a central place for faculty information and to discuss some
mediating role.[7] Out of these discussions grew the idea of a tripartite
commission to handle disciplinary matters. This proposal, presented
to the full college-faculty meeting that afternoon, was quickly
accepted by the administration. As the threat of violence on campus
grew, especially when a group of counterdemonstrators surrounded
Low Library and tried to prevent people and food from getting
inside, the faculty meeting in Philosophy Hall transformed itself into
an ad hoc committee in an effort to become a "third force" between
the protesting students and the administration. This committee had
three aims: to prevent violence among students; to prevent police
from coming onto the campus; and to negotiate the specific demands
being made, principally the gymnasium. The ad hoc faculty group
had no clear constituency. The meetings were held almost around the
clock in the Philosophy lounge, and as crises developed, votes were
taken among those present. While many of those present were junior
faculty, the heart of the body was a fifteen-man steering committee,
made up principally of individuals who were politically liberal in
orientation, who had studied radical movements, and who had some
experience in the study of "comparative politics."[8] Few of them had

[7]The initiative in this matter was taken by the writer of this essay and
Professor Eugene Galanter. For a detailed account of all the actions, and the
various factions, both student and the faculty, see the informative article by
Dankwart A. Rustow in *The New Leader*, May 20, 1968.

[8]The members of the steering committee were: Alan Westin (government),
chairman; Alex Dallin (government), Dankwart Rustow (government), Immanuel
Wallerstein (sociology), Terence Hopkins (sociology), Allan Silver (sociology),
James Shenton (history), David Rothman (history), Robert Fogelson (history),
Walter Metzger (history), Robert Cumming (philosophy), Sidney Morgenbesser
(philosophy), Robert Belknap (Russian literature), Seymour Melman (industrial
engineering). The writer was out of town when the Ad Hoc Committee was
formally created, but when he returned on Saturday, he was "co-opted" to
membership. All except one of the committee were tenured professors; nine
were full professors.

any illusions about SDS, but they were united in two convictions: (1) if the police were brought in, the student body would be "radicalized," thus giving SDS the victory it wanted; and (2) there was a majority of protestors who were not of SDS, but had joined the action because of the issues, and these students might be convinced to leave the buildings peacefully if the administration would negotiate. About 200 faculty members signed a statement proposing a halt in the construction of the gymnasium and the transfer of discipline to a tripartite body. They also promised that if the students evacuated the buildings, they would not hold classes until these proposals were accepted.

On Thursday, at midnight, Vice President Truman appeared before the Ad Hoc Faculty Committee and stated, rather abruptly, that because of mounting tension on campus and fights between demonstrators and nondemonstrators, the administration was asking the police to clear the buildings. The response was a storm of boos and cries of "shame," and the faculty present voted unanimously to interpose themselves between the police and the students in the buildings. Taken aback by this reception, Truman reconsidered and called off the police. He told the Ad Hoc Committee, in effect, that finding a way out of the situation was now up to them.

For the next few days, the Ad Hoc Committee suggested a variety of formulas to mediate the dispute. A considerable body of sentiment on campus swung behind the committee.[9] Yet the faculty group encountered intransigence on both sides. Although construction on the gym had by now halted, the university insisted that it could not make any further statements because of legal complications. More important, while the administration agreed to the creation of a Joint Disciplinary Committee, President Kirk refused to surrender to it "ultimate disciplinary powers." The students in the buildings, fearful of what this might mean, held fast to the demand for amnesty.

[9]While student sentiment during a changing and explosive situation is difficult to determine, a referendum organized by the student services societies gives some indication. While the organizers of the poll stated at the time that it had been impossible to conduct it on a sampling or organized-referendum basis, the tally compares in all respects with the results of a poll taken six days after the police action by the Bureau of Applied Social Research at Columbia. According to the account in the *Spectator* of Monday, April 29, of 5,500 ballots the following responded thus: (1) In favor of amnesty for all students involved in the demonstration of the last three days: Yes, 2,054; No, 3,466. (2) To end the construction of the gym: Yes, 4,093; No, 1,433. (3) To end the university's ties with IDA: Yes, 3,572; No, 1,855. (4) In favor of the demonstration tactics used by the SDS and SAS thus far: Yes, 1,325; No, 4,124.

The Failure of Mediation

By Sunday, it was clear that the mediation efforts of the Ad Hoc Committee had failed. Spurred by information from the mayor's office that unless a break in the dispute came by the next day the administration would probably call in the police—and the committee members were given a vivid account of how brutal such police actions might be—the Ad Hoc Committee decided to "impose" a solution on both sides. It drew up a settlement that, it stated, would be a "bitter pill" for the administration and the students, but that represented a "just" arbitration. It called for continuing the suspension of work on the gymnasium, with no further action to be taken unless reviewed by community groups; it proposed that final disciplinary power be lodged in a tripartite judicial body; it rejected amnesty but stated that in light of the fact that the students had acted collectively, there would not be individually different punishments—thus making sure that strike leaders would not be singled out for heavier punishments—but uniform penalties would be applied to all. Again, since it was unlikely that all the demonstrators would be suspended, in effect this meant that all the students would be placed on probation.

A massive effort was made all day Monday to mobilize support for the Ad Hoc Committee position. Within a few hours, 2,500 students including almost all the established student leaders on campus, had endorsed the proposals. Prominent figures in New York's political and community life sent in statements of support. Faculty emissaries met with the administration and with the Student Strike Coordinating Committee to persuade both sides to accept. The students were warned, as forcefully as possible, that police action was imminent. The administration was told that if the students accepted the faculty proposals and the administration rejected them, the faculty would stand before the buildings if the police came.

All these efforts also came to nothing. The administration did make a conciliatory gesture in which it warmly endorsed the action of the Ad Hoc Committee, but it refused to accept community review of any future decision on the gymnasium, nor would the President give up his final disciplinary powers.[10] The Strike Steering

[10]To illustrate the legalism which ensnared many of the administration's actions, in his testimony before the Cox Committee, Vice President Truman noted that a serious question had arisen about what disciplinary powers could be delegated by the president or the trustees under the university's charter. He pointed out that Columbia was operating under the original colonial charter, which antedates the establishment of the New York State Board of Regents. Thus Columbia is the only university in the state that does not come under the

Committee rejected the Ad Hoc Committee proposal out of hand; at the end, in a typical gesture, they even refused the faculty negotiating committee the courtesy of a written statement. Instead, they insisted that they be allowed to read their own statement before the faculty body. Despite the unanimity of the Strike Steering Committee, however, it was later revealed that the Ad Hoc Committee proposal had been accepted, in part, by the students at Fayerweather, who in a "counterproposal" dropped the demand for amnesty and suggested that the issue of discipline be submitted to a "bipartite" faculty-student committee. The leaflet listing these counterproposals stated: "The above rough proposal was voted by the majority of strikers in Fayerweather Hall to be forwarded by the Strike Steering Committee for consideration by the rest of the liberated community." As it turned out the Strike Steering Committee, dominated as it was by SDS, did not circulate the Fayerweather proposals. Nor did the SDS leaders pass along to a number of the buildings the full import of the faculty warnings.[11] The SDS leadership certainly wanted the police to come. As one of them said later: "The eyes of Berlin were upon us and we wanted the police to come in and drag us out." They did.

The Bust

The irony is that the more extremist of the demonstrators, politically and rhetorically, escaped the main brunt of the police savagery, but the moderates did not. There is little doubt that after a while the police action did indeed turn brutal, and as many bystanders as participants were hurt. The police command had assured the administration that a "minimum" amount of violence would be used. Everyone, particularly the mayor's representatives

---

jurisdiction of the regents. Truman said that efforts to revise the charter in one detail might have opened the way to revision of other portions of the charter, and the university wanted to avoid this.

On reflection, I would say, too, that the tone of the ad hoc document was preremptory, and given the need to extend the time, and to reduce tension, the imposition of a deadline was a mistake. By firing up both sides in this way, the committee's effort probably served to sharpen the confrontation. I shared in this mistake.

[11]Equally relevant was the students' intense suspiciousness of the "outside world," which their self-exile under siege conditions generated among them. When Professors Peter Kenen and Seymour Melman tried to enter Fayerweather, Melman, who has been active in SANE and left-wing causes and who had spoken at SDS rallies at the sundial, thought the students would listen to him. But he and Kenen were met, as they put it, with "naked distrust and paranoia."

who were on hand, was mindful of the blacks in Hamilton. In fact, it was only after the mayor's representatives could be sure, after a check throughout the community, that Harlem would take no action, that the signal to bring in the police had been given at all.

The administration had made many efforts before April 30 to negotiate with the black students in Hamilton. Percy Sutton, the black Borough President of Manhattan, went into Hamilton at Kirk's request, but departed without telling the administration what he had learned—an action that led some administration people to believe Sutton had advised the students to stay. Kenneth Clark, the black psychologist at the City University, and a member of the New York State Board of Regents, entered Hamilton with Theodore Kheel, the labor mediator, on Monday afternoon. While the black students in Hamilton decided to stay, it was made clear that they would put up no resistance. When the police came, including by protocol a black patrol, the students in Hamilton walked out quietly, through the tunnels in the building, to the waiting police vans. In Mathematics Hall which was dominated by the Maoists, kooks, and hippies, there was little resistance and few students were hurt. The same scene was repeated at Low, where the SDS leadership had congregated. Ironically, the worst incidents of brutality happened in Avery and Fayerweather, in which the moderate students predominated. Having wavered before, the students in these buildings now seemed intent on "proving their manhood," and they resisted bitterly. As the police were forced to clear them out of barricaded room after barricaded room, they became more savage. But one part of the police action that had nothing to do with the clearing of the buildings was largely responsible for the intensity of campus reaction the following day.

Except for Hamilton, all the buildings being cleared were on the north side of College Walk. On the south side, almost a thousand students had congregated to watch the action, many of them inevitably jeering and taunting the police. Once all the buildings were emptied, the police were assembled in a line on College Walk, facing the students. They were then suddenly ordered to clear the field. Without warning, the police—enraged by the jeers and taunts they had been hearing—charged the students in front of them, flailing away with their nightsticks, running after the students fleeing across the field, and clubbing those who failed to move swiftly enough. In all, about a hundred students were hurt. But it was not the violence itself that was so horrible—despite the many pictures in the papers of bleeding students, not one required hospitalization. It was the capriciousness of that final action. The police simply ran wild. Those who tried to say they were innocent bystanders or faculty were given the same flailing treatment as the students. For most of the students, it was their first encounter with brutality and blood, and they responded in fear and anger. The next day, almost the entire campus responded to a call for a student strike. In a few hours, thanks to the New York City Police Department, a large part of the Columbia campus had become "radicalized."[12]

A New Idea: "Restructuring"

The day after the police action, the joint faculties on Morningside Heights met for the second time in the history of the university.[13] On the Sunday before the buildings were cleared, the joint faculties had met and overwhelmingly adopted a formal vote of confidence in the administration. Now, two days later, the mood of the senior faculty had changed. Although a motion expressing support for the administration was introduced, a substitute motion, introduced by a group from the Law Faculty, took precedence and carried the meeting. It called for the creation of an executive committee that would be empowered to take "needed steps to return the university to its educational task." It was clear that the faculties no longer had complete confidence in the administration, and wanted their own means of expression.

Not only had the faculty mood changed, but that of the students as well. The new Executive Committee met that evening and

[12]In all, 705 persons were arrested; exactly how many were arrested in the buildings, and how many on South Field after the police charge, it would be hard to say. Of the total arrested, 181, or 26 per cent, were not connected with Columbia. Of the 524 identified as registered Columbia students, 400 (or 77 per cent) were undergraduates. Of these, 239 were from Columbia College, and 111 from Barnard, the remainder from General Studies. In effect, almost 10 per cent of the college student body was arrested.

[13]Columbia University is a strange congeries of institutions, as a result of its long history and growth. Barnard College and Teachers College students receive Columbia University degrees, but the two institutions, though on Morningside Heights, are not part of the Columbia Corporation and each has its own trustees. The medical faculty, the School of Public Health, the dental faculty, and the School of Social Work are members of the Columbia Corporation but are not on Morningside Heights. This makes it difficult to be exact about the total number of faculty and students of "Columbia University." The faculties on Morningside Heights comprise the college; the graduate schools, divided into three faculties of science, philosophy (including the humanities), and political science (including the social sciences); and the professional schools: law, business, engineering (which includes an undergraduate college), architecture, journalism, and the school of arts (writing and the performing arts). In addition there is a College of Pharmacy, which is neither on Morningside Heights nor a member of the Columbia Corporation.

the next day with about forty student leaders. Few of them had been in the buildings and few had supported SDS. But now all of them supported the strike, and a new, overriding issue was raised which had not been heard before: the need to "restructure" the university —"to structure" has become an acceptable, in fact a highly favored sociological verb, these days. SDS had been making political demands, and few of these student leaders were interested in them. But they now felt that the archaic organizational arrangements of the university, and the exclusion of students and faculty from the decision-making processes, even in consultative capacities, had now to be changed.

The question of purpose was soon to divide the students. At the start, SDS sought to capture the strike movement. The Strike Committee—a carryover from the committees in the occupied buildings—announced that "any" group of seventy students could send a representative to the enlarged strike committee. It was a shrewd move, consonant with the idea of smashing "bourgeois student" power, since many of the established student leaders (e.g., the board of managers of Ferris Booth Hall, the Student Union) had no specific "constituency." It also meant that a student could often vote several times, in different capacities (in the dormitories, as a member of a club, or as a member of a departmental student group), in electing a representative to the Strike Committee. Within a week, about sixty students had been elected to the Strike Committee, and while some double counting was inevitable, the total represented—presumably 4,000—was still impressive.

It is the very nature of any extremist movement to keep things churning. It must maintain activity and excitement in order to maintain a zealous morale. But the police "bust" had been an exhausting emotional experience for everyone on the campus, and shortly afterward some of the tension began to ebb as the questions of how to "restructure" the university came to the fore. The executive committee of the faculty had been instrumental in setting up a Fact Finding Commission, under the chairmanship of Archibald Cox of the Harvard Law School, to hold hearings on the causes of the recent events. It had persuaded the Board of Trustees to set up a panel to inquire into the organization of the university. It had begun to create a large-scale summer study program to evaluate different plans of university organization. To SDS all such activity was a threat, because it raised questions requiring research and answers, it asked for various student programs and proposals, it raised the vexing issue of "complexities." As the faculty statements pointed out, an institution as complicated as Columbia could not be overhauled in a day or by the flick of a rhetorical phrase.

SDS responded to all this, on May 17, by uniting with some local tenant groups to seize a Columbia-owned apartment building on West 114th Street. It charged the university with "colonialism," and with creating a "white ghetto" on Morningside Heights by "deliberately forcing the removal of almost every black, Puerto Rican and Oriental" from the neighborhood. A black flag was raised over the building, and the students demanded that the building, more than half-vacant since it would before long be torn down and the site used for a new school of social work, be used for community housing. Within a few hours the police cleared the building and area without violence.

The effort by SDS to keep things churning inevitably created tensions within the Strike Steering Committee. At least half of the committee was not interested in the political aims propounded by SDS. Their concern was, genuinely, with the reorganization of the university. When Mark Rudd began making appearances at Brooklyn College, and calling upon Columbia students to demonstrate there, and when SDS issued proposals for support of other direct-action measures, a split developed within the Strike Coordinating Committee, and one group, representing about half the total, left to form The Students for a Restructured University.

Hamilton II

It was at this point that the administration decided to assert its authority by suspending four of the leaders of SDS. The move was technically in accordance with the procedures set up by the new Joint Disciplinary Committee, which had been created after the first police action. The timing of the suspension, however, was ill-considered. Its result was Hamilton II.

On May 23, four weeks to the day after the first sit-in, about 250 students took over Hamilton Hall. This time the demonstrators were white. The Students for a Restructured University, which now claimed to represent 3,000 students, declared that it would not participate. A majority of those who did sit in chose to do so for the symbolic reason of making a protest. But once the building had been taken, the SDS leaders began to argue that it was necessary to stay and force the police to throw them out again. At first only 25 students wanted to stay and 150 to leave. But the SDS leadership refused to accept that vote and after several hours of debate, the majority of those inside Hamilton were shamed into staying.

After ten hours, the police moved in at 2:30 in the morning and quietly cleared the building. The action was peaceful, but the students, having been brought to a fever pitch, needed some cathartic release. The entry of the police on campus triggered an emotional reaction among hundreds of students who, in the pre-dawn hour, roamed the campus, hurling bricks at the police, smashing windows, and lighting fires in several university buildings. President Kirk gave an order for the police to clear the campus. A larger force of police was called in to contain the students. Savagery on both sides erupted. About 68 persons were injured, this time including 17 policemen; 174 persons were arrested.[14]

The action of the police again brought a surge of sympathy for SDS—though this sympathy was somewhat tempered by disapproval of the vandalism of a number of "kooks" and by the vengeful burning of a history professor's notes. The Students for a Restructured University attacked the administration for "provoking" the disturbance by starting the disciplinary action, but refrained from commenting on the fact that such action was not final and still subject to review by the Joint Disciplinary Committee, was responded to so violently by the SDS. A *schadenfreude* judgment was made by a writer for the "underground" newspaper, *The New York Free Press*, who, chortling over the fact that the administration had "played into the hands of SDS," wrote:

> It is part of the philosophy of the radical left that the "Liberal Establishment" when confronted with ideological political force "cannot act reasonably even for its own ends . . . and when pressured will make mistake after mistake after mistake." Fortunately for the radicals at Columbia, this prophecy turned out to be especially true in the case of Grayson Kirk.[15]

[14]Of those arrested, 46, the single largest group, were outsiders; of the remainder, 45 were from Columbia College, 23 from the Graduate Faculties, 17 from Barnard, 15 from General Studies, and a total of 23 from all other units of the university. Five faculty were also arrested.

[15]That writer continues: "At about 4:30 A.M. hundreds of tired students gathered around the Sundial where Dean Platt 'regretfully' announced that President Kirk had given the order for the police to move in and clear the campus.

"Exhausted students who had been dragging themselves from place to place suddenly woke up with the announcement. One girl who had been just about to leave for her apartment said, 'That makes me feel as if I'd just gotten a shot of adrenalin.'

"Students immediately rushed to the barricades to prepare themselves for the coming struggle. Had Kirk at this point stationed five uniformed policemen in each of the academic buildings and not provoked the students with a confrontation, a Strike leader privately commented, 'the whole thing would have broken up and everybody would have gone to bed.' "

Life Imitates Art

After Hamilton II, the violent passions began to subside. Examinations were suspended, and in the college any student who wanted it could obtain a simple pass grade if he notified his instructor. On the grass, in the spring sun, the Strike Education Committee now devoted itself to "counter-classes" as part of a new Liberation School. The rules were simple:

> The question of expertise of the leader(s) of a counter-class is to be determined by the (relevant) community of faculty, students and others together. This implies that anyone (including undergraduates and custodians) will be allowed to run a counter-class as long as the community of students, faculty and others in his alleged area of expertise recognize him.

Anyone who wanted to, could give a class. The teacher was not to stand in front of the class and each person, including the teacher, was supposed to take no more than his proportion of the time, so that if there were twenty persons present, each person, including the teacher, would take only one-twentieth of the time. Leaders of Trotskyite sects flocked to the campus to hold courses on the "History of the Russian (and other) Revolutions." Professors *manques* analyzed the contradictions of capitalism; and lay psycho-analysts and lecturers, whose usual audience is "Over 28, Singles Only" clubs, spoke on "Intimacy games, their meaning, the individual and society." Others did their "thing," which had one Phyllis Deutsch giving a course in Arabic Belly Dancing ("dress to move freely") and Howard Press lecturing on "Culture and Constraint Dimensions of Freedom in Marx, Freud, Marcuse, Reich." And amidst all the din, one student gave a course on "A Slightly-less-liberated Talmud," in front of Earl Hall, the religious counselors' building; why not, for as he explained to Professor Sidney Morgenbesser, it was a commandment and a blessing to teach Talmud anywhere.

It was, we were told, 1848 all over again, the revolution of the students. But if it was 1848, then history had begun to imitate art rather than itself. The model had been laid down by Flaubert in *A Sentimental Education*, his novel about 1848. In the Rue Saint-Jacques, the Club de l'Intelligence, whose chairman is the incorruptible pedagogue Senecal, is debating the aims of the revolution:

> The audience showed great respect for their chairman. He had been among those who had on the 25th of February demanded the immediate organization of labour; the next day, at the Prado, he had urged an attack on the Hotel de

Ville; and since it was the custom for figures of that period to model themselves after a pattern—some imitating Saint-Just, others Danton, others Marat—Senecal tried to resemble Blanqui, who was a follower of Robespierre. . . .

"My turn!" cried Delmar.

He leapt on to the platform, pushed everyone aside, and took up his usual pose. Declaring that he despised such mean accusations [against actors] he dilated on the actor's civilizing mission. Since the theatre was the centre of national education, he was in favour of reforming it. First of all, there should be no more managers and no more privileges.

"That's right! No more privileges at all!"

The actor's performance inflamed the crowd, and the air was thick with revolutionary proposals.

"Down with academics. Down with the Institut!"

"No more missions!"

"No more matriculation!"

"Down with university degrees!"

"No," said Senecal, "let us preserve them; but let them be conferred by universal franchise, by the people, the only true judge."

Microcosm II—a Commentary

The Columbia "student rebellion" is now passing into the mythos of revolutionary history. It is being linked, in temperament and impulse, with the outbursts against authority that marked working-class action in early nineteenth-century England (the Luddites), the violent opposition to industrial discipline in Victorian England (the Chartists), and the anarchist plots of the early 1900's. Along with the Sorbonne and Berlin, Columbia will serve for historians as a notch in the recurrent cycles of radical social movements. And there can be no doubt that the Columbia disorders reflect a reaction to some deep-running structural changes in our society. But the more difficult question is why the imp of the *Zeitgeist* happened to land at this time, in this place.

As I have indicated earlier, what happened was unexpected, even by the instigators, and accidental. There was no long history of angry, unresolved conflicts that had been boiling for some time and had to explode. The administration had not been repressive; if anything, it had been, in disciplinary matters, at first lenient and then wayward. The manifest issues had impinged little on the consciousness of the students. Those issues that were raised did not seem salient: the IDA was already being studied by a university committee as a result of previous protests; the gymnasium, while a nagging thorn to the black militants of Harlem, had not aroused much attention on the Heights. There were latent grievances and discontents, as are present in most institutions; and there were serious shortcomings in the administrative and decision-making procedures of the university that arose out of its sprawling and uncoordinated structure. But students, and even most faculty, were not really aware of these.

In short, before April 23, few people assumed the issues to be important, and even fewer would have justified the extreme tactics which, as means, were so disproportionate to the ends allegedly being sought. But during the events and since, history has been quickly rewritten in order to make it seem that the university was repressive and unresponsive, so as to give a cast of desperation to the action of the students, as though no other course was open, or because the issues were so crucial.

Events make history, but how does one explain the trajectory of events? How is it that, on one campus at least, the politics of confrontation and the tactics of extreme disruption were able to evoke so large a student response as to make once marginal issues become so immediate and burning, and questions of ends and means, once so central to a liberal philosophy, be waved away as irrelevant? How could an administration, tolerant to a fault and even avuncular in its responsiveness to students, albeit in a fumbling way, become, after a series of fitful indecisions, so punitive as to make a fortuitous conflict with the police seem to be the culminating event in a chain of purposeful confrontations?

What this suggests—in answer to the first question—is that a considerable portion of the student body, in the course of becoming "radicalized," underwent a "conversion experience" so intense and embracing as to blot out all qualifying and self-critical thoughts about the nature of their challenge to the university, and—in answer to the second—that the administration experienced a reaction so traumatic as to make the reassertion of formal authority the sole criterion of its policy. Locked into this double confrontation, the only resolution for both sides was force. How and why this happened I am not sure can be made clear; I can only try.

Liberalism in Crisis

The ethos of an institution embodies its legitimations, and the ethos of Columbia is liberalism. There is complete academic freedom. A teacher, even assistants and preceptors, teaches his own courses without any interference, and gives a staff course in his own way without supervision. To my knowledge, no administrator or departmental chairman has ever dropped into a man's course to "observe" his teaching. Most of the faculty is, politically, liberal. The men who give Columbia its reputation—Lionel Trilling, Meyer Schapiro, Ernest Nagel, Richard Hofstadter—have been in the forefront of liberal causes for more than thirty years. A number of Columbia's leading political scientists and law professors—Roger Hilsman, Zbigniew Brezinski, Richard Gardner, Charles Frankel, William Cary, Wallace Sayre—have served in recent Democratic administrations. In the year-and-a-half before April 23, 1968, a group of ten leading professors, led by Fritz Stern, the historian, and including Vice President Truman, had worked actively to reverse the nations' Vietnam policy. In the college and the graduate faculties, a Republican is a rarity. A poll revealed that 70 per cent of the faculty favored withdrawal from Vietnam before President Johnson's statement.

The student body itself, cosmopolitan and coming from parents in the professional class, is largely liberal. More than 900 students work in the Citizenship Council, an extracurricular activity that has devoted itself in recent years largely to service— tutoring and community organization—with the poor and in Harlem. Several hundred students were in contact with pacifist organizations such as the War Resisters League, the Fellowship of Reconciliation, and the Resistance—the more so since, under the new draft regulations that went into effect in June 1968, grad- uate students no longer received deferments, and college students were likely to be drafted right after graduation. This had heightened apprehensions on campus.

But in the last two years liberalism itself, particularly in the student movement, had come under severe attack. The Vietnam War, it was argued, had grown out of "liberal anti-Communism." The restlessness and militancy of the blacks was taken as a portent that peaceful social change is ineffective. The Great Society was mocked for the inadequacy of its domestic programs.

That political liberalism was in crisis was quite true, but perhaps not for the reasons given by the student Left—in fact, for reasons that would not be to its liking. For if there is a single source for the crisis of liberalism—apart from the Vietnam War—it is owing to the complexity of our social problems, to the linked nature of change and a lack of knowledge or adequate research about where and how one can effectively "cut into the system" in order to direct social change. The old simplicities about "more" schools and "more" housing, or even "better" schools or "better" housing, have not proved very useful in breaking the cycle of poverty or in dealing with Negro family structure. For those given to moralisms or "sophis- ticated" chatter about "power," such talk about complexities is irritating. Either they regard it as an evasion of the "real" problems, or they retreat from any analysis by simply insisting that more money will solve any problem, or, in the case of the New Left, they insist that the entire society is sick and corrupt and that "the system" must be overturned in one fell swoop.

The Students for a Democratic Society was itself in a great quandary. During the previous five years it had become steadily more "left," yet it felt itself to be increasingly frustrated. SDS had its first flowering in the civil-rights movement, but that movement had now become exhausted. SDS then turned its attention to "community organizing" and sought to build interracial "unions" of the poor in a dozen cities; but these efforts had been fruitless. It had its own "identity crisis" in not knowing whether the students were a "class," or how they stood in relation to the "means of production." (Some SDS members, more theoretically minded, latched on, interestingly, to the idea propounded originally in France by Andre Gorz and Serge Mallet of a "new" working class, made up of technicians and professionals—a left-wing version, so to speak, of the post-industrial society.) But for most of them, there was simply the tension and rancor fed by the war, and the attraction of the propositions, distilled second-hand from Regis Debray, that it was sufficiently revolutionary to act without any program, to act simply for the sake of the revolution. In this spirit, they conceived themselves to be guerrillas in the urban society, and for their field of action they chose the university.

The University as Microcosm

SDS sees the university as the microcosm of our society. If the society is sick and corrupt, so is the university. Having made this assertive leap, SDS sought to document this charge with "evidence" of the university's "complicity" in the war. The moralizing of belief leads to the vulgarization of politics, for if politics is seen as a case of *either/or*, one needs rhetoric that is simplified and does not admit of complication or compromise. SDS found its rhetoric in a primitivized and stilted Marxism, rooted in a conspiracy theory of "hidden networks of power," in which all motives are economic and all actions are sinister.[16]

[16]In an extraordinary brochure entitled "Who Rules Columbia?," published by the self-styled North American Congress on Latin America, but distributed widely by SDS, the effort is made to show the "nexus" between Columbia and the "military-industrial complex." Thus in one section we read: "It was General Dwight D. Eisenhower and Grayson Kirk who brought Columbia University's financial support for defense or defense related projects from less than 1% (in 1945) to about 48% in 1968." The statement typically confuses the total of *all* of Columbia's contracts with the federal government with "defense or defense-related" contracts. Of some $55 million in Federal government contracts, comprising about 48 per cent of Columbia's operating budget as of March 31, 1968, $22.9 million was from the U.S. Public Health Service, and

What SDS could not do to the larger society it could attempt against the university: to wreck it. A university, after all, is essentially a defenseless place. It commands no force of its own, other than the reluctant power of expulsion, and commands its loyalty through the moral authority growing out of the idea that the university is a special institution in our society, drawing its grace from the most "sacred" source of rights in a free society—the commitment to open inquiry and truth. Even so, the SDS militancy was largely verbal—until the barricading of Hamilton Hall by the blacks—an open defiance of the university by individuals who had no regard for its intellectual and scholarly role, but saw it only as a secular power on the Heights overlooking Harlem. The occupation of the buildings by SDS had a largely different consequence, for here, directly and for the first time, the moral authority of the university, qua university, was being denigrated. Talk had now passed. The tear in the social fabric had now been made. The SDS had taken the first step in becoming guerrillas.

First Deeds, then Words

What of the other students, the four hundred or so who did not belong to SDS but who, in the five days, followed SDS into the buildings and stayed until the police got them out? This is a group that shares the underlying vague, inchoate, diffuse dissatisfaction with our society and its liberal culture, the more so because of the Vietnam War. Many of them disdained the SDS and its self-inflated posture of revolution. But they were restive—the undergraduates because of their new status in the draft, the graduate students because of their subordinate positions in the departments—and, in the demonstration of the inadequacies of liberalism in a liberal institution, they were receptive to protest actions against the administration. But few of them, before the events, ever would have conceived of themselves as occupying buildings and justifying such means that were so disproportionate to the manifest ends. It was their unexpected action—and the failure of the administration to differentiate them from the SDS—that gave a very different coloring to the events. Why did they act as they did?

---

went almost entirely to the Medical School. The total from the Defense Department was about $12 million—of which $9 million was from the Navy for the maintenance of two laboratories concerned with oceanographic research, one of which is devoted to basic or "pure" research concerned with mapping the ocean's bottom, and one of which, whose scope is being reduced, was devoted to classified research.

Freud once remarked that you commit yourself first in words and then in deeds. This is a curiously rationalistic description of the way people change their views. The revolutionary psychology is more subtle: first you commit yourself in deeds, and then you find the words to justify the action. But the first leap has to be a big one, a tearing down of a major taboo. In this case, the very audacity of seizing a building by the blacks was the bold act that preempted many doubts, for the implicit meaning was communicated: if such drastic steps are being taken, something must be wrong. The way then is open for others. In the contagion of excitement, there is a stampede to action; in the call of one's friends there is involvement with a group; in the polarization of antagonists there is the tension of impending conflict which keeps one firm no matter what the silent or wavering doubts.

The deed having been done—the acting out of forbidden impulses—the words came next. Along with the occupation of the buildings there was an extraordinary barrage of propaganda— sustained, concentrated, intensive, repetitive, simplified—all of it making one or two reiterated points: Columbia was the "intersect" of a corporate-military-CIA nexus to advance American imperialism, and Columbia was guilty of "institutional racism" in its neighborhood policy. All of this was "documented" with the corporate affiliations of the university's trustees and the connection with IDA, and with the charge that Columbia in its "expropriation" of the neighborhood had expelled seven, eight, or ten thousand families from Morningside Heights, all of them black or Puerto Rican. These were the themes of numerous leaflets and of a half dozen or so newspapers sympathetic to the New Left which were widely distributed on the Columbia campus.

In this hothouse atmosphere of frenetic excitement, in which the world had shrunk to the dimensions of a single campus, and students felt themselves to be actors in a great historical drama ("Columbia is at the beginning stages of the revolution" was the intoxicating refrain), there was a massive shift in the frames of reference of hundreds of students. Most of us, implicitly or otherwise, work from some basic premises about a society, the values which make some actions seem right or wrong. When such premises are codified, given a moral content and often an antagonistic stance, it becomes an ideology, a formula that allows an individual, without further doubts about his premises, to make a whole series of related judgements about new circumstances. Ideology, thus, is a cognitive map with a built-in set of emotional judgements and rationalizations. What happened to hundreds of students during those last five days of April—the imprint of the conversion experience as a result of their impulsive commitment to action—was this shift in social perceptions, a shift given greater vividness by the *eclaircissement* of Columbia as a malevolent institution, by the dramatic revelation of hidden "secrets," the tearing down of old beliefs and the substitution of a new, stark "reality." In short, what we had here was a classic illustration of the contagion phenomenon of a mass that Gustav Le Bon described so graphically in *Psychologie des Foules* in 1895.

Any new set of beliefs requires some confirmation of its validity by some "significant others," or by a testing of reality. At Columbia, one legitimation was quickly supplied by members of the New York literary "establishment," who were ecstatic at having a real revolution on their doorstep. Norman Mailer threw a large fund-raising party.[17] Dwight Macdonald wrote a "begging" letter to his friends for money in support of SDS. Moreover, the fact that the French students at Nanterre had begun occupying their university buildings, in an action that spread quickly to the Sorbonne, gave the Columbia students the heady sense of participating in an international movement of historic scope, and this identification strongly reinforced their belief that their actions were legitimate.

But the acquisition of new beliefs or judgments also requires confirmation at the cognitive level, some real test of the intellectual validity of the new conception. This can—in more neutral areas and in quieter times—take the form of intellectual debate about the consistency of the argument, the quality of evidence, the congruity with other beliefs, its place within a larger theoretical or intellectual structure, and so on; reality testing also takes the form of prediction, and the falsification of such judgments becomes the basis for the beginning of disbelief. Where emotions are deeply involved, such testing is never wholly persuasive, of course, but it is still necessary, if only to rationalize earlier action when a glimmer of disbelief or disillusionment has set in.[18]

[17]Radical history has the unfortunate habit of repeating itself in pop form. In 1913, Wild Bill Haywood of Wobbly fame had a party thrown for him, during the Paterson strike, by John Reed at Mabel Dodge Luhan's house, an event that went down as one of the "glories" of Greenwich Village history. More than fifty years later the scene was replayed in Brooklyn Heights.

[18]Most conversion experiences are superficial or temporary, and if the surrounding social environment is powerful enough, or retains its legitimacy, or if the new converts become repelled by discordant elements of the new belief, or disillusioned in the character of the new prophets or leaders, or feel they have been manipulated, there is a quick erosion of the new belief, and the converts feel betrayed or angered. Where conversion involves a "leap of faith" to a sharply different set of counterbeliefs, religious and political movements protect themselves from reality testing by "encapsulating" themselves from the hostile environment. In the nineteenth century this often took the form of utopian colonies physically separated from the dominant social environment. In the

The accusations—and beliefs—of the students were never challenged by the administration: in part out of bewilderment with their whirlwind appearance and their patently intellectual simplifications, which the administration thought few would believe; in part because the administration was enraged at the tactics used—holding a dean hostage, rifling the president's files, raising of red flags, barricading of buildings, and refusing, initially, even to meet with the vice president and discuss the issues. Thus, there was no intellectual debate, and the "reality testing" was provided by the police. The "bust" confirmed the students' new beliefs. Whatever psychological guilt or unease was felt about the demonstrators' coercive and disruptive tactics was dissolved in the payment of broken heads and spilled blood. As the students saw it, the administration resorted to force because it could not answer them. With the police action, the administration lost a large part of its legitimacy—its moral authority—which had previously commanded the loyalty of students and faculty.

The University as a Community

In a hard and brilliant piece in *The New Republic* of June 1, 1968, entitled "Revolution and Counterrevolution, (But Not Necessarily about Columbia!)," a rather Machiavellian essay written from the balcony, Zbigniew Brzezinski coldly analyzed the mistakes of the Columbia administration and faculty. It is worth quoting him at length, though I shall take issue with his analysis:

A revolutionary situation typically arises when values of a society are undergoing a profound change. . . .

twentieth century this has taken the form of adopting a sharp "combat posture"—it is no accident that the extreme right and the extreme left glorify combat (one directly in the form of war, the other in the form of revolution) as the highest virtue.

At Columbia the "hothouse" nature of the events and the experience of danger reinforced the sense of solidarity and encapsulation which engulfed those in the buildings. The use of the word "commune" and the shared way of life that prevailed created a *Gemeinschaft*, intense and personal, which made it difficult for doubters to leave—particularly in the face of an impending "bust"—and made it easier for the leaders to manipulate those in the buildings. In such an atmosphere, the one who is most "left" or "radical" has a psychological advantage over any others who may raise questions of compromise or doubts. Many students who were only vaguely "left" or "liberal" came under the psychological pressure of having to prove their political *bona fides* by suppressing their doubts and giving assent to the actions.

The crisis of values has several political consequences of relevance to revolutionary processes. First of all, it prompts ambivalent concessions by the authorities in power. The authorities do not fully comprehend the nature of the changes they are facing, but they are no longer sufficiently certain of their values to react in assertive fashion—concessionism thus becomes the prevailing pattern of their behavior. Secondly, increasingly self-assertive revolutionary forces begin an intensive search for appealing issues. The purpose is to further radicalize and revolutionize the masses and to mobilize them against the *status quo*. . . .

The critical phase occurs when a weak spot has been identified, appealing issues articulated, and the probe becomes a confrontation. At this stage the purpose of revolutionary activity is to legitimize violence. If the initial act of violence is suppressed quickly by established authorities, the chances are that the revolutionary act itself will gain social approbrium; society generally tends to be conservative, even in a situation of crisis of values. Thus a revolutionary act is likely to be condemned by most, provided it is rapidly suppressed. If the revolutionary act endures, then automatically it gains legitimacy with the passage of time. Enduring violence thus becomes a symbol of the authorities' disintegration and collapse, and it prompts in turn further escalation of support for the revolutionary act. . . .

An important role in this revolutionary process is played by legitimist reformers and intellectuals. Intellectuals by their very nature are unwilling to pick sides, since they are better at identifying gray than siding with black and white. In a revolutionary situation, they are particularly concerned with not being stamped as counterrevolutionary conservatives. . . . Accustomed generally to dealing with established authorities, they are more experienced in coping with the authorities than with the revolutionary forces. Thus, in the process of interposing themselves, they are inclined to apply most of their pressure against the established authority, with which they have many links, than equally against established authorities and the revolutionary forces on behalf of reformist appeals. In effect, irrespective of their subjective interests, the legitimist reformers and intellectuals in a revolutionary situation objectively become the tools of the revolutionary forces, thus contributing to further aggravation of the revolutionary situation and radicalizing the overall condition.

When faced with a revolutionary situation, the established authorities typically commit several errors. . . . They display an incapacity for immediate effective response, Their traditional legalism works against them. Faced with a revolutionary situation, instead of striking immediately and effectively, they tend to procrastinate, seeking refuge in legalistic responses. . . . An early confrontation would work to the advantage of the authorities, since mass support begins to shift to the revolutionaries only after the situation has been radicalized. . . . When finally force is employed, the authorities rarely think ahead to post-use-of-force consequences, concentrating instead on the application of force to the specific challenge at hand. They thus neglect the important consideration that the use of force must be designed not only to eliminate surface revolutionary challenge, but to make certain that the revolutionary forces cannot later rally again under the same leadership. If that leadership cannot be physically liquidated, it can at least be expelled from the country (or area) in which revolution is taking place. Emigrants rarely can maintain themselves as effective revolutionaries. The denial of the opportunity for the revolutionary leadership to re-rally should be an important ingredient of the strategy of force, even if it is belatedly used. . . . Finally, established authorities often fail to follow up effective violence with immediate reforms. Such reforms ought to be designed to absorb the energies of the more moderate revolutionaries, who can then claim that though their revolution had failed, their objectives were achieved. This is very important in attracting the more moderate elements to the side of the authorities.

Now, there is much that is true here: an authority which is unsure of itself is bound to hesitate and lose its effectiveness. The democratic regimes of Europe in the 1930's did succumb in part because of their failure to control private violence by the Fascists and Communists. If the university were a microcosm of society, his points would be well-taken. *But the university is not the microcosm of the society; it is an academic community,* with a historic exemption from full integration into the society, and having an autonomous position in order to be able to fulfill its own responsibility, which is to conduct untrammeled inquiry into all questions. If the university is a community, asking for special loyalty from its members, how can it sanction the clubbing of its students?

It was SDS which initiated the violence at Columbia by insisting that the university was the microcosm of the society, and challenging its authority. After some confusion, the administration, in its actions, accepted this definition and sought to impose its authority on the campus by resorting to force. But in a community one cannot regain authority simply by asserting it, or by using force to suppress dissidents. Authority in this case is like respect. One can only *earn* the authority—the loyalty of one's students—by going in and arguing with them, by engaging in full debate and, when the merits of proposed change are recognized, taking the necessary steps quickly enough to be convincing.

The true difficulty is that the Columbia administration, both in its experience and in its conceptions of politics, was ill-equipped for either the Machiavellianism of Brzezinski or the politics of persuasion that, I think, would have served the university far better. The administration leaders, though they are reputable political scientists, were familiar only with the American political system, in which one operates either legalistically or by "making deals." Neither Kirk nor Truman had any "feel" for the volatility of social movements, or for the politics of ideology. The administration above all failed to understand the *dynamics* of the student protest: that whatever reason there may have been for early police action, when the buildings were seized by the hard-core SDS members, the subsequent surge of political support on the part of 500 other students—most of them liberal, moderate, pacifist, and not members of SDS—

effectively changed the *political* character of the situation. The failure to make the necessary distinction between these students and SDS, and thus to understand that these students were not wreckers but were now trying to express their inchoate grievances against the university, permitted SDS to call the tune—which, in the five crucial days of the occupation of the buildings, it did.

This led to the second turning point—the first was the seizure of Hamilton by the blacks—the calling in of the police. Thus the SDS was able to prove the truth of an old revolutionary adage that no demonstration is successful unless it compels a repression. For the strategical intention (as Howard Hubbard showed in "Five Long Hot Summers and How They Grew," *The Public Interest*, 12 (Summer 1968), even when the tactic is nonviolence, is to provoke brutality on the part of the opponent, and thus win the moral—and psychological—case. The lesson of Berkeley four years ago, and of Wisconsin earlier in the academic year (when the police were called in to clear an occupied building and ran wild) is that such repressive force is self-defeating. The Columbia administrators may have known about Berkeley and Wisconsin, but they did not show it.

What Might Have Been

What would have happened had the police not been called in—if, for example, the administration had simply shut down the university while trying to meet with the students and discuss the questions they had raised? In all likelihood—a view admittedly strengthened by hindsight—the students would have split badly among themselves: in part because of the deep differences among them; in part because of the manipulativeness of the SDS leadership which, as it became increasingly dominated by a Maoist faction, was lying to, and thus alienating, its own supporters. The nature of an emotional "conversion experience" is that the new converts, anxious to prove themselves, insist on purity of motive and selfless zeal on the part of their leaders. Disillusionment in such circumstances can be as quick as conversion. SDS had no real interest in any specific program, or in reconstructing the university. But actual reform had motivated many of the students in Avery and Fayerweather, and when they began to discuss these issues, or to question the insistence on "amnesty" by the "revolutionary leadership," many were shocked at the savagery of the response against them. A sensitive graduate student who was a member of the Strike Coordinating Committee, David Osher, has written about this state of affairs in the pacifist publication *WIN*, for July 1968. Radicalization, he writes, in effect attitudinal change, is a delicate and fragile process. It can be reversed, and depends on the good faith and sympathy of the individual. The distrust engendered by the unresponsiveness and lack of candor of the [strike] leaders and the overemphasis on amnesty (which whether or not it was a proper demand, was unsellable even to many of the strikers) worked against radicalization. . . . People and buildings changed their positions at different times and responded in various ways. Some caucused, some passed resolutions, some people were upset and quietly left. Ultimately people inside as well as outside the buildings were polarized, and a number of intimate observers felt that if the cops had not come Monday night an internal rebellion would have developed inside the buildings during the next few days.[19]

After the first police action there was an immense storm of support for the dissident students, and a general strike effectively cancelled most of the classes in the college and the graduate school. But the tensions that had been latent within the Strike Committee became evident as well. SDS had no program, only "tactical issues," and could only try to whip up other incidents. The students who had been angered by the police action began talking of the need to "restructure" the university and explore the role that they, as students, could play in the university. The Faculty Executive Committee began to take an active role in initiating studies on the ways in which the university could be reorganized.[20] In a leaflet

[19]In his account, Oscher describes the tensions within the strike movement:

"Although all the buildings held meetings, had steering committees, and had representatives on a central strike steering committee, power within the strike did not lie in the buildings. Power lay in two bodies, Strike Central, the bureaucracy which resided in Ferris Booth Hall (the unliberated student activities building), and the Central Steering Committee. Both of these groups appeared to be dominated by Progressive Labor-oriented [i.e. Maoist] Columbia SDS leadership. . . . Once they had gained a position of power, the monopolizing of information by those meeting and working in Ferris Booth Hall facilitated their keeping it.

"Strikers in each building depended on the Central Steering Committee for news concerning the positions of allies in other buildings. No one wanted to fink out on the other building, but few knew how the other building felt. At times this was the normal product (and problem) of occupying separate buildings, but in other cases, as in Low Library, leaders censored incoming and outgoing information. While that case may be extreme, buildings were played off against each other. ('Do you want to cop out on your brothers in Hamilton?')"

[20]A news analysis in the Columbia *Spectator* during this period called attention to the change. In the article Paul Starr wrote: "As the Strike Committee moves aimlessly in the midst of its own bureaucracy, making little progress toward achieving its demands, conducting a successful but paradoxically ineffectual strike, and staging confrontation on peripheral issues to keep its

distributed to the students, the Faculty Committee said that the tactics of provocation must give way to the politics of reconstruction, and that students had a large role to play within the university. Credibility had begun to revive among the students. The Strike Committee itself was divided and finally did split on this question, and the majority left the SDS-controlled strike to form the Students for a Restructured University. The SDS itself seemed close to becoming a shambles.[21] At this point the administration, without consulting the Executive Committee of the Faculty, suspended four strike leaders, and out of this confrontation arose Hamilton II, the second uncontrolled police action, and a renewed attack on the administration by the moderate students. Whatever chance the administration had had of winning over the moderate students who wanted the restructuring of the university was lost in this headlong effort to suspend the strike leaders.

In initiating the suspension the administration was—belatedly, by Brzezinski's standards—seeking to assert its authority. It was, to be fair about its own dilemmas, under enormous pressure from a "constituency" of its own—alumni, other universities, and some trustees—to take "action" and demonstrate its "decisiveness." But even in these circumstances—in part because it still did not completely recognize the need to engage students in debate; in part simply for the lack of an adequate apparatus—the administration's public relations were singularly inept. The university never presented its own case for the gymnasium: how it had sought to enlist some Harlem participation but had foundered, partly because it could not deal effectively with a community that itself had no coherent structure or leadership. When the gymnasium plans were completed,

troops together, the executive faculty committee has begun to cast itself as the productive and positive force driving at significant change.

"In a sense the faculty committee is trying to reverse roles with SDS. During the occupation of the buildings, the strikers were the only group with a substantial program. Their opponents all seemed defenders of the status quo, and the most conspicuous part of their opposition was a faction that seemed to have no understanding whatsoever of the problems facing the University. SDS held the initiative and clearly controlled the issues that were before the students, if it did not control opinions students held on those issues.

"That, however, is now changing. The strikers are no longer presenting the issues that are being debated. They are no longer the only group with a program for change. Instead, they are now in a position where they, not their opponents, appear obstructionist and negative. The executive faculty committee instead of SDS is proclaiming itself the vanguard."

[21]This view is confirmed by a review of strike tactics by the SDS leadership in *New Left Notes*, the national SDS weekly, for June 16, 1968.

the ministers of five of the largest churches in Harlem, as well as Dr. Mamie Phipps Clark, the wife of Dr. Kenneth Clark, and the director of the Northside Center for Child Development, had publicly endorsed the project. But few students in the university knew this. Nor did the university make its case—a legitimate one—for its own needs in the neighborhood. The university itself, as a provider of jobs and as a great intellectual resource, was finding itself choked for space; students wanted more faculty, and wanted the faculty to be available for more sustained contact—yet little faculty housing was available. Any urban environment is necessarily subject to change, and tenants do not have "absolute" rights to apartments, especially slum apartments; the balance of rights should be determined by appropriate planning for the area and the city as a whole.22

But the major lapse of the administration was its failure to respond to the evident desire for structural change which became manifest so rapidly once the buildings were seized. There was probably no one at Columbia University with a surer sense of this need than David Truman. In his report as dean of the college, in June 1967, before the sudden shuffle in which he became vice-president and provost, Truman had quietly pointed out the defects of the existing arrangements, and had proposed a new integrative structure which would have brought together the liberal-arts portions of the university—primarily the college and the three graduate faculties—and given them an effective voice and leadership in the university as against the professional schools, which had set the pace of expansion in the previous decade. In his year as vice-president and provost,

22The question of how many persons have actually been dispossessed has become a numbers game. In an article in *The New Republic* for May 18, 1968, entitled "Columbia's Real Estate Ventures," James Ridgeway wrote that "*Since World War II*, Columbia and the *other* [institutions on Morningside Heights] methodically pushed out 7,500 residents, most of them poorly off . . . many of them black or Puerto Ricans." In the *Ramparts* account of "The Siege of Columbia," this became: "The population displacement wrought by *Columbia's* institutional programs in Morningside Heights amounted to almost 10,000 people *in the last decade. . . .*" (italics added)

According to Morningside Heights, Inc., a group of ten institutions including Columbia, Union Theological Seminary, and St. Luke's Hospital, as of June 1, 1957 the ten institutions owned 151 parcels of land, containing 3,561 apartments at the time of purchase which, after renovation or removal for new buildings, contained 3,072, or a loss of 489 apartments. Of the 107 buildings which Columbia itself owned, there was *a net loss of 166 apartments*. These would be apartments in which individuals were evicted for new institutional building. In the retained buildings, Columbia and the other institutions gives preference, when apartments become free, to its own personnel.

Truman had begun to rebuild some weak departments and to revamp the central administration. But Truman worked cautiously, cards close to the chest, and consulting only a few senior persons, instead of involving the faculty and even the student body in broad discussions. And given the sensibilities of Grayson Kirk, who was close to retirement, and the exigencies of the first large-scale centralized fund drive in the history of the university, it is evident that Truman was constrained in effecting the changes that he wanted to bring about. The consequence was a lack of boldness in leadership when, psychologically, it was needed more than ever.

The Romantic Spasm

The New Left, as a social movement, is passing through a phase ranging from protest to resistance to desperation. Over the past few years it has modeled itself on the Black Militants, just as the young middle-class rebels of the 1930's aped the Revolutionary Proletariat. But the Blacks themselves are in a bind: no matter how much the leaders rant against The System, a huge "constituency" wants "in," and the effectiveness of any continuing black leadership is the degree to which such gains can be achieved. The rhetoric and the threats are levers for bargaining. Black Power, if it has any meaning, is a device for the redistribution of privilege and power, not for total revolution.

The New Left in contrast, wants "total" change in the society. But is hoist on the dilemma that it has no effective vision of a "counter society," other than the ephemeral "participatory democracy"—which, in hothouse revolutionary situations such as Columbia, quickly gave way to cadre organization and manipulation —and as a "total" movement it does not want to bargain. Worse, being a tiny minority it has no lever for change other than disruption. Disruption in the society at large is at present impossible; hence The New Left has been forced to retreat more and more into the university and to resort to more grandiose dreams and more megalomaniacal visions. The title of an article by Tom Hayden in *Ramparts* is entitled "Two, Three, Many Columbias"; he does not explain the title, but the allusion is clear to those in the know: Che Guevera's call to create "Two, Three, Many Vietnams" in Latin America. It is a call for guerrilla action. In that curious merger of apocalyptic language and practical instruction that forms the catechism of the revolutionary, whether Nechayev or Debray, Hayden writes:

> Columbia opened a new tactical stage in the resistance movement which began last fall: from overnight occupation of buildings to permanent occupation; from mill-ins to the creation of revolutionary committees; from symbolic civil

disobedience to barricades resistance. Not only are these tactics already being duplicated on other campuses, but they are sure to be surpassed by even more militant tactics. In the future it is conceivable that students will threaten destruction of buildings as a last deterrent to police attacks. Many of the tactics learned can also be applied in smaller hit-and-run operations between strikes: raids on the offices of professors doing weapons research could win substantial support among students while making the university more blatantly repressive.

Such desperado tactics are never the mark of a coherent social movement, but the guttering last gasps of a romanticism soured by rancor and impotence. The SDS will be destroyed by its style. It lives on turbulence, but is incapable of transforming its chaotic impulses into a systematic, responsible behavior that is necessary to effect broad societal change. In fact, its very style denies the desirability of such conduct, for like many chiliastic sects its ideological anti-nomianism carries over into a similar psychological temper, or rather distemper. It is impelled not to innovation, but to destruction.

But the questions it raises—the challenges to hierarchical decision-making and the desires for broadened participation in the institutions that affect their lives—are real ones. They reflect the more generalized sources of student unrest which themselves arise out of world-wide structural changes in advanced industrial societies —the imposition of "organized harnesses" in a technological society, just as, more than a hundred years ago, a "machine-paced harness" was imposed on a rurally transformed industrial working class. In both instances the reactions have been familiar: an anarcho-syndicalist mood of rebellion, which today is psychologically joined to the rebellion of the color-shaded agrarian *tiers monde* against the world's cities. In the post-industrial societies of tomorrow—in which the university is, I would claim, *the* paramount institution—the problems of decentralization, of the balance between technical and political decision-making and of greater participation, will be pressing ones. I shall discuss these broader questions in another article. But in the world of the university, as the experience of Columbia demonstrates, these problems have already come to the fore, and are now on the agenda.

The issue of disruption and of the character of the university are one. The authority of a university is not a civil authority but a moral one. It can deal with disruptions—or its threats—not by invoking civil force but by rallying an entire community to establish common rules of common procedure. Disruptive students can only be contained by a faculty and by other students, not by the police. The nature of a university, as a moral community rather than as a political society is its openness to all points of view within the primary values of the search for truth and the maintenance of open procedures. Hence confrontation politics—as a means of imposing a particular political point of view, and particularly through coercion —is inadmissible. But all this is only possible when a university makes the fullest commitment to being a participatory institution, to an extent consonant with its full responsibilities. This means, of course, neither student power nor faculty power nor any such shibboleths, but the definition of areas of rights and powers and responsibilities appropriate to the division of function and place in the university itself. Unless it takes those steps, convincingly, to enlarge that participation, the university—and Columbia—may be forced to the wall by those who, in the words of Fidel Castro that the New Left has adopted, are "guerrillas in the field of culture."

University of Chicago

Strategies of Protest: Developments in Conflict Theory

Donald W. Light, Jr.

During the past decade, this country has witnessed an impressive increase of nonviolent protests, accompanied, however, by little analysis of how nonviolence and passive resistance work. In her introduction to *Conquest of Violence*, a lucid exploration into nonviolence, Joan Bondurant writes,

> That the suffering and sacrifice of recent years in civil rights movements around the world have made no advance towards a philosophy of conflict, has its own significance. Why, indeed, have civil rights movements given rise to so little reflection upon the nature of the politics of nonviolence? Perhaps we are bound by a paralysis born of intensive preoccupation with the pressing issues of the day.[1]

Sociologists have been refining theories of conflict, but as Lewis Coser notes in his most recent contribution to those theories, few empirical studies have applied hypotheses generated by conflict theory to see how useful they are.[2] This paper intends to explore the formal properties of certain nonviolent conflicts and to apply some theories of conflict to a recurring social form, student protests on college and university campuses. To date, social scientists have concentrated on the social origins and personalities of student protesters, rather than on the structure of the protest itself.[3] Here we shall focus on the strategies of protest itself and their effects on each party and on the outcome, for a given protest still harbors a mysterious quality for both sides participating, as if it were an animal with a life of its own. Indeed it does have certain regularities built into its structure.[4]

The Importance of the Issue Protested

Before proceeding further, we must distinguish between two kinds of nonviolent direct actions which are often confused, *satyagraha* and *duragraha*. Both terms were most fully explored in the writings and practices of Mahatma Gandhi and are still useful today. *Satyagraha* (truth-seeking) is a technique of pursuing the truth which requires selfless, total commitment of the participant.[5] One must retain strict adherence to the truth and never waver from it, yet readily admit that one's truth is limited or erroneous. It is not possible to seek truth without nonviolence; for only in nonviolence can one display his love of his opponent and his good faith on which common truth can be sought. *Satyagraha* assumes that each party holds a limited view of the truth and that together both parties can find a larger truth; yet one must be ready to die for what he believes if his opponent attacks him rather than coming to some understanding. The method of reconciliation is not compromise (the main Western tactic), but rather finding a common truth.

Duragraha (nonviolent harassment) is not an interaction with the opponent as in *satyagraha*, but a technique of harassment. For Gandhi, *duragraha* is done either out of weakness because the party wishes to be violent but lacks the power, or as a preliminary tactic before violence. Thus, in intent if not in tone, *duragraha* is not nonviolent, although it appears to be. The litmus test arises when there is a fundamental difference between the two parties. As described above, the technique of *satyagraha* is designed for just such a basic difference in the truth. In contrast, Gandhi observed that *duragraha* in this case merely leads to a bitter stalemate or to violence; for no effort is made to seek a larger truth. It also weakens respect for law and confidence in democratic processes. Gandhi, in using *satyagraha*, respected law and due process even though he broke the law when he thought it necessary.

From this discussion, it is clear that virtually no Americans use *satyagraha* as a technique. Civil rights demonstrations, student protests, and other such phenomena employ *duragraha* and display the attitudes which accompany it. We shall call this technique *directed resistance*, because the term *passive resistance* fails to convey the activity of this technique.

That *directed resistance (duragraha)* only succeeds, if it does, when there is no fundamental disagreement between the parties is not only a definition on Gandhi's part, but an observation. Directed resistance is a technique of persuasion, and therefore the nature of the issue protested becomes very important in determining the nature of resistance and its outcome. This resistance is directed against authorities to render change, but much of the outcome depends on the response of the surrounding community. In almost all cases, one can assume that the authorities will initially refuse to cooperate with those protesting, so that the climate of the community affects what concessions will be made on the issue protested.

From observing many protests on campuses, one can list the issues of protest which are most common and rank them in order of community sympathy. To a large extent, the community in this case is the faculty and general student body. Listed from greatest to least sympathetic consensus are the four issues which are singly or in combination the foci of almost all student protests in the past several years:

Repugnance of serious disruption of university life, especially by physical invasion;

Support of student campus rights or of adequate educational facilities and opportunities;

Advocacy of relevant education for minority groups;

Opposition to the university's cooperation with or obligation to government.

The first item means that if either side can define the situation as disruptive or as an invasion, it will gain strong community opposition against the other side and strong support for its position, even if that position is not too relevant to campus disruption. The outcome of the Berkeley protests in 1964 illustrates this point. The initial issue was free speech (the second issue on the list), which received some sympathy from faculty and the general student body. The arguments included attacks that the university was being co-opted into the military-industrial power structure, but they did not seem to evoke popular support. However, after the governor had the administration bring large numbers of police onto the campus, attack students and arrest them, great community support came forth, not only against the "administration's" tactics, but in favor of the position of the Free Speech Movement.[6] That this first issue receives greatest sympathy is unfortunate; for it puts a premium on making ends (amnesty, unwarranted force) of means and losing sight of the original goals of reform. This occurs because first, the authorities define the protesters as fundamentally different from them, and then those resisting see themselves in the same terms. The authorities have rightly defined them in terms of their latent violence, as Gandhi noted.

Both the second and third items represent the major thrust of recent protests in American society, to expose the discrepancy between values of individual freedom or equality and the hierarchical structure of American institutions. This attack was first made against Southern racial laws.

In general, Americans have a bad conscience about the civil rights of minority groups, and most colleges today try to "give them a break." Recent demands by black students for much more than a break receive some sympathy, but only within limits. One hears, "I can understand how they feel, but asking for one hundred Negro freshmen is discrimination in reverse."

Least sympathy goes to those opposing university cooperation with the government, because so many faculty and so much of the university receive funds from the government, and because this relationship has never been a basic issue in American culture. Several observers have sensed that the Vietnam protests differ in this basic way from protests for civil rights.[7]

Ever since 1964, student protests tend to be understood in terms of the Berkeley protests of that year. They were so well-publicized and so thoroughly studied that it sufficed to say that a given demonstration was "another Berkeley," "not quite like Berkeley," or "a little Berkeley." Yet if the experiences at Berkeley have any relevance to later demonstrations, they are as an historical antecedent. This is shown by the clear change in what issues were prominent among protests, a shift from more local to more national ones. Starting in 1966, the emphasis shifted from free speech and remnants of the McCarthy era to the university's ties with the government. The year 1966 is a better marker than 1965, because, though students at Berkeley protested against a Navy recruiter in November-December 1965, it was in the spring of 1966 that a national series of protests against university cooperation with the Selective Service occurred. Moreover, the Berkeley protest against allowing a Navy recruiter on campus was conducted in terms of free speech; the administration refused an anti-draft group the same privileges.[8]

As expected by the ranking of issues according to community support, these demonstrations against university cooperation with the government experienced mixed and much hostility. It was in this period, from 1966 to 1968, that new strategies of protest emerged; these are described below. Starting in the spring of 1968, more protests have been for university cooperation with the black community, most directly by admitting more black students, but also by extending to policies towards black urban areas and to the study of Afro-American heritage. Because of the efforts of Dr. Martin Luther King, and his assassination, these protests have been mixed, sometimes directly, with anti-Vietnam protests.[9]

Directed Resistance

For purposes of reference, let us describe a typical demonstration on a college campus. It begins when students claim that a policy or action of the authorities is unjust. There is talk about it, and some attempt is made to get the policy changed. The authorities appear to the students to be intransigent or indifferent, and they consequently depict the authorities as arbitrary and themselves as direct or indirect victims of the authorities' actions. A demonstration ensues, and we are here concerned with serious action such as resistance, sit-in, and other forms which entail more than verbal protest. In a few cases, the authorities meet the demands of the protesters, and the demonstration ends.[10] More typically, the authorities (including faculty) regard the protest as intolerable behavior, and warn that protesters will be removed, arrested, or severely punished. In other words, they change the primary issue from the one being protested to the disruptive act itself. At this point, three outcomes are possible. Under official pressure, the protesters may desist from demonstrating.[11] Little modification of policy follows this capitulation. If the students are determined, they stay, and the demonstration is broken up by force.[12] Here the protest may end, and the record shows little policy change over the issue of protest. Rather, the authorities feel they "won." Finally, the students may stay, be arrested, and rally for another demonstration. This pattern can be repeated many times, as re-demonstrations are held and more police are brought in. Two changes occur in this last outcome: the central issue becomes use of force and violence rather than the protest issue, and the demonstrations escalate rapidly. Examples of multiple, escalated protests include the demonstrations at Berkeley in 1964, Waseda (Japan) in 1966, Rome in 1966, Berlin in 1967, and Columbia in the spring of 1968.[13]

Directed resistance (*duragraha*) is a nonviolent confrontation of an aggrieved party against those in authority, which occurs when other, legitimate means of protest fail. While both parties may be nonviolent, at least the aggrieved party is. However, the aggrieved may be very aggressive in seeking and provoking the enemy. Thus, the authorities can be more passive in behavioral terms than the aggrieved.

In directed resistance, the idea of two parties takes on a special meaning; for the aggrieved party sees itself at some level as part of the same community as the party it opposes. Considering the hundreds of student protests and the thousands of participants in recent years, one is impressed with how little violence has been initiated by protesters. Sabotage, assassination, or outright war assume very different relations between parties than does direct resistance. It is the technique of the insider. By the same reasoning, as student protesters come to be defined as outsiders, they tend more to initiate violence.

Directed resistance is a tactic of persuasion in which each side tries to define the situation for the larger community. The aggrieved define it in terms of an unjust policy or action; the authorities justify their policy and define the situation in terms of unreasonable disruption by the protesters. As the protest becomes established, it takes on the features of a game with utility curves for each side. These curves change as the issues change. For example, if the authorities succeed in persuading the community that the protest is unnecessarily disruptive, it will win over the community, because that issue stimulates greatest sympathy. If, however, the authorities arrest the protesters quickly, the definition of the situation may change to the unnecessary use of force, as it did in the Berkeley protests of 1964. Such escalation, brought on by the authorities, also increases cohesion among the demonstrators and attracts sympathetic bystanders to their ranks.[14]

In directed resistance, how the authorities judge the conflict issue affects the shape of the protest. Whether they see the stated issue as genuine or "fabricated" will determine whether they take the protest issue seriously, and whether they will therefore negotiate seriously about it.[15] This decision affects how much respect the authorities have for the aggrieved party. Insofar as the authorities regard the conflict as unrealistic, they will be outraged by the "inexcusable disruption" of the protest and will be more likely to take severe measures. If, however, the protest is mild, they will tend to disregard it. In either case, little policy change over the protest issue is likely to occur.

The authorities also decide whether the issue is, for them, basic or not. Conflict has a positive function, states Lewis Coser, if its goals and issues do not contradict the basic assumptions on which the relation is founded.[16] Apparently Coser does not consider *satyagraha* in his propositions on conflict. If the authorities feel the issue is basic, the conflict will be protracted, and directed resistance will lead to a bitter stalemate as Gandhi observed. Those resisting, by the choice of their weapon, have defined the issue as real and not basic to the relationship.

The Stand-Off

Not only are the Berkeley protests of 1964 an historical antecedent to new issues, where the secondary issues of 1964 emerged as the primary ones of 1966-1968, but the Berkeley experience also led to a new and effective strategy on the part of college administrators.

One lesson of Berkeley for many administrators was not to complicate the issues. Berkeley's officials got into a quagmire by arresting students, sending in police and by other such acts beyond settling the original issue. Underlying this feeling that it is best not to complicate matters is a law of nonviolent conflict. *The more passive party has a distinct advantage in persuading others of the justness of its cause.* The mistake of Berkeley's officials was not to raise new issues, but to raise the kind of issues they did, namely to become more aggressive and violent than the Free Speech Movement. People who suffer for a cause in which they believe earn a certain amount of respect and support.

This advantage of relative passivity is one reason why authorities try to make protesters appear to be more aggressive than they are. For example, when authorities break up a sit-in, they will describe those sitting in as active and minimize their own aggressiveness. Pulling apart and dragging off limp sitters is described as, "Students blocking entrances and obstructing traffic were removed by the police." By the same token, protesters will respond to arrest and violence with self-righteous shock. This does not mean that the shock is not genuine. Throughout this paper we are dealing with social and structural regularities—Durkheim's social facts, which are not often calculations of individual actors. The authorities sincerely feel, for example, that to sit in a doorway is "blocking," and the gerundive describes the aggression of the act. Likewise, they sincerely feel that the sitters "were removed," and the passive voice conveys the appropriate tone. In a similar manner, protesters who know they are breaking rules or laws are genuinely, experientially shocked when the authorities descend upon them.

The advantage of the more passive party could diminish if violence became a more acknowledged part of our culture. Violence appears throughout the American fabric, but the nation's self-image is a peace-loving one.[17]

The *law of passive advantage* suggests that if the authorities are passive, the protesters will be defined as the aggressors and thus start at a disadvantage by their very act of protesting. This implication is true, except when the protest issue has wide sympathy in the community. Then the authorities will appear weak and ineffectual, as in Gandhi's salt campaign.[18]

The stand-off is a form of directed resistance where the authorities refuse to take action against those resisting, but they also refuse to yield to the demands made. In a typical case, the aggrieved party resists and the authorities cry foul. They claim they stand ready to negotiate as soon as the demonstrators cease their "irrational and coercive actions." In this case, the demonstrators usually end the protest themselves, and the authorities lightly reprimand them. If the authorities remain passive until the aggrieved party ends the demonstration, there is less chance of a policy change than if the protest is forcibly ended. Chances of policy change are decreased, because for the stand-off to terminate, the definition of the situation which prevails must be that of the authorities.

The stand-off has laws of its own. There is an inherent *law of capitulation*, to wit, that the protesting party must "see the light," "be reasonable men," and stop the demonstration so that negotiations can proceed.[19] In one corner stands the aggrieved party which claims that certain matters are unjust and that the authorities refuse to change them or even talk about them. In the other corner sits a gentle but energetic party which claims it is more than ready to talk, but which refuses to be bludgeoned into talks. As time passes, the authorities repeat their willingness to negotiate; it is up to the resisters now to show that they are men of good faith and fair play by stopping their protest and joining in negotiations. In time, even those members of the community who are sympathetic to the protest issue begin to feel that the demonstration has served its purpose. "You've made your point. Now stop demonstrating and negotiate." With more time passed, the authorities emphasize that they are losing patience, and the community feels that the protesters "are more interested in demonstrating than in finding a solution to this problem." Against such psychological warfare, the aggrieved party weakens; for internal cohesion depends on a clearly defined enemy.

The stand-off has a built-in time limit, described in the paragraph above. The longer the stand-off lasts, the more ground the protesters lose. If, however, the stand-off ends quickly, as it often does, then its laws are irrelevant. But the stand-off itself structurally favors the authorities because their definition of the situation gains credence.

The stand-off is an unstable form of directed resistance, as indicated by the time limit. Carried to the end, it soon leads to capitulation by the protesting party. In the one example I know in great detail, this took about three days.[20] Today, for reasons stated below, it would most likely take longer. The stand-off protest at the University of Chicago in early 1969 lasted sixteen days; one at Brandeis University in January, 1969 ended in capitulation after ten days. Short of capitulation, the stand-off can transform itself into aggressive resistance or violence by the frustrated demonstrators, an outcome more frequent as relations worsen. A thirteen-day sit-in at Sir George Williams University in February, 1969, turned to $2,000,000 property damage as a way of relieving the stand-off pressure. It could change to open violence on both sides. Finally, the authorities could retaliate, perhaps by arresting the students or by breaking up the protest. This last alternative is the most frequent, but the fact that it was preceded by a stand-off redefines the retaliation. If the authorities arrest or haul off demonstrators near the beginning of the demonstration, they run the risk of losing the sympathy of the community and appearing as intransigent, rigid dictators, just as the protesters described them. At the same time, they will probably make the protesters more entrenched, more cohesive, more determined. If, however, the authorities call in the police after having waited some time for the protest to end and after making several overtures to negotiate as soon as the students stop demonstrating, then the action will seem justified. While before, they would be seen as assaulting aggrieved members of the community with unreasonable force, after a stand-off the same action will be considered as subduing irrational belligerents who refuse to be reasonable or negotiate. The community may even come to see it as the authorities' duty to remove a disruptive element from the community.[21]

From the perspective of those protesting, the social psychology of the stand-off inflicts severe wounds. It quickly splits the group into the "all-or-nothing militants" and the "let's negotiate moderates." The stand-off takes away the enemy. The protesters unite as a fraternity to fight against the forces of evil, and suddenly those forces yield, like punching the tar baby. Moreover, the opponent claims he is not against them and will negotiate now, concluding that only the pro-testers themselves prevent their wishes from being fulfilled. Members of the fraternity begin to sense that they are their own worst enemy.

The protesters gradually sense that their 'disruptive' acts have overshadowed their basic demands in the eyes of the community. When they talk to faculty they find that the faculty is so preoccupied with the disruption that basic issues are not discussed. The students become dispirited as they see the community become hostile. Note, however, that the time limit in the stand-off is not the same for the protesters as it is for the community. In coming to this despondency, the protesters lag behind the community. This differential means that if the authorities send in police in the middle of a stand-off, they may have community support yet enrage the protesters and make them more determined. All of these effects from disciplinary action depend on the severity and scope of the action. As a general rule, the more severe and/or larger the disciplinary action, the longer the authorities must tolerate the stand-off to justify it.

The stand-off tends to have a regular aftermath. In a stand-off, the protest issue is less likely to be taken seriously by the administration, especially as time passes and their definition of a disruptive situation prevails. When a stand-off completes its natural course, the students are left with a sense of failure and internal disunity. There often seem to be no channels left for them to communicate or express the deep sense of injustice which still remains concerning the protest issue. While the administration has won the battle, it is not clear of trouble unless it makes concrete steps to settle the protest issue. Usually, only minor, vague steps are taken, such as a joint committee to investigate the problem. Students, then, become bitter and hardened, and the next protest is likely to last longer and be more ugly.22

The University of Chicago — A Case Study

To illustrate the theoretical points which have been made about nonviolent strategies of conflict, one sit-in at the University of Chicago serves admirably. In May, 1966, a protest and sit-in against the ranking of men for Selective Service took place. It was the first major protest focused strictly on the university's compliance with the federal government. In December, 1965, the students at the Berkeley campus of the University of California protested against the presence of a Navy recruiter on campus, but largely because the administration refused to give equal privileges to other, anti-war groups from outside the campus. The Chicago example also illustrates the pure case of a stand-off, perhaps the first. Finally, the sit-in at the University of Chicago, while less known than the Berkeley protest a few months earlier, stimulated over a score of "sympathy" protests across the nation in what was the first national sweep of university protests. It dramatically opened a second era of demonstrations against university-government connections.

No one at the University of Chicago believed that there would be a sit-in that spring of 1966. Even a junior member of the faculty who knew many leaders of the protest said, "I was in Woodworth's about ten days before the protest, talking to another faculty member about how there would not be a Berkeley at the University of Chicago . . ."[23] Of course there were warning signs—are there ever no clues in retrospect?—but they were not seen, partially because people at Chicago associated large protests with Berkeley, and the University of Chicago did not seem like Berkeley. The University of California at Berkeley is part of a mammoth state university system which accepts a wide spectrum of students. In 1964, the Berkeley campus alone included 27,000 students, two-thirds of them undergraduates, and about 1800 faculty members. The faculty is very research oriented, and the University as a whole has a graduate research tradition.

At the University of Chicago, about 9000 students, one-fourth undergraduates, study under 1080 faculty members in the venerable 'Gothic' buildings.[24] The campus is private, highly select, and intellectual. Although Chicago has proportionately fewer under-graduates, the college has a great tradition of teaching and close student-faculty relationships. The entire tone of the two campuses contrasts sharply. Chicago is small, quiet, gloomy with many single figures moving within private worlds against harsh weather and a naturally severe environment. The University at Berkeley dominates its environment, and one sees clusters of students throughout Berkeley, lots of motion, and an openness which California weather induces. No one knows how much campus atmosphere affects protests, but the predictions that there would be no sit-in at the University of Chicago were made on just these kinds of comparisons.

Faculty and administrators at the University of Chicago also felt that the educational and political atmosphere of their campus differed from that of Berkeley. They accepted the image of impersonal, abusive, computerized education which discontented students on the Berkeley campus had so graphically portrayed in the mass media. And because of the behavior of Berkeley's administration during the 1964 protests and before, most students and faculty at the University of Chicago felt that Berkeley's administration was personally unresponsive and politically restrictive.[25]

In contrast, the University of Chicago boasts of a grand tradition in the liberal arts. The Hutchins' college fostered many innovations in college teaching, some of which were widely copied. It featured a personal education with faculty who had been selected especially for the college and who loved to teach. The ideals of Robert M. Hutchins still live at Chicago, and during the year 1965-1966, extensive discussion and planning had taken place about restructuring the college so that its offerings would be still more relevant to the modern world. Politically, the students did not feel constrained, and they frequently made admiring remarks about how the faculty had fought the loyalty oath in the 1950's.

How, then did a major protest arise at the University of Chicago? The question can never be answered directly, but a partial answer occurred when a faculty report was issued in the winter, recommending basic policies on housing. The administration lauded the report and put it on the agenda for official approval. Immediately students on the left began to accuse the administration of railroading the report, of trying to get the report approved before students had a chance to read it. Although the student newspaper devoted many pages to the report and its discussants, student pressure continued and the approval of the report was postponed. In reality, the faculty committee who issued the report had spent hundreds of hours listening to students' ideas on housing, and the report acknowledged the students as the source for most of its good ideas.

In short, the experience revealed an ingrained and intense distrust of the administration that was not wholly rational.[26] Students focused their suspicion mainly on the administration, not on the faculty who wrote the report, and they felt that administrators did not listen to them.

Finally, in May 1966, undergraduates staged a "sleep-in" on the campus lawn to protest illegally the housing policies. They were met by administrators who brought out refreshments and asked what the students wanted. Almost all of the student demands were shown to be incorporated in the new housing policies—an illustration of the extent to which the housing committee had tapped student sentiment on living arrangements. With nothing to protest and rain besides, the sleep-in quickly fizzled.

Two weeks later the sit-in began, and many student leaders said that the failure of the sleep-in increased feelings of frustration and impotence that had made students determined to have a large, successful protest. The administration had "seduced" them once with punch and friendly conversation, but it would not happen again. The basic distrust and antagonism had to be expressed in some manner.

The example of Chicago illustrates a fundamental prerequisite for protest. Protest occurs when the authorities are seen as arbitrary and unresponsive; for *protest is basically a unilateral response to an arbitrary force.* As the comparison of the Berkeley and Chicago incidents shows, this perceived rigidity is more important than the commonly attributed causes of protest, such as university size, size of classes, quality of teaching, quality of facilities, and political restrictions. Many institutions suffering from one or more of these problems have had no large protests, and small, liberal, high-quality institutions have. A sense of institutional rigidity can arise in very different environments, because student activists on a given campus are part of a national movement and have a national consciousness. They are cosmopolitans, not locals, and they tend to cast local problems or characters into a national syndrome.[27]

The one quality which consistently makes universities and colleges protest-prone is not university size, etc., but academic and/or social prestige. Such institutions are more likely to have large numbers of children from upper middle class and professional homes. These students are most prominent among political radicals.[28]

With a background of student hostility towards the administration, a major, substantive issue emerged and gave the protest its impetus. Since 1964, the attention of liberal students had shifted from civil rights to the expanding war in Vietnam. In 1965, radical leaders stated that the civil rights movement was dead, and the black power movement grew. The Students for a Democratic Society (SDS) turned to injustices of the war, and in the summer of 1965, they held a conference on the draft. During that fall, SDS held numerous meetings at the University of Chicago, where the small audience discussed the inequities of the Selective Service. At the same time, the national office of SDS moved to Chicago near the University.

During the Winter Quarter, some members of the college staff began to question the use of grades in relation to the draft. This was a *faculty* problem—whether grading a student carried a moral burden of judging a person eligible for fighting, and possible death, in Vietnam. Some faculty felt this burden and discussed it in sections of a famous Hutchins course, Social Sciences II. Thus a number of undergraduates openly discussed in class this moral issue.

Faculty concern over the Vietnam conflict increased. A Faculty Committee on the Problems of Foreign Policy formed and became more active during the first part of 1966. Six faculty particularly concerned about draft deferment based on grades met with a high University official and made the following recommendations, listed in descending order of preference.

1. The University should refuse to issue grades to the Selective Service. If this action is claimed illegal, that claim should be examined and challenged.

2. The University should gather with other top universities and discuss the joint withholding of grades from the Selective Service.

3. If the University does not want to withhold grades, the University should issue a public statement condemning the use of academic information for Selective Service.

4. If the University does not want to take a position as a body, it should institute a mechanism whereby faculty would not have to issue grades.

5. As a minimum, the University should sponsor a national conference on the Selective Service.

These suggestions were confidentially discussed by the faculty Council and its executive Committee during February, March and April. The conclusions, issued May sixth, included action on the second of these suggestions.[29]

While a number of students had been concerned about draft deferments, student initiative did not begin until April, 1966. A group of undergraduates, many of them not political activists, persuaded two young faculty men to give a course entitled *The Moral Basis of Political Decisions.* Most of these students became leaders of the sit-in. Specific political action leading to the sit-in began in the response to a press release by General Hershey announcing the Selective Service test and the use of class ranking for college deferments.[30] Throughout April, students had forums and meetings about the issue of rank in class. Attendance at SDS meetings grew rapidly. Radical SDS leaders came to prominence and tried to negotiate with the administration about not ranking undergraduate men. The University reiterated its policy of providing class rank to Selective Service boards at the student's request.

Thus an issue new to student protests had been created. The focus had shifted from faculty concern about giving grades to student opposition at being ranked. Fundamentally, the argument states that in matters of life and death, all men are equal. It is immoral to rank one man above another. If a student gets good grades, for example, he is exempted by the Selective Service for that reason only, and he puts fellow students lower in class standing, exposing them to the draft. Thus, the Selective Service pits student against student, and the ultimate stakes are death.

Students were feeling guilty about their privileges. Earlier that year the Student Health Service reported a rapid increase among graduate students of "anxiety over privilege." Then undergraduates began to approach a few faculty members, saying that they did not want to compete against others for deferments. Yet, these same students did not want to fight in the war and kill. Taken together, these two positions would force them to almost certain induction, followed by refusal to serve military duty. In other words, for moral reasons they would trade an outstanding college education for a prison sentence. The most serious of them were horrified by the choices they faced.

At the University of Chicago, the protesters explicitly demanded that the University refuse to cooperate with the Selective Service, and the rhetoric accompanying the demand advocated that the University be an independent moral force in society, in this case by condemning evil policies in Vietnam. This demand challenged structural features of university and society which most people take for granted. Moreover, the policy sought was probably illegal, claimed the University attorneys. Protesters at Chicago also wanted a voice in making policy decisions relevant to students. This second demand seems a part of the first one, in that students could not trust the University to be a responsive moral force or to represent their interests.[31]

Because the protest at the University of Chicago raised new and radical questions, few sympathized with it. Most Americans, including academicians, assume a limited cooperation between the university and the government, a relationship which the students felt had gone too far. To complicate matters, the students as a group were confused about the issues, and faculty quickly found illogic in student position papers. Some senior faculty also found a no-rank stance irresponsible, because it would give students an advantage over those in weaker colleges if they sought deferment through the national Selection Service examinations. Also, some argued, a student with a D average is as morally equal to an A student as he is to a Negro drop-out living three blocks from the sit-in. Therefore, one cannot oppose rank without opposing student deferments. Not until after the sit-in did the Students Against the Rank persuade its mixed membership to take this fearful but honest stand.

Between the radical nature of the issues and the lack of clear arguments, the sit-in at Chicago could not rally emotional or intellectual support for its position, either within the academic community or in the general public. The faculty was disgusted with the sloppy thinking of protesters, and few took the issues seriously. Moreover, the students who had banked on strong faculty support, forgot that the draft is an age-specific (but *not*, to the surprise of some, a sex-specific) issue. Unlike free speech, the draft does not affect faculty directly. The faculty on the whole ignored the demands of the sit-in, and many felt that rank was a bogus issue created by radicals in order to gain greater student power in the University. Ironically, most of the faculty and administration strongly opposed the sit-in because it disrupted University life and breeched the tradition of free speech. Protesters could not have been more disillusioned. While they suffered for morality, life, and death, the University was preoccupied with order. On the other hand, those opposing the sit-in felt the students were acting like bad and confused children.

While the issues and their social context were important in defining the nature of the conflict that soon followed, other forces shaped the sit-in at the University of Chicago and its outcome. The students, frustrated by attempts to negotiate, rallied, formed a group, Students Against the Rank (SAR), and decided to sit in the administration building if calculation of the rank were not at least postponed until the fall. Conflict is ultimately a power relationship, and students had felt powerless before a seemingly arbitrary administration. One miscommunication particularly intensified this impression of intransigence. On April 12, 1966 the faculty council met and, as the ruling body on academic affairs, made (with slight changes) it the University's official practice that information on rank would be released only at the student's request.[32] This meeting was confidential, and like many bodies, the Council distributed its minutes just before the next meeting. Consequently, many faculty and most senior administrators did not know that a policy had been made or what the policy was. Those who knew could not tell. Since no official policy on class ranking for the Selective Service had previously been made, no one even knew who had authorized the practice.[33] Therefore, protesting students got "the run-around" from administrators, who gave flat statements mixed with confused answers. The minutes came out the day before the sit-in.

The formation of SAR made once powerless individuals feel powerful enough as a group to force their demands on the University. The transformation was exhilarating.[34] The students gained almost a class consciousness.[35] As their movement grew, it became more intense and idealistic, until they demanded a confrontation.[36] Although the group was increasingly hostile towards the enemy and internally cohesive through this effort, its members exhibited glee, comradeship, and enthusiasm. This illustrates the importance of distinguishing group hostility from individual hostility in conflict theory, while the Simmel-Coser approach assumes they are interdependent.

The SAR delivered its ultimatum and University officials recoiled from its blunt, imperative tone. The die was cast, and on Wednesday, May 11, students began to gather for a rally. A heavy rain drove them into the lobby of the administration building, and by five o'clock about 450 people were spreading throughout the building. As employees, Deans and officers left, the crowd cheered and jeered. By that night, the students had secured all exits, including the President's private elevator. The University did not resist, and the students were delighted with their instant success.[38]

For two days the sit-in continued full-force. Some students left; others replaced them. There were many people coming and going, students, maintenance men, the press, and speakers. Day and night a teach-in continued in the lobby while other areas were designated for eating, studying and sleeping.[39] Students, faculty—both sympathetic and unsympathetic—and administrators spoke about the issues. The protesters and visiting speakers debated policies and tactics, and on Friday, May 13, the SAR voted to leave the building of its own accord, with a token force remaining as a symbol of opposition. The group had been convinced that the object of persuasion (not coercion) was the faculty rather than the administration and that faculty were as repulsed by the sit-in as administrators. Over the weekend students organized to canvass each faculty member and to persuade him of their views about the rank and student power.

On Monday, May 16, the employees did not return to their desks in the administration building; the administration considered the building still occupied by the token force of protesters. Students were shocked. By leaving the building, they felt they had made a major concession towards conciliation and they expected the administration to do likewise. Rather than infuriating the students, as happened at Berkeley, the University's firmness disspirited them. That evening SAR met to decide what to do. Respected faculty spoke and told them as before that negotiations were not possible under conditions of coercion. With "childlike eagerness" the students listened and then voted to remove the token force. Officially, they had held the building for over five days—more than they planned. Now they left the building entirely and turned to persuading the faculty to vote against the ranks.[40]

What occurred in the five days of demonstration can be best understood in terms of the structure of a stand-off. The administration did not take the rank issue too seriously, and to their audience the students sounded at first like complaining, then pleading children. Very few faculty or administrators could understand why the rank issue would touch students so deeply, and theories of outside agitators quickly arose.[41] Moreover, the Chicago administration, learning from administrative errors at Berkeley, controlled the conflict by letting the sit-in occur without retaliation. Thus SAR bore the onus of escalation and invasion, and the students appeared to the University community to be rash and unreasonable. Slowly, through informal talks with members of the faculty, through speeches made by guests in the lobby of the administration building, the protesters sensed that the faculty did not understand their arguments and that the University community was overwhelmingly against them.42 In the end, they grew despondent about the effectiveness of the sit-in, and they ended the sit-in without a single concession by University officials. This decision took hours and hours of painful discussion, but was finally made. As the students began to see themselves and their "coercive" action as extreme, moderate voices gained greater attention, and by the weekend when they decided to leave the building and to canvass the faculty, the leadership had officially changed to a more moderate one.

To understand the undermining experience which led to capitulation, one must recognize two channels of communication which occur in any dialogue. One channel consists of what each person expresses overtly. At the same time, each person may express covertly or not at all other thoughts he may have. At the University of Chicago, persons on both sides of the conflict used a second channel to express informal feelings and thoughts which differed significantly from their overt statements about the sit-in and its issues. Official university statements reaffirmed the University's position on the rank issue and deplored the sit-in. Meantime, an ad hoc council of senior officers met daily assessing, worrying, and seeking solutions. Members of this group met constantly with leaders of the sit-in or spoke at the sit-ins as individuals, and informally they conveyed a willingness to negotiate once the students stopped being "coercive." They expressed a sympathy for the students' cause and a repulsion at the military calculation of life. Representatives of the University expressed privately to protesters their failings and those of the institution; yet no such statements or sentiment became part of the official posture.

Students were especially responsive to these sympathetic and concerned communications by esteemed members of the University community.43 Because many students value intellectual pursuits and plan to get advanced degrees, these men served as career models for them. At the same time, these men told the protesters that the protest was ruining their university, and these remarks touched the considerable loyalty students had for the college if not the University. The general feeling among most protesters was, "We don't want to destroy the University; we just want to stop the rank."

Students Against the Rank, like the University, issued strong statements; the hard line dominated the written mode of both sides. Informally, however, many moderate students were quite concilia-tory in tone as the community became more hostile. Thus, one could see how the unity of SAR dissipated as faculty and administrators focused more on the coercion of the sit-in and less on the issue of rank. SAR was united against the rank, not against being coercive or damaging the University. There were even rumors that opponents of the college were using the sit-in to press for an end to under-graduate education.

The effect of redefining the situation in this manner is that a large group of participants emerge who are hard on the initial issue (rank), but soft on other emerging issues (destruction). On the other hand, a number of participants remain determined to get their demand satisfied at any cost. In estimating the enemy, they distrust the conciliatory tones which University officials use informally and point to the official reiteration of old policy. The phenomenological experience of a protester in this situation is almost schizophrenic. All around him he hears different voices threatening and coaxing: "Your behavior is intolerable." "We are deeply concerned about the inequities of the draft law." "You are destroying the University." "As soon as you get out of the building, we can talk this over." "Call the police and have them all arrested." "For God's sake, get out before everyone falls at each other's throat."

Conclusion

This paper outlined, with the help of an extensive illustration, two main strategies of protest used by students and administrators in the past few years, if not longer. From informal observation, it would seem that the structure and process of almost all such demonstrations in this country since 1964 fit these models. As strategies with certain, distinctive features of their own, these forms of conflict may be able to be applied to other phenomena than the one used here. Such an analysis, however, is always historical, and new forms of student protest may arise. Certainly there is every sign that protesters will become harder and protests tougher. While administrations have succeeded in "winning" protests, either through the stand-off or negotiation or force, they have paid too little attention in the aftermath to the initial demands. This has created a credibility gap, and students increasingly feel that the most reasonable approach to a problem is to be "unreasonable," and the best way to negotiate is not to.[44]

In conclusion, I would like to comment upon the Simmel-Coser theories of conflict. Mainly in the footnotes, these have been used both to clarify the dynamics of certain conflict situations and to explain some of the events at the University of Chicago. Professor Coser writes that he would like to see more empirical testing of conflict theory, but certain problems make such an undertaking difficult.

The Simmel-Coser approach to conflict is largely social psychological; yet much of the writing reflects a formal, structural frame of mind. One difficulty in testing propositions rests in the definition of certain key terms, such as "basic" conflict, "realistic" conflict, and "in-group." The meaning of these terms cannot be pre-established, for their meanings vary with each individual conflict. Therefore, many of Coser's propositions are not hypotheses but definitions themselves. To propose that conflict may serve to reunite two groups, unless the issues contradict the basic assumptions upon which the relation is founded is a definition of basic conflict, not a testable hypothesis.[45]

It is impossible to test hypotheses using these terms if they are treated as if they had a life of their own. This does not mean the terms are irrelevant; to the contrary, they reflect distinctions which real persons and groups make when in conflict. For the concepts to bear greatest empirical fruit, they should be used within a phenomenological framework. For example, does either side see the conflict or some part of it as nonnegotiable and basic? "Basic conflict" should not be defined beforehand. Again, who sees whom as an out-group, and how do the borders of groups shift? Simmel and Coser make us sensitive to the distinctions found in conflict situations, but they do not emphasize the perceptual character of many of those distinctions.

The Simmel-Coser theories present another problem for empirical testing. They form a network of propositions so interwoven that empirically any outcome can be explained. This is partly due to the definitional problem stated above: if the conflict reunites, it was not basic; if it cannot be resolved, the conflict was basic. But part of the problem comes from the network quality. If the conflict was not resolved, was it basic (Proposition No. 7), or does it indicate a stable relationship (Proposition No. 8)?[46] If students protest vigorously and refuse to negotiate,[47] is it because the conflict is non-realistic (Proposition No. 3) or because the students are fervent in their cause (Proposition No. 12)?[48] If one hypothesizes that conflict with out-groups increases internal cohesion (Proposition No. 9) and one finds a great deal of internal conflict within the protesting group, does that challenge the hypothesis or validate another hypothesis, that the closer the relationship, the more intense the conflict (Proposition No.6)?[49]

Beyond these general problems of testing conflict theory, passive resistance and the stand-off exhibit qualities which differ from other forms of conflict. In terms of the Simmel-Coser conception of conflict, these strategies lead to peculiar experiences, where cohesion may not form in face of the enemy,[50] where participants may experience great intra-personal confusion as they are pulled in different directions by their conflicting loyalties,[51] where associations may not form[52] or where the group may accept any sympathetic person and exclude few deviants.[53] As these forms of protest persist, more study is needed of their social psychology.

Footnotes

[1]Quoted from Joan V. Bondurant, *Conquest of Violence: The Gandhian Philosophy of Conflict* (Berkeley: University of California Press; revised edition, 1965) page v.

[2]See Lewis A. Coser, *Continuities in the Study of Social Conflict* (New York: The Free Press; 1967), page 8.

[3]See the entire issue of the *Journal of Social Issues*, XXIII, 3 July, 1967; *The Contemporary University: U.S.A.*, Robert S. Morison, ed. (Boston: Beacon Press, 1967); Kenneth Keniston, *The Young Radicals*, (New York: Harcourt Brace, 1968); "Youth, Change and Violence," in *The American Scholar*, Spring, 1968, pp. 227-245; Charlotte Weissberg, "Students Against the Rank," Master's Paper, Dept. of Sociology, University of Chicago, 1967.

[4]I am indebted to Richard Flacks, Assistant Professor of Sociology at the University of Chicago, for starting me on this study as part of the Youth and Social Change Project. The theoretical aspects of the paper have been improved by the comments of Lewis A. Coser. This study has been conducted under the grateful support of an N.I.M.H. pre-doctoral fellowship, No. 7-FL-MH-25,333-04.

[5]This discussion of *satyagraha* and *duragraha* is derived from Joan V. Bondurant, *op. cit.*, pp. 1-40.

[6]By the same token, faculty at the University of Chicago upheld the administration's opposition to a student sit-in by 90 per cent to 10 per cent, because they saw the students as seriously disrupting university life. No police were employed in that five-day sit-in, which took place in May, 1966. The faculty also supported the administration's position on the original protest issue, which concerned the ranking of males for Selective Service. In this manner, faculty as a group seem highly consistent across issues and events; they oppose strongly action by either side which seriously disrupts the university or college.

Students assume naively that the faculty and they are kindred spirits of intellectual values against a corrupt, crass administration. However, faculty often oppose students when the issue at stake does not affect their lives. Faculty are in a different life position than students, and their primary interest is to be protected and left alone.

[7]For example, see Daniel Katz, "Group Process and Social Integration: A System Analysis of Two Movements of Social Protest," in the *Journal of Social Issues*, XXIII, 1 January, 1967, pp. 3-22; Irving Howe, et al., "The Vietnam Protest," in *The New York Review of Books*, vol. 5, no. 8, November 25, 1965, page 13.

[8]See Sheldon S. Wolin and John H. Scharr, "Berkeley and the University Revolution," in *The New York Review of Books*, vol. 8, no. 2, February 9, 1967, pp. 18-24.

[9]The linking of black power demands and anti-government issues, such as was seen across the nation in the protests of April 16 and 24-26, 1968, is no surprise. The tone and issues of anti-government protests have closely paralleled those of the civil rights movement. In the early period, up to 1966, students were demanding their civil rights on campus, to be treated like adult citizens, and disciplinary rules changed considerably during that period. As Negroes began to realize that power politics were the real demon behind abortive civil rights, both the black power movement and the students turned to unpopular attacks on the structure of American institutions. This period, 1966-1968, wrought little change for either group, and a new, tougher phase of attack can now be seen in both groups. While blacks claim that they can run their part of the city better than whitey, student protesters feel they can run the university with greater integrity than the administration. The bitter feeling at the Columbia University protest and in the ghetto is to destroy or take over, the two logical extremes of opposition. This view, of course, represents only the leading, militant edge of both groups.

[10]For one example made visible, see "200 Students Win in B. U. Lockout," *Boston Herald Traveler*, April 25, 1968, page 1. The lockout lasted only twelve hours.

[11]Students at Brandeis University protested against the presence of an Air Force Recruiter and also against new university rules restricting demonstrations. The administration threatened punishment, and the demonstration ended in a few hours.

[12]For example, in October 1967, students at the University of Wisconsin in Madison, filled a building lobby and were roughly removed by campus and city police. The shock of police force ended the demonstration.

[13]There are three standard books on Berkeley: Hal Draper, *Berkeley: The New Student Revolt* (Grove Press, 1965); S. M. Lipset and S. S. Wolin, eds., *The Berkeley Student Revolt* (Doubleday Anchor, 1965); M. M. Miller and Susan Gilmore, eds., *Revolution at Berkeley* (Dell, 1965). At present, the only account of the Waseda demonstrations is "The Sociology of a Student Movement—A Japanese Case Study," by Michiya Shimbori in *Daedalus*, Winter, 1968, pp. 204-228. My knowledge about the university strike in Rome, 1966, comes from conversations with visiting students who were there. For a summary and review of the events at the University of Berlin, see Joseph Wechsberg, "Letter from Berlin," *The New Yorker*, November 18, 1967, pp. 165-216. A couple of books describe and analyze the demonstration at Columbia University, *Up Against the Ivy Wall* by the editors of *The Columbia Spectator* and *Crisis at Columbia* by the Cox Commission. See also Jimmy Breslin in *The Boston Herald-Traveler*, May 3, May 13, 1968; *Ramparts*, June 15, 1968, pp. 26-39; *The Public Interest*, Special Issue "The Universities," No. 13, Fall 1968.

[14]See Lewis A. Coser, *The Functions of Social Conflict* (Glencoe: The Free Press, 1964), pp. 139-149. When such escalation occurs, both sides divert their attention from the initial protest issues to matters of sheer power and violence—"our" justly sought power and "their" unwarranted violence.

[15]*Ibid.*, pp. 48-54. Objectively it is almost impossible to determine whether a given conflict is, in Coser's terms, "realistic" or "non-realistic," not only because

the criteria for such an evaluation are ideological, but also because both elements exist in tension with each other. See "The Ins and Outs of SNCC," by Nancy Stoller, *Studies in Brandeis Sociology* (Waltham, Mass., 1966, mimeograph), pp. 20-21.

16Coser, *op. cit.*, pp. 72-80. Again, the decision whether a certain conflict is basic or not reflects the posture of the assessing party. Here and in the preceding footnote I am suggesting that what judgment is made about the realistic or basic nature of the conflict tells more about the party than about the conflict in some objective way. How these judgments are made serve as indices of the attitudes which the opponent brings to the conflict.

17See "Is America by Nature a Violent Society?" *The New York Times Magazine*, April 28, 1968, pp. 24 ff. Such an upsetting question is not discussed often in the mass media.

18For a summary, see Bondurant, *op. cit.*, pp. 88-104.

19The quotations in this paragraph are from interviews of faculty and administrators during a sit-in at the University of Chicago in May, 1966. However, very similar phrases and stages can be found in accounts of almost any student protest. See, for example, accounts of the protest at Columbia University, April-May, 1968, in *The New York Times*. Parallel quotations will be found on page 30, April 24, 1968; page 50, April 26; page 28, April 29; and page 34, May 1.

20Students Against the Rank, University of Chicago, May, 1966. An account of this sit-in follows.

21There are always limits to such propositions. If the university shot all those who participated at a sit-in, this act would probably be seen as unjustified, even against unreasonable protesters. Thus, the definition of the situation sets boundaries to conflict even as types of conflict structure the situation and its definition. The psychology and dynamics of the stand-off did not appear in the protest at Columbia University, because its administration did not use stand-off tactics. Despite an official emphasis from the second to the seventh day of protest that violence would be avoided at all costs, police action was a major element from the first day. In fact, the on-campus demonstrations began in response to the arrest of a student by city police. From the third to the tenth day, numbers of city police were present on campus, and barricading against massive assault began in the second day. In this and other ways, the protest at Columbia was like the one at Berkeley in 1964. See "Reflection of Berkeley," by Fred M. Hechinger, *The New York Times*, May 2, 1968, page 47M.

When the focus of a protest turns from the original issue(s) to uses of force, a stand-off posture of "let the students get tired" will not succeed. Strategically an administration should either rapidly compensate for whatever force was used or forcibly end the protest. The former has clear advantages in negotiating if the issues are respected. If students are serious about having their demands satisfied (rather than wanting a maximum of disruption and destruction), it is tactically preferable to avoid issues of violence and force as long as possible.

22The bitterness of effecting no change can be seen in the protest on the Berkeley campus in 1966 (following 1964) and at the University of Chicago in 1967, 1968, and 1969 (following 1966). When black leaders participate in student demonstrations, they bring to them a hardness and intransigence which few whites can feel so deeply and personally.

In general, student protests are becoming more aggressive, more demanding, less compromising. One cannot tell whether they will become truly violent. So far, student protests have caused surprisingly little damage for their scale. Large-scale violence as a form of protest has grown rapidly in recent years, but so have stronger forms of non-violence. The Poor People's March on Washington in the spring of 1968 was the first Gandhian campaign in this country of recent times. As we have seen, *satyagraha* is a much more powerful form of non-violence than *duragraha*.

[23]This quotation was transcribed from a taped interview, one of several which I conducted with faculty and administrators during and after the sit-in at the University of Chicago, in May, 1966. Other sources of information for this case study include participation in the student protest, interviews with leaders of the protest, papers and histories of the protest written by faculty and by protesting students, and the *Maroon*, the University newspaper. See also the article by Richard Flacks in this volume.

[24]The central quadrangle at the University of Chicago, its only point of focus, looks a few centuries older than it is.

[25]See John Searle, "The Faculty Resolution," in Miller and Gilmore, eds., *op. cit.*, pp. 92-104.

[26]Georges Sorel presents a penetrating analysis of the nature of political myths in *Reflections on Violence*, translated by T. E. Hulme (New York: Collier, 1961) pp. 26-56. The main features of such myths can be seen in this case; that they stand as wholes and must not be analyzed into parts, that comparing them to reality is irrelevant, because they do not make immediate claims on reality.

Quoting Renan, Sorel writes, "A man suffers martyrdom only for the sake of things about which he is not certain." (44-45). Sorel states, ". . .the myths are not descriptions of things, but *expressions of a determination to act.*" (50, emphasis is mine.)

[27]I am indebted to Professor McKim Marriott for this analysis.

[28]Seymour Martin Lipset comes to the opposite conclusion from an institutional argument. He seems to think protests are largely about educational facilities. John May correctly writes that the facts do not fit Lipset's conclusions in the *American Journal of Sociology*, *73*, 5, March 1968, pp. 631-633.

[29]Towards the end of the sit-in, the University announced that it would sponsor a conference on the draft, but no reference was made to the above list of recommendations. The following fall, the conference was held, and its proceedings are printed in *Draft*, Sol Tax, ed. (Chicago: University of Chicago Press, 1967). The conference was boycotted by some protesters, because its theme refused to consider whether armed forces were necessary or not.

[30]For a general background on the events of this time and the issues of the draft, see Richard Flacks, Florence Howe, and Paul Lauter, "On the Draft," *New York Review of Books*, VIII, 6, April 6, 1967, pp. 3-5.

31The logical extremes of this position are either to take over the university and have no administration or to destroy the university. As student demonstrators have become more adamant, these extremes have become more visible, and both are heard in protracted demonstrations today.

32The 'policy' changed from sending class rank to local draft boards unless otherwise directed by the student, to sending the class rank only upon the request of the student.

In fact, the policy was not changed, because no policy had existed, and because the "new policy" exactly paralleled the old practice. Since the Korean war, sending ranks had been administrative routine, done only upon the request of the student. No one whom I interviewed, from the highest to the most junior offices of the University, was aware of these facts. Administrators kept referring to the University's "past policy" but could not tell me the exact nature of that policy.

These unfortunate errors of knowledge are often the basis for mistrust, as they were in this case. Students concerned about the draft could never get an accurate answer on what University's policy was, because none existed and officials defended their vague knowledge with rigid postures.

33Thus, in reality, the students were correct to attack the administration and not the faculty Council, for ranking was an administrative procedure, and no one could tell them the faculty had recently made it an official policy. One dean, who was constantly asked about the University's position, related his frustration at knowing that "something" had been decided on April 12th, but at not being able to find out what happened from colleagues who had attended the meeting.

Faculty and administrators were irritated by SAR attacking the administration. The more generous saw it as stupid; the less regarded the action as a deliberate distortion by radical students to perpetrate a mass bid for student power.

34For a theoretical discussion of the group-forming and group-binding functions of conflict, see Coser, *op. cit.*, pp. 33-38, 87-95.

35 See Coser, *Continuities . . .* , pp. 22-34.

36The character of SAR is well-described by Coser's discussion of Simmel's fine statement, in *Functions. . .* , pp. 111-119. Such a group tends to search for enemies with increased fervor. *Ibid.*, pp. 104-110.

37I am indebted to Nancy Stoller Shaw for this analysis, found in her paper, *op. cit.*, pp. 24-25.

38Throughout the five floors, very little damage was wrought. After the sit-in, the president estimated costs of lost time and rentals at over $100,000 and indirect costs of grants and donors lost at over $1.5 million.

39One of the most interesting phenomena of recent student movements is participatory democracy. The Simmel-Coser theory of conflict defines a serious problem for groups in conflict with outside forces. Under such circumstances, great internal cohesion is demanded by the group. Very little deviance is tolerated. (Coser, *op. cit.*, pp. 87-104). Yet conflict usually exists within a group, and safety-valve institutions are important for preserving the group. In the case of student protest groups, the inner-group tensions are increased by the newness of the group, the diversity among its members, and the severe pressures individuals feel during a demonstration.

Participatory democracy serves to handle these multiple tensions and conflicts at a time when high group cohesion is required. By its principles, any member can speak for as long as he wishes on any issue. All decisions are made by the general body, not by an executive committee. To formulate a plan of action may take many hours of deliberation, but the process insures that the feelings and loyalties of all are considered. This forum is often expanded into a general teach-in; so that when no business of the group presses, others may speak about the issues of the day. This also permits great deviance while retaining overall cohesion of the group. As a form of high group cohesion, participatory democracy is not characterized by the Simmel-Coser formulation. Participatory democracy is a way of maintaining high cohesion in face of an external enemy, yet allowing great internal conflict and adjustment.

[40]For the next week, students opposing the rank talked to faculty members, especially those who held positions on the faculty Council. On May 24, the Council voted 32-3 for a two part resolution favoring the present policy of rank, commending the administration, and recommending disciplinary action against future disruptive acts. On May 27, the faculty Senate met for the first extraordinary session in University history. While not a policy body, it expressed its sentiment 85% in favor of the policy on rank with 5% abstaining, and 60% supporting the administration's posture with 30% abstaining. A minority of faculty and the protesting students severely criticized the way this meeting was conducted.

[41]These theories of outside agitators centered mainly on SDS, which had moved its national headquarters from New York to the south side of Chicago.

[42]One SAR student wrote the following summary of an interview with a professor: "*all* her colleagues . . . are utterly appalled at the incredible stupidity of our tactics in taking the Ad(ministration) Building.

"Not only will she not support us; she won't talk to us until we get out. She says being in here is killing our stand.

"She says ranks are formed and always have been. They're used for many purposes, including job applications for ---- students. Absurd to say, don't form them. It's unjust to students who *want* their rank sent in not to have such a rank.

"But foremost in everyone's mind is our militant taking over this building. She says we're fools to listen to soft-heads like (names of faculty). They're in an even smaller minority of the faculty than we are of the students.

"Don't bother talking to her again while we have the building.

"Also, she says we're ignorant and stupid and childish to protest Administration. Faculty made the decision, not the Ad. Faculty senate has no voting power, so it's even stupider tactics to talk to them about voting for us. Stupid was her favorite word for us."

[43]This analysis of student receptivity to faculty appeals was first put forth by Richard Flacks.

[44]Compare this analysis with that of Kenneth Keniston, "Youth, Change and Violence," *op. cit.*

[45]Coser, *op. cit.*, page 80.

[46]*Ibid.*, pp. 72-85.

47This "refusal to negotiate as a group" phenomenon was reported in the *New York Times* (4/24/68, p. 30) at the initial demonstration at Columbia University.

48Coser, *op. cit.*, pp. 55-60, 111-119.

49*Ibid.*, pp. 87-95, 67-72.

50Contrast with Coser's treatment of Proposition No. 9, *ibid.*, pp. 87-95.

51This effect of the stand-off is not treated in Coser's book.

52Contrast Proposition No. 16, *ibid.*, pp. 139-149

53This occurs largely because of participatory democracy. Contrast with Proposition No. 10, *ibid.*, p. 95-104.

Duke

"It Ain't Over Yet": Activism in a Southern University

Allan Kornberg and Joel Smith

The University as a Vulnerable Institution in Mass Society

Almost twenty years have passed since Philip Selznick[1] posed the question of how, in the struggle for power in mass society, the integrity of culture-bearing institutions could be preserved when they become targets in political combat. He noted that both elitist and democratic theorists share the belief that a mass society is one in which the mass does not permit elites to perform their traditional cultural functions, that is, the maintenance and transmission of cultural values and standards within a society.[2] Since both groups of theorists are agreed that the mass is inherently unqualified to perform these tasks, a kind of cultural vacuum occurs; not because of any dearth of superior individuals, but because such individuals, in the radical leveling that occurs in mass society, are no longer able to give cultural direction to society.

Institutions of higher learning, as sources of cultural development and as custodians of current cultural values, have been particularly sensitive and vulnerable to the mass process. The universities have learned to adapt themselves, but the adaptation has been costly. Specifically, when mass characteristics appear in a university we find that: the faculty is unable to reach the students as persons but merely trains them as experts; conditions for the emergence and sustenance of intellectual elites on the campus are poor; the faculty adapts itself to the mass character of the institution; standards of conduct and of nontechnical achievement deteriorate; and the meaning of the university as a culture-bearing institution is increasingly attenuated.[3]

One manifestation of this cultural attenuation is that, although both the behavior of students and faculty becomes increasingly less affected by major cultural symbols, they may develop a compulsive attachment to the symbols as such. Outside the university, the symbols of higher education and their institutionalized embodiments (although not their meanings) also become precious to the mass, who are easily susceptible to the blandishments of those who manipulate such symbols. In fact, under certain circumstances the mass can become the university's most aggressive defenders, being prepared to use any means against the university's purported enemies. When such conditions exist, when educational values are stereotyped, when symbols and meaning become divorced, and when their content can be manipulated with impunity, then acts taken in the name of educational values, in fact, violate their spirit.

According to Selznick, mass behavior also is associated with an activist interpretation of democracy and with increasing reliance on force to resolve social conflict. Social disintegration entails the breakdown of normal social restraints and the established channels of action. This breakdown frees the mass to engage in direct unmediated efforts to achieve its goals and to try to seize the most readily accessible instruments of action, for example, the "invasion" of the buildings of a state university. The goal of such tactics, especially when they are used before any significant mass character emerges in a target such as a university, is precisely to break down feelings of deference for the rule-making body and to prepare for extra-legal methods of intimidation. Like other aspects of mass behavior, activism is thus a result of the withdrawal of deference ascribed to established institutions. But, as has already been suggested, such institutions (particularly of higher learning) are likely to be defended, often at great cost of life and resources, because they have come to reflect society's self-image. "They define its aspirations and its moral commitments; they are the source and receptacle of self-respect, of unique identity. No enemy is so dangerous as he who threatens these valued principles and structures . . . the haloed reverenced symbols of public weal, the last bastions which dare not be surrendered, without which life itself seems worthless, cast down to a melancholy level of hopelessness and despair."[4] Although in this paper we will address ourselves to student activism at Duke University, we also will try to speak to the more general points that are made in Selznick's essay on the vulnerability of culture-bearing institutions in mass societies.

Our use of Selznick's analysis is motivated by the many suggestive insights for interpretation that it affords, and, hopefully, these will be apparent throughout the discussion. The crucial concepts, such as "elite," "mass society," and "culture-bearing institutions" are clearly ideal types whose utility rests on their analytic helpfulness rather than on the accuracy with which they reflect reality. One of the more useful facets of his analysis is its suggestion that society becomes more mass-like as its members feel they have access to rights and responsibilities more directly (as a consequence of homogenizing ideologies and behavior) but, nonetheless, feel a continuing incapacity or incompetence for playing their newly emerging responsible roles. It is under these circumstances that the culture-bearing institutions come under a pressure that was never absent but is now magnified to a qualitatively different level. They are deflected from their traditional goals and the general demand develops for them to provide entree and prescriptions for efficacious actions for the emerging segments of population gaining equality of rights and responsibility with the older holders of power.

It is doubtful whether American universities ever have approximated the "community of scholars" model or whether even a minority of colleges have been the idyllic and sheltered preserves of the upper middle class, great teachers, and paternalistic deans. Student and faculty activism did not spring full-blown from the brow of SDS; colleges struggling with their finances long have accepted students (and faculty) whose scholarship and conduct were questionable; and administrators and university lobbyists, in their eagerness to please rural-dominated legislatures, long ago created extension departments and gave credit-bearing courses in hamlets in which there were few scholars and even fewer books.

As was suggested above, it is also doubtful whether American universities and colleges ever have been autonomous institutions—in the sense that they have neither been subjected to nor have they responded to the importunings of special groups. The establishment of essentially technical and training schools, such as agriculture, business administration, education, engineering, forestry, journalism, medicine, and nursing, alongside and sometimes within the traditional liberal arts framework (not to mention the more exotic and academically questionable departments of physical education, police administration, hotel management, and conservation management that proliferate in so many large state universities), indicates that a majority of universities and a substantial proportion of colleges have been responsive to the expressed needs of society. The fact that they have been willing to legitimate mass demands (even if this has meant lowering existing academic standards and/or granting special dispensations and privileges to selected groups of students) constitutes, in a sense, *prima facie* evidence that American culture-bearing institutions for at least two generations have had to accommodate themselves when sufficient and sustained pressure was applied to them. Therefore, the pressure currently being applied by student and faculty activists and their outside supporters to university authorities to make their institutions meet the needs of blacks, the Third World, or the amorphous "community" may be viewed as a continuation of a well-established process.

One of the concomitant features of elite institutions seems to be that they are somehow or other unconcerned with routine maintenance functions. As expressions of the luxury possibilities of societies whose surpluses allowed them more than a minimal subsistence existence (cf. analyses of the emergence of science, a priesthood, education concomitant with the development of the city), historically they were often arenas of the rich (e.g., the dilettante scholar, the patron of the artist). As these elitist functions have become routinized in institutional form, this combination of circumstances, regardless of its specifics, has helped sustain the attitude that money and the market place are sordid, and has led in turn to inadequate ancillary supportive services and personnel inadequately financed. As altruists engaged in altruistic endeavors, the elite professionals and their co-workers are supposed to be indifferent to the material goods of the market place. To coin an aphorism, "shabbiness is the proof of goodness and total commitment."

Activism at Duke University:
An Overview

Duke University has shared many of the experiences of elite educational institutions since the indenture of James B. Duke transformed it from a small Methodist college into a university with national visibility and stature. Despite the presence of a distinguished faculty in the College of Arts and Sciences and in the Medical School and the fact that the student body was integrated in 1961 and the faculty in 1966 (no small feat for a private Southern university), Duke is probably better known for its nationally ranked basketball and football teams and for the grandeur of its Gothic and Georgian architecture than for its academic excellence and social conscience (until 1968 the best remembered student incident involved a march by an irate group of students on the home of former President Hart and his hanging in effigy because he had refused to extend the Christmas vacation so that they could watch the football team play in the 1961 Cotton Bowl).

Certainly, as one report of the 1968 mass demonstration termed a "Silent Vigil" makes clear, "the Duke campus seems by no means a likely place for a student uprising on behalf of Negro workers seeking recognition for their union. The Gothic spires, gargoyles, and greenswards of West Campus . . . and the 18th century Georgian style . . . remind one of traditional values and provide an incongruous setting for activist behavior."[5] Nevertheless on Friday evening, April 5, 1968, the day after the assassination of Dr. Martin Luther King, some 450 students and a handful of younger faculty members marched to the home of President Douglas M. Knight and presented him with four demands: 1) that he sign an advertisement to appear in the Durham newspapers calling for a day of mourning for Dr. King and asking Durham citizens to do all they could to bring about racial equality; 2) that he resign from the segregated Hope Valley Country Club; 3) that he press for the $1.60 minimum wage rate for non-academic employees (the existing minimum of $1.15 was not scheduled to rise to $1.60 until 1971); 4) that he appoint a committee of students, faculty, and non-academic employees to make recommendations concerning collective bargaining and union recognition.[6]

Although in two hours of discussion with the group's leaders the President assured them he shared their concern over the current racial crisis, he nevertheless refused to meet their demands. And, in a memorial service for Dr. King the next day in the Duke Chapel, he insisted that no one individual, not even a university president, could make university policy. However, he did indicate that he would establish a broadly representative University committee on the problems of the non-academic employees. Unmoved by his speech, some 200 students followed it with a protest, the Silent Vigil, on the Main Quadrangle of the University. Further, a large proportion of the group that had marched to the President's house the night before remained in his home even after they learned that the President was suffering from exhaustion and a possible relapse of hepatitis and had been ordered into seclusion by his physician. Not until Sunday afternoon (and only at the urging of their chief faculty advisor, John Strange, an assistant professor of political science and an alumnus of the University) did they consent to join the students already on the Quad. Thereafter, with their numbers rapidly multiplying, the Vigilers brought blankets and sleeping bags to the Quad, made arrangements to serve meals (they eventually fed 1,400 demonstrators with chicken and pork chops on Wednesday night) and to meet other personal needs, and settled down for an indefinite stay.

From the beginning, the Vigil was characterized by stringent self-discipline (ground rules included no talking, no eating except at snack or meal time, no sunbathing, no conversation with spectators, no singing except at specified periods, and no responding to harassment) and superb organization; the students' ability to set up an information center, a lost and found center, a medical center, a transportation pool, cleanup crews, and even a banking service almost overnight was truly impressive. It led one faculty member to comment that "forty years of arranging Homecomings and Joe College Weeks *does* make a difference." Except for a handful of black students, those taking part were white, mostly Protestant, upper middle class, and of all hues and persuasions politically.

On Monday the black maids, janitors, restaurant employees, and hospital orderlies—organized in Local 77, a "union" that had been trying unsuccessfully for more than two years to obtain recognition from the University administration as the employees' bargaining agent—voted to strike. All but the hospital workers left their jobs and set up picket lines. In turn, the members of the Vigil called for a boycott of all University-run dining halls and also organized a class boycott.

By Tuesday the number of Vigil participants had grown to well over 1,000, and the handful of elected leaders, together with their faculty advisor, John Strange, were now negotiating with the Chairman of the Board of Trustees, Wright Tisdale, who had replaced Dr. Knight as the University's chief negotiator. Telegrams of encouragement and support were received from William Styron, Eugene McCarthy, and the late Robert F. Kennedy. Over $2,000 were collected by students to help finance the Vigil and the strike; the faculty of the Divinity School asked the administration not to give them whatever funds might be set aside for them for salary increases in the next year, but to use it instead to help raise the wages of non-academic employees; and Howard Fuller, a leader of the activist segment in Durham's black community, told the Vigil that their action was keeping Durham from exploding into the kind of violence that characterized other American cities in the wake of the King assassination.

On Wednesday both the executive committee of the Board of Trustees and the faculty Academic Council made known their positions on the Vigil. The Chairman of the Board told the Vigil that wages for non-academic employees would be advanced to the $1.60 minimum two years ahead of the legally required schedule. Although he skirted the issues of collective bargaining and union recognition, he apparently was sufficiently moved by the assembled students to clasp hands with them and sway to the words of "We Shall Overcome." The Academic Council, meanwhile, instructed its executive committee to join with University officials in considering the problems of the non-academic workers, including the question of the "nationally accepted right of collective bargaining." They also urged members of the Vigil to return to their classrooms and laboratories. After an all-night talkathon, including an emotional 2:00 a.m. confrontation in the Chapel between a group of students and the Chairman of the Board of Trustees, the Vigil voted to suspend the demonstration on the Quad, to continue to support the worker strike by boycotting campus cafeterias and by picketing, and to reconvene if the collective bargaining issue were not satisfactorily resolved within ten days.

During that period, the Trustees agreed to the establishment of a kind of internal NLRB. The procedure worked out by a faculty committee set up by the Academic Council calls for a five-man faculty committee (Duke University Employee Relations Advisory Committee) to arbitrate and decide (subject to a veto by the University's President) any disputes that arise between employee councils, to be elected by the employees, and the University. Accordingly, the non-academic employees ended their strike, the students decided not to resume their protest, and one observer summed up the events of the week thusly, "Duke appears to have come through its crisis unhurt and with the morale of many students and professors higher than before. The Duke experience has, in fact, been exceptional. The student demonstrations were directed to unselfish goals, were joined in by a substantial part of the student body, and, except for the occupation of President Knight's home, were conducted with restraint and deescalated at every critical juncture."[7]

Apparently student activism at Duke, if not ended, at least was "on ice." However, in October rallies again were being held on the Quad, petitions were being circulated, and a boycott of political science classes was being proposed because the contracts of an instructor and an assistant professor in the political science department who had been active participants in the Vigil were not being renewed. Although the initial furor was occasioned by the two men's association with the Vigil (other members of the Department also were involved), the focus for criticism soon became the structure of decision-making in the political science department, and, indeed, throughout the University. Editorials in the student newspaper, *The*

Duke Chronicle, asserted that the failure to re-hire the two faculty members merely was symptomatic of a more general malaise throughout the University, the undemocratic nature of decision-making within the structure of the University and the inability of students to affect procedures that bore upon them as students.

Although a Political Science Union of undergraduate majors was quickly formed and similar organizations in other departments were called for, the protest faded. Relative peace ensued until the occurrence of Black Week (February 3-10) celebrations sponsored by the campus Afro-American Society. During the course of the week, the theme of which was the "Beauty of Black," President Knight revealed that a black advisor would be hired for black students and that a summer remedial program would be provided for black students having need of such a program. He took the opportunity to announce that he was resigning from the segregated Hope Valley Country Club (one of the original demands made by Vigil participants).

It also was learned that the Afro-American Society was to be given office space, that a black barber was to be hired for the University barber shop, and that "Dixie" was no longer to be played at University functions. He left open, however, the disposition of demands by black students for more "Black Studies" courses, saying only that such recommendations "will require careful study before we can determine the best solution to the problem."[8]

Ten days later, students and faculty on their way to early morning classes learned that a group of approximately thirty black students[9] had entered the administration (Allen) building; had forced the clerical help to leave their offices; had barricaded themselves within a portion of the building; and had threatened to burn the University records if the police were called to eject them. And, despite an attempt by the Provost (ironically, Dr. Knight was in New York that morning seeking funds from the Ford Foundation for a Black Studies program) to get them to negotiate an evacuation and then an ultimatum from him at 3:30 that they *must vacate* the building or be ejected by the police, they did not leave until 5:30 p.m. By that time an emergency meeting of the faculty learned from Dr. Knight, who had been summoned from New York, that the black students had made thirteen demands,[10] that he would not consider any of them while the black students continued to occupy the administration building, that the police had been called, and that they would be employed if the black students did not voluntarily leave.

In the tragicomic sequence that followed, the black students left the building; they were followed down Campus Drive away from the Main Quad by their white supporters and a crowd of interested observers; the police moved in from their assembly point in Duke Gardens and began to surround the administration building; the crowd turned around and proceeded to the Main Quad chanting, among other things, "It ain't over yet," "Sieg heil," and "Pigs off campus." Several police cars then drove through the crowd, and a number of angered students banged on the cars and tried to set one afire. The crowd of supporters of the black demands together with other interested spectators (most of whom were not supporters) began to shout at the police; the police opened up with a barrage of tear gas—the police said they used gas because bricks and other objects were hurled at them, the blacks and their supporters claimed the gassing was unprovoked. As a result of the melee that followed, forty-five people were reported to have required treatment at the emergency room of the University hospital, two of them police.

By Saturday an *ad hoc* faculty committee that had been established by the Academic Council the night before the seizure (to look into the problems of black students) had been meeting almost continuously for three days. Finally, after a three-hour meeting Saturday night between representatives of the Afro-American Society, the faculty committee, President Knight, the Provost, and Howard Fuller (the black community leader who also had been prominent in the Vigil), it was announced that most of the black students' demands had been met and that the administration had "pledged itself to work toward some form of all but one of the others."[11]

However, a few days afterward (February 20th), in a published letter to the Durham Chief of Police and in similar letters to the Governor and to the Mayor of Durham, President Knight praised the police and the state highway patrol for their "proficiency" in handling the trouble that arose on campus after the black students' evacuation of the Allen Building. He also denied that the administration had "given in" to the black students, saying that a number of the demands had already been acted on before the black students seized the building, but that they had not been fully informed of this fact. Predictably, his statement angered both the black students and their white supporters in the faculty and student body, and as this is written, a minority of younger faculty members have formed a Free Academic Senate open to all members of the Duke academic community "who share a common commitment to a humane vision of the University and its purposes." In addition, the editorial staff of the *Chronicle* has called for a restructuring of the decision-making apparatus of the University and the creation of departmental unions including undergraduate and graduate students in all disciplines, and a group composed largely of graduate students, the Student Liberation Front, has started a strike fund on the assumption that the employees' councils (established after the Vigil) that are to bargain collectively with the University's Personnel Policy Committee will not operate successfully. In summary, there has been a considerable polarization of opinion and feeling between students and faculty, students and administration, faculty and faculty, some faculty and administration, and some non-academic employees and administration.

This course of events has been kaleidoscopic in contrast to the longer-run changes in the general character of the institution. At the institutional level, significant changes in the quality of faculty, students, and instruction have taken place during a forty-year period which has seen a transformation from an undistinguished, denominational, liberal arts college to what is now (depending on prejudice) *the* or *one of three* leading private universities in the region.

The changes over these years have been of the sort experienced by most major academic institutions. The faculty, especially those recruited within the last decade, pay more than lip service to the shibboleths of research and publication. A substantial number tend to be discipline- or specialty-oriented in the sense that they ascribe greater value to acquiring prestige and visibility in their respective disciplines or specialties than they do to becoming campus notables. Virtually all members of the faculties of the Medical School and the "hard" sciences are funded with "soft money" (i.e., their salaries and research funds come from federal granting agencies such as NIH and NSF). A substantial proportion of the social science departments also look to granting agencies, public and private, to fund their research, to pay for "released time" from teaching, to provide them with summer salaries, to enable them to travel to conferences and colloquia, and to provide them with clerical, technical, and the other kinds of assistance that currently are considered a virtual *sine qua non* by professors engaged in serious ongoing research. Of necessity, involvement in site visits, in reading papers, in acting as consultants, and so forth has meant they frequently are off campus one or more times a semester. Relatedly, a smaller proportion of their total time is spent in preparing and delivering lectures than was previously the case; the current "normal" teaching load for social scientists, for example, is approximately half of what it was ten years ago.

This is not to suggest that faculty engaged in research and related activities, with or without grants, are poor or even indifferent teachers. In fact, for most the opposite is the case. It is to say that one of the realities of the modern university with serious pretensions to national stature (and Duke is such a university) is that many of the most creative and productive faculty members are *de facto* teaching graduate rather than undergraduate students, offering courses in specialized areas in which they have special competence as opposed to giving instruction in survey-type courses, and engaging in the kinds of prestige-giving activities described above. In this sense they are what Selznick termed "highly specialized." To the extent that they identify psychologically with a group (their discipline, sub-discipline, or specialty) outside their university and engage in activities (such as research) that limit their person-to-person inter-actions with students and faculty colleagues, they are also what Selznick called "segmental participants" in their university community.

It may be noted that in addition to these highly specialized professors, Selznick also predicted that "demagogues" would become increasingly prominent in faculties, and Duke has its share of, if not demagogues, then radical faculty members. These individuals are most frequently seen addressing activist rallies on the Quad, planning strategy and tactics with their student advisees, or deep in conversations with the black non-academic employees of Local 77. Not unexpectedly, they are the faculty who actively joined in the Vigil or were its most vigorous and vociferous supporters. They also made up the majority of a small group of faculty who walked out in protest from the February 13th emergency faculty meeting after the President revealed that the local police had been summoned and would be used, if necessary, to get the black students out of the Allen Building. Since that time, they have continuously called for total amnesty for the black students involved; have condemned the administration for its use of the police and for its insensitivity to the needs of students and of non-academic employees; and, as was previously indicated, have established a Free Academic Senate whose avowed purpose is not to compete with the established Academic Council of the faculty but rather "to exert a reforming influence on it through its structure and its commitments."[12]

Most of this young radical group of faculty members are instructors and assistant professors, recent or soon-to-be Ph.D.s in history, political science, philosophy, and the humanities. Because almost none of them enjoy tenure, they and their student allies, especially those on the editorial staff of the *Chronicle*, fear that the "power structure" will punish them for their political beliefs, either by having their merit increases withheld or by not renewing their contracts. They have, therefore, waged a rather vigorous campaign in the *Chronicle* to alert other faculty and students to the danger of this happening. A typical example of this campaign is a recent "news" story in the *Chronicle* headlined "Young Faculty: Exodus in History." The story reveals that an activist assistant professor in the history department has resigned to take a better-paying job because of a dispute with his senior colleagues over renewal of his contract and goes on to say that "one full professor vowed at a cocktail party this summer 'We're going to clean out that nest of young radicals over in East Duke.' "[13] Although it is extremely doubtful that such a statement ever was made (it has such a fine false Victorian ring to it), it does illustrate how difficult it is to achieve a community of scholars, even if "community" is defined in terms only of a relatively small faculty.

Politically, the Duke faculty attitudes range from strong conservative (primarily among the physicians in the Medical School) through moderate-conservative (the other professional schools), moderate-liberal (the hard sciences), liberal (most of the social sciences and humanities), to strong liberal and radical (a minority of the social sciences, humanities, and some of the Ph.D.s in the Medical School). Faculty attitudes toward student activism, black or white, range from hostility and disgust (throw the bastards out!) through annoyance (how can we work in these conditions?), confusion (what do they want?), paternalism (they'll grow out of it, in the meantime they need our guidance), and sympathy (these are our best kids) to vigorous support (you have wrought a revolution!).

The undergraduates are also a mixed bag, although they are not as heterogeneous a social or political group as are the faculty. In terms of social background, the majority are of upper middle class status, Protestant, and of Western or Northern European ethnic background. Although a substantial proportion of each incoming freshman class are "in-state residents" or else live in the South, the proportion of students recruited from outside the South has been rising steadily in the last ten years (e.g., in 1959, 45 per cent came from outside the South; in 1964, 47 per cent; and in 1968, 54 per cent). The SAT scores of incoming freshmen also have risen sharply in the last decade; the average SAT score was 572 in 1959 and 647 in 1968.[14] In this respect, Duke University differs from what Selznick had predicted would be the norm in universities in mass society. According to him, universities would have to adapt themselves to the demands of mass society by permitting participation on the basis of lower standards and conduct. That this has not been the case is explained, in great part, by the fact that, unlike larger universities, both public and private, Duke has not established departments such as hotel management, police administration, or even physical education, nor is it likely to in the future. Further, until recently, the conduct of students has been exemplary; newly arrived faculty frequently find that the courtesy and deference that undergraduates exhibit toward authority figures in the faculty and administration is a rather novel change from their previous experiences.

Politically, the majority of students probably occupy a position at the center or slightly to the right of center of the con-tinuum, although there probably was considerable support among undergraduates in the 1968 presidential campaign both for Mr. Wallace and Senators Kennedy and McCarthy.

In a feature story that appeared shortly before the Vigil, the undergraduate student body was characterized by a faculty member as belonging to the "timid generation." By this he meant that, although Duke undergraduates do not lack definite opinions on current social and political issues, for a variety of reasons (principally, a desire to compete successfully in what they regard as a microcosm of society) most have hesitated to take an overt position on or to become involved in emotionally exhausting political and social causes because such involvement is time-consuming and has a deleterious effect on their grade point averages. Given the moderate and conservative ideological positions of the majority of the undergraduates and their supposed hesitancy to become involved in matters not directly related to academic success, how can the participation of approximately a third of them in a demonstration that sought higher wages, the right of collective bargaining, and union recognition for unskilled black workers be explained? Empirical observation and interviews with a number of student participants and with faculty and administrators who were involved in the Vigil suggest that many of the students who took part were deeply shocked and burdened with guilt over Dr. King's death. The Vigil was seen by them as a means of "bearing witness" and of "atoning" for the assassination. Administration members, in particular, offered "guilt expiation" and "emotional fervor" as motives for student participation. Indeed, the Vice President for Institutional Advancement, in an address to a group of Greensboro, North Carolina, alumni that was widely distributed, cites essentially these motives in the "official" explanation for the Vigil: "It is difficult to describe the vigil to anyone who did not see it. The only thing in my experience to which it is analogous is an old-fashioned revival or camp meeting, but the vigil was much more orderly, and highly disciplined. I believe we had on our hands a group of students who were very like new converts, and who saw their mission as that of converting others."[15]

As was previously indicated, all but a handful of black students remained conspicuously apart from the Vigil, and it is interesting that they also believe that guilt was the primary reason for the participation of their white student colleagues. For example, when asked by one of the authors why more black students had not participated in the Vigil, a former president of the Afro-American Society said, "We didn't kill Dr. King. We had nothing to feel guilty about. Besides, it was their thing and we wanted to let them do it."

Whether or not atonement for guilt was the principal motive for student participation in the Vigil, it is apparent that until very recently a majority of even the most active undergraduates have been what Edward E. Sampson[16] termed "constructivists" rather than alienated youth. That is, to the extent that they become involved in social and political affairs either within or outside of the University, they seek to work within the existing social framework rather than to reject society and either withdraw from it or try to destroy it. Parenthetically, it may be because most activists viewed the seizure of the Allen Building and the threat to burn the records as an act at least symbolically aimed at the destruction of society, that many who had participated in the Vigil of 1968 condemned the action of the black students in 1969.

Despite the relatively limited support by average white students for this act, the number of activists who may be said to be in active rebellion against the "system" has increased gradually in the last year. It is these students who are now taking the lead in trying to restructure the decisional processes within the University so that students, younger faculty, and black non-academic employees can play a significant role in policy-making. Selznick noted that mass-oriented elites who advocate activism and employ unorthodox pressure tactics normally try to break down feelings of deference for the established rule-makers preparatory to employing extra-legal methods for intimidating them.[17] Although even the most active white students (but not black) until recently have largely refrained from employing the viler insults and obscenities used by activists at other college campuses, they now *have* begun to apply pejorative labels such as "pig," "racist," and "fascist" to their opponents in the faculty and the administration.[18] It is not inconceivable, were there to be another more serious clash in which police were called by the administration, in response, let us say, to the seizure of one or more buildings or the disruption of the operation of the University hospital or the computer center by black non-academic employees, students, and their white supporters, that such obscene expletives would be employed, as would be the threat of force and violence.

It should be noted, however, that the majority of students, active and passive, still trust and defer to both the faculty and the administration. The President is generally regarded as a politically liberal, sensitive, and humane individual who, unfortunately, is himself trapped in a system he did not create and that he cannot control.[19] And, unlike the situations at Berkeley and Columbia, he is accessible to students, if not always to all faculty members. During the Vigil and the aftermath of the seizure of the Allen Building, several hundred students marched to the President's house, were graciously received by him, and were able to question and converse with him for several hours. The relative accessibility of the President and other top administrators and their willingness to give students a sympathetic hearing may account, in great part, for the relatively favorable image that most students still have of them.

Credit for this image is largely due to the Dean of Students and his staff and to the Assistant to the Provost responsible for Student Affairs. Although, even at Duke, the decline of *in loco parentis* and the tendency for individuals at the top of the administrative hierarchy to make decisions in areas that formerly were the prerogative of the Dean have weakened him, he and the middle tier of administration just mentioned continue to provide both a catharsis for student grievances and a channel for their communication with top decision-makers. It is true that there have been increasing complaints by activist students that the Dean and his staff invade their privacy, limit their social activities, and serve as buffers and "fall guys" for those above them. Nevertheless, they do not regard them as a barrier to their (students') playing a really decisive part in policy making. Rather, it is the Board of Trustees who are perceived as the villains.

Most activist students regard the Board as a self-perpetuating oligarchy, completely out of touch with them and their aspirations. They feel the Board neither trusts nor respects them. Worst of all, it will not take them and their claims seriously! The students' assumption is that their ideas concerning the direction the University should take, and the policies it should espouse, are *at least as valid* as the Board's, and they are quick to point out that the Trustees' views of what are the best interests of the University frequently are not unrelated to their (the Trustees') own. For example, the supposed opposition of certain Trustees toward collective bargaining and unions for non-academic employees is widely interpreted, even by non-active students, as being rooted in the Trustees' corporate and personal positions as large-scale employers of non-union labor. The facts that the Trustees are dispersed, distant, difficult to communicate with, but yet all-powerful because they make the *really* important decisions (it will be recalled that it was the Chairman of the Board of Trustees rather than the chief academic officer, the Provost, who negotiated with the leaders of the Vigil after the President became ill and withdrew), make them an ideal scapegoat and help reinforce the notion that the administration and, particularly, the President really are good men who could be counted on to do the right thing (i.e., accede to activist requests) if *only* they were not held captive by the Board.

Regardless of whether he is their captive or whether he willingly refers policy questions to the Trustees (or, rather, the executive committee of the Trustees) for resolution, it does appear that there is close and continuous consultation between the President and certain Board members on policy issues. But the Board of Trustees is only one of the publics to which the President and his administrative colleagues must be attentive. Since Duke is a relatively young institution and a majority of alumni still live in the South (the region from which they were initially recruited), and since many of these alumni are also economic and social conservatives, during apparent crises such as the Vigil and the black student seizure of the Allen Building, they want to know what is going on at *their* University. Why is the administration permitting a small group of radicals and agitators among the students and faculty to destroy the institution they love? When is the President going to show some real leadership and expel the radical students and fire their leaders in the faculty?

Nor are the alumni the only ones concerned with campus affairs. There is also the Durham community, white and black; the Governor and the members of the state legislature (the capital is only fifteen miles away); and because of Duke's prominence and position of leadership within the region, there are also other economic and educational elites who follow events at Duke and the nearby University of North Carolina very closely.[20] All of these publics are capable of exerting considerable pressure on the administration and the Trustees and of escalating relatively minor incidents into major events. One may assume that the majority of the members of these groups possess only a vague notion of what a university's functions are or understand how delicately balanced the relationship between students and faculty, between students and administration, between faculty and administration, between academic and ancillary personnel, and between a university and the surrounding community must be if a university is to remain sufficiently autonomous to maintain its viability. Nevertheless, they are not loath to make suggestions, and the panaceas that they offer—such as expelling, jailing, or drafting radical students, purging radical professors, passing legislation that would control who may or may not teach or even speak on a campus, hiring faculty for reasons other than their professional competence, waiving entrance and scholastic requirements for black students, establishing a Black Studies unit within the University that would be academically and administratively independent, hiring and retaining faculty on the basis of their "correct" ideological beliefs and/or popularity with students, creating new curricula on the basis of relevance for current students, having the University perform social welfare functions, and making the University "sensitive" to the needs and wishes of the community—might well cure the University of its current malaise, but they undoubtedly would destroy its integrity as an educational institution. The upper middle class student activist who mounts violent demonstrations on behalf of radical faculty members whom he wants retained and who rationalizes his behavior in terms of "academic freedom" or a "free university" has no more understanding of those concepts than the unlettered layman who demands that these same faculty be fired or otherwise punished for their radicalism, and who also rationalizes his request in terms of "the University." To the extent that such demands increase in frequency and intensity, it would be ironic if the greatest threat to Duke University came from those elements who, at present, would most like to "save" it!

Summary and Conclusions

We began this paper by citing Selznick's predictions with respect to universities in which mass characteristics have appeared. Using Duke University as our empirical referent, we have tried to demonstrate that some of Selznick's predictions have been realized but that others, at least until recently, have not. Thus, for example, we have shown that, in certain respects, the Duke faculty has *not* been able to reach students as persons but has merely trained them as experts. If there is blame to be apportioned for this state of affairs, some of it obviously must rest with the faculty. As is the case in other leading educational institutions, many of the most productive faculty members are what Selznick terms "segmental participants" in the University community; they are absent from the campus periodically, they teach less, and what they do teach tends to reflect what they rather than *students* are intellectually interested in or committed to.

In any event, if faculty members have not responded in supporting fashion to the repeated pressure of student demands, it may be because the demands of the very same students, independent of their explicit content, reflect two contradictory themes. One of these, in Selznick's language, is an anguished demand to return to the older style of the university and has taken the form of requests (which have been granted) for fewer classes, seminars, and more personalized instruction generally. In contrast to the attempt to make the university at least approximate the traditional model of a community of scholars pursuing knowledge and propagating values that are timeless if not transcendental, are the demands for relevance, for palliative courses and programs designed explicitly as surcease for the needs and pressures of the day, but destructive of the university's more traditional role. The prognoses for this dialectic remain unanalyzed and, in this light, the absence of adequate faculty response is not surprising.

In part, however, the blame also rests with the student body, in that a majority of the undergraduates seemingly are interested largely in pre-professional and pre-business career training. In the last decade an increasing number have come to learn something about themselves and the world they live in. And, as they do, some have been seized with the desire to transform it into what they feel would be a better world. It is from their ranks that the activists have come. Most of the activists (and the less active students as well) are motivated by altruism; higher wages and unions for non-academic employees are not things they personally are likely to benefit from. A fairly substantial number also sympathize with the goals, if not the tactics, of their black student colleagues. The rhetoric of the black students, their demands for freedom, dignity, and control over their own lives, fall on the sympathetic white ears of students who see themselves pursuing the same ends.

It is also true that the Duke faculty has, more or less, accommodated itself to such activism, particularly when the student goals appear to be selfless and humane. Other than for a small group of young faculty, however, it has been far less willing to support activist goals when they entail extra-legal or unorthodox tactics. Thus, the coalition that existed between student participants in the Vigil and a majority of the faculty ended when the black students seized a University building, threatened to burn records, and their white sympathizers organized a sympathy strike on their behalf. As it becomes increasingly apparent to even the most liberal faculty members that student activism may spread to their classrooms and that for a (still) small cadre of student activists the goal is power in decisions that affect the faculty (as well as students and non-academic employees), they will awaken to the fact that their interests and those of the students, not to say the non-academic employees, are not as congruent as they had imagined! It is, therefore, unlikely that any but a handful of the faculty will continue to condone and support student activism if that activity is directed toward areas that the faculty regards as its prerogative.

Until very recently, Duke has been able to maintain conditions which sustained intellectualism, research, teaching, learning, and training. The environment has been such that the established order of relationships among groups in the University community and between the University community and the larger society has been taken for granted. Now these relationships must be defended. Increasingly, the administration and the faculty have been called upon by student activists and certain of the non-academic employees to justify their traditional role and prerogatives. The administration also must justify and defend what happens on campus to their constituents outside the University—the Trustees, the alumni, and the several attentive social groups in the region. In turn, the latter requirement increases the administration's difficulty in dealing directly with specific activist demands. With the Trustees, alumni, and others figuratively looking over his shoulder, the President's response to, let us say, the black students' demand for an autonomous Black Studies program or a request for higher wages by non-academic employees, must take into account the reaction his decision is likely to evoke from his other publics. That this latter consideration is a relevant variable in administrative decision-making is revealed by Vice President Ashmore's statement on the Vigil to the Greensboro alumni,[21]

In the weeks immediately preceding the assassination of Dr. King, the more militant Negro leaders in the Durham community were reported to have given up on further conversations with the white community. Reports of imminent, widespread violence were prevalent, as were reports of the organization of vigilante groups among segments of the white community. Duke officials had been in close communication with city officials on these problems for many months, and it was our conviction that any violence in town would probably affect Duke, and that any violence at Duke would undoubtedly spread throughout Durham.

It would appear, therefore, that recent decisions made by the President (or members of the administration acting on his behalf) were not only responses to the students' action but also were conditioned by his perceptions of what the other publics' reactions would be to what he and the students had done. Such constraints, not unnaturally, can result in decisions which enrage both the activists and their opponents (witness the furor caused by public statements that the University had acceded to the black students' demands and that they had made no concessions to the blacks). More important, in the long run, is the cumulative deleterious effect that such decisions are likely to have on the President's influence base; neither the activist students' trust in him nor his more conservative constituents' patience with him are infinite.[22]

Upon reflection it seems rather remarkable that the events we have chronicled have taken place in a small, private, Southern institution with an almost totally white upper middle class student body and faculty. Their occurrence, in one sense, is indicative of the strong liberal strain, not only in the University community, but also in the surrounding area. It is difficult to imagine such events having taken place in another institution in the "Old Confederacy." In another sense, the events and actions also reveal the strong hold that traditional social and academic values and processes still have. The hostility that the two major instances of student activism generated both within the University and outside it reflect the latter tradition.

This particular combination of a strong but not broad strain of liberalism and strong and deep conservatism has a potential for future conflict which, in duration and intensity, could equal or even excel that experienced at institutions like Wisconsin, Berkeley, Columbia, and San Francisco State. The fact that, until now, white student activists and a substantial proportion of the blacks have been willing to work largely through "proper channels," to rely on "due process," and to eschew extra-legal or unorthodox tactics does not mean that they will continue to do so. For one thing they have observed that the proper channels are more likely to respond with alacrity to their requests when unorthodox protests are employed *or even threatened.* Further, it is doubtful whether they take seriously administration and faculty claims that they already were in the process of acting on, or had already granted, student requests when their protests occurred and that the unorthodox pressures employed were, therefore, neither necessary nor productive. (A number of students have probably asked themselves how frequently a faculty-administration committee meets at 8:30 on a Saturday evening—as the *ad hoc* faculty-administration group did meet two days after the seizure of the administration building.) One could argue, therefore, that if enough student activists and others in the University community become *convinced* that mass action, no matter what it entails, is likely to prove effective, or alternatively, unless it can be demonstrated that such action is unproductive or even counter-productive, then it may well be, insofar as further activism of a more radical type is concerned, that the crowd of students who, after they left the administration building, chanted "It ain't over yet," were correct in their prediction. It may not be over.

For an institution in the mid-course of adaptation, simultaneously under conflicting pressures from many different publics to move forward and backward at one and the same time, the next rounds of activity should help clarify the nature of student activism. Whatever form action does take, the nature of the targets should be most revealing. If the targets are segments of the University for which there would be a rational basis (whether right or wrong) for seeing them as instrumentally connected to the issues at hand, then continued activism may be essentially constructive and supportive. If, on the other hand, the targets are not so related and are, perhaps, even selected because of their non-involvement with the issues, we shall have testimony that this activism is indeed a first wave attack on a vulnerable institutional chink in a "rotten" society. As apt as are these remarks for interpreting events at Duke University, they are appropriate to a degree for all universities.

Footnotes

[1]Philip Selznick, "Institutional Vulnerability in Mass Society," *The American Journal of Sociology*, 56 (1951), 320-31.

[2]Selznick, 321.

[3]Selznick, 321.

[4]Selznick, 329.

[5]Luther J. Carter, "Duke University: Students Demand New Deal for Negro Workers," *Science* (May 3, 1968), 513-17.

[6]At the same time, other members of the group were out in the surrounding area successfully collecting an unusually wide spectrum of faculty signatures for the related statement to appear in the Durham newspapers.

[7]Carter, 517.

[8]*The Duke Chronicle* (February 4, 1969).

[9]The estimates of the number of students involved ranged from fifteen to fifty. In a letter to the University's lawyer, the Afro-American Society listed the names of sixty of their members whom they claimed had occupied the Allen Building, *Chronicle* (February 27, 1969). The University eventually charged twenty-five black students with violating the "Pickets and Protests" regulation promulgated by the administration in the summer of 1968.

[10]Initiation of Black Studies program controlled by black students; a black dormitory; reinstatement of black students who had to withdraw because of academic difficulties; an increase in the black student population to equal 29% by 1973; a black advisor selected by black students; black students admitted solely on the basis of high school records; an end to police harassment of black students; more black representation in University power structure; financial reassurance for black students; an end to the grading system for black students; earmarking of fees for a black student union; self-determination of working conditions by non-academic employees; and total amnesty for all black students involved in the sit-in.

[11]*Chronicle* (February 17, 1969). The single exception was the question of amnesty for the students who had occupied the building.

[12]Minutes of the February 20, 1969 Meeting of the Free Academic Senate.

[13]*Chronicle* (February 25, 1969).

[14]Data do not include freshmen admitted to the School of Nursing.

[15]Frank L. Ashmore, "A Crisis in Conscience," a speech delivered to the Greensboro Alumni Association of Duke University, April 24, 1968.

[16]Edward E. Sampson, "Student Activism and the Decade of Protest," *Journal of Social Issues*, XXIII (1967), 4-5.

[17]Selznick, 329.

[18]Illustrative of the new activist rhetoric at Duke is the editorial column written in reaction to the introduction of police onto the campus on February 13. It begins: "Judging from Thursday's events, the men who run this University—that is, the Board of Trustees, the President and the faculty—are not

only unfit to run it.[sic] They are intellectually unfit to set foot on its campus.

The Trustees, small-minded, bigoted men who control this place from their nouveau urban empires in North Carolina and elsewhere, decided that it was time to show the uppity blacks and radical whites exactly who rule at Duke.

They said 'jump!' and the President of this University jumped.

The President of the University, in turn, presented a faculty dominated by reactionaries, crackpots and mediocre careerists with a *fait accompli*—and said 'jump!' The faculty, in their zeal, jumped so fast that they had to ask 'how high?' on the way up.

Had they acted with any integrity whatever, and refused to justify and dignify the administration's immoral actions, the entire episode might have been prevented. But they didn't. They laid down like they were told to, and made believe they were enjoying it. They had a choice between law and order—and they chose order." Mark Pinsky, *Chronicle* (February 15, 1969).

In view of the fact that student speakers at open campus forums on the Quad have publicly exhorted each other and their cohorts by calling the faculty pigs and by offering a program to rid the University of all faculty members over forty (because they stand in the way of the few decent younger members of the faculty), these printed remarks are relatively mild.

19The view that the President himself is "locked into" the system was best expressed by one of the four student leaders of the Vigil. Jack Boger told the President, "An old order is changing—we cannot allow institutions that are amoral, good men who can't take moral stands because of something they can't control . . . We must take a stand in this situation. We'll stand behind you if you take a stand," *Chronicle* (April 8,1968).

20A more extensive analysis than can be attempted here would be needed to explore the consequences of the symbiotic relationship that exists between these two major institutions. Its strength and rate of interchange rise and fall but it is almost always a not inconsiderable element in the course of events. For example, in relatively happier days, the state's late and unlamented "speaker ban" law for state institutions was forcefully attacked at propitious moments by President Knight when the University of North Carolina presidents involved could not take such actions themselves. There is now much clear evidence that radical students and their organizations at the two schools coordinate and cooperate (just as the institutions themselves do) and recent actions and statements of the Governor suggest that he has adopted this same mode of thought.

21Ashmore, "A Crisis in Conscience," 3-4.

22That this patience may be ended is suggested by a letter to the Duke faculty from President Knight dated March 8. In it the President revealed that the Board of Trustees in their meeting of March 7 had created, at his request, the new post of Chancellor to oversee internal University affairs. He made it clear that "The President will continue to be the chief executive officer of the University." However, his duties will now consist of "maintaining major relations with most foundations, national organizations, alumni, and with special external individuals or groups with a major potential interest in the University." The Chancellor "will be the chief operating officer for the internal affairs of the University . . . and the President will participate in such matters when they are referred to him by the Chancellor."

Stanford

Sit-in at Stanford

Irving Louis Horowitz and
William H. Friedland

On Thursday, May 9, 1968, the Associated Press wire service released a story that was picked up by newspapers from Boston to Los Angeles. The story read in part:

> Topless dancer Vicki Drake has won a preliminary election for presidency of the Stanford University student body. In an unprecedented turnout Wednesday, the students voted 1,575 for Miss Drake and 1,252 for runner-up Dennis Hayes. . . . The photos of her unclad, 38-22-36 figure, which Miss Drake and a number of her supporters tacked up early in her campaign disappeared in less than an hour and reportedly now are lodged on the walls in and around the campus. Vicki declared after the victory that she had run for office only because of her interest in Stanford.

Such a release could easily have led the American public to believe that the only change really taking place on university campuses across the country was an escalation from panty raids to topless co-eds. In contrast to the violence and sit-down strike at Columbia University taking place at the same time, the news must have relieved many people who had begun to wonder out loud what had turned the "silent" student generation of the previous decade into political and moral militants. But a less reassuring response to the wire service release appeared in the *Stanford Daily* of the same day, May 9th. The campus newspaper presented a somewhat different conception of what was newsworthy at Stanford that week.

Fifty-six and one-half hours after they walked into the Old Union with only themselves for support, over 650 student demonstrators peacefully departed last night with an unprecedented vote of support for their demands by the Stanford faculty.

The Academic Council, assistant professors and above, met yesterday afternoon and early evening for three and a half hours, and recommended after heated and emotional debate, that the proposed suspension of seven Central Intelligence Agency demonstrators be set aside by President Wallace Sterling. The Council also asked, in a vote of 284 to 245, that no students be penalized as a result of the current demonstrations in the Old Union. The Council strongly urged the demonstrators to leave the building.

The Council recommendations, which passed largely with votes from the humanities, sciences, and medical school faculties, supported a comprehensive plan for reformed judicial structures which the Committee of 15 created early Wednesday morning.

Affluent campuses such as Stanford are large enough to support both the absurd dramatics of topless dancers and the confrontational politics of militant demonstrators. Although the wire service release tells us a great deal about what the media think interests the American public, the fact was that at Stanford, Miss Drake provided only the frosting on the cake; center stage was occupied by a much more serious drama that had already taken place on many campuses, that would be followed by others, and that would increasingly capture public attention.

What made the events at Stanford so meaningful was neither the extent of violence nor the degree of militance. The Stanford sit-in struggle is worth telling for its universalistic quality. It contained most elements of student rebellions throughout the nation. The Stanford case is also illuminating for what it presaged for the future; it forewarned the United States about what could be expected from the student generation.

Causes—Legal and Symbolic

The issue at Stanford was not the invasion of the old union, the destruction of campus property, nor freedom run rampant. The strategy was not violent insurrection nor arson. No attempts were made to fashion goals for a new society. The broad and underlying issue, as all concerned knew, was the measure of student power on campus. In a real sense the student demonstrations and the sit-in provided the measure. The discipline of the student demonstrators, no less than the results of the sit-in, demonstrated the social realities of student power better and more dramatically than any administrative actions or faculty resolutions.

In this sense Provost Richard Lyman was correct in stating that the struggle had become symbolic and not only concerned setting aside the conviction of seven anti-CIA demonstrators, but also the structure of university relations *per se.* In the rush to politeness which followed the student resolution to sit in, this aspect of Provost Lyman's assessment was minimized by formal proposals asserting faculty respect for Stanford's present administrative authorities. Yet, the fact remains that the settlement, which involved faculty support and administrative acquiescence, increased legitimation and recognition of students' real power. The demonstration offered direct justification for the symbolic belief that students not only have the right to participate in decision-making but also the right to determine the policy of a major university.

Perhaps the most accurate assessment of symbolic and long-range goals involved in the Stanford sit-in was given voice by Professor of Religion Michael Novak. In response to the administrative officials' continual pleas to students to meet and reason together, Professor Novak replied, during the height of the strike on Tuesday:

I commend both the wisdom and the courage of the students who are sitting-in at the Old Union. They show political wisdom, because they rightly understand that the issue is one of power: the power of students to determine their own affairs. Where one group has almost all the power in an institution, one must be suspicious of appeals to "reason." For "reason" in such contexts usually means docility to the way those in power perceive things. Students have very little power in the university; hence their views are not often taken to be "realistic." Realism is defined by those who exercise or defend present power. By sitting-in, however, the students create a new factor in the situation, which the "realistic" must take seriously. In this way—and often in this way alone—do human beings make progress in genuine communication. The old "realism" must be altered. The new realism must take into account a new consciousness and a new power. The students' sitting-in today, by their courage, are creating this new consciousness and this new power. Many of us are grateful for their creative act.

Finally I would like to call attention to the fact that the substantive issue amid all this debate is not legal or procedural. It concerns the university's ties to the CIA and to other government agencies. What do we students, faculty, and administration wish our university's qualities to be? The seven convicted students should not be penalized, they should be commended, for awakening us to Stanford's moral responsibilities when no one else cared. That is what education is all about.

The 56-hour confrontation had various causes and occurred against a background of events that also contributed to the specific forms that developed. Long-range and immediate problems, played against a series of on-campus and off-campus issues, created tactical considerations which contributed to the unfolding of the Stanford demonstration in unique ways.

In contrast to events at other campuses, the immediate cause of the Stanford demonstration was legalistic in character. It had to do with the issue of double jeopardy, whether students, having charges dismissed against them after due process, can be retried on the same grounds. This legalistic "injustice" provided the basis for the student cause and significantly broadened support within the student body even when tactics of the radical sector of students were not endorsed. Student grievances on local issues rather than community or national political grievances triggered the Stanford uprising.

Underlying the immediate issue was the more general question of the nature of justice and of student equities within the university. Like many other high-quality universities, Stanford placed responsibility for student conduct with faculty committees, while reserving ultimate decisions for the administration. In challenging a specific legal decision involving the retrial of students, the Stanford demonstrators began to come to grips, albeit inchoately, with the generic relationship existing between different units of the university—a triad composed of the faculty, the administration, and the student body as a collective entity.

Underlying the Stanford dispute were broader issues related to the university position in the broader social structure, a system with which many students have become disenchanted, if not totally alienated. The Stanford demonstration illustrated the process whereby national political issues—which cannot be effectively confronted by student militants—become translated into local issues. Without conscious intent or forethought, the Stanford demonstration revealed how an issue of breadth and distance such as the Vietnam war is made a meaningful local issue. Despite demonstrations, silent vigils, teach-ins, mobilizations, and other activities that have involved the energies of many college students, the Vietnam war has always been a difficult issue to come to grips with within the university. Proposals, for example, to suspend normal instruction and devote classes to discussions of the Vietnam war have always been combatted on the grounds that such action will not resolve the war. The implicit point is that the formal academic program of the university is as irrelevant to the war as the war is to the university's academic program.

Even picketing the campus recruiters of the Central Intelligence Agency or Dow Chemical is a somewhat distant event for most students. However, when the forms of justice are violated in a normative sense in response to such picketing (through what is considered to be "double jeopardy"), then the issue of an unpopular war is translated into a basis for student demonstration, and obtains wide support in the student body even if some disagree about specific tactics.

Before discussing the sit-in itself, we shall consider the background and peripheral causal phenomena which helped determine the degree of militance of the demonstration, and the social solidarity exhibited.

First, one should note the Black Student Union (BSU) victory several weeks earlier. The BSU demanded greater admission of and participation by black students, and used threat mechanisms to achieve its demands, demands which included hiring more Negro faculty and administrators as well as black supervision over entering Negro students. The easy resolution of these demands in favor of the black students provided a demonstration of the possibilities inherent in a student strike. However, the striking students failed to consider the limited nature of the black student demands. These demands after all were for separatism rather than for domination. What they also left out of the reckoning was that the Black Student Union had a social base of support in the Negro community, particularly in the East Palo Alto ghetto area. As one of the demonstrators observed during one of the sit-in meetings, the action of the black students bore an implicit threat that "a group of East Palo Alto studs would invade the campus" much as had been done at San Francisco State. The absence of such community support has become noticeable in recent struggles, not only at Stanford but also on other campuses. In any event, the tactics and the demands of the Black Student Union certainly provided a model for the Stanford demonstrators as the black power movement has provided a model for student activists in general.

Second, a general politicalization of the student body had taken place in 1968. In California, widespread hostility to the Vietnam war had given birth to the Peace and Freedom Party, which provided an outlet for Left-oriented students. The campaign to support Senator Eugene McCarthy for the Presidency had "turned on" a host of other students for whom the politics of the Peace and Freedom Party were either too militant or too marginal. The McCarthy campaign provided a legitimate outlet for students disaffected with the war and searching for a critical stance more in keeping with their moderate inclinations. Although the momentum of student participation in presidential politics declined slightly with President Johnson's self-removal from the campaign (as on other campuses, there were widespread spontaneous manifestations of collective delight on the Stanford campus when the president made his announcement), that momentum was not completely lost. Since the Stanford demonstration was triggered by the suspension of students for picketing CIA recruiters, one can see the relationship between national political questions and campus issues. Throughout the sit-in many "McCarthy for President" buttons and some Kennedy buttons were worn. For a number of students the sit-in seemed a natural extension of the national campaign to either end the war in Vietnam or limit that war by eliminating the most conservative candidates from office.

A third cause of the demonstration was the phenomenon of *in loco parentis*, that set of informal norms which absolves the college student in America from usual responsibilities to law and authority. Students respond in a highly ambiguous way to *in loco parentis*. On one hand, they fully realize the advantages of differential treatment at the hands of police and university officials, but on the other hand, they resent this special paternalism as precisely what must be eliminated if students are to receive equal treatment in university affairs.

More than one Stanford student, both in writing and in speaking, alluded to *in loco parentis* and insisted upon equal treatment before the law even if it meant fewer "superficial" advantages. The Stanford Student Union President, Cesare Massarenti, in the Monday noon rally which sparked the initial burst of protest, flatly opposed *in loco parentis*. However, even if the students did not particularly relish their protected position, the administration felt responsible for them as quasi-legitimate offspring. In a university comprised of upper-middle-class young people, combined parental influence is sizable, particularly in the state of California. Parents would hardly take kindly to the administration's sending police in to beat the skulls of their children. The administration had to manipulate a rapidly maturing student process of politicalization, while serving its inherited legacy, both financial and ideological, as the guardians of errant as well as aberrant youth. As a result of this contradiction, the administration was unable to call upon the public law to the fullest degree. It had to grant privileges and prerogatives—including the forcible entrance and takeover of one of their own buildings as the center of headquarters for a student sit-in.

The students, for their part, although they resented the system of *in loco parentis* and the concept of obedience before the abstract paternal rule of the President or Provost, were shrewd enough and capable enough to make use of the contradictions of *in loco parentis*. Their attempt to gain equal treatment for students as members of an adult citizen population made use of the special privileges and prerogatives enjoyed by students since medieval Europe. A basic cause of the sit-in, *in loco parentis*, also served as an institutional protective covering for the students during the sit-in.

Currents and Cross-Currents

On November 1, 1967, between 50 to 100 students participated in a demonstration against a recruiting agent of the Central
Intelligence Agency. This demonstration was prototypical of
hundreds of confrontations on campuses throughout the nation
between anti-war students on one side, and recruiters for the
CIA, Dow Chemical, and military programs on the other. In
these demonstrations, students usually attempted to impede the
recruitment processes and inevitably came into conflict with the
university's administrators. This is what happened at Stanford.

At first the students attempted to occupy the west wing of
Encina Hall and to prevent the potential interviewees for the day
from reaching the CIA recruiter. However, after Dean of
Students Joel Smith informed them that they were violating
university policy on demonstrations, they withdrew to the
surrounding grassy area to continue their protest without
disrupting any of the interviewing going on within. Ten days
later, Dean Smith brought charges against ten of the participants.
The case was first heard by the judicial council of the Associated
Students' Union of Stanford University. After a considerable
length of time, the council found all ten students not guilty on
the grounds that the university policy on demonstrations was too
general and therefore unenforceable.

However, their decision did not go unchallenged. The not-
guilty decision rendered on February 19, 1968, was followed by
a letter on February 21 from Dean Joel Smith to Professor
Howard R. Williams, the chairman of the interim judicial body,
in which exception was taken to the decision of the ASSU
judicial council. A copy of the notice of appeal was sent to the
student respondents, and a hearing was granted by the IJB
(Interim Judicial Body). Disciplinary action against two of the
students was withdrawn, but a hearing was scheduled for the
remaining seven for April 30, 1968. This faculty board hearing
was held *de novo*, that is, entirely anew, without reference to
the previous ASSU hearing. The grounds for so doing were the
refusal of the student judicial council to surrender possession of
the tapes of the previous hearing. The consequence was that the
seven students were again tried on exactly the same charges.

The IJB ruled that the university policy on campus
demonstrations was entirely enforceable and therefore the
decision rendered by the ASSU judicial council an erroneous one.

Professor Howard R. Williams then outlined the IJB's
decision. Each respondent registered as a student at Stanford
University was suspended. The extension of the previously

scheduled hearing by the IJB prevented final disposition of the matter until after registration for and substantial completion of the current quarter; therefore the suspension was not to take effect until the end of the current quarter. The suspended students would then be deprived of the privileges of registering for course credit, of attending classes or working in university laboratories, or of receiving financial aid. The period of suspension was to terminate on September 1, 1968, for five respondents; for the other two respondents, whose earlier proceedings had been found to violate university policy on campus demonstrations, suspension would terminate January 1, 1969. Finally, each student was placed on disciplinary probation for the balance of the second quarter of 1968 and would remain on probation for the first two quarters for which he registered after his suspension period expired.

The IJB decision set the stage for the student demonstration. On the morning of Friday, May 3rd, Stanford President Wallace Sterling and other administrative officials of the university met with Cesare Massarenti, President of the Associated Students of Stanford University (ASSU) and other student leaders. Student leaders did not think this meeting was productive and called a rally at White Plaza, the center of most student demonstrations and political gatherings at Stanford.

Only about 150 students attended the Friday noon meeting, but it quickly moved towards action when a proposal to shift to Building 10, where President Sterling's "Downing Street" office was located, was made by Marc Sapir, one of the students given a lengthy suspension by the IJB. The students temporarily sat-in in protest in front of President Sterling's office, but decided to plan a larger-scale action for the following week.

The tone of the coming demonstration could be sensed in the words of some student speakers, ASSU president Massarenti, who had been active in the 1962 student protests in Italy, called for construction of a mass movement around the issue of the suspension. A veteran of Berkeley's Free Speech Movement, Steve Weissman, foreshadowed a key element of the confrontation about to take place. Emphasizing that a demonstration had to be sufficiently militant "so that students have to choose sides," Weissman argued that "the best thing Stanford students do is to be concerned." Thus, "veterans" of past student struggles provided ideological support for events to come.

The student protest was to be given its first definitive form in front of President Wallace Sterling's office. Four basic demands were formulated in the give-and-take discussion that characterized student protest decision-making during the entire course of the

demonstration. The four demands, which were iterated and reiterated during the subsequent few days, were:
1. The IJB decision calling for the suspension of the seven students should be set aside. 2. The IJB must be disbanded immediately. 3. In its place, an appeals board would be created, composed of four faculty members, four student members, and a law student selected by the eight to be chairman. 4. The appeals board would consider appeals only from defendants.

What is striking about these demands is that only one was concerned with the suspended students; and that tacked on to this demand were proposals for reshaping the judicial procedures of Stanford with respect to student behavior. Implicit in the third demand was the issue of student power, that is, the relative weight to be given to students and faculty in disciplinary procedures. Also entailed was the termination of the power of review of these decisions held by the president. The students wanted any decisions to be final and residual in the proposed new appeals body.

The students demanded that President Sterling meet them at a noon demonstration at White Plaza on Monday, May 6th, and respond to their four point program. Having made these decisions, the students adjourned their brief sit-in and moved into preparatory actions for the Monday rally.

The IJB action and the Friday meeting warned the campus community that action was forthcoming. In an attempt to head off potential student action, different parts of the campus establishment began to firm up attitudes and positions, most of which appeared in the Monday morning issue of the *Stanford Daily*.

Perhaps the most serious statement was issued by the President, J.E. Wallace Sterling. He pointed out that: "Issues this complex are not going to be resolved in White Memorial Plaza, this noon or any other noon. Issues this ambiguous are not going to be resolved in answer to an ultimatum." Indicating that the orderly process of judicial review would be worked out by the campus community to the satisfaction of all but a few "zealots" of the "far Left" and "far Right," the President went on to make a shrewd observation, the implication of which he was apparently unable to follow through with. He pointed out that the issues themselves had changed a good deal. "When the problem first arose and until fairly recently, it was viewed as a controversy about the judicial system. It has become clear in the last few months, as the result of hard work by the members of the Committee of 15, that we must simultaneously resolve closely linked issues of rule-making and judging. Two different kinds of bodies, one to make rules and another to pass on alleged violations of the rules, are now being discussed in the

Committee of 15. Both kinds of bodies are intended to include students."

This is as close as any member of the administration came to acknowledging that the major issue was in fact student power and not simply judicial reform, but the President seemed to negate his own observation by concentrating the remainder of his public statement on the juridical aspects with no further mention of the judgmental features of the crisis. Perhaps the most significant feature of the statement was his conclusion, when he had to face the question of the anti-CIA demonstrators directly. On these specifics he once more reserved both rule-making and judging as a prerogative of presidential office. Not only did President Sterling's communication to the Stanford community exclude the students from a decision-making role on this sensitive issue, but it also excluded the faculty as well. He frankly stated that "the Interim Judicial Body's recommendations in the CIA demonstration case are now before me. Accordingly, I am inviting each of the defendants in that case individually to present any facts he may wish to bring to my attention before I decide to accept, modify, or reject the recommendations of the Interim Judicial Body."

As if in anticipation that his position would not be accepted, and that he, the President, would need the support or at least the legitimation of the rest of the community, Sterling closed with an indication that "a meeting of the academic council would be convened for 4:15 p.m. on Wednesday, May 8th." Sterling also used his open letter to invite the President of the Student Council and one other student officer to appear at the faculty meeting on Wednesday to present their claims. The President did not foresee that when this "committee" did meet it would not certify administration policy but would ratify the correctness of the student complaints.

The student body's attitude towards the need for strike action, or at least for overtly militant action, was undoubtedly reinforced by the essential agreement on the question of procedure of the spokesmen for the faculty with the administration. For the involved faculty seemed quite satisfied, if not enthusiastic, about the performance of IJB. The quasi-official campus faculty spokesmen also seemed even less informed than the administration about the collision course the school had embarked upon. Law faculty response only hardened student attitudes. Typical statements appearing in the *Stanford Daily* were those of William F. Baxter, Professor of Law, speaking for the "conservative" faculty and the statement by Kenneth J. Arrow and Leonard I. Schiff speaking for the "liberal" members of the faculty. Professor Baxter pointed out that in his opinion, "on the afternoon of Monday, May 6th, serious damage may be done to the generally successful pattern of student-faculty-administration negotiations, over university government that has prevailed at Stanford for several years." While he expressed his hope that the damage could be averted, he did not indicate what the successful pattern of negotiations had been in the past, or what was wrong in the present. Indeed, he went on to indicate a rather wide permanent divergence of opinion between these three bodies— administration, faculty, and students.

Professor Baxter felt the demands of the students that the conviction of the anti-CIA demonstrators be set aside, that a new judicial body containing a large number of student representatives be established were threats to the community, and that even the students were not really convinced or even hoped that they would be accepted. He concluded by saying that "In any sizable community one must expect and cope with some member or persons who seek trouble, and even violence, for its own sake or for their own personal aggrandizement. Demonstrating in support of demands known to be unacceptable is a tactic of such persons. If they are very few in number, the processes of negotiation and accommodation can continue. If their number is large, such processes fail, and the community must accept its destruction or government by dictation and force." In this way a key member of the faculty indicated his disbelief in the sincerity of student demands and his corresponding belief that any mass show of force or any mass action would somehow entail anarchy and destroy law and order.

The behavior and stated attitudes of the liberal faculty also did little to encourage students that a genuine assessment of their demands would be made. The statement by Kenneth J. Arrow and Leonard I. Schiff, both with national academic reputations, read as follows: "Great issues are at stake, that can be settled to the satisfaction of students, faculty, and administration. To accomplish what is possible, time is required and reasonable discussion must be continued. Open discussions in White Plaza and meetings like that between representatives of students, faculty, and administration on Friday afternoon have their parts to play in arriving at settlements. Demands accompanied by deadlines, sit-ins, and forcible destruction of academic activities do not; they are destructive of the good will that exists in the overwhelming majority of the three constituencies." The statement by these two influential figures concluded by pointing out that although they spoke for themselves, "we are confident that we represent nearly all of our faculty colleagues in urging patience, and abstention from the use of force. We believe that any other course will merely delay the institution of the changes in student-faculty-administration relationships that all agree are needed and toward which all are working."

Since no part of the administration or the faculty would accept the idea of setting aside a judicial body decision made by faculty members—even faculty members who were extremely close to the administration in ideology if not in organization—a hardening of student attitudes over the weekend was inevitable.

The Committee of 15 (more commonly called the "C-15"), which had been organized almost three years earlier to deal with a variety of questions involving issues of student participation in decision-making at Stanford, was composed of five administrators, five faculty members, and five students. The C-15 had performed some useful work, but if its production were to be judged by normal faculty standards, it would have been refused tenure. While most of the reasons given for its lack of action were reasonable, the fact remained that student judicial procedures had remained unresolved. Thus, the IJB decision focused attention and criticism on the Committee of 15.

Tom Forestenzer (a student member of the Committee of 15 for two and a half years) represented the dominant student viewpoint toward the situation—or at least, the viewpoint of enough students to effectuate a demonstration. His statement is of particular interest because in the name of the students he gave vent to the sorts of attitudes which made a confrontation inevitable whatever the ideological bases of those who came to be the sit-in leaders. Mr. Forestenzer espoused vigorous combat with the existing system and support for the potential student action, whatever such action might involve—"not as a result of the recent outrageous IJB decision, but because the IJB itself is a perfectly accurate representation of how the administration has systematically excluded students from any positions of power and responsibility over student affairs." He noted that "I" in the IJB stood for the word "interim." "Interim is a useful word for those in the administration who hope that student demands for such radical innovations as trial by jury of one's peers are temporary and sporadic outbursts of fickle youth. The IJB has been interim for no less than three years. During those three years I was personally involved in several efforts to establish a plain old JB, with half student-faculty representation."

After accusing the Committee of 15 of procrastination, particularly the administration delegation to that committee, Mr. Forestenzer went on to what undoubtedly was the core of the entire issue, namely, the exploitation of students *per se*, and not simply the sentencing and temporary expulsion of seven of their number.

Behind this intricate quadrille are harsh realities which I now enjoy expressing. The sentence passed on the CIA demonstrators is vicious, but it is no more brutal than the year-to-year, day-to-day treatment of students at Stanford whenever they rock the boat. Every time an interim solution is adopted (which is the same as saying that students are barred from choosing their own representatives to such vital panels as the IJB or the SES or any presidential advisory board), that patronizing Dean or Provost says: "Golly gee, I wish we could do this because I'm really on your side, but we're in a bind." What he is really saying is, "Go to hell."

The weekend at Stanford was clearly a busy one for a small number of administrators and campus militants; both groups were preparing for action. Since a number of the students proposed for suspension were graduate assistants belonging to the local chapter of the American Federation of Teachers, AFT officers were busy conducting a telephone poll of its members on Saturday, May 4th. It was decided to strongly support those AFT members who were to be suspended, but there was less agreement as to what should be done in the case of a sit-in. This was left to the individual members of Teachers' Union.

Sunday evening, a meeting of the students was organized to plan for the Monday demonstration. This meeting, itself the product of a mounting wave of agitation following the Friday meeting, attracted over 200 students.

A number of key decisions made at the meeting shaped subsequent events. The four demands formulated on Friday were reendorsed and students agreed that the demonstration would stick firm for all four demands and not be satisfied with only the first demand. A tactics committee was elected. This group of nine students was composed of eight graduate students and one junior and included students in general studies (the one undergraduate), political science (two students), mathematics, law, sociology, communications, medicine, and Latin American studies. The weighting of the Tactics Committee toward the graduate students, although the students present were predominantly undergraduates, indicated a shared deference toward the greater experience of the graduates.

A curious note of the Sunday meeting was the presence of Willard Wyman, the Associate Dean of Students. Wyman was recognized by the students present, and discussion centered on whether or not he should be permitted to remain. Ultimately no action was taken to remove him from the meeting—which served as a precedent for student attitudes in future meetings and actions. These meetings displayed strikingly democratic characteristics during the entire period of the demonstration.

Monday, May 6th, found the campus girding its loins for battle. Students arriving on campus were greeted by news of the Friday sit-in, by headlines in the *Stanford Daily* that President Sterling had rejected student demands, by statements and letters on the *Daily's* inside pages, and by the mimeographed leaflets of student militants calling for attendance at the noon rally at White Plaza.

A major characteristic of any significant political event is the development of some symbolic focus around which action can develop. In this respect, the demonstrators were aided by an unwitting administration. Forewarned that the Old Union, presently a second-echelon administration building, would be the target of student demonstrations and potential takeover, the administration decided on a peculiar course of action. On Monday, at the very time that the students gathered in White Plaza to hear the complaints of their colleagues, the administration locked the building. Not only did they lock out the students, but they also emptied the premises of all staff and, in effect, locked themselves out. The lockout was performed with chains and a master padlock on each of the doors. This visible representation of administration intransigence to student demands also provided the students an opportunity to take over the building and to remove the symbols of the administration lockout, in this case the chain and locks, and the campus police timidly stood guard while the campus went mad.

When the administration refused to address itself or be addressed by the constituency which it served, its ability to retain campus management became minimal if not impossible. Thus, the focus as well as the problem shifted from the administration until the very end of the strike itself; once it locked itself out of its own building the initiative it had begun with evaporated quickly. The issue of the strike became problematic, simply a question of how many students could be mobilized in the public arena rather than whether a strike could be restrained by the play of major forces within the administration or faculty. As one graduate student of economics, Frederick D. Berger, put it: "Refusing to negotiate under pressure will lead only to greater pressure, that is, violence."

While the Stanford events were certainly far less violent than similar student outbursts elsewhere, it would be a mistake to think that no violence occurred at all. The administration building was broken into; there was a considerable amount of scuffling between campus police and student strikers. And while no one was seriously hurt, great potential for violence remained during the rest of the sit-in period. The school decision to open the administration building made under the *fait accompli* pressure of student invasions of the building, was the most moderate course of action open and minimized violence. Free access to the building guaranteed a forum for the expression of militant students' demands and provided a key channel of communication among all sectors during the strike period.

Attended by well over a thousand persons, some of them curiosity-seekers, the Monday noon rally on White Plaza was relatively brief. It was soon clear that no administration spokesmen would appear to discuss the four demands prepared by the students. After some brief talks by student leaders, including one by ASSU President Massarenti informing the students that the Tactics Committee had not recommended strong action, there was a general movement from the Plaza to the Old Union, located adjacent to the Plaza. This movement was not a spontaneous one; the militants had agreed to shift the meeting to the Old Union to confront representatives of the administration if none presented themselves at the White Plaza meeting. However, the speakers urged the students not to break or destroy property; the memory of Columbia was lucid in the minds of the students, and the essentially legal character of the student demands was evident to their "tactical" leaders.

What was to become a major characteristic of the Stanford strike was announced policy from the start. The students were disciplined and restrained. This restraint was evident even in the way in which the Old Student Union building was penetrated. Surrounding the building at a variety of key points, they made a number of attempts to get into the building. Several students attacked the molding of one of the windows on the ground floor and attempted to pry it open. A slight tap on the glass with the tool that one of them was using would surely have broken the glass; however the care that was being exercised showed that they would avoid destruction of property even at a minor level. Several students formed a human pyramid to raise another student to a tile roof from which he could, and in fact did, climb in through an open window on the second floor. At a third doorway, students lined up and respectably, if loudly, negotiated with the campus police captain who stood guard. At this point a minor scuffle between police guards and students took place; the immediate willingness on both sides to negotiate student entrance to the building enabled a non-violent condition to prevail.

At roughly 1 p.m., or one hour after the meeting at White Plaza, the building was opened. A student sawed the chain off the door handles, and removed the symbol of administration intransigence. The students filed in; many sat down and others stood milling around discussing tactics. Outside the building on the grass and in the graceful fountained court, an amplifier system was mounted. At the original rally the lack of amplification had made the students advocating the strike appear weak. Setting up an amplifier made possible attracting and dealing with large numbers of students who were unwilling to enter the building but who somehow felt involved —particularly those who supported the demands but were unprepared to occupy university property.

That the demonstration was not merely a political act but a new form of good times became clear with a performance of the Stanford Guerrilla Theater immediately after occupation. The Theater offered an allegory in which Irving Impotence, the prototypical Stanford student, was unable to "make it" with Sally Stanford until she was attacked by President Sterling, acting on behalf of the CIA. Once Irving perceived what was going on and rescued Sally, he was able to finally "make it," not unlike the way Clyde Barrow finally succeeded with Bonnie Parker in the movie. The scene then shifted to where the President and the Dean were discussing the need to castrate Irving and having grabbed and made off with him, raised their knives only to be interrupted by the narrator for the Guerrilla Theater, who asked the soap opera question: "Will Irving be castrated? Or will he find his manhood again? Tune in tomorrow." This bit of *ad hoc* fluff ended with a brief but inconclusive meeting, after which many students left the premises. About 3 p.m., however, in a matter begun in the Old Union, a whole series of decisions were made. The revolt began to take clear focus for the first time.

The atmosphere of carnival that pervaded the Old Union and its Court should not be minimized. Throughout the action was a tone of theatricality, of the entertainment value of the political act. In a romantic revolutionary sense the demonstration represented politics as poetry. In fact the sit-in represented mass psycho-drama as much as mass politics. The strike was an operational way of providing 1,000 characters in search of a drama with a good time and a good part. It might almost be said that the theatrical aspects were prearranged, since administration, Establishment faculty members, and radical students all seemed at the outset, at any rate, to be creating a drama that would lead to confrontation rather than seeking a pragmatic solution to the problems immediately at hand.

But all was not fun. As the afternoon wore on, a series of meetings began in which the demonstrators started living out a new kind of politics. Confrontation involves approaches different from those found in standard American political life. Thinking in formal political terms has led all too often to terminated communication between demonstrating students and their elders in the administration and faculty. Nor is communication facilitated when administrators see Bolshevik menaces or other conspirators in the deepest recesses of the student revolt. When student rebels meet openly and reach tactical decisions on questions of enormous import with associate deans present, charges of conspiracy make them wonder about the motives of the accusers.

The key element in the Monday afternoon meetings was the nature of the political indoctrination of many individuals who had joined the demonstration. This indoctrination primarily involved the development of the "correct" norma that should be part of the demonstration. Emphasis was placed upon spontaneity rather than on planning. The inevitable confrontation with university officials became defined as involving the entire group of student demonstrators. Because, in fact, administrators are unwilling to negotiate with several hundred students, smaller groups were chosen. However, the members were defined as messengers rather than representatives. In this way, the anti-parliamentary bias was kept intact.

Even the familiar processes of political socialization had special twists. Cooptation, political recruitment, socialization, and concern for tactics and the role of leadership were handled by student leaders more in terms of what they learned from Harold Lasswell than from Vladimir Lenin. Sit-in leaders seemed to be menaced by the experience of the old Left, and also by the intellectual confrontation with political theorists who, if they had not necessarily convinced students of the role of pluralism in American politics, at least had convinced them of the necessity for maintaining democracy within their organizational ranks.

The students introduced to the sit-in several new approaches which represent changes in political tactics. These tactics are perhaps restricted to student use; they would probably work poorly with a more heterogeneous class grouping. But the common experience of undergraduates in large classes taught mainly in sections by graduate students, and of graduate students as the donkeys of day-to-day instruction, has in fact created great homogeneity of opinion within the students' ranks. Similarly, many students who have not previously experienced sit-ins seemed to grasp intuitively the need to deal with the peculiar exigencies of such situations quickly and effectively.

Student speeches tended to be relatively short; when the concept of brevity was violated, stony silence or indications of physical disconfort indicated that the audience was bored with any lengthy address. The sentence structure used in the debate and conversation tended to be quite simple; the usual convoluted expressions that faculty members find characteristic of many students were absent in this situation. Finally, many students who rarely spoke in a classroom situation found themselves speaking to the other demonstrators, even addressing large numbers of students and urging them to a specific course of action.*

Several key elements in consensual action politics became evident at the outset. Not only is the physical shape of argument different from addresses by elites to masses, but the audience response is vocal and clear. It does not usually take place unless a speaker says something outrageous or is outrageously boring; rather, reaction tends to come after the completion of the remarks by the speaker. The norm of free speech is strong among the student activists and, indeed, tended to be a crucial aspect in the gathering storm. Throughout the meetings of the demonstrators, expression of dissenting views was strongly encouraged. Not only were the demonstrators' microphones used to denounce them but also to call their opponents to meetings.

As the meetings continued, the norms of the rebellion began to be worked out. With the foyer of the Old Union crowded with students, it soon became uncomfortably warm. Tins of soda and bottles of fruit punch began freely circulating among the demonstrators. Although it was hot and people were thirsty, each person took a small drink and passed the container on. The shared excitement of risk as well as shared minor travails and tiring hours of sitting on hard floors through endless hours of tactical discussions soon were a key element of the "new ethic."

As the afternoon wore on, the question of confrontation with the university administration was uppermost. A committee of students was rapidly chosen to talk to Provost Richard Lyman. What would be the shape of the evening's activities became clear when students learned that the Provost was willing to meet with them and to discuss issues with them but that he was concerned with the choice of place of the meeting. He was unwilling to meet them within or near the confines of the Old Union—appropriately subtitled: "Student Service Center." Some of the students on the committee were impressed by the "reasonableness" of the Provost's willingness to talk, but others wanted the administration to meet them in or near the demonstration site of the Old Union.

---

*We will be referring to the pattern of decision-making followed by the students through most of the demonstration as "consensual action." Our choice of the term is deliberate and, perhaps, unfortunate. We feel the need to distinguish the kind of politics engaged in by the students from the "politics of consensus" defined by elitist politicians. The consensual action of the students was closer to the kinds of consensus search that occurs in small-scale societies and collegial social groups where the norms of social cohesion are strong. If anything, the consensual action of the students was closer to the decision-making of African tribes than of Modern American political parties.

Increasingly anxious to broaden their base and to bring larger numbers of students into the sit-in, the demonstrators decided upon a meeting of the campus student body for 7:30 p.m. Messengers were sent to various living units to alert students. At the same time, the Provost's meeting was scheduled for 8:30 p.m. at Stanford's Memorial Auditorium, a five minute walk from the Old Union. A clash between the two meeting times was therefore averted and the drama was staged for two different physical sites.

By 7:30 p.m., several thousand students had gathered in the courtyard of the Old Union and had distributed themselves on the porticoes and roofs of the surrounding buildings. The meeting had a number of fraternity men and athletes who had responded to the call for a meeting by organizing themselves for a heavy turnout. The list of speakers was smaller, but the presentation of conflicting views continued.

The group's size and newly introduced heterogeneity made consensual action impossible and the "normal" style of American politics, the presentation of and voting on motions, prevailed. Where majority-minority decisions have to be made, it became possible for skilled organizers to manipulate decisions. At the evening meeting, however, the organizational tactics of old Left politics were noticeably absent. There was no discreet placement of speakers in the audience. There was no attempt to continue meetings indefinitely so that only hard-core radicals remained. There were no efforts at parliamentary tampering, but rather a simple statement that a variety of interest groups was involved and core principles were at stake.

At this critical evening meeting of the entire campus student community, a series of votes was taken in rapid-fire succession. First, a motion to separate the demands to the university administration and vote on them one by one was defeated. Second, a motion to consider the four demands *en bloc*. This was accepted. Third, a motion endorsing the tactics of the militants in seizing the administration building. This bitterly contested item was in fact voted down by a roughly 60-40 ratio. And fourth, a motion demanding protection against prosecution of the students who had participated in the building seizure. This was accepted. As the meeting concluded at 8:25 p.m., the militants found that although their key tactic had at least for the moment been repudiated by a constituency that they themselves had assembled, their demands had been sustained.

The student militants thus had campus support for their demands but not for their tactical handling of those demands. While a sector immediately attempted to point out that one cannot vote matters of conscience, the fact remained that the entire voting procedure had involved matters of conscience. It was also on this basis that the militants decided to attend the meeting in the Memorial Hall Auditorium.

The older generation's inability to deal with consensual action was clear at the evening meeting. Stanford's Memorial Auditorium was packed to its capacity of 3,000. On the stage with Provost Lyman were two faculty members and the Dean of Students, a key figure in the events leading up to the protest. The discourse was academic: restrained and polite. The proceedings were dominated from the stage: members of the audience were told that they could ask questions after remarks by the members of the panel. The presentations were made calmly, as if to emphasize the rational framework within which the administration was operating in contrast to the implicit irrationality, haste, and ill-considered judgment of the students.

Provost Richard Lyman chaired the meeting and was its first speaker. Beginning with an overwhelmingly sympathetic audience, he finished in a wave of applause. His position was eroded, however, from that point on. Addressing himself to the four demands, Lyman rejected the first demand—that the IJB decision for suspension not be accepted—by saying President Sterling did not want to act until he had consulted individually with the "defendants." He went on to reject the demand that the IJB be disbanded, pointing out that it is a thoroughly legitimate body. "To grant its demolition under the kind of pressure we now have would be a sad commentary on our times," he added. The third demand, for an appellate board composed of four faculty members and five students, would be met "in spirit" when the Committee of 15 presented its recommendation—which at that Monday meeting Provost Lyman thought would be six weeks in the future. Finally, Lyman said that the fourth demand could only be heard on appeal from the defendants to the appellate board; and that it also could not be met, because the ASSU judicial council is the creature of the legislature and this would mean that the student legislature would have undue power over all other sectors in the community. The Provost either would not or could not yield even on minor points, much less on the major issues at stake.

Lyman was followed by Professor of Law William Baxter, who emphasized his presence as an individual faculty member rather than as Chairman of the IJB. Professor Baxter pointed out the need for the rule of law, unless "we were to accept the premise of coming home to find someone else occupying our bed"—an untenable position, "at least not without our permission." Calculated to amuse the students with its sexual connotations, it fell flatter than cheap pornography. Baxter's reasoned argumentation avoided the accusations which had been made against legal procedures which had been followed for nearly three years with no significant success. For his part, Professor Hubert Marshall of the Political Science Department and Chairman of the Committee of 15 argued that the C-15 could be expected to make an announcement of new judicial procedures at almost any moment.

While the meeting in Memorial Auditorium was going on, the student demonstrators in the Old Union assessed the votes which had just been taken and debated whether they should be bound by the decision condemning their tactics in seizing the Old Union. After considerable debate, they concluded, with some exceptions, that the vote required them to abandon the Old Union. Perhaps the fact that the scene of action had shifted to Memorial Auditorium also contributed to the decision, but whatever the reason, the bulk of the demonstrators left the Old Union and drifted into the Provost's meeting.

The arrival of several hundred students changed the character of the Provost's meeting. Where the audience had previously been dominated by conservative students, faculty members, and a heavy representation of visibly older people, the demonstrators' arrival seemed to give courage to elements in the audience that had been sympathetic to the demonstrators but silent. Increasingly, the Provost lost the support of the audience as the demonstrators began to demand greater participation in the Memorial Auditorium meeting. Why, the Provost was asked, were students' representatives not present on the platform? The Provost responded that he hardly had any procedure to select representatives, considering the many factions of students. But this was not a satisfactory answer. Nor did some of the Provost's acerbic comments (for which he is justifiably well-known at Stanford) on student demeanor sit well with the student rebels.

As the momentum against the Provost built up, reasoned but impassioned statements were heard from the student members of the Committee of 15. These students, representing varying political persuasions, called upon the Committee of 15 to meet on a continuous basis until revision of conduct procedures could be completed. They threatened to resign unless their proposal was accepted by faculty and administration members of the Comittee. The student members' action served several notable ends: (1) it rebuked the Provost's slow and easy approach; (2) it provided the coalition of conservative faculty and administration and faculty with a face-saving device whereby the "results" of the Committee of 15 could be meshed with the demands of the students for amnesty.

The academicians and administrators on the platform were prepared neither intellectually nor ideologically to deal with a continuous and sustained barrage of student criticism. In a situation pregnant with opportunity for conversion into a familiar give-and-take—the teach-in—members of the panel were unable to shift to a different mode of discourse. The teach-in format would have had definite advantages from the point of view of the administration; it could have served as a significant substitute for the occupation of the Old Union. There would have been disadvantages to a teach-in, of course. At any rate, the Provost was unable to gear himself for the possibilities of change and took refuge in a statement about the "different diurnal schedules" of his generation—confirming student prejudice about the differences between the generations. Thus, at 10:15, the panel, led by the Provost, decamped and abandoned the platform to the students.

At the conclusion of the Memorial Auditorium meeting, a spontaneous event occurred, as the students drifted back to their fortress in the Old Union. The Old Union had never been completely abondoned by the demonstrators; a group had held the building pending the outcome of the meeting at the Memorial Auditorium. Nonetheless, the administration had lost its last opportunity to resolve the strike on its terms. If student legitimacy demanded that the demonstrators go and listen to the administration position, confrontation politics demanded that they return to the building they had captured during the day, since the administration was refusing to talk on equal terms.

The late evening sessions following the fiasco at Memorial Auditorium in the main concerned formal arrangements for the maintenance of the building. Groups were set up to police the grounds, to maintain a certain amount of rigor in sleeping arrangements, to arrange for seminars, classes, and discussion groups. At this point realization that a long-range stay in the building was possible took hold; with this realization, the social consequences also became apparent.

The logistics of the Old Union made possible some easy solutions to problems which had plagued the Columbia revolt; the Old Union directly faced Tresider Memorial Union. The student union's cafeterias meant that the problem of food was minimal. Students could easily be rotated in and out of the Old Union; there was no crush to bring food to the striking demonstrators. In fact, the movement to and from the "headquarters" was remarkably uncontrolled and unsupervised.

By the end of the evening, the students had begun to live their revolution. Unlike rebels of the past, this generation is *not* alienated from their peer group—they swing almost as a strategy. While serious discussions on the focus and tactics of power have their place, the students see little virtue in suffering for its own sake. They do not mind being identified with millennialism or with early Christianity, but they repudiate the protestantization of American culture typified by their elders of all religions. While many were deciding matters of tactics, and others were working out arrangements for living quarters, a dance got underway to round out the evening. The earth-shaking rock groups now standard on American campuses provided a kind of relaxation previously unheard of in the crucible of revolution. The first evening ended as it had begun, with the practice of politics as poetry, instead of the traditional politics of poverty. The students were, after all, true to the affluence of their class backgrounds.

As the sound and fury of the rock bands died away, signs of intensive organization became manifest. Education committees, press committees, food and drink committees, and a host of other essential operations were set up, all plugged directly into the Tactics Committee. By making the key coordinating group a "Tactics Committee," all questions of principle, all matters of ultimate ends were left open to debate—ideology joined organization as a "happening." Naivete became a reasonable "style" and not just a low degree of political consciousness.

The next morning was more or less devoted to arranging for the second noon rally. This time it would not be held in White Plaza but in front of the Old Union. This time the acoustics were good, the loudspeakers were working, and the audience could hear from any part of the lawn or the interior of the Old Union building. Patterns of internal organization established Monday evening had already crystallized to the point that certain students had such specialized jobs as policing the ashtrays, cleaning the floors, and yet others picking up junk strewn about this court. No "status" demotion was possible, since no system of status promotion was tolerated.

The paramount fact was that the Old Union had indeed become a center of gravity that could no more be ignored by the opponents than by the participants. Leaflets pro and con were in abundance.

One leaflet, "Moderation or Occupation?", which was widely distributed, without molestation of any sort, read:

Last evening in response to Cesare Massarenti's call for a mass meeting, over 1,200 students gathered at the Old Union for a discussion of issues and tactics. They overwhelmingly rejected the occupation of the building as a tactic to settle the IJB dispute. Today this tactic continues to hinder the normal function of university business and threatens to silence the forces of moderation. We must pledge our support for rational negotiated settlement with the university in a spirit of good faith. Let us, the silent majority, express our confidence in the negotiation process by wearing a white armband until the occupation ends.

The demonstrators circulated a leaflet giving the program of "Seminars: Relevant Here and Now." Some of the courses were as follows: Latin American Student Movements; University Administration and Corporate Power; On Doing Good Overseas; The Spanish Student Movement; The Sociology of Lenny Bruce; *Sgt. Musgrove* as Political Drama; Black Panthers (Tapes and Discussion); Stanford Imperialism; Malcolm X; Radical Community Living; and Leninism Today. Everything from the final speeches of Martin Luther King and Malcolm X to the social satire of Lenny Bruce could be heard in a cacophony of sound, live and recorded, in the Old Union. These activities served not only to pass the time but to create a climate of relevant education that students wanted the whole Stanford plant to be aware existed.

The second noon meeting was attended by over 500 students, most favoring the sit-in but with a smattering of opponents. The session began by flogging the press for its coverage of Monday's events. An announcement was made that the press committee set up the previous night would be available, and to straighten out the record a press conference would be held later in the day.

Next, a leader of the student sit-in, Steve Weissman, a former leader of the Free Speech Movement at Berkeley and hence a veteran "professional student" endowed with a mystique of action, provided the rationale for the reoccupation of the building. He pointed out that had the vote gone to continue the sit-in at the mass rally Monday evening, students would not have felt compelled to sit in. By the same token, he felt that the vote against the occupation tactic was no more binding on the demonstrators. Weissman acknowledged the personal remarks directed at him by Provost Lyman at Memorial Auditorium the previous evening and went on to talk about that meeting. It was Weissman's opinion that the meeting had indeed been a communication mechanism, one which the administration had not expected to work out the way it did, for it had only demonstrated anew the paternalism which was being protested by the student sit-in. It also illustrated the depth of student hostility for the administration and in so doing informed the members of the administration of the seriousness of the situation. Weissman then went on to advise the administration how to save face. The essence of his position was that either via the Committee of 15 or the Faculty Council meeting scheduled for Wednesday, the administration could extricate itself from its untenable position. He pointed out that mechanisms for solving the problems were available; the students simply wanted their demands to be met—others could claim victories. His speech, a key one, ended with a demand for amnesty for the demonstrators.

The demand for amnesty was the product of the experiences of the students who had seen select students singled out after other demonstrations for special prosecution and disciplinary action. At Columbia University, that demand had also represented a key issue dividing the students and the administration. The demand for amnesty illustrates some of the terminological inexactitude that can develop with relatively inexperienced student leaders. Even for some of the students themselves, the term had a negative meaning, connoting an admission of guilt. What was intended by the demand was that no single student should be prosecuted, that all should be held equally responsible for the sit-in. The more accurate, and classic demand: "no victimization" did begin to replace the amnesty bid, and the latter phrase tended to remain in use only among those who opposed the demonstration. At the final stage in the sit-in, the "no victimization" slogan was legitimated by a statement of complicity signed by many students acknowledging their participation in the sit-in. The move from amnesty to non-prosecution reflected the demonstrators' growing assurance and also was a move away from the inherited campus struggles that took place four years earlier at the University of California in Berkeley, or three thousand miles away at Columbia.

The next speaker, Mark Sapir, one of the expelled students, announced that Provost Lyman was in the audience and that he could talk to at least four of the proposed suspended students right there in front of the entire student audience if he wished. The statement triggered the first activism of the meeting. People began clapping in cadence and standing up until most of the audience was clapping rhythmically and demandingly. This went on for two minutes. The chairman then announced that Provost Lyman's response had been to walk out. Sapir continued by pointing out that he, Sapir, would be glad to explain his participation in the CIA protest movement and also what had been going on during the past twenty-four hours of demonstrations and, finally, what would happen if the demonstrators did not win their demands. Although Sapir never made this first threat more explicit, escalation was a thought to which many other students were addressing themselves.

The following speaker was Tim Haight. Mr. Haight, who had the good fortune of combining hip language with a radical rhetoric, was listened to attentively. His key point was that nothing prevented the administration from using the Old Administration building for its bureaucratic purposes; that the students, while they intended to continue the occupation, did not in any way intend to prevent the administration from carrying out its work. All the student demonstrators wanted were discussions with the administration.

What gave particular poignancy to Haight's remarks was that on the same Tuesday morning, two of his letters appeared in the *Stanford Daily* under the title, "Two Letters of Conscience." Both were remarkable for the universal expression they gave the quality of mind and conscience of student opposition that led to the sit-in. The first, addressed to the Selective Service System, Local Board No. 95 in Los Angeles, read in part:

> I can no longer cling to the sanctuary of the university while the people I most respect are turning in their cards. To me the Selective Service System is an embodiment of the coercive forces our materialistic, racist, sexless, and soulless society has used to push people of basic decency and dignity into molds unfit for human beings. You want us to be killers, or workers, or technological innovators, so that America can lead the way in changing a beautiful planet into man's progeny and his products. Worse than that, you wage senseless wars, exploit people, and discriminate in savage ways.

The second letter was addressed to Professor Edwin D. Barker of the Scholarship Committee at Stanford, notifying Mr. Barker that he had returned his draft card to the local board and that he was forthwith announcing his rejection of his grant money. This letter too is worth citing:

> Although the pursuit of truth is a noble venture in itself, it cannot be carried out in isolation. You are in the madhouse with the rest of the crazy people, and withdrawing to a corner to do good work will not change that. If you and professors like you would tell this society and its government that you would do nothing for it unless it made immediate, genuine, and lasting commitments to wipe out the blots on America, change would come. Society needs you.

The letter then concluded with a critique of faculty performance that summed up the feelings of the majority of the protestors.

> But if you won't accept that, you will discuss the fine points, and check the methodology, and run it through the computer. By that time the extensions of your system will have murdered and degraded millions more and perhaps have destroyed the world. How do you do it? How do you segment your life so that you can be the good professor in the corner of the arena, while the emperors direct their games? I hope one day to come back to work with you again, but there are more important things right now.

After a few more speakers discussed the "more important things" (tactics for future struggles), and announcements were made of afternoon seminars, Eckhard Schulz, a graduate student in engineering from Weisbaden, Germany, stood up to announce another meeting in Bishop Auditorium on Wednesday in the Graduate School of Business. Its purpose was "to try to unite those groups who oppose the tactic of the sit-in." Schulz referred to the meeting on the previous Monday night, and the vote of the students disapproving of the occupation of the Old Union. He further objected to "demands" being made on the administration, leaving implicit the notion that he agreed with their content but not with their style. He proposed that those disagreeing with the sit-in should let the administration know this by an act of their own. Schulz was followed by Fred Cohen, a demonstrator, who urged the students opposed to the tactics but in favor of the demands of the anti-CIA demonstrators to organize their own protest. His point was that the demands should be met irrespective of the tactics of different student groupings. Students who feel like Mr. Schulz should protest and take action in *their* own way, he pointed out.

The next speaker, James Forester of the Medical School, introduced a new factor which was to be extremely important in the final settlement. He emphasized the unity which existed about the demands for setting aside the suspensions and for amnesty. He announced that the Medical School faculty would put strong pressures on President Sterling to ease the penalties, if not to remove them. As it turned out, even Mr. Forester underestimated the consensus which prevailed among the Medical School faculty, which rested not only on a righteous indignation but on the feeling that disciplinary action against a Medical School student should be taken by the Medical School and not by presidential dictum. Forester concluded that the sit-in on Monday was justifiable because it brought the issues into focus and to the attention of the college community. While he was unsure as to the correctness of the reoccupation, he felt that this was not an issue of great moment, in the light of Provost Lyman's Memorial Auditorium performance.

That the Stanford protest was not an isolated event but one of many protests at campuses across the United States became clear when the chairman of the meeting read a telegram of support from the Northwestern University students who had successfully concluded their own sit-in the previous week. This telegram was received with cheers, after which a proposal was introduced to have an open-house for the faculty on Wednesday, between two and four in the afternoon, just prior to the Faculty Council meeting. As it turned out, many of the faculty availed themselves of the opportunity to speak with demonstrators directly.

The next student, Richard Arnold, reported that the Santa Clara Central Labor Council had sent a night letter to President Sterling asking him to meet with the American Federation of Teachers' local chapter. Arnold expressed the need for external pressure group techniques that would result in greater community action such as had been achieved by the Black Student Union earlier. The dilemma was that such external groups were largely mythical in character; community consensus did not form to back the students, but it did remain amorphous and was not directed against them. In some measure the reason for this lies in the *Palo Alto Times'* sensitivity to the general community spirit and its desire to respond positively to university community needs, including many of its student readers on campus. The local newspaper took a position not unlike that of conservative faculty members, namely, leaving open the claim for judicial review of the anti-CIA demonstrators, while deploring the tactics. If the community was not alerted to the exact nature of the struggles, they at least were defused in terms of possible action against the demonstrators. The absence of hostile local press relieved pressures on the administration to take precipitous police action, which they were clearly loath to commence in the opening stages of the sit-in.

The final speaker of this meeting was Assistant Professor Robert Polhemus of the English Department who read a letter being circulated among the faculty. It declared the Monday evening meeting in the Memorial Auditorium a communication failure and asked that another be held in which: (1) the platform would be shared among a wide spectrum of views on the controversy; (2) the audience would participate and would not be formally limited to asking questions; (3) the meeting would not be suspended arbitrarily but would be of sufficient length to permit a full airing of all issues; (4) the moderator would be nonpartisan, if possible; (5) an attempt would be made to achieve some agreement and solution. He noted that non-faculty support for the sit-in demonstrators would indeed mean a black day for the university, and concluded by urging students to contact faculty members in their offices or homes to explain their position. Polhemus' letter made a noteworthy thrust at Provost Lyman. For the first time a faculty member connected up, if only tenuously, student struggles with the nature of the administrative handling of the university bureaucracy as a whole.

Professor Polhemus was one of a small number of faculty members who were willing to speak out on the issue in favor of the student demands. But even his statement had an aura of legalism and neutrality rather than the kind of partisanship that the students had felt they could expect from at least a portion of their faculty. Unexpected support for the students did come from a mild and gentle member of the mathematics department, Professor Robert Finn, whose statement was surely one of the more unusual events of the day.

It seems to many students a world of futility and of terror. It is a world which the students neither created nor chose. Yet it is they who will have to bear its burdens. It will be for them a kind of taxation without representation, in which the taxes are paid in blood—the blood in the veins of those who must fight, and the blood on the hands of those who devise and operate the machines to produce the bombs and missiles and jelly gasoline, and the gases and chemicals and germs. Our college youth have been exposed since birth to the unsavory spectacle of their elders busily preparing the annihilation of the universe for private profit. And they are now constrained to witness the complicity and silence of their university on this central moral issue of our time. They are right if they feel that a university which is unable or unwilling to disassociate itself from the development of instruments of torture, murder, and mass destruction or with the loathsome activities of the CIA is a university whose highest officials should be called to account. In this situation it is the millitant students whose actions reflect the real best interest of all of us and it is those who are content to let matters slide who betray us. It is love for their university as distinguished from its buildings, that motivated the CIA demonstrators and which motivates these students now. Their actions will not destroy the university; they may instead rejuvenate it.

The general mass meeting came to an end and the chairman announced that those who had to go to class should do so, while those who had no classes ought to move back into the Old Union. One curiosity of the entire demonstration was that classes went on; students continued to meet in White Plaza and at Tresider Memorial Union. The normal routines of the university were in fact only slightly disrupted, for the action was limited to the sit-in at a single building and no attempt was made to generate either a strike of students or a disruption of normal academic activities.

The noon meeting and subsequent afternoon events took place against a background of the meeting convened in response to the demands of the student members of the Committee of 15. Much of the C-15 meeting, which continued into the night, was devoted to informal seminars and to the continuing discussion of tactics.

The tactics sessions contributed significantly to the development of social solidarity and political socialization. Particularly in the afternoon hours of Tuesday, the second day of the sit-in, a new articulate group of rank-and-filers began to emerge, able to express themselves from the floor on all manner of tactical and strategic issues without hesitation. Indeed, unlike the faculty, students had a remarkable ability to accept criticism universalistically rather than personally, and without malice. The contrast between student sobriety and faculty pique was remarkable enough to discomfit students who were shocked to realize that even in their manners they were not necessarily inferior to the faculty.

Typical was a discussion Tuesday afternoon which concerned whether students should leave the Old Union prior to the Wednesday faculty meeting. Not only were faculty members present unable to indicate what students' attitudes should be if the faculty vote went contrary to their demands, but also, when students plied their professors, some of them wearing "McCarthy for President" buttons, many indicated a lack of faith in faculty sentiments, or in the faculty's ability to function as an autonomous body apart from administrative needs. The faculty participation on the IJB and their virtual absence from strike activities reinforced student hostility toward and alienation from them. When faculty members did come to the Old Union, they usually advised the students to leave or made a five minute Cook's tour of the premises and then departed, having satisfied themselves either of the curiosity of the event or its hopelessness.

In response to criticism, one of those recommended for suspension, Mark Sapir, backed up by David Pugh, a student "radicalized" by the struggle, tried to speak in behalf of the students and to note that the sit-in was not coercive but representative; not violent, but non-violent; not intended to cajole but to protect the interests not only of the students, but of the community as a whole. Sapir pointed out that "to leave the building and seek re-entry at a later date would mean real violence, real confrontation. It would also alienate the affections of student support more thoroughly than anything before that."

The sentiment for continuing the sit-in no matter what the Committee of 15 reported or what the Faculty Council decided was overwhelming. The lines had hardened by the second day; the tactics meetings emphasized the gulf between the demands for law and order and demands for setting aside the penalties inflicted by law and order.

The highlight of the Tuesday events was the attendance at the sit-in of David Packard, a Stanford trustee and President of Hewlett-Packard Corporation of Palo Alto. Mr. Packard, listed as one of the wealthiest men in America in the May 1968 issue of *Fortune* magazine, was clearly the *coup* of the student evening. He pointed out that "If you get into these confrontations, you may lose everything you have gained. Keep working with us, and you will find a good solution to this." Packard continued by noting, "We are willing in principle to allow you to have a larger voice, but not at this point to decide everything." Packard called for a partnership approach. He said, "We don't want the type of thing we had at Columbia University. I came here to gain a better understanding in case the trustees have to decide anything in this matter—and I hope we don't."

Mr. Packard expressed fear not so much of student power to win its demands, but of its power to disrupt the operations of a major university. The collective conscience inspired by the shutdown of Columbia also provided a sense of solidarity in the hall that evening. While liberal faculty members such as Professor Gavin Langmuir of the History Department, Professor Walter Meierhoff of the Physics Department, Professor Lucil Ruotolo of the English Department, and Professor Lorie Tarshis of the Economics Department, all echoed Mr. Packard's call for harmony and partnership, students' resolve stiffened. Even many of those who had earlier argued for a more moderate and legalistic approach had become convinced that the sit-in tactic was the key to any future student success.

The second day of the strike thus ended with a statement from an important member of the Board of Trustees which ostensibly called to the students to abandon their sit-in; it could just as easily have been read as a warning to the administration not to allow the situation to become another Columbia. The reference to involvement by the Board of Trustees was not easily ignored by the administration. A final resolution was also submitted by the Committee of 15, recommending a judicial overhaul, but this resolution more properly belongs to the events of Wednesday, since those who were still awake were not notified of what had transpired at the Committee of 15 meetings until 3 a.m. By that time the two-hundred-odd children, grown into young men and women, were sleeping with a grim discipline that belied the activities of their waking hours.

Wednesday, May 8th, the final eventful day of the strike, saw the important decision-making of the sit-in shift from students and administrators to the faculty. The recommendations of the Committee of 15 were based on faculty ideology and orientation. Wednesday was also the day of the Academic Council meeting. Indeed, as the events unfolded, support for the Committee of 15 resolution became contrasted with support of the resolution to the Academic Council submitted on behalf of the faculty of the Medical School by Professor Halsted Holman. These two documents were, in effect, statements which pitted the "ethics" of the Medical School against the "rules" of the Law School. The judicial overhaul was in the best tradition of the legal profession, and the resolution to the Academic Council by the Medical School was in the best tradition of mass democracy.

The Committee of 15 proposal voided the key issue which precipitated the crisis—the proposed suspensions of the CIA demonstrators. It urged the President to "make his decision . . . independently of previous decisions." The bulk of the Committee's proposal, however, was taken up with spelling out in detail a revised judicial procedure. In contrast, the Holman resolution focused upon the immediate demands of the demonstrators and called for setting aside suspensions and penalties against the sit-in students.

In a sense, the statements were really two ships in the night, passing each other untouched. In part this was because the Committee of 15 represented long-range as well as legal interests, whereas the Medical School resolution was concerned with resolving the problem that had polarized the Stanford campus. That the issue became centered on these two resolutions is primarily due to the instinctual impulse of administrators and faculties on large university campuses who find refuge in the form of law rather than in any formal juxtaposition of the two sets of statements.

The students pointed out the peculiar dilemma which had arisen when they stated that, despite their support for the Committee of 15's final statement, "the Committee failed tragically to meet the specific grievances which the current demonstration protests." The Medical School resolution to the Academic Council addressed itself to precisely these specific grievances. Its similarities to student demands for amnesty were clear. In fact, the Provost recited the student demands later in the afternoon and matched them up against the Medical School resolution to show how proximate they were.

But as these faculty activities began to take shape and to dominate the events of the day, they did so at least symbolically behind the backs of the students, since the students were pressing on with the sit-in and counter-actions. The main work of the demonstrators on Wednesday was oriented toward convincing the faculty to support their demands. Students were delegated to visit with the 900-odd members of the Stanford faculty, while faculty members were given an "open house" at the Old Union headquarters.

The students opposed to the sit-in, who had simply reacted to the sit-in demands for the previous 48 hours, began to mobilize organized action on mid-Wednesday. The demonstration had kicked off a number of individual actions, but not until Wednesday did the students opposed to the demonstrators coordinate their opposition. The relative degree of impotence of the student supporters of the administration (or opponents to the demonstration) is worth noting. It is often stated that demonstrators represent a minority of the campus without appreciating the degree to which administration supporters represent a smaller and certainly less coherent faction of the campus community. In point of fact, one real victory of the demonstrators was their ability to mobilize a "middle" sector of the campus community that had never before participated in the political life of Stanford. In a sense, the organization of a meeting in support of the administration represented an alternative to and a test of student sit-in organizational styles.

The meeting of the administration supporters was held, appropriately, at the Graduate School of Business. Although the fire marshal charged around the aisles as if the meeting was the same scope and magnitude as the one held Monday evening at Memorial Auditorium, it was far from it. Attendance was sparse; by a head count (mid-way in the meeting) there were not more than 212 people in the Business School auditorium, including adults, photographers, and perhaps a third of the audience who were either demonstrators or supporters of the sit-ins.

The purpose of the meeting was primarily to obtain a mandate, a seal of legitimacy, for a five man group to speak to the community in the name of the people present, plus the 2,000 students who, the audience was informed, had signed the anti-sit-in petitions.

The master dilemma of those students supporting the administration was, of course, the absence of an articulated position. The leaders of this meeting were unable to agree on very much aside from their opposition to the continued occupation of the Old Union. Equally significant was their failure to prepare for what might have been a significant meeting by obtaining a parliamentarian or, even better, having a chairman with some experience in parliamentary decision-making. The chairman of the meeting, Eckhard Schulz, announced that the *modus operandi* for the counter-demonstrators' meeting would be parliamentary procedure. It rapidly transpired that the chairman had far less grasp of the niceties of *Roberts' Rules of Order* than many others present.

Chairman Schulz's announcements that the meeting was "closed" except to participants who deplored the tactics of the demonstrators stood in sharp contrast to the open quality of the demonstrators' meetings, where Schulz himself had spoken several times. The lack of any grass roots feeling was made plain by the fact that the seal of legitimacy was endowed on Eckhard Schulz himself and five other students. The leaders showed no agreement on any points other than their deploring the tactics of the demonstrators. They requested that a vote of confidence be given their leadership, which would be limited to a two week period, after which they would reconvene and have another meeting.

Schulz revealed the hopes which the administration was placing on this meeting when he attempted to show how important the session was for students. Contacts with the administration, he said, had shown that the students selected by this group would be given representation in the various transactions that would take place. Shades of the notorious strike-breaking formulas of the "proletarian thirties" were implicit in Schulz's recital. By obtaining a vote of confidence, it slowly became clear, the five "leaders" (the term continually used by Schulz) would be able to provide support for the administration from an organized and constituted body of students.

The awkwardness of student participation on terms set forth by the administration became manifest as organizational inexperience when a full five minutes of discussion was required before one person in the audience had the sense to move a vote of confidence in the five proposed student leaders.

When the discussion from the floor opened, however, no sentiment jelled. The meeting floundered for several minutes until Mr. Shanahan got up and repeated what Eckhard Schulz had said, in a more concise form. He sat down to some applause, the first and about the last to be heard at the meeting. Shanahan was followed by a motion to close debate which was put to a voice vote and adopted, with about twenty in agreement and fifteen opposed. At this point, several of the pro-sit-in demonstrators tried to get the floor and began to tie the chairman into parliamentary knots. A student opponent of the demonstrators finally proposed that Mr. Shanahan become the chairman of the meeting, but since he did not want to, and Mr. Schulz did not want to relinquish the chair, the meeting limped on. A vote of confidence in the leadership was finally adopted amidst confusion as to whether the vote was one of confidence in the five leaders or a vote to close the debate.

After students finally obtained a vote to close the debate, a series of confusing votes on the main motion, the vote of confidence, followed. Finally, a hand vote was taken with the results being 96 in favor and 18 opposed. From this point on the strategy of the sit-in delegates to the anti-sit-in meeting was to have the size of the actual vote recorded. Mr. Shanahan spoke angrily to the effect that they did not pretend to say that the majority of the student body was present. A British student proposed that the number voting on the resolutions be incorporated into any report. His proposal, strangely enough, was adopted by a voice vote. The countering response came from the floor when one of the audience pointed out that the leaders chosen represented not just the people present but the 2,000 signatories to the various anti-demonstration petitions.

The next resolution, that the anti-CIA demonstrators not be excused from punishment, revealed the weakness of the opponents of the sit-in. This resolution brought a severe response from a student member of the Study of Education at Stanford, a committee organized to investigate educational innovation—a man who had been in the sit-in himself. He departed from the meeting. Mr. Shanahan then dealt with some of the moral issues this student had raised, pointing out that students could have moral discussions anywhere they like but not in university buildings. This brought general applause, but applause touched with some derision. Amidst increasing chaos as the time for termination of the meeting drew near (the hall had to be vacated by 1:00 p.m.), votes were taken. The resolution to punish the CIA demonstrators failed. The meeting was dismissed with a motion to adjourn amidst shouts to the effect that the meeting should be declared a farce.

Back at the Old Union, demonstrators had decided to use both the outside court area and the interior portions of the building. The contrast with the meetings of the anti-demonstrators was staggering. The demonstrators had already received preliminary reports about the meeting of the anti-demonstrators and shrewdly decided to ignore it as totally ineffective—as in fact it had been. The demonstrators' meeting was casual, relaxed, unhurried. The demonstrators were aware that the crucial faculty meeting was about to take place, but the relaxed tone reflected their feeling that they had done their work; now it was up to the faculty. There was considerable speculation about what the faculty would do. The demonstrators did not exactly have a noble impression of faculty sentiments, but they did have a keen appreciation of how a faculty could perform decision-making roles even against its own will.

In a leaflet distributed to the faculty as they entered the meeting hall, the students reiterated their four demands. The statement emphasized that the faculty had to decide whether to pay attention to the Committee of 15 proposals or to the main issue of the suspension of the demonstrators. The leaflet read in part:

> We have overwhelmingly rejected the Committee of 15 proposals as humiliating, obscurantist, and antithetical to the substance of our demands and demonstrations, because the proposed student conduct legislative council and the proposed Stanford judicial council are designed to be stacked against the students, with all power still residing in the President. He would control this judicial council by a simple 5-4 majority. He has a clear advantage in the proposed legislative council. The sections on interim regulations for student conduct, the judicial aid defendant cooperation, and alternative student procedures help to expose this proposed court as kangaroo-like in nature. Your meeting was called to take action concerning the suspension of seven demonstrators. This, and not the C-15 recommendations, remains the central issue.

Interestingly, this particular document was not authoritative. Signed "Students Against Political Suspensions," it represented the work of a few of the most radical of the demonstrators. Yet it must be said in all fairness that as the meeting of the faculty developed, it was indeed a choice between the Committee of 15 approach and that taken by the Medical School. The extreme radical posture had in fact accurately estimated the situation as it obtained at 4:15 p.m.—when the faculty convened.

The faculty seemed to be an unwilling power elite being compelled to make a decision which would be binding on both the administration and the students. The impotence of the powerful was never better demonstrated than that afternoon.

The meeting became the major watershed in the struggle inadvertently rather than through design. This was not only because it marked a decisive victory for the students by giving them a voice in the tri-partite university but because the faculty members were compelled to face the issues of faculty power as decisively as the students were confronting the problems of student power.

The specific format of the faculty meeting initially called for consideration of a motion proposed by the Executive Committee of the Academic Council. The motion endorsed, in effect, the decisions which had been rendered earlier that day by the Committee of 15, urging the Committee to put its proposals for judicial revision into final form as quickly as possible. This resolution also called upon the students to vacate the Old Union. Thus, the Executive Committee focused faculty attention, as predicted, on the Committee of 15's work. In contrast, a resolution introduced by Professor Halstead Holman called for setting aside the CIA suspensions and for not acting against the demonstrators. The discussion was lengthy and acrimonious; the faculty's decision was one in which great stakes were manifest.

Although it took five hours for the meeting to run its course and for the resolution favoring the students to be adopted, the central conclusions of this meeting were clear. First, the faculty in the main perceived student demands as a loss rather than as a gain to their own power as a faculty. This was certainly the case with those 245 members who voted against the Medical School resolution. This was also true of many of those voting in favor of Holman's resolution, since the vote was not so much a pro-student vote as an anti-trouble vote. This became especially clear in the constant reiteration that the vote did not represent a critique of the admin-istration. In fact, the following day a group of the more distinguished liberal faculty, including Gabriel Almond, Robert McAfee Brown, William A. Clepsch, Philip Dawson, Halstead Holman, Donald Kennedy, David Levin, Mark Mancall, Davie Napier, Louis W. Spitz, and Lorie Tarshis, in a letter to the Stanford community explained that while they had voted affirmatively on the resolution, they were disturbed by two inferences:

At no point did we intend our actions as a vote of no confidence in the administration. We expressed a difference of opinion—a very deep difference— but we believe it to be the essence of the democratic process that reasonable men may disagree on the next one. Consequently, we reaffirm our full confidence in President Sterling, Provost Lyman, Vice Provost Packer, and other administration officials with whom on this occasion we may have differed. And we look forward to working under their leadership in building Stanford's future.

At no point did we intend our action as an encouragement for sit-ins or civil disobediences. These do not seem to us the appropriate methods for determining university policy. Nor do they create the kind of atmosphere conducive to fruitful dialogue and real learning and they should not be contemplated except in the most extreme circumstances, when all other means of communication have clearly broken down.

It is clear that faculty members perceived that this vote was crucial. An informal sample of those that did not attend or those who attended and chose not to participate showed that reasons were not related to apathy or lack of concern. Rather, there was profound fear among faculty members that going on record either for or against the proposal would cut them off from the university community as a whole. The vote represented an end to the politics of ambiguity—an end brought on by external and unwanted pressure.

If votes of individual faculty members were revealed, the consequences could have been profoundly negative. Faculty members cherishing their credit with students might have found it rendered into bankruptcy; or colleagues might have taken issue with one another's vote. It is all too easy to accuse faculty members of not having courage. While some of them do not, the more central point is that this kind of a vote forces decision-making roles upon men who prefer dialogue to resolution.

A third point is that the vote did have a bitterness reminiscent of a deadlocked party convention. Yeas and nays were often spoken emphatically and belligerently, while at the other end of the spectrum some whispered their votes in the vain hope that no one would pay attention. This of course was hardly possible, since the vote was taken on roll call, and each member of the faculty was polled separately and individually.

Fourth, to a great degree the genuine issue became transformed into a symbolic one. The Provost in particular chose to transform the issue of student amnesty into one of confidence in administration policy. If this transformation of values did not shake the vote loose from its moorings, it did embitter administration with faculty, and, even more, faculty with each other.

There seemed to be a last-minute administration ploy to break up a faculty intent on avoiding "trouble" (defined as either a prolonged student strike or as an invitation to the police to solve the strike through armed force). The points used were: (a) the faculty was ill-informed of the issues; (b) the faculty should have considered the resolutions of the Executive Committee of the Academic Council as a first order of business; (c) the faculty was not equipped to act as a committee representing the whole on delicate matters of law. When this approach had no apparent effect, the Provost then indicated in the strongest terms that a vote to set aside the IJB convictions would amount to a "repudiation" of his own position. This only accentuated divisions in the faculty rather than alleviating them. Indeed, it seemed as if the moral backs of the faculty stiffened as a result of the Provost's insistence on a roll-call vote. Any vote-switching after the preliminary results had been announced would have resulted in a severe loss of prestige for the faculty.

The Provost failed to take into account that by making the vote on the demonstrating students a vote of confidence by the faculty in the administration, he shifted the burden of the issue from student power to faculty power. And a faculty possessing the relative autonomy of Stanford's faculty could not be coerced (an often used and abused word during the sit-in period) by such a heavy-handed tactic. Thus, the roll-call vote proved to be an exercise in futility. It merely guaranteed that the faculty would seize upon this issue to register its own claims to university-wide power—however tenuous those claims might be either in fact or in expectation.

The faculty meeting of Wednesday afternoon had a precision and formal elegance that was as unexpected as it was unintended. The insistence of Provost Lyman's call for a roll-call vote, "given the extremely serious nature of the vote, and how it reflects directly on the confidence this faculty has in the administration," made it possible to connect professional lines of endeavor with political attitudes in a way most unusual for "men of knowledge."

Only 515 of the roughly 930 faculty members eligible to vote exercised this option. An estimated additional 100 either decided to abstain or left the auditorium prior to the vote. In any event, no more than 60 per cent of those eligible actually participated in the voting. Those absent or abstaining were randomly distributed; that is, no one school seemed to be disproportionately overrepresented or underrepresented. The final tally was approximately 281 in favor of the "Holman Resolution" and 233 against it.*

---

*Our own tally showed 285 in favor, and 245 against. However, we will use the "official" figures, since they form the basis of the breakdown by school on the final vote.

A second fact to be noted is that the vote of the Academic Council was by various "faculties"; thus it was possible, however crudely, to gauge the differential response to student demands. There was a remarkable degree of bloc voting (which will herein be defined as a minimum of two-thirds voting either for or against the Holman Resolution). The strong "yea" vote was given by the Faculty of Humanities and Sciences, and by the Faculty of the Medical School. The strong "nay" vote was supplied by the Faculties of the Business School, Engineering School, and Law School. The one faculty conspicuously divided on an almost equal basis was the Faculty of the School of Education. Since a majority of the faculty is contained in the schools voting approval for the Holman Resolution, with the marginal "deviant" ballots cast somewhat canceling each other, the student petition was acted upon favorably, although the tallies were close.

ACADEMIC COUNCIL VOTE ON THE "HOLMAN RESOLUTION"

University Division or School	*Vote*		*Percentage*	
	Yes	*No*	*Yes*	*No*
Graduate School of Business	0	18	0.0	100.0
Earth Sciences	3	16	15.8	84.2
School of Education	11	10	52.4	47.6
School of Engineering	29	56	34.1	65.9
Humanities and Sciences	149	74	66.8	33.2
School of Law	2	18	10.0	90.0
School of Medicine	80	24	76.9	23.1
Food Research Institute	2	4	33.3	66.6
Computer Services	5	5	50.0	50.0
Miscellaneous Officials	0	8	0.0	100.0
TOTALS	281	233	54.3	45.7

Any model of explanation of the faculty voting pattern would have to take into account the following "local" factors: (1) The school's high status as a relatively recent member in the elite of American universities. (2) The school involvement in those university activities which may be called "service-oriented" in contrast to conventional "intellectual-oriented" roles. (3) The school's upper-class student population, as measured by values and attitudes, and as reflected in the departmental affiliation of those students who participated in the sit-in.

Most of the impetus for Stanford's meteoric rise into the elite of American universities has come from its professional schools.

The Engineering School has utilized the largesse of federal project research funds and the accessibility of technologically oriented industry in the Stanford Industrial Park and at the Stanford

Research Institute to develop a first-rate faculty and a renowned graduate education program. Many of the faculty in the School of Engineering are intimately involved with the corporate activities of the area, either (or both) in advisory capacity or in entrepreneurial roles. Lockheed Corporation, Philco Corporation, and Ampex Corporation are just three major firms utilizing the engineering output of Stanford—both of its faculty and its graduating students. However, the wealth and relative independence of the engineering faculty has permitted them a degree of political independence that reflects itself in the fact that nearly one third of its faculty did in fact vote *for* the Holman Resolution.

The Business School, capitalizing on Stanford's unique position as the only quality private university on the West Coast, has developed programs heavily funded by the corporate structure of the area, particularly the California industrial base. On the other hand, lacking either the status or the expertise of the engineers, the degree of its commitment to the general ideology of the Board of Trustees is more complete than that exhibited by the engineers.

The Law School, for its part, had always been strong enough not only to segregate itself from other parts of the university system, but to announce that segregation by remaining on the semester system while the rest of the campus went on the quarter system. In this way, lawyers-to-be as well as law professors are as effectively isolated as the Medical School is innovative. Thus, the structural and organizational parameters of the Law School are clearly distinct from the rest of the campus, and its conservatism is in effect a function of its organizational separatism.

To this must be added that traditionally the Law School at Stanford meted out justice and punishment to students and performed a parliamentary and adjudicative role on the campus for the administration. A student victory would not only immediately threaten its own decision-making powers, but would represent a long-range threat to a system whereby the School of Law has had special access to the administration. For these reasons the Law School became as profoundly the pole of conservative opinion as the Medical School became the pole for liberal opinion.

There have been factors systematically built into the growth of the Medical School which render less problematic the intellective-service dualism. First, the Medical School was moved from San Francisco to a new physical plant on the Stanford campus in 1962. This move was widely criticized as "Wally's Folly" (reference to President Wallace Sterling). The School was given little chance of surviving in a non-urban setting apart from massive, centralized hospital, laboratory, and medical facilities. To counter this criticism, the faculty and staff of the Medical School, from the first day of operation in Palo Alto, sought to institutionalize innovation as a means of raising quality and quieting criticism. That practice has resulted in a highly flexible and unorthodox curriculum, a fifth year of study that allows students to work in other areas of the University, and a faculty that is vitally concerned with the political and social life of the nation as it relates to the health and welfare of individual citizens.

The Medical School at Stanford is thus known as an innovating institution in its graduate program as well as in the areas of medicine. Faculty and students of the School of Medicine participate in a culture far closer to the social science and humanities orientations of most graduate students than one finds in other medical schools. Instead of conventional anti-humanistic, anti-behavioral science biases found elsewhere, the Stanford community exhibits reverse biases.

An additional factor may have been that the most "famous" student suspended was a Medical School product, and there was a strong belief in the School of Medicine that if punitive measures such as suspension were to be taken, the School should either make the decision or at least be consulted by the University administration. The anti-CIA "case" thus became a test case for the autonomy of the School of Medicine.

The School of Education is considered one of the finest in the country, but the fact that it still suffers from academic snobbery within the Stanford community means that its identification with university affairs is tenuous and diffuse. This is reflected in an absence of any consensus in the School of Education's vote. The tension between student support for the demonstrators and administrative opposition reinforced status anxiety, reflected in the fact that the School of Education had the poorest proportional attendance at the meeting.

The influence of the School of Humanities and Sciences with administration, faculty, and students has waned as that of the professional schools has risen to national eminence. Suffering from reduced levels of importance and holding firm to its traditional role as guardian of learning, the faculty of Humanities and Sciences tended to identify with the students against the professional schools' faculty and the University administration, and cast a largely positive vote on the resolution.

If part of the vote can be explained in terms of organizational and innovative patterns and special relations within the university system, the vote of the faculty also tended to be very much along classic lines of rich and poor, with the wealthy faculty—in the areas of engineering—opposing student demands, while the less well paid but equally distinguished faculty in the humanities voted heavily on behalf of the students. Social scientists tended to cleave along department lines and exhibited little patterning. This may simply represent the differential positions occupied by the social and behavioral sciences within the university hierarchy, with high range, high status social scientists tending to oppose student demands, and social scientists in less enviable positions tending to support such demands. On the other hand, this also requires qualification.

An alternative mode of analysis of the voting behavior of the various faculties is possible by examining the task performance of the different schools. Here the Medical School and the School of Education must be treated as deviant cases. As we have noted, innovation has caused the Medical School to move in a direction of task identification and performance that is more closely allied with that of the School of Humanities and Sciences than of traditional medical schools and professional schools in general.

Generally, the professional schools are more service-oriented. Stanford's strength in this area coincides with the recent acceptance of this dimension as a valid measurement of overall university quality. The work of the professional schools may be seen as more instrumental than that of Humanities and Sciences; it has greater "use" or "marketability" for non-university interests. This is where the wage differential model is most applicable: the work of the professional schools—as opposed to that of Humanities and Sciences —is more "valued" by tne non-university society. There is a clearly defined reward system in society for individuals in these professions, which is monetarily greater than for Humanities and Sciences people. Further, the university is only one institution among many where the professional school faculty member can work. The Humanities and Sciences faculty member is usually more limited in finding an institution that can utilize his skills without demanding a radical reformation in the nature of his task.

This suggests that the loyalties and values of professional school faculty are substantially different from those of Humanities and Sciences faculty. Professional school faculty, because of their service orientation, are less concerned about ideology or the value of the university *per se*. For them, the university is only an employer, and their purpose there is completion of tasks. Thus, one could expect these persons to respond to the sit-in as a dangerous violation of law and order and to consider all issues and questions in terms of their consequences for the restoration of peace. If the price of this peace is such that the university is unable to function or that they are unable to work there without further disruption, if the nature of the university is radically altered by the means used to restore order, they know they can leave it. Humanities and Sciences faculty do not have this option; they have to live with the university. And because these persons are also concerned about the nature of education and other such "abstracts," they are vitally concerned with preserving harmony as well as order, and are more liable to engage in critical thought that might suggest other ends or more basic issues and questions.

The overriding fact was that the suspensions of the students were unequivocally set aside by the vote of the Academic Council; however this was read by the administration and faculty, the students perceived the results as a victory for their militants. It not only legitimated student power; it also provided semi-legitimation for the tactics of the radical students—which is precisely what administration spokesmen recoiled from in horror.

In the immediate aftermath of the faculty meeting, the demonstrators in the Old Union had to make a decision. While the faculty had voted for the essence of their demands, they had no assurance that President Sterling would accept recommendations from the faculty. The students seemed unaware of how implausible the administration position had been made by the faculty vote. Not all of them were willing to acknowledge the vote as sufficient a victory for them to withdraw from the building. Interestingly, H. Bruce Franklin, the most trusted faculty supporter, seemed uniquely appreciative of the magnitude of the student victory.

The discussion lasted for several hours before the decision to leave was made with an overwhelming majority. In keeping with the spirit of the faculty decision, students reached the decision quickly; by 10:00 p.m. Wednesday night, the students had policed the Old Union and departed, bringing an end to their demonstration.

The conclusion of the sit-in did not mean that everything had been said. The stance toward the recommendations of the Committee of 15 concerning the structure of a judicial system was still a subject of debate. To continue discussion, it was agreed to hold another noon rally—this time, once again in White Plaza—on Thursday, May 10th.

The Thursday noon meeting might be considered a means by which students cooled out their demonstration and phased out their *ad hoc* political organization. The focus was on the Committee of 15 proposal, which met with a mixed reaction from the demonstrators, but which was later endorsed by the student legislature.

In essence the Committee of 15 established a new basis of legal equity that gave not only students but faculty a larger voice in the administration of student affairs than in the past. To be sure, the administration itself may prefer this turn of events, since it often performs caretaker services in the area of student control by default rather than by desire. Among the essential points in the statement of reform of the student judicial system, the following seem most important.

First, greater equity was established between faculty and students in handling cases of student discipline with the faculty having six members to the five of the students. Second, the Committee's proposals were not to be construed as limiting in any way the power of the Board of Trustees or the authority delegated by it to the President of the University. Third, the powers of the Dean of Students in handling cases was limited, since he would no longer be in charge of presenting evidence nor for the conduct of cross-examination; thus the Dean was no longer in the position which exacerbated conditions and could lead to the difficulties such as those with the anti-CIA demonstrators. Fourth, the pontifical significance of the Law faculty was limited. This was indicated by the provision that the chairman of the Stanford Judicial Council would be chosen by the President from the faculty of the Law School; the chairman, however, would only have a vote to break a tie. Given the degree to which the Law School is an important segment of the Stanford conservative tradition, the Committee of 15 resolution had made a major decision on this point.

The position of the students was best summed up by Eric Triesman, who pointed out, "What we have got now is nothing, but by the passage of the C-15 plan we at least have the possibility of getting what we want. Giving power to the faculty is better than leaving it in the hands of the administration."

If the Thursday student rally was ostensibly called to discuss the Committee of 15 proposals, it rapidly broadened into more generic discussions of whither and whether students. Steve Weissman, one of the sit-in leaders, called for an escalation of confrontation politics to gain two new goals—student involvement in faculty tenure appointments and in presidential selection. "We have to take the power away from the trustees. We must demand not only that students sit in on the committee for presidential selection but that students vote in referendum on any choice of that committee." Whether Weissman's statement was intended as an immediate demand to be acted upon or whether it was an attempt to develop an organizational foothold for future struggles presented an ambiguity. He concluded by noting: "Students need confrontation politics so they will not be coopted into the consensus of decision-making."

The faculty representatives at this meeting vigorously defended the Committee of 15's resolution. Professor Sanford Dornbush of the Sociology Department reviewed the state of the demands with more optimistic conclusions than did the students. He felt that it was inconceivable that President Sterling would override the Academic Council's recommendation and indicated that he doubted seriously that the President would take the CIA demonstration case back through the new procedures when and if they were established. He maintained that everybody had misread the propositions in the Committee of 15 report and then went into a discussion and a defense of that report. He argued, among other things, that the faculty wanted a faculty member to have the casting vote because they wanted decision-making to remain in the hands of the faculty in case of a basic split. When questioned as to why the faculty opposed student-originating jurisdiction, he responded that students could then decide against the interests of other segments of the community and disequilibrate the system from their point of view.

This statement was followed by Professor Marshall's summation of the decision-making process in the Committee of 15. Hubert Marshall, perhaps influenced by the general metaphysical tone of student statements, went into an analysis of three types of power which existed at Stanford: legal power, which resides in the trustees; real power, which is partly held by the faculty and the administration; and finally, residual power which the students used when they staged the sit-in. He went on to note that when employed residual power can work, but that it cannot be done very often. He concluded pungently by noting that, "You can't have the reality of power, but you can share it with the faculty." Professor Marshall never quite got to the point of whether the power of the faculty either corresponds to or supersedes the legal power of the Board of Trustees. It is therefore not certain whether he meant to say, as his statement suggested, that the students can perhaps at best share a sense of powerlessness with the faculty.

The sharpest attack on the proposed new legal structure came, appropriately enough, from Tim Haight, who having resigned both from the Armed Forces and the university the previous day, was not about to accept any palliatives. "We're still not equal, just like the black people. The C-15 plans maintain the *status quo* and we will not get our kind of power unless rational discussion allows us to be equal. It is either this or the streets." The final speaker, H. Bruce Franklin, in effect abandoned the theme of the Committee of 15 recommendations entirely and sought to refocus the issue as one of relating the university to the broader masses in the outside world. Franklin put the issue most directly: the struggle of the students was only a part of larger struggles in society; it was the job of the students to take up those larger issues and come to grips with them.

At the end of the Thursday meeting, the campus returned to normal except for a brief shock wave created by a semi-public speech by Herbert Packer, Vice-Provost of the University. Professor Packer, who is Professor of Law, had been invited to address the annual meeting of the Stanford chapter of the American Association of

University Professors on May 13th. This invitation had preceded the Stanford events, but Packer's address focused exclusively on the demonstration, with a bitter attack upon the faculty members supporting the Holman Resolution. Coming as it did, as the campus began to settle into the end-of-semester routine, his address opened a number of wounds. Vice-Provost Packer hurriedly appended a letter to his address suggesting that he had perhaps been carried away by events. The issue simmered heatedly but quietly for several days and then faded away.

The aftermath of the letter revealed, however, that while the niceties of everyday functioning called for faculty and administration to recreate the *status quo ante*, serious damage had been done to the normative climate of the university by the demonstration, the administration's handling of events, and the faculty meeting. As the term drew to a close, the ostensible quiet on the campus could not hide the fact that the return to school in September would bring new issues and possibly new confrontations. The triad of students, teachers, and administrators had hardened. Coalitional politics was still possible, but cooptation was now nearly impossible.

Berkeley

Protest + Police = Riot*

Rodney Stark

In defiant defense of the behavior of his police during the Democratic National Convention, Chicago's Mayor Richard J. Daley told the press, "the policeman is there to preserve disorder." While this was obviously another of Daley's legendary malapropisms, the

*This study was done under a grant from the Ford Foundation to the Center for the Study of Law and Society. I should like to thank colleagues at the Center who gave me vital critical advice: Philip Selznick, Sheldon Messinger, Anthony Platt, Elliot Currie, Phillippe Nonet, Jerome Skolnick and Carole Joffe.

mayor came much closer to the truth than is generally recognized. The police *are* a major cause of violence and disorder, particularly that which has broken out on our college and university campuses.

Bluntly put: students have developed a passionate hatred of the police, and the police, in turn, hate students with equal or greater intensity. The confrontation of the two almost inevitably leads to disaster. Consequently, the arrival of the police in strength on campuses, and their subsequent deployment and behavior, has transformed innumerable small student protests into mass demonstrations and then on to violence and rioting. Typically, any violent potential in student protests has remained latent or at least minor until the police have been used in force: bringing in the police to prevent violence usually precipitates it. Worse yet, in the crisis following police intervention the issues raised by student protest are ignored, energy and resources which ought to have been devoted to resolving these issues are diverted, and the integrity of our academic institutions is gravely compromised. In this report I shall try to explain why and how this happens.

I will begin by reviewing several recent episodes, establishing the sequence of events in the escalation of protest, in order to demonstrate the provocative effect of the police. Then I will characterize some important features of contemporary policemen: their hatred of student protestors, their propensity for violence, their tactical incapacities to deal with demonstrations, their misunderstanding of academic places, and the ways in which society has abused the police by making them a repressive stand-in for urgent reforms. Next, I will deal with student views of the police and try to explain the almost hysterical reactions to police on campus. To clarify these generalizations I shall then present a detailed analysis of the recent widespread disorders on the Berkeley campus to show how these factors operated to generate needless disorder, injury, violence, destruction, and tragedy. The equation is: protest + police = riot.

Before taking up these questions, several matters must be emphasized. This report is not meant either to indict the police or to condone all student activities. Frequently the police have tried their best to do a thankless, dangerous, and nearly impossible job. And often, too, student protestors have behaved abominably. But if tranquility and the preservation and evolution of our educational institutions, rather than vengeance, are our goals—and I think they are—then it must be recognized that police attempts to repress student protest have been a terrible and costly failure. I do not advocate peace at any price. But it seems demonstrable that those who see bayonets and repression as the road to salvation have no sense of price at all.

Finally, in writing this report I have intentionally tried to avoid questions of the merit of the specific demands made by student protestors, in order to concentrate on the implications of the use of the police. But it would be dishonest to pretend I am uncommitted. Thus, some general remarks about the issues to reveal where I stand, and why, seem appropriate.

Student protest has moved through three distinct phases in the last several years. I was strongly on the student side during the first; opposed to them during the second; and generally sympathetic with student demands in the present, or third, period.

The first period, which began with the Free Speech Movement at Berkeley in 1964, comprised student protests against the arbitrary, unresponsive, and restrictive nature of academic institutions. The issues were real, and most faculty members and students, at least at the better schools, supported the demands for reform.

The second period of student protest was radical rather than reformist and was at least partly a result of the fact that the great hopes of institutional reform built up during the initial protests went unfulfilled. During this radical period, much of the earlier mass support withdrew. Suspicion grew that the radicals had no genuine concern about the issues they raised, that they raised them only to attract mass support and that they did not want a settlement. The campus majority is overwhelmingly reformist, not revolutionary; the conflict between reform and revolution is basic. The fact that urgent matters of reform were raised by the radicals was a source of confusion: there was strong support for the issues, but at the same time there was antagonism towards radicals because it was felt they didn't really believe in what they said.

In the fall of 1968 student protest entered a third phase. Radical leadership was supplanted by black and other non-white minority spokesmen. Subsequently, there has been a return of mass reformist support based on a new confidence that the issues are real: that minority students want what they say they want. Furthermore, there is widespread campus belief that the demands are reasonable and ought to be met. Increasingly, the student and faculty majorities are convinced that what the minority students are asking is that the campus serve their needs in the same way that the white middle classes have always been served. Unfortunately, these demands are misunderstood by most of the public, especially politicians, as asking for special treatment instead of simple parity with the special treatment which white society presently enjoys.

Intrinsically, it is no more or less frivolous to teach Swahili than to teach French. If it is the proper business of colleges to prepare students to be community leaders, it is no more proper to produce leaders for the white community than for the black. And if it is proper that the community served by academic institutions controls them—as boards of upper class, white trustees and regents are meant to do—then it is equally proper that minority communities exert some control over those sectors of the campus meant to serve them.

These are the present issues. They are often lost in the furor over protest. But the furor itself mainly reflects the fact that the issues are not being dealt with responsibly.

Some Recent Cases

During the first two months of 1969 student protests in support of black and third-world student demands occurred at many American colleges and universities. A careful reading of reports from a number of these campuses supports two main points: the appearance of police on campus greatly increased support for the protest and solidified student factions; disorder and violence increased greatly after the police were called in. Indeed, I am even tempted to say that the amount of violence and property damage increased exponentially with the number of police present.

Consider the following examples:

1. *The University of Wisconsin*: A protest in support of a list of 13 demands for black studies began with the calling of a class boycott of Feb. 8. According to all press accounts the boycott received little student support (there are about 500 black students at Madison in a student body of 32,000). That night approximately 600 militants—black and white—demonstrated ineffectively at the field house where a basketball game was being played. For the next two weeks the boycott call continued, but the students remained apathetic and it appeared the protest was running out of steam. Then the city mayor intervened and called the national guard to the campus. The effect was dramatic. By noon at least 2,000 students were demonstrating where only a handful had picketed before. Insults and taunts began to be exchanged with the guardsmen. By 1 p.m. the student crowd had grown to at least 4,000, and the guard used tear-gas on them. That night, perhaps 10,000 students staged a torchlight march to the capitol, and a major crisis had been precipitated.

2. *Sir George Williams University, Montreal*: Black students, many of them from the West Indies, sitting-in at this Canadian University heavily damaged the computer center *after* police entered the building to drive them out. Prior to the use of police, the people sitting in had been non-violent, awaiting negotiations with the administration on their grievances.

3. *Duke University*: Black demands were put to the administration of this North Carolina school during the week of Feb. 17.

Among the demands was a request for a campus-wide ban on the tune "Dixie." Several days later, 60 of the school's 80 black students (out of 7,500 total enrollment) occupied the administration building. The administration gave them a one-hour ultimatum to leave the building. The black students agreed to negotiate as the hour passed. But by then Durham city police arrived in force. The blacks decided against confrontation and left through a rear exit. The police then surrounded the empty administration building. But the effect of the presence of police was to produce a crowd of 2,000 previously non-demonstrating, *white* students who, in turn, surrounded the police. All the black students were now absent, but a stand-off ensued between police and the white students. Something was thrown at police (they claim several rocks, the students claim wads of notebook paper) and the police charged the students, clubbing them and then using gas. Five white students were arrested and 25 were hospitalized. The next day a massive and angry student boycott of classes began. Even white, Southern students react passionately to police on campus.

4. *The University of Chicago*: This is a telling counter-example. On Feb. 21, 60 student protestors left the administration building which they had occupied for 16 days in an effort to force the university to reverse its decision to not rehire an activist, but non-publishing, woman sociologist. President Edward Levi chose to remain firm, reasonable, but utterly cool. He gave no press conferences, issued no statements, but quietly continued to push through reforms to expand the role of students in faculty hiring. These reforms won faculty and moderate student support, thus isolating the rebels from mass support. But in many incidents the rebels have dragged along without support until the police were used. Indeed, student rebels often hope to maneuver administrators into heavy-handed repression and policing in order to generate mass support. But Chicago administrators refused to fall into this error. Indeed, one official said, "We were prepared to lose that building or any other building by occupation or by arson right down to the last stone rather than surrender the university's ability to govern itself without the police, the courts, or the Guard."[1] Fortunately, Chicago has long ago won autonomy from trustees and can withstand public pressures for police repression. As a result, the original 400 sit-inners shrank to 60 and then gave up instead of swelling to 10,000. Chicago may face future problems which cannot be solved so easily. But at least in this instance they did not resort to the police and a crisis did not develop.

Chicago is not the only school which has accomplished a peaceful settlement with demonstrators this year. Reed, Brandeis, Pennsylvania, and Swarthmore, among others, did not resort to police in the face of militant black protests, and all eventually found solutions without disorder. It is instructive that all were private institutions and thus relatively immune to the current political climate which seems to force public colleges and universities to resort to repressive measures rather quickly. Once the police enter the picture the possibilities of a just solution, and even of maintaining order, rapidly recede. I shall take up some of the reasons why this is so.

The Police

Material which I collected, while a consultant to the National Commission on the Causes and Prevention of Violence, gave overwhelming testimony that student demonstrators and black militants arouse extreme hatred, fear, contempt, and anger among the police. Thus, the recent merger of black and student protest is, in the eyes of most policemen, a sinister merger of evil, subversive, and perverted elements. Such language may strike the reader as shrill, but unfortunately it is accurate. Let us consider some evidence.

All recent studies of the police are unanimous in reporting that the majority of American policemen are deeply prejudiced against black people. Recently, an excellent empirical study conducted for the President's Commission on Law Enforcement and the Administration of Criminal Justice by Donald J. Black and Albert J. Reiss, Jr.[2] provided overwhelming systematic evidence that these estimates of police prejudice are accurate. Observers who rode with a sample of policemen in three northern cities recorded hearing *72 per cent* express "considerable prejudice" against blacks. Police views of this matter were *not* solicited, but were merely noted when voluntarily expressed. The examples presented make it clear that these observers found intense and bitter hatred of black people rampant among the police. Other examples of virulent prejudice abound in the literature on the police. For example, nightsticks and riot batons are commonly referred to by the police as "nigger knockers."

There is similar unanimity, in reports on the police, that they violently hate student protestors. In the judgment of psychiatrist John P. Spiegel, director of the Lemberg Center for the Study of Violence:

> To the Irish or Italian police officer of working class background, black-skinned activists and youthful protestors are the embodiment of everything that is alien, evil and destructive of the American social system. Militant youths and black militants are perceived not only as un-American, but also non-human. Ruled out of the human race, they become non-persons and therefore deserving of intense attack, as one would attack a rattlesnake.[3]

Spiegel's judgments are supported by many qualified observers and much evidence. Here is a vivid account of his feelings given to a *New York Post* reporter by a policeman who had participated in a violent dispersal of yippies from New York's Grand Central Station during the summer of 1968:

> Here's a bunch of animals who call themselves the next leaders of the country ... I almost had to vomit ... It's like dealing with any queer pervert ... or any of those other bedbugs we've got crawling around the Village. As a normal human being, you feel like knocking every one of their teeth out. It's a normal reaction.[4]

Similarly, a recent study of the police by *Fortune* concluded that "most policemen view young radicals from middle-class backgrounds with especially intense moral repugnance."[5] The editors of *Time* reported: ". . . police tend to be appalled by abnormal behavior and rebellions against authority. Most scorn long hair. . ."[6]

To sum up: the police harbor intense hatred of blacks and rebellious students. Thus, when college administrators consider bringing the police on campus they must realize that they are bringing in an armed body of men who harbor powerful antagonisms against those with whom they are called upon to deal, and the sight of whom will infuriate students.

It must also be recognized that the police have repeatedly shown that they are unable to conduct themselves with discipline and restraint when confronted with mass protest. On the basis of an intensive study that I am completing on the police, I have been forced to conclude that there is virtually no internal authority or discipline within the present-day American police departments. An ironclad rule among the police that misbehavior will never be admitted or reported means that infractions go unpunished. Thus, the police have considerable impunity to act freely against demonstrators: they will not be punished for what they do, so they can do as they like. And what they would like to do is beat some respect into these "niggers," "radicals," "hippies," "draft dodgers," "perverts," "commies," and "nigger lovers."

Not only during the Democratic National Convention, but also during a wild police attack on a peace march the previous April, it is reported by impeccable witnesses that Chicago police officials were running after their men, cursing them, ordering them back into line, trying to pull them off victims, all in vain. Even more important than the fact that the rank-and-file police refused to obey their commanders is that afterwards they were not punished. Their disobedience must have been greatly influenced by the fact that they did not expect to be punished, and their propensity to act this way again must have been greatly reinforced by the fact that their expectations were borne out. Indeed, even in Berkeley, after a public admission by the city manager of police misconduct last July, there were no indications of disciplinary action.

Thus, when we speak of restoring law and order to campuses we must consider the frequently proven fact that the police cannot maintain order among themselves.

This is hardly to deny the importance of the policing *function*. Clearly, society requires some power of coercion against violence and destruction. Unfortunately, the police too often cannot provide such coercive power in a useful manner, and the policing function is inadequately fulfilled. College administrations must make the horrid choice between no police and dangerous police. Could the American police be counted on to behave with the courage, discipline, and firmness displayed by U.S. Justice Dept. marshals during student violence over the admission of James Meredith to Ole Miss, then college officials would have an important resource available in the present times of trouble. During September, 1962, about 200 U.S. marshals faced a howling mob of 2,000 students for seven hours and stood firm under barrages of bricks and sporadic sniper fire without ever breaking their lines or attacking, despite the fact that 29 marshals sustained wounds. Recalling this episode, it becomes clear how little we have come to expect of the police. Now we somehow condone wild-swinging attacks on unarmed students and a great many injuries and brutalities if a couple of stones are thrown at the police from the student ranks.

A major factor in the hostility of police towards student protesters is their misunderstanding of the aims, motives and capacities of students; a second is their misunderstanding of the nature of academic places.

Police periodicals, pamphlets, and manuals, as well as the pronouncements of prominent police spokesmen, are unanimous attributing student demonstrations to a sinister and subversive conspiracy. This is not a recent development in response to the nationwide activities of SDS—the most widely cited and "authoritative" police report on the 1964 FSM at Berkeley, prepared with the aid of then Berkeley Police Chief Addison H. Fording and published in the respected *Police Chief*, the official publication of the International Association of Chiefs of Police, attributed the FSM demonstrations to "the guiding hand of communists and extreme leftists."[7] Quite simply, the police do not comprehend the issues which mobilize mass student protest and see it all as symptomatic of a "communist master-plan to destroy society."

Recent interviews with policemen from a number of major cities reveal almost universal belief that demonstrations were the work of subversives.[8]

The following remarks by a San Francisco officer are representative:

> I believe that most of these young kids that are involved in these demonstrations are just dupes. I think there is an organized conspiracy, supported by Communists, to disrupt this nation. I read a book by an ex-FBI agent, I can't remember the name of the book, but in it he said there were six different methods by which the Communists are attempting to disrupt this country, and I think he was right. I can't see anything to refute his claims. I think that we need the right to assembly and to demonstrate for people who have legitimate grievances, but I do not think that most of these demonstrators we have now do have legitimate complaints.

That police believe demonstrations are the work of conspirators is confirmed by their underestimation of the resources of the student sub-culture. Their analyses of various demonstrations are filled with references to the "mysterious" abilities of the students to organize, to produce signs, leaflets, sound equipment, bail money, and the like. These are taken as evidence that the students must be getting coaching from "veteran agitators." But such talent is commonplace on our campuses. Talent and its training is what colleges are all about; the police might as well see evidence of conspiracy in the fact that mass campus protests also have available persons who can solve matrix equations, read Sanskrit, and build atomic bombs.

In like manner, the police do not understand the nature of academic places. As Jerome Skolnick has made clear, the police, like the military, have extremely restrictive conceptions of order and are trained to regard anything slightly out of the ordinary as suspicious —a potential threat to order.[9] Colin MacInnes stresses this same characteristic of the English "copper:"

> The true copper's dominant characteristic . . . [is an] almost desperate love of the conventional. It is untidiness, disorder, the unusual, that a copper disapproves of most of all: far more, even than of crime which is merely a professional matter. Hence his profound dislike of people loitering in streets, dressing extravagantly, speaking with exotic accents, being strange, weak, eccentric, or simply any rare minority—of their doing, in fact, anything that cannot be safely predicted.[10]

This description of what is most threatening to police conceptions of order could be taken as a description of academic places.

Unconventional dress has always been part of the campus scene, and the dress of today's students is extremely different from that of conventional persons. Campuses are places where people are meant to loiter, where arguments and exotic language are valued. The more academic the atmosphere of a school, the more it will appear to the police as a disorderly freak-show. No wonder they are enraged at the sight of it all.

To conclude these comments on the police, something must be said about their present predicament. No observer of the police doubts that they are under increasing strain because they are increasingly being given tasks well beyond their resources.

Since the publication of the Kerner Commission Report there is no longer much reason for anyone not to understand the nature of the social ills underlying the symptomatic violence of the black ghettos. But while we all know what needs to be done, little or nothing has been done. Instead we toss the problem to the cops while we temporize: keep the lid on and maybe someday we'll do something, we seem to say to the police. Meanwhile, it is the American policeman as well as the black citizen who must daily pay the next installment on society's inaction and indifference.

Similarly, the police can do little to ameliorate the reasons for student protest. But when protest is met with police, it becomes a police problem. They cannot grant Third World students their college. The police can *only* form skirmish lines, make arrests, bust heads and throw gas. If this does not contribute to peaceful settlements of disputes, it is still the only contribution the police are able to make.

In short, we have forced the police into the unenviable role of acting as repressive stand-ins for necessary political, social and academic reform. If they cope with this impossible situation by venting their rage on the most apparent and available source of their predicament—blacks and student demonstrators—we should not find it surprising, only tragic.

The Students

Today's students, both black and white, hate the police as passionately and even as blindly as the cops hate them. Anyone who has stood in a student demonstration when police arrive has experienced the immediate tide of almost palpable wrath that sweeps through the crowd: the pretty middle class co-eds beside you begin muttering obscenities about the "pigs," their faces flush and contort, and you know they believe they are gazing upon the face of unmitigated evil.

Several days after the televised coverage of the rampages of the Chicago police, the Gallup Poll asked a national sample of Americans whether they approved or disapproved of "the way the Chicago police dealt with the young people." 55 per cent of Americans approved, while only 31 per cent disapproved. However, among two major groups in the population, the Chicago police did not get such overwhelming backing: only a minority of persons (47%) under 30 approved of the police and only a tiny proportion (18%) of black Americans approved. Furthermore, a poll of young people conducted by *Fortune* several months later found that college students overwhelmingly disapproved of the behavior of the Chicago police.[11] Thus, anger at the police is not confined to a few radical students and black militants. *It is the predominant feeling on the contemporary campus.*

These feelings are a major factor in campus protests. The appearance of the police activates violent emotions which escalate both the volatility and the size of student protests. In combination with the intense anger of the police towards the students, the situation immediately becomes volcanic.

Why do students refer to the cops as pigs? How did this implacable anger develop?

Student hatred of the police has been building for a long time. In the beginning it was kindled by the abominations of southern law enforcement against the civil rights movement. Indeed, these atrocities, many of them televised, outraged the nation and produced the major civil rights legislation of the sixties. The effect on youth was especially deep because their commitment to the movement was profound. Furthermore, youth retained its commitment when the civil rights drive turned northward. Again the typical response to sit-ins and demonstrations was police repression, and student experience (at least vicariously) with police violence grew to include northern police as well as southern. This experience was further expanded with the growth of the peace movement. While middle class America could and did doubt that the police had really misbehaved in their dispersal of peace marches, students knew better. They (or their friends) were the ones dispersed. Furthermore, while President Johnson could ignore the Kerner Commission Report, and thus minimize its impact on many adults, students read it in classes and student publications took it very seriously. The students knew that the report—produced by prominent members of the establishment—made serious charges against the police. Thus, in the eyes of students it had become increasingly obvious that the policeman is not your friend unless you are white, short-haired, and apathetic about the primary moral and political questions of our time.

Furthermore, students have been in much closer contact with the black community than has the rest of white society. The anguished cries of brutality coming from the ghettos have long been heard by students.

Then there was Chicago. The main consequence of the Chicago police riot during the Democratic Convention, and the subsequent hard line of Mayor Daley, has been to corrupt relations between students and the police for years to come. Now they expect the police to be used against dissent. Now they expect the police to be brutal. For many students the possibility of working within the traditional political system was permanently destroyed by nightsticks and tear gas on the streets of Chicago.

Recently, I stood amid thousands of Berkeley students gathered on a grassy slope across the street from University Hall where Governor Ronald Reagan and the Regents were meeting. It was the morning after the Governor had activated the National Guard to assist police in the campus crisis. Across the street hundreds of uniformed police stood in solid ranks facing the students. Hundreds more stood in reserve.

A girl next to me said loudly: "Do you know where we are?"

"We're in front of the West Gate," someone answered.

"You're wrong," she said. "We're standing in Grant Park and that building across the street is the Conrad Hilton."

This brief sketch barely outlines the process through which students have come to see the police as the enemy. But the important fact to be recognized is that, however it came about, American students do believe that the police are violent, brutal, and repressive. It hardly matters if the police in a particular confrontation behave impeccably—students are not prepared to dismiss the past very quickly. Even more unfortunate is the fact, as the revolutionaries among the students well know, that the police can almost certainly be counted on to mishandle their assignment and turn all the suspicion and hostility of students into blinding anger. Inevitably, it would seem that at the very least a few officers will break formation and beat up a student before the eyes of the crowd. When this happened recently at Berkeley, a young sorority girl standing beside me, who was only a spectator and had earlier been indignant about the use of the word "pig" on a picket sign, began screaming: "Oh, God, they *are* pigs, they *are* pigs!" The next day I saw her in the picket line.

The growth of student anger against the police has recently escalated conflict to a more dangerous level. Non-violence, as a doctrine rather than a tactic, has lost its force. Increasingly often a few students *do* throw stones and firecrackers at police formations. But, more dramatic and dangerous, when the police now attack student crowds, there is a good deal of fighting back. At Berkeley recently when a patrolman ran from his formation into the street and began to beat a student, another student ran out of the crowd and knocked him down, then both students fled into the crowd. Later, when the police threw tear-gas canisters, instead of fleeing the students grabbed them and flung them back. Other groups flanked the police and tipped over their unguarded vans.

Student demonstrations have long been wrongfully called riots. Events during the Free Speech Movement at Berkeley in 1964-65 were often called the student riots at Berkeley, despite the fact that the students never departed from absolute non-violence and passive resistance. But today student demonstrations often do become riots.

The students, black and white, are filled with hatred of the police. The police are filled with hatred of students and blacks. We mix them at our peril.

Berkeley: "Cops Off Campus"

An analysis of recent events at Berkeley provides a concrete picture of the process by which interaction between police and students turns protest into campus warfare. This report is based on my own observations of events, interviews with a number of participants and observers, public statements by strike leaders and university officials, and press and television reports.

Frankly, when I began my investigation of events at Berkeley I did not expect to reach the conclusions I did. Having recently devoted considerable time to studying the police, I anticipated that their basic hostility towards students caused them to "over-react"—to use the current jargon—to student provocations. But this expectation was not borne out by the evidence. It was mainly the police who provoked, and the students who reacted. A careful day-by-day reconstruction of the continuing crisis permitted only the conclusion that the disorders were almost totally in response to prior police provocation.

Time and again the police were used with very little reason, and time and again their arbitrary, massive and too often brutal performance spread and intensified the student protest. It is difficult to see how such a long and consistent series of tactical blunders and morally repugnant acts could have occurred. The record suggests that university officials had little or no voice in decisions concerning the use of the police. But what of those who did have the control? Their behavior is only made comprehensible by assuming either that they knew nothing of the real situation or that they acted maliciously to provoke the worst possible crisis. Admittedly, these are grave charges. But consider the evidence.

The specific protest which culminated in a series of violent clashes between students and police began peacefully and with little support in late January, 1969. On Monday, Jan. 20, spokesmen for a coalition of non-white students ("we are black, brown, yellow and red") organized as the Third World Liberation Front (TWLF), announced that a strike to protest delays in the creation of a black studies program would begin on Wednesday, Jan. 22, unless the administration moved rapidly to settle their grievances. A list of demands published by TWLF the following day mentioned the creation of an ethnic studies department. Shortly thereafter the central point in the TWLF demands evolved into the creation of a Third World College, devoted to ethnic studies, which would enjoy virtual autonomy, and within which TWLF students would exercise considerable authority over hiring, admissions and courses.

The same day that TWLF announced its intentions to strike, it received support from American Federation of Teachers local 1570, made up of graduate student teaching assistants. AFT 1570 voted to begin a work stoppage on Wednesday.

The university administration countered with a review of recent accomplishments to improve Third World representation and participation in the institution and with reassurances that the ethnic studies demand would receive positive action. But Chancellor Roger W. Heyns refused to alter normal committee actions in order to act hastily.

So the strike was begun as scheduled. Approximately 300 persons were on picket lines at the noon peak. The picketing was orderly and university administrators and plainclothes campus police were on hand to direct students around the pickets. Officials estimated that campus-wide class attendance was down no more than five per cent. Thus, although the aims of the strikers were respected by most students, it did not engage their active support. This seems to have stemmed from several factors. Most students believed that the administration was proceeding in good faith to meet the demands. Secondly, the TWLF excluded whites from their meetings which left many white students feeling that the strike was neither their business nor responsibility. Thirdly, the overwhelming majority of Berkeley students and the faculty believed that the TWLF demands were not the real reason for calling the strike at this time. Instead, most believed that the strike at Berkeley was mainly symbolic, a necessary show of solidarity with TWLF students at San Francisco State College who were struggling on in their long and bitter strike. In light of calls for aid from S.F. State strikers, the actions at Berkeley were judged to be devoted primarily to the expressive needs of TWLF students vis-à-vis their respective constituencies.

Thus, the first day of the strike produced only a small turnout and had little or no impact on the daily routine of the university. The picket line in Sproul Plaza and token pickets at a few other places were the only evidence that a strike was in progress, and many students entered and left the campus without ever seeing a picket.

That night the strike was dealt a serious setback. The campus was shocked by the burning of Wheeler Auditorium, the largest lecture room on campus, as a result of alleged arson. TWLF leaders and spokesmen for AFT 1570 denounced the arson as wanton and senseless and denied all responsibility for it. The AFT statement said: "The burning of Wheeler Hall after a day of peaceful picketing . . . is clearly contrary to the interests of Third World students and, if an act of arson, was apparently intended to discredit the strike."

The mass of students, according to an account in the *Daily Cal* (the student paper) of man-in-the-street interviews, "generally reacted with disgust and anger today to the fire." Nevertheless, students were inclined to accept TWLF denials and to blame the arson on Telegraph Avenue "crazies." All Berkeley is aware that the city houses some extremists who try to escalate crises through acts of violence and destruction. Furthermore, the campus has been beset by bombings and arson attempts for the past several years, long before there was a TWLF. Indeed, on Sunday, Jan. 19, when TWLF met to take their strike vote and hammer out policy, there had been unsuccessful arson attempts on both Wheeler Auditorium and on the Student Placement Center. Knowing these facts, the students, unlike the press and probably the Regents, could see reasonable grounds for believing TWLF denials.

Nevertheless, the strike suffered badly. Summing up the second day of the strike, the *Daily Cal* headline read:

Fewer Pickets:

Cold Wind, Wheeler Fire
Cut Down Strike Support

Class attendance was reported back to normal. Pickets dropped below 300. From then on the strike went down hill. Friday, the third day of the strike found even fewer pickets out. All strike activity was suspended for the weekend. Monday saw further erosion of support. AFT 1570, the TA union which had begun a work stoppage in support of the strike the previous Wednesday, now took a strike vote and it failed to carry. The *Daily Cal* reported: "Picket Lines Remain Small."

Clearly, the TWLF strike was fading. It had never been much, in terms of support or effect on campus activity. Student opinion had been further offended by some tough talk by strike leaders about possible violence. This is an important point: violence by protestors drives away potential mass student support, without which protest is doomed to impotence.

But with the strike ebbing away, the incomprehensible occurred and a recurrent pattern was begun.

Tuesday again saw a very small picket line in Sproul Plaza, and, perhaps as a result, TWLF leaders adopted more militant tactics. Students were no longer permitted to pass through the picket line at Sather Gate, but were directed to walk around it. For a while deans, administrators and plainclothes campus police directed students to avoid the line and intervened in several hassles between pickets and a few non-striking students who angrily refused to circle the line. Technically, this was obstruction of a public thoroughfare and thus the pickets were subject to dispersal or arrest by the police.

It must be emphasized that the importance of Sather Gate, both for the strikers and for the administration, was symbolic, not practical. Although it is the main thoroughfare leading from Sproul Plaza into the heart of the campus, the gate is flanked on either side by smaller footbridges, which were not obstructed by pickets. Furthermore, there are countless other points of access to the campus. Thus, blockage of Sather Gate was at best a minor inconvenience. TWLF spokesmen emphasized the symbolic nature of their new tactic—the symbolic importance of Sather Gate was to be used to demonstrate to the campus the depth ot TWLF students' commitment to the strike. Unfortunately, the symbolic importance of the gate was also highly valued by the police and the campus administration. Instead of responding on practical grounds—the lack of any practical need to maintain access through the gate—they found this symbolic challenge to their authority unacceptable. Thus, a symbolic act by the strikers was transformed by police actions into a powerful strike tactic. Throughout the course of the strike, whatever police force was necessary to keep the gate open was used.

Consequently, at noon the picket line was declared illegal and off campus police were summoned to disperse it. Approximately 100 outside officers arrived and marched onto the campus only to find the picket line had already dispersed. There were no arrests, but the cycle had been launched. Following the arrival of the police a stink bomb was thrown into a classroom in Dwinelle Hall, several striking students entered classes and attempted to disrupt them and there was minor vandalism in Dwinelle and Barrows Halls. Twenty policemen rushed into Dwinelle when black students allegedly broke a window and tipped several cigarette urns. But the major event was simply the massive presence of the police, marching here and there in a public show of what many students regarded as impending police repression. Knots of students formed to watch the police, and they were obviously disturbed by the sight. New life was injected into the lagging TWLF strike.

The next day (Wednesday, Jan. 29) the effects of calling in the police were translated into bodies on the picket line: "1,000 Students Stage March Around Campus," reported the *Daily Cal* in a headline. Suddenly the number of protestors had *trebled* from its opening day high point. Again the police were called in and dispersed the picket line in Sproul Plaza.

And the next day active support doubled. More than 2,000 students demonstrated throughout the day. Again the police appeared, and the first arrests occurred. Two persons were arrested. One was Jim Nabors, a black student strike leader. The second was also a black student. TWLF spokesmen said he was not involved in picketing, but was simply walking from a class carrying his briefcase. This created a slight odor of police bigotry.

On Friday serious efforts were apparent on the part of both strike leaders and the university administration to cool down the situation. There was some reduction in the size of the demonstrations, and the police were not called out.

It seems reasonable to assume, in light of later public statements, that the university administration had wanted all along to play it cool and avoid antagonistic confrontations. But unlike the University of Chicago, the Berkeley administration was not able to take many risks to preserve campus peace. The Regents, led by Governor Ronald Reagan, an outspoken advocate of running campuses at "the point of a bayonet," had been for some time systematically reducing the discretion of campus executive officers to deal with protest—a process which was further accelerated later in the course of the crisis. One presumes that Chancellor Heyns was under terrific pressure to get tough and to use the police. To make matters worse, Heyns had no authority over outside police. He only had the power to decide whether or not to call them for aid in a given situation, but once called they were completely independent. As one campus official put it, "We have only the power of persuasion over the police, but they're not in much mood to be persuaded."

As a consequence, Heyns was apparently reluctant to use the police, and the police, when called, tended to make a massive show of force, as if to make up for "lost" time.

The pressure on Heyns to get tough became public over the weekend, despite the fact that the campus had been peaceful without a police presence on Friday. Alameda County Sheriff Frank Madigan publically released a letter to Governor Reagan, in which he threatened to refuse to continue furnishing police to the campus unless he was given a free hand to crack down. The Sheriff lamented the fact that the university refused to take action against known evil-doers. He called for the declaration of a "State of Extreme Emergency," in order to enable him to "control criminal conduct on the campus." The legal effect of such a declaration is to remove authority to call on the police from the university and give the decision to Sheriff Madigan, who suggested that he knew much better how to deal with TWLF dissidents than did an irresolute administration.

The university countered that they had called in the police whenever necessary and that they had "attempted both to protect legal picketing, and to protect people's right of access to campus."

This surfacing of a behind-the-scenes struggle between the administration and others over the use of the police was seen as a bad sign by many, because it seemed unlikely that the university could win such a dispute. That the administration was not winning seemed evident in the fact that outside police had come on campus three days during the previous five. This was further confirmed on Monday. Despite the fact that Friday had been peaceful, police came on campus in large numbers. At 12:30 the picket line in Sproul Plaza was declared illegal. Subsequently, the line was dispersed several times—only to reform. Some stones were thrown at police lines. Then strikers moved noisily through the campus with the police tagging behind. A new level in escalating the crisis was approaching.

It arrived the next day (Tuesday, February 4). The *Daily Cal* account of the day began:

Violence and arrests reached a new peak yesterday as police and students fought in the latest chapter of the . . . TWLF strike.

At least 20 persons were reported injured in a "rock throwing, club swinging melee" that broke out when police tried to arrest some students in the picket line across Sather Gate, at the end of Sproul Plaza. Twenty persons were arrested. After the violent dispersal of the picket line at Sather Gate, strikers marched in a serpentine line through the campus. Three flying squads of police broke up the line, and the students then followed them jeering as they marched back to Sproul Plaza. This was too much for some of the Alameda County Sheriff's Deputies, who wheeled around and waded into the students with their riot batons. The students scattered and eventually left.

On Wednesday (Feb. 5), the university administration was deprived of all authority over the police. Governor Ronald Reagan held a news conference and declared a state of "extreme emergency," thus turning the control of the campus over to Sheriff Madigan. Reagan told the press: "I just feel we have come to the end of the road in depending on local law enforcement by campuses. It isn't good enough any more to wait until rocks are flying and beatings start and then come in and restore order."

The state of emergency also gave Sheriff Madigan control over permitting noon rallies, a daily Berkeley occurrence regardless of whether there is a strike or a demonstration going on. It was immediately announced that rallies were temporarily suspended.

For the remainder of the week and half-way into the next, the campus remained rather calm. Strike leaders exerted all their influence to keep the demonstrations large, but very cool. The police, on the other hand, also seemed to be trying most of the time to avoid trouble. On Thursday there was one arrest. On Friday, with 1,000 marchers watched by 80 policemen, confrontations were avoided by both sides and there were no arrests.

When strike activities resumed on Monday the numbers on the picket lines were down from the previous week. Again there were visible efforts to keep things cool and the day passed quietly, but with two arrests. The *Daily Cal* described the pickets as "much less militant" than before.

Meanwhile, in Sacramento further clues to the intense conflict between university officials and the governor over the use of police were offered by Governor Reagan in a speech delivered immediately following a private meeting with University President Charles J. Hitch. Reagan chose this occasion to criticize the Berkeley administration for not getting tough. "For a long time I hoped the academic forces cooperating with law enforcement would take emergency steps. Somehow this never happened."

Tuesday and Wednesday produced only quiet picketing by increasingly smaller numbers and passed without incident. But it was too good to last. On Thursday the police made a series of moves which can only be described as those most likely to restore militance, greatly increase mass support for the strike, and to escalate violence and destruction.

First, four squads of police moved across Sproul Plaza and dispersed a line of about 300 pickets who had been circling on the bridge area behind Sather Gate. The pickets left without incident. Off to one side of Sather Gate was a tiny circle made up of 17 teaching assistants from AFT 1570 who were conducting an informational picket line. According to faculty witnesses, the line did not at any time disrupt normal traffic through the gate.

Nevertheless, Sheriff Madigan, who was present to supervise a force of by now 150 officers in the plaza, plus numerous plainclothesmen, made the decision for mass arrests. Suddenly the 17 TA's were surrounded by police and taken away under arrest.

Immediately, students responded. There was vandalism in the Bear's Lair, a nearby campus cafeteria, and in the library. The police resumed their earlier tactics of sweeping the students out of Sproul Plaza. A chanting line of students formed at Sather Gate, only to be broken up by a squad of highway patrolmen. A total of 36 persons were arrested during the day. One of these arrests soon became a police brutality scandal, which further inflamed student feelings about the police.

Clifford Vaughs, a Los Angeles radio reporter was arrested and dragged away by police. Witnesses report that Vaughs was severely beaten by officers as they took him into Sproul Hall. Once in the basement of Sproul, according to a number of eyewitnesses, some of them university secretaries working in Sproul Hall offices, the police systematically beat Vaughs while he begged them to stop. Shortly thereafter the bloodied reporter was taken to Herrick Hospital where he was treated for head injuries. The fact that Vaughs is black seemed an adequate explanation to students for this apparently wanton action by police.

That night, AFT 1474, the faculty union, met and, although they voted not to strike, voted to join the picket line—clear evidence that strike support had spread and intensified.

The next day picketing was considerably increased from the day before and faculty members appeared on the line. The police seemed restrained, perhaps shocked by the response to their agressive tactics of the day before. There was only one arrest.

Following the weekend break, despite heavy rain, strikers staged a large march across the campus. There were three arrests. The university announced that the ban on rallies was being extended. An announcement made by public affairs officer Richard P. Hafner made clear the source of the decision: "The police are charged with law enforcement on the campus which includes the authority to cancel public meetings if they are estimated to endanger public safety."

The next day began peacefully. The strike crowd was 1000 strong, and the noon hour peak passed without incident. But at 2 p.m. Alameda Sheriff's Deputies moved to clear the steps in front of Sproul Hall. In the group was Jim Nabors, a prominent black strike leader. The deputies arrested him on the spot and then made a bloody, public mess of the job. Here is the *Daily Cal* account:

Deputies surrounded Nabors, and began to lead him off when several hundred students moved to intercept him. The deputies waded into the crowd, swinging their clubs and chasing many down Sproul steps.

At this point Nabors was able to wiggle away from his captors, but he was quickly tackled by an officer of the California Highway Patrol. According to eyewitnesses Nabors was then pinned to a bench by several officers and viciously beaten into unconsciousness by several others.

[Nabors later said he was not unconscious and this part of the story was retracted]

As Nabors was beaten the crowd in the plaza area swelled to several thousand and a number of people began to shout "Pigs off campus!" or threw mud at the police.

Thirteen people were arrested and there were minor acts of vandalism on the campus.

Meeting that night, AFT local 1570, the TA union which on January 27 had voted not to strike, now passed a strike motion by a margin of five to one!

The next day (Wednesday, February 19) the crowds were huge. The series of police actions, the widespread reports of beatings administered by police in the basement of Sproul Hall, the public beating of Jim Nabors, club-swinging forays into the picket lines, the mass arrest of TA's, and the massive public presence of the police had finally mobilized a mass base for the strike. But it was the police, not TWLF demands, that was the gut issue. Many students now demonstrated in support of "Cops off Campus," who had hitherto shown little commitment to TWLF demands and who disapproved of much that had gone on previously. But this was "a whole new ball game," as one student I spoke to put it. "The Alameda County fuzz have been running over this campus raising hell and that has to end right now. Look at these Nazis standing there in their goon-squad gear. They hate us so bad they can hardly stand still. Well, they haven't seen anything yet. This is Berkeley!"

Again and again I heard these same sentiments on Wednesday. And the crowd grew and the anger grew. Students kept telling each other that there would be no running and no going limp when the police struck. "I've been beat up twice by the cops when I was limp," a muscular graduate student said, "from now on they're going to have to earn their bread." He was wearing a crash helmet and had a lead-loaded sap inside his jacket.

Minutes later, the police moved out a sweep-line from their stations along the side of the plaza and confronted the students. They were immediately encircled by chanting ranks of students who stood about 20 paces away. A few rocks were thrown. A number of cherry-bombs were tossed at the feet of the police and the students roared each time one exploded and caused several policemen to jump into the air. Then the police line was withdrawn back to the side of the plaza and the long picket circle, containing perhaps 3,000 people with at least another 1,000 bystanders, began snaking through the plaza again. Ultimately twenty-four arrests were made.

But Thursday, the next day, was the day of reckoning. The Board of Regents was meeting on campus. The press reported that they were preparing to overrule the chancellor of the San Diego campus and to fire elderly radical philosopher, Herbert Marcuse. (They didn't.) The picket lines began forming about 11 a.m. and by noon there were several thousand marching. Ranks continued to grow. Students seemed even angrier and many of the police were obviously livid. They snarled answers to simple requests about where one should walk.

By 1 p.m. the demonstration included perhaps 3,000 people (a far cry from the several hundred of a few days before). Then it was announced that the demonstrators would march across the campus to University Hall where the Regents were meeting (Governor Reagan was thought to be attending, but he did not attend until the next day). The march set out. This move caught the police by surprise and, as observers of the police realize, surprising the police can be dangerous—rattled policemen are likely to become violent policemen.

The march left most of the police behind guarding one side of the now nearly deserted Sproul Plaza, while ahead, at University Hall, there was only a token force. Arriving at University Hall, just moments ahead of the first police reinforcements, the students were able to "liberate" the street unopposed—University Hall is not on the campus proper but across Oxford Avenue from the West Gate. The streets on two sides of University Hall were solid with students chanting "We Want Reagan," while perhaps 1,500 more students looked on from the grassy slope across from University Hall. Police reinforcements began pushing the marchers back, and, to the surprise of many, the students cooperated with great speed. Clearly, the students were still determined to protest peacefully.

But this determination was almost destroyed by a sudden incident. A small group of policemen in yellow rainsuits, hurrying from Sproul Plaza in the rear of the marchers, burst down the sloping lawn behind student on-lookers and headed for the intersection which had just been cleared of students. These policemen were in a towering rage and were probably afraid because they were so few. They rushed through the students on the slope and charged at the intersection. Several passed very near me and they were shouting obscene threats; their faces were contorted and they brandished their riot batons. Their charge into the intersection almost led to disaster because, although the students had cleared the street, *they had formed dense lines along it in doing so*. Thus, this arriving squad of cops came up behind these dense lines, unseen until the last moment. But the students scattered in front of them, many darting out across the street to join the lines on the other curb.

And then it happened. *Several officers of this squad broke from their line and ran after the fleeing students.* One officer, now far away from his companions, caught a student in the middle of the street, pulled him down from behind and began to beat him with his nightstick in front of thousands of onlookers, hundreds of whom were much closer than the rest of the police squad. Almost immediately a young man with long black hair, wearing an army surplus fatigue jacket, dashed into the street and knocked the officer flat. Then, both he and the other student fled into the safety of the crowd. For a long, tense moment it looked as if the officer might draw his gun and other cops began moving around; but he got up, returned to his formation and the crisis passed. After that, the students shouted their sentiments about Governor Reagan and the Regents and then marched back to Sproul Plaza, where the mass picketing began anew. But the incident in the street had changed the mood. The students had again seen a policeman behave like a "pig," and had seen that the new anti-pacifist mood was not just talk—a student had decked a cop and rescued a fellow student. And the police had seen it too. Understandably, they put a different construction on the incident.

Still, after reorganizing into their circular picket lines upon returning from University Hall, the students seemed orderly and no different from before. The police lined one side of the plaza and students obeyed instructions to keep their lines moving in an orderly fashion. It was so obvious that the picketing would simply continue for awhile longer, and then disperse as usual, that at 3:00 p.m. I left to record my notes on the day's activities. It seemed certain that the students planned to remain orderly and I simply couldn't imagine that the police would do anything to push them into action. Such a move would be tactical idiocy. Who would conceive of turning a noisy, but orderly, picket line into a mob? Patently, I underestimated the police, because the police did blunder into a confrontation and generated a full-scale riot moments after I left.

Here are excerpts from the *San Francisco Chronicle*'s eye-witness account of what occurred, which a number of independent and qualified observers deem accurate:

A full-blown riot—shrouded in a swirling haze of tear gas—erupted on the Berkeley campus of the University of California yesterday and raged until nightfall.

Violence broke out sporadically through the morning and early afternoon, climaxing in a roaring, rock-hurling rampage shortly after 3 p.m.

Several thousand striking students and their sympathizers had been jammed in Sproul Hall plaza when a minor incident—involving a flower—ignited the mass and brought a barrage of tear gas canisters from Alameda County deputy sheriffs and California Highway Patrolmen.

Students retaliated by pitching some of the containers back at officers. Windows in Sproul Hall were broken and the acrid smoke billowed into the administration building forcing all occupants to flee.

Police chased the coughing, choking students out of the plaza and into streets adjacent to the campus where more tear gas was thrown.

Observers reported that scores—possibly hundreds—of tear gas canisters were thrown. Police brought in pepper foggers, motorized machines that spray vast clouds of gas and emit an eerie hum.

At least 15 persons were arrested, all but a couple of them after the rampage began. The charges ranged from blocking a public way to assaulting an officer and inciting to riot.

It was difficult to determine how many had been injured—probably more than 30.

. . . at the stroke of 3, with students packed into the plaza, for no apparent reason 20 patrolmen moved out of Sproul Hall to break up the crowd.

As the officers split the students into two groups, half to the west and half to the east, cherry bombs began to fall from the second floor of the Student Union. Then some students let go with rocks and small groups of officers became isolated within the crowds of hostile students.

There were numerous skirmishes as officers and students battled hand to hand.

At 3:30 p.m., a running student tossed a purple flower at one of the officers. He was grabbed, clubbed and carried off, and it was believed that this incident turned the already aroused student throng into a furious mob.

They surged toward police and the officers retaliated by trying to rout them with tear gas.

The cannisters flew back and forth, from police to students, exploding at intervals.

Driven by clouds of gas into the streets of Berkeley, the students surged down Telegraph avenue for a block, then turned and massed in the street.

Stores closed. Motorists left their cars where they stood. Residents of the area, who live in apartment houses and hotels, huddled in the lobbies of their buildings, wet cloths over their faces.

Rocks, bottles, and gas cannisters were vollied at police, and students gathered cardboard cartons, burning them all along Bancroft Way.

The crowd overturned two police vans after first breaking the windows with rocks.

The shouts rose: "The cops have had their riot. We're going to have ours."

Late that night Governor Reagan activated National Guard units to aid police in maintaining order.

The next day (Friday, February 21) tear gas and pepper gas hung heavily in the air over Sproul Plaza. After an hour of standing I began sneezing continually, as did many of those around me. The crowd began gathering in mid-morning. By 11 a.m. several large picket circles were operating. Looking down Telegraph Avenue I could see a heavy and steady flow of people towards the campus, evidence that it was going to be a big crowd despite news accounts which made it sound as if the National Guard were occupying the city (they were not in evidence). The students were mobilized and militant.

A leaflet distributed by TWLF announced that the picket lines would march from Sproul Plaza and hold a rally at West Gate, on the grassy slope across from University Hall where many had stood the day before.

The march began at 1 p.m. and proceded with astonishingly good order to the West Gate. Despite the ban on campus rallies, the Berkeley Police Department showed the good sense to grant a permit. The march would have been attempted in any event and someone was wise enough to prefer a peaceful assembly to a riot.

The students were angry, but determined to demonstrate the capacity of the TWLF to exert effective leadership. It was an uneasy march over. Many students carried gas masks. White-gowned medics led the way.

As the students formed up on the lawn outside West Gate, facing University Hall where Gov. Reagan and the Regents were meeting, they looked across at massive lines of police. Hundreds more policemen could be seen on the roof of the parking garage across the way. The crowd, at least 4,000 strong, was packed tightly together awaiting events. There were suspicions that police from Sproul Plaza might move in on them from behind. The police across the street repeatedly formed into large, military formations and marched out to replace segments of their lines. The first such march caused the students to get ready for a police charge until they realized it was merely a formal changing of the guard. After that they relaxed.

What followed was an uneventful demonstration with the usual dull speeches, punctuated only by cheers for various visiting police units—the San Francisco Tactical Squad was loudly and sarcastically cheered—and an obscene parody of a football cheer for Gov. Reagan—"Give me an F!" "F!" "Give me . . ."

After that the demonstration dispersed without incident.

During their meeting the Regents added potent fuel to the campus fire by announcing tough new rules, among them the mandatory interim suspension of all persons suspected of rule violations during campus emergencies, with no penalty less than suspension, dismissal, or expulsion upon conviction. Thus, the discretion of the university administration to use judgment in acting for the best interests of the academic community was further sharply curtailed.

Monday there were few police in evidence and the student activities consisted of peaceful picketing.

That is where things stand as of this writing. It is not my intention to explain why the TWLF strike occurred, to record its history or predict its outcome. This analysis has one purpose: to show how the use of police and the misbehavior and misjudgments of the police were a mainspring in escalating a relatively small protest into a major series of riots which threatened the existence of a university community.

A study of events provides strong evidence that this is in fact how it happened at Berkeley. The first police action came as the strike was dwindling away and had virtually no student support. Student reactions against the use of police immediately produced 1,000 demonstrators and made the strike a going operation. Again the police were used and the next day the strike gathered 2,000 supporters. Again and again this pattern was repeated. From Feb. 7 through Feb. 12, the picketing was uneventful, the massive crowds produced by earlier police actions began to melt away and soon the picket line was down to several hundred again. Then police changed tactics on the 13th, dispersed the main picket line, arrested the harmless 17-man TA picket line, beat a black newsman, made 36 arrests, and produced a massive series of confrontations, thus renewing campus militance. Once again strike leaders helped cool out the crisis, and though the crowds remained large, peace prevailed. Then the police moved against the crowd and publicly beat a black strike leader and set off the whole battle once again. From there on, events escalated rapidly, until Friday, Feb. 21, following the terrific riot of the day before. It was once again the TWLF, not the police, who restored the peace.

These conclusions, based on the timing of events, are overwhelmingly supported by an enterprising interview study of student opinion conducted by Timothy W. Armistead.[12] The study was based on a brief questionnaire distributed among the spectators in Sproul Plaza on Feb. 19 and 20. The data show that the presence of police and their behavior was producing anger and growing support for the strike among *non-striking* students. 64 per cent of the non-striking students who responded said they now regarded the police as the primary issue; 61 per cent said they would not be present if the police were not there. Indeed, 20 per cent reported growing commitment to the strikers cause, even though they had not become more sympathetic to TWLF demands, simply in response to police violence. One student wrote that earlier in the strike his glasses had been broken by a striker. But now he supported the strike. Many others described similar conversions. All indicted the police.

Whatever one feels about the merits of student protest, and despite the fact that one may abhor student violence whether or not it follows aggressive police actions, it is obvious that the use of the police did not restore order or tranquility. The declaration of emergency turned the campus into an armed camp, but it resulted in chaos, not order. On pragmatic grounds the tactic of police repression of student dissent is a dismal and dangerous failure.

Not only did police action spread support for the strike until large numbers of students became involved, leading to violence, injuries, and destruction; it had a profound impact on student attitudes. The number of students who have surrendered all hope in the ability of our institutions to reform themselves and who have turned to radical solutions doubled and redoubled during the confrontations with police. It is becoming increasingly common to hear students say that it takes a faceful of tear gas or a bash on the head in order to see the truth about our society, to see that it is rotten and repressive and must be torn down. For those of us who still believe that the only real hope for humane institutions is orderly reform, the police are allies we can ill afford.

Before this case against the use of police can be rested, an important counter-argument must be examined. After all, didn't the students intentionally engage in vandalism and violence in order to force a police confrontation? And can the University just sit back and ignore these blatant acts? Consequently, was there any alternative to calling in the police to quell the violence?

Prior events on the campus provide some basis for judging the worth of this argument. As registration began for the fall quarter (1968), the Regents provoked campus opinion and violated the norms of academic freedom by moving to prevent Black Panther leader and distinguished author Eldridge Cleaver (now a fugitive) from giving 10 lectures to a course organized under an experimental program of student-initiated classes. The eventual action of the Regents was to deny university credit for the class. A student protest aimed at securing credit began and more than 100 students, most of whom were enrolled in the course, were arrested after a few-hour sit-in. The students offered no resistance. The next day the campus braced for a massive outburst of sympathy. But the noon rally in Sproul Plaza was dominated by radicals and street people, who talked of violence and revolution, led a march around the campus, perpetrated some vandalism and then barricaded themselves in Moses Hall, where they did considerable damage. When police moved in, many radicals who had spoken of a pitched-battle fled, and 72 were arrested. Their actions destroyed all possibility of continuing the protest. The students would not support wanton destruction and violence.

Similarly, the intermittent talk of violence by the TWLF alienated mass student support. Had they pursued such a course they would quickly have isolated themselves from the mass of students to such an extent that legal sanctions could have been used against them with student approval. Of course, had they not continued they would only have been a peaceful protest, certainly tolerable on the campus. But, probably because they had no operating room due to pressures from the Governor and the Regents, the administration brought in the police early and whatever vandalism or violence could be laid to TWLF was invariably counter-balanced by evidence of police misbehavior and abuse. Furthermore, there was no recognition of the fact that much stone-throwing and window-breaking was not perpetrated by TWLF, but by juveniles and assorted "crazies" who lurked on the fringes of the action. Thus, student opinion was outraged by arrests of TWLF leaders and pickets who obviously had not committed the misdeeds. It became a common complaint among students that some kid would come up behind the demonstrators, throw a rock over them at the cops and run, and then the police would arrest and/or beat up someone from the front of the crowd.

Whatever abuses were committed by the TWLF, they were always mitigated and even over-ridden in the eyes of students by counter-abuses by the administration and the police. It is a moot point whether the TWLF would have engaged in excesses that would have isolated them from the campus community. But in point of fact the administration was unable to wait for such a moment. Instead, the police continued to move in, and gatherings were continually declared illegal and arrests made. And the inevitable beatings. Whatever else one can say, these were tactics bound to produce a massive student revolt.

Reaping the Whirlwind

Anyone who sees the main lessons of this report as bearing on counter-insurgency tactics for more effectively suppressing student protest has not understood it and does not understand the essential features of academic institutions.

Obviously, there are some implicit lessons here for more effective use of the police, if their presence is unavoidable: no provocative deployment; no massive shows of force; no marching into demonstrations to serve arrest warrants; no dispersal of non-violent crowds—the protection and orderly management of crowds, not their destruction; and the use of faculty and students as official observers to inhibit police violence. All these suggestions follow from the evidence and could be discussed at length. *But these proposals miss the real issues.*

The use of repressive power, even if it could be made effective, is a Pyrrhic approach which threatens the integrity of academic institutions. It may be feasible to maintain institutions such as prisons on the basis of massive coercion, but to envision an academic institution maintained by bayonets, police lines and the suspension of campus gatherings is not merely perverse, it is hopelessly self-defeating. Such an institution cannot in principle or in practice be called academic.

Of necessity, institutions devoted to ideas, reflection, and the pursuit of understanding are based precariously on consent, rational procedures, and mutual good faith. Such a system of relationships and procedures is necessarily aborted by repressive action. Moreover, even normal educational activities become impractical, as well as improper, in an atmosphere of confrontation, impending violence, and massive police presence. For many members of academic communities, such conditions are themselves regarded as urgent educational matters requiring the suspension of normal instruction. Indeed, the simple fact that some members of an academic institution feel they must risk confrontations with the police in order to get a hearing of their grievances testifies that the internal arrangements of that institution, vis-a-vis basic academic values, are ossified or badly deformed.

This is hardly to suggest that the *police function* is incompatible with campus life. Rape, burglary, vandalism and the like are properly a police problem on campus as well as off. Similarly, student activity which represents a serious threat to the integrity and safety of the campus is properly a police problem. But when issues, rather than acts, are the main basis of conflict it becomes urgent that university administrators recognize that what is at stake is the ability of the institution to govern itself and keep faith with its basic values. Sometimes, for the sake of these larger interests, some risks must be taken and some inconvenience and even abuses accepted.

Unfortunately, partly as a result of the general political climate, university administrators are often unable or unwilling to run any risks for the sake of their institutions. But broken windows, blocked gates, picket lines, and even a burned building or two in themselves pose little internal threat to the existence and character of academic institutions. As has historically always been the case in America, the real threats to higher education lie in repression, usually by off-campus forces that want to "save" the colleges from Darwinism, Socialism, sexual immorality, drugs, or protest.

Repression remains the popular antidote despite its obvious practical failure and institutional dangers. Public opinion polls show virtual public unanimity behind policies to get tough with dissident students and faculties.[13] Politicians exploit these sentiments— legislative hoppers are clogged with bills proposing a mad variety of measures to increase the scope of police power and repression. Some have proposed fencing campuses and admitting only properly "cleared" students through guarded check-points. Others speak without qualm of putting several armed National Guardsmen in every classroom if that's what it would take to stamp out protest. A Southern college president recently told the press that he would keep his campus open, even if he had to expel every student.

With the devastating insight of the young, students have been telling us the real issues all along. Clearly the first step is: "Cops Off Campus!"

Footnotes

[1] Quoted in *Newsweek*, Feb. 24, 1969, p. 23.

[2] "Patterns of Behavior In Police and Citizen Transactions."

[3] Quoted in the *New York Post*, Nov. 12, 1968, p. 53.

[4] *Ibid.*

[5] A. James Reichley, "The Way to Cool the Police Rebellion," *Fortune*, Dec. 1968, p. 111.

[6] Oct. 4, 1968, p. 26.

[7] April, 1965, p. 10.

[8] The interviews were conducted by Sam McCormick, former Los Angeles policeman, for the Center for the Study of Law and Society, University of California, Berkeley.

[9] Jerome H. Skolnick, *Justice Without Trial: Law Enforcement in Democratic Society*, New York: John Wiley & Sons, Inc., 1966.

[10] *Mr. Love and Justice*, London: New English Library, 1962, as quoted in *Ibid.*, p. 48.

[11] Jan., 1968.

[12] "Police on Campus and the Evolution of Personal Commitment: A Survey of Non-strikers' Attitudes During a Berkeley Confrontation," forthcoming.

[13] See, for example, the results of the California Poll published in the *San Francisco Chronicle*, Mar. 4, 1969, p. 6.

Two

The Spokesmen:

A Spectrum of Opinion

The articles in this section are position papers: strong, often polemical, arguments for a particular point of view. They are mainly the work of men who have not only pondered their views, but who have acted on them. Represented here are the competing ideologies which *are* a primary manifestation of the crisis in higher education.

In choosing these authors we tried to cover a diversity of points on the political spectrum. Certainly, in terms of range, we have been successful. Yet, we would have been even more pleased had more of our conservative and more of our black writers been able to respond. As it stands, the white and left perspectives predominate. Nonetheless, the conservatives are favored by two excellent spokesmen, Dr. Max Rafferty, Superintendent of Public Instruction for the State of California, and Dr. S. I. Hayakawa, acting President of San Francisco State College. The black militants are represented by the articulate statements of Professor Nathan Hare, former head of the Black Studies Department at San Francisco State, and Stokeley Carmichael and Charles V. Hamilton. Black moderates are represented by Roy Wilkins, Executive Director of the NAACP, and Melvin Posey, a University of California graduate student active in the affairs of both the BSU and NAACP. Todd Gitlin, Robert Chrisman, Bill Barlow and Peter Shapiro represent the left position of the continuum.

The importance of these works is not derived from a veridical appraisal of student crisis, but from the fact that the ideas they embody are the ideas that are being hurled against each other in the struggle for power in higher education.

Several of the articles dealing with Black Power do not relate directly to specific crises, or even to the general issue of student dissent, but they are critical for an understanding of what Black Power rhetoric—which has been much distorted in the popular press—really means.

Education in Ferment*

S. I. Hayakawa

I am completely overwhelmed with the warmth of your welcome. I don't know what I have done to deserve it, but I must have done something, and I am trying to review in my mind what it could have been and why it is so important.

What I am learning from your responses and the response of many other people to my actions at San Francisco State College is that higher education is far more important than I had ever imagined. You know, many of us go into college professorships in order to lead a tranquil and blameless life; however, I find that that life is not tranquil, and that I am always blamed for everything.

So many of the important changes of our culture come from the universities. The great scientific work being done at Berkeley and Stanford and UCLA and USC and MIT and CalTech—all these things are changing the face of the world. In the social sciences and the humanities, the moral and social problems of our times are argued, heatedly debated, researched; so that in a sense the colleges and universities are the testing grounds for new ideas as the world changes. And perhaps . . . the central importance of the universities to our time (perhaps they are as important to our time as the medieval church was to the middle ages) is why these conflicts concern everybody so very, very much. When they see great institutions like Columbia University and Berkeley (San Francisco State College doesn't belong in quite the same league with them) . . . , when they see institutions like these being threatened by internal disorder, faculty disaffection, violence, all sorts of things

---

Editors' Note: The following speech was presented to the Commonwealth Club of San Francisco in January, 1969. After being introduced to the Club, Dr. Hayakawa received several minutes of sustained applause.

The Editors have made several modifications in the speech, in accordance with Dr. Hayakawa's instructions, and it therefore is slightly different from his presentation to the Club.

that seem to have no place whatsoever on a college campus, they become deeply concerned.

How I happened to become president was a curious story. I got to agonizing about this whole question of disorder on campuses in 1964 with the FSM movement in Berkeley. I simply *agonized* over it, and I have agonized over every such event ever since, all the way from Berkeley to Oshkosh State College in Wisconsin. And I suppose it is because I had agonized about it vocally to Dr. Dumke at one time or other, and wrote him memoranda on what I thought about it, that suddenly I found myself pinned with the job last November. I just felt a moral compulsion to accept.

Everyone has asked me at one time or other: "What's it all about? Why is there this tremendous uproar?" We are approaching the end of twelve continuous weeks of turmoil at San Francisco State College. What's it all about?

It seems to me that there is a systematic plan to bring this college to a halt, as there was to bring Berkeley to a halt or Columbia to a halt, as a prelude for an attack on all higher education. I think that the higher educational system is definitely threatened by a planned attack. It isn't just student disaffection. Of course there is discontent, and of course there is an enormous amount of social change that lead to frictions that lead in turn to impatience for rapid adjustments. But behind all this I think that there definitely is a plan to bring to a halt, or to destroy, one of the nerve centers of our culture, namely the universities.

Why do I say this? Well, I say this because so many of the arguments people have about what's going on at the college revolve around some basic inaccuracies; that is, people have been seeing all our troubles in an erroneous light, and I think people have been at some pains to see to it that the problems are seen in that erroneous light. That is, a lot of people think that the current disorders have to do with racial conflict, and the strikers and their supporters say that they are fighting in order to get a Black Studies Program or an ethnic studies program and things like that. Now, the truth is that we had 22 black studies courses in operation at the beginning of this semester (Fall, 1968). And the Trustees, months ago, approved plans for a Black Studies Program and the details of this curriculum were all but completed before the strike began November 6th. And on December 6th, a month later, I had the pleasure to announce the final approval by the Council of Deans of a Black Studies Department leading to a degree with a possibility of a major in that subject, appointing a head to that Department and enabling the whole thing to be operative. And still the disturbances went on, on the part of both students and faculty, as if nothing had been done. And almost two months after December 6th, when the official statement went out, people were still walking up and down saying that Black Studies must be implemented.

What's holding it up? Nothing but the strike itself. Nothing but the determination of those who, knowing that the demands have been met, still continue to act as if they had not been met in order to continue the disturbance. Our other ethnic minorities in the loosely organized "Third World" say they are fighting for their specialized programs. But you know, some of the Third World people are being paid at San Francisco State College to develop new programs in that area and they have not yet submitted any practical proposal. All this has been authorized, personnel have been appointed to research this matter; there is hardly a piece of paper to show for it yet, but still they demand an ethnic studies program, which no one has as yet outlined.

And so what's behind all this? It seems to me that the truth was revealed the first day of the strike by Black students and faculty leaders, copied shortly after by . . . the "Third World" leaders. The entire episode was an attempt, it seems to me, to seize power. By seizing power I mean ignoring the ballot box and the advocacy of mob rule. Mob rule is the old-fashioned name for what is now called "Participatory democracy" in some left-wing circles.

We saw the nature of the struggle and the caliber of most of their leaders yesterday, when I believe 449—or is it now 483—people were arrested on our campus for deliberately staging an unlawful rally and then refusing to accept college and police orders to disperse; so they all got busted. The leaders deliberately invited the administration to call the police. That action on the part of the police to surround them and arrest them, by the way, was done with such skill and finesse, it was an amazing and beautiful thing to see. And no purpose was served by that huge demonstration yesterday other than this: to attempt to create enough disorder so I would take alarm and announce the campus closed, which I did not. Additionally, it interfered, in the last week before examinations, with the studying and the reading of thousands of students who wanted to go to classes to complete their courses and get their credit for the semester's work.

The groups of revolutionaries have been in the Library messing up the books, throwing them around, putting them in the wrong shelves, throwing them on the floor, taking them out, and returning them again in great batches, completely confusing our library system and preventing other people from working. What purpose is served by this kind of thing other than revolution? And I say, in all seriousness, the important issue here is *not* racial discrimination, is *not* the problem of the disadvantaged minorities, because according to these revolutionaries, it seems to me, they want to keep the minorities as disadvantaged as possible so that there will be more grounds on which to argue for revolution.

So after twelve weeks now, we see the radical student groups no larger than they were when they started, and so the revolution has not been very successful. Occasionally we see small visiting groups from other campuses present at San Francisco State College to get their initiation in revolutionary activities: pinheads from Sonoma State, knuckleheads from San Jose, and savages from Berkeley. And we also see a group of faculty members hitchhiking to the student-initiated turmoil to press their selfish demands for more money, less work, and free parking, for God's sake. I will come back to that matter of less work a little later on.

Even in the midst of this crisis, it seems to me that the future doesn't look too bad. The faculty strike problem is now in the hands of the Trustees and the courts; impatient and irate students and parents are in the wings to demand from individual teachers an accounting of their commitment to fulfill their teaching contracts, and we find the student radicals and faculty militants backed into a situation where they now know they cannot succeed. And meanwhile, behind the scenes, the law is moving steadily to deal with violators, and we, in the Administration, are planning for the kind of action we envisage as necessary to maintain the instructional process. And as a result of the dedication of our Deans and the vast majority of our professors to their tasks, we will start the second semester on February 17th, somewhat handicapped to be sure, but we are going to start it, and we are going to have a very fine swinging college going again starting with the second [Spring] semester.

There may be some real differences in how we operate next semester. We are still weighing all this, but we are going to get started and we are *not* going to be stopped. One student told me the other day that she is due to get her bachelor's degree in June this year, and she is going to continue to come to class if she is the last student there, and I assured her that we would keep the college open for her if she *were* the last student there.

The one important thing, above all, that the revolutionaries want is the shutting down of the college. That's why I get messages every day, practically: "Look at the bloodshed, look at the turmoil, look at the terrorism, look at the condition of the campus, people can't study in an atmosphere like this, close down the college for God's sake, close it down!!" I don't fall for it. I am not closing it down.

But up to this point I have only talked about necessary actions in the face of crisis. I want to look ahead a little bit to what I would hope San Francisco State College would ultimately be. In order to explain that, I guess I have to say something about my own education and therefore about my own sympathies and prejudices.

Many years ago, in fact before the San Francisco earthquake, my father was a young immigrant boy in this city, about eighteen years old, working in the kitchen of the father or grandfather of some of you around here. And when he first visited me in Mill Valley a few years ago, he looked at my house with great pride and said that this was the kind of house he used to enter through the servants' quarters. I grew up during my high school years in Winnipeg and I went to college at the University of Manitoba, a tax-supported college that offered a college education to people who otherwise could not have been able to afford it. A college very, very much like San Francisco State College, a "streetcar college."

The idea of a streetcar college that makes education available to those who otherwise could not afford it has always fascinated me and has always engaged my sympathies. After I got my PhD, the first teaching job that I had was in the University of Wisconsin Extension Division. This was during the depression years. And the University of Wisconsin and the legislature of that state, in its wisdom, decided during the depression, when so many young people were unemployed, to extend the University into places where it had never been before. So I taught with the first wave of the Extension Division teachers at the University of Wisconsin's new centers in Wausau, Merrill, Waupaka, Rheinlander, Two Rivers, and all sorts of ungodly places, through the winters of the late 1930's. And there I learned what it meant to take a University away from its tree-lined campus at Madison, Wisconsin, into small town public libraries, into spare meeting rooms in the back of fire halls, etc., to teach history, geography, freshman composition, and the like. The idea that you would take the University out to the people excited me very, very much at that time, and it still does.

And so, in a sense, this is what attracted me about San Francisco State College from the very beginning when it was located on its old campus on Laguna, near the Mint. This was a college in the heart of a city, reaching out directly to the people who needed it—the children of recent immigrants, the children of the working class, the children of the rising middle classes. The college and the education it provided was the thing that made possible social mobility, the heart of the American experience. I was a little regretful when we moved out to the Lake Merced campus because I felt we were getting away from the city, that we were getting too suburban. However, life at the Lake Merced campus was pretty good anyway. But at the same time as I understand the advantages we have out there, I also have dreamed of the possibility that maybe San Francisco State College could also extend itself back again into the heart of the city. And I have also thought of this because we have many, many people on our faculty in all of our departments, in education, sociology, psychology, literature, in nursing and home economics, who are deeply interested in the problems of urban people. I have often wondered if it wouldn't be a wonderful thing if we could extend our campus into Hunter's Point, into the Mission, into the Fillmore, into Chinatown, and have additional extension centers all over town. Start out with little store-front extension universities, like store-front churches, if necessary, and build bigger centers later on. But is it not possible to do what we used to do at the University of Wisconsin Extension and just move out into the places where they have never had a university before? As you all know, there is an enormous increase in the rate of Chinese immigration into this city as the result of recent changes in the immigration laws. Should we not be serving that Chinese community better than we now are? Should we not be in the Fillmore helping the small business man and many Negro business men and Mexican-American business men in the Mission district, who don't have the kind of business administration background that they often need? And shouldn't we be building schools of business administration in various parts of the city to help the small business man? Should we not be out in the community among the Mexican-Americans, among the Central Americans and South Americans of whom there are very large numbers in the city? Should we not be taking the college and its opportunities to people, not just the young people, but to adults? One of the most exciting things about San Francisco State College is its large adult population: the women who married before they completed their education, now have a couple of children growing up and have a little time to take extra courses; the young men, sometimes middle-aged men, who made a discovery as they grew to maturity that they are in the wrong line of business and would like to trade their present occupation for something else. One of the very exciting things about teaching at San Francisco State College is, as a matter of fact, the number of mature men, of over thirty, who will shake hands with you at the end of the semester and say I want to thank you, I have just quit my job and I have taken on an entirely different line of work. And this process of self-discovery in mature people is another of the processes that go on in adult education.

I think about the University of Wisconsin at Milwaukee now where the Library is open 24 hours a day to meet the needs of an urban population, because people work at different hours of the day and night in a big city like this. Why shouldn't we have an extension center and a University library, a college level library, that can serve all these people who want to study?

You know, I have all sorts of day dreams. I have an idea of taking over, if we can, somehow—I don't know how you go about these things, because I have never been a college president before—I want to know if we can get Fort Mason or the old Mint, or something like that. I don't know how you grab these things, anyway, and convert one of them into a great big extension center.

Now take the matter of the old Mint. I learned that it would take about $1,300,000.00 to completely renovate it and make it a usable building. Wouldn't it be terrific to have that as the San Francisco State College extension center? How many working people would be able to use that, day and night, as a source of additional training and inspiration. In other words, I want to think of a college such as San Francisco State, not as a great prestige University like the University of California at Berkeley, with heavy requirements on all its faculties for research and publication. I want to think of San Francisco State College as it properly belongs between the junior colleges with whom we should be working and the universities, a place mainly for teaching, and much teaching at the University level, but still with close, close contact at the junior college or community college level.

And this is why I have little patience with a nine-hour teaching load which the American Federation of Teachers is demanding. I think we should continue to have our twelve-hour teaching load. A nine-hour teaching load is entirely appropriate for Berkeley, but not appropriate for us. As a matter of fact, a twelve-hour teaching load is one of the nicest, softest jobs on earth. And they say, you know, that it takes three hours of out-of-class time for each hour of lecture, and it is sometimes true, but it is sometimes true, also, that you go over your own notes in ten minutes and get into the classroom and you're all set.

But I would like San Francisco State College to dedicate itself to *teaching* and to relate itself profoundly to the community around us. I am happy to hear from Mr. Yong Han San (formerly Consul-General of the Republic of Korea, from 1949 to 1960, and now a naturalized American citizen): "I am happy to inform you that over fifty Korean students at San Francisco State College are not participating in the mis-named revolutionary organization, the 'Third World Liberation Front.' These Korean students came from Korea to receive Western education in all lines of subjects at great expense to be used in Korea. Their parents sacrificed greatly in financing them to get an education in America, but these anarchist trouble-makers and fake professors—that is, they are fake because they are striking and agitating—are greatly hindering their education."

Well, I would like to say to Mr. Yong and I would like to say to everyone else who is concerned about students and young people at San Francisco State College that I am determined that San Francisco State College shall continue to perform its function. We shall also continue to perform the very, very important function of being an advisory group to the Secondary Education System in the Republic of Liberia, which is one of our great projects. So, with services to Korea and the Philippines on the one hand, and to Liberia on the other, and to all the people of San Francisco and people of the United States on the other hand, we are intimately connected with the daily work, the daily careers, of the masses of the people of America.

Now, a lot of people say that the trouble with the State Universities is the Trustees—they are so reactionary, conservative, routine-minded, and so on, that they are terribly tight with the money, and therefore that's why we have all our problems. I can't entirely believe that. I am sure that there are certainly very reactionary and hide-bound people among our Trustees but that's not the problem; it seems to me the central problem, and I think it is a problem for Berkeley no less than for us, is that the State Colleges and the Universities must regain the confidence of the taxpayer by demonstrating that they are able to run themselves. And once we have earned that confidence, by showing that we can operate the schools, I am sure that the public, not only the taxpayers but the business community of San Francisco and in the State of California, will be glad to be far more generous to us than they have been. Because, I am sure the business community understands this even better than I, that investment in people is the most important investment you can make, because the future of California rests upon the enlightenment and the education, the talents and the skills, in the people of the next generation.

So to ask for this investment in people is a very, very simple thing to ask. And more and more research nowadays shows that wherever the educational level is high, wherever the level of skill and talent is high, there the whole level of the culture is very high and the culture manifests itself in its best forms in those situations.

Now, since colleges are an important source of social change, I have asked that if we do gain the public's confidence at San Francisco State College and elsewhere, I would hope that the warm welcome that you have extended to me today, the attention with which you are listening to me, can be translated from applause into hard financial help for our colleges. I would like you to help me to get that old Mint building and refurbish it. I would like to have the support of the business community in researching the needs of this city so that we can expand our educational services wherever they are most needed, with the advice of business, of industry, of banking and investment, and the advice of our public school system and our adult education systems. Where can we be of the most help to the entire community? How can you get involved in solving the problems of this great city? I think that it is important to our community to expand the services of San Francisco State College all over the San Francisco Bay Area. It is certainly as important to do that as it is to replace Candlestick Park.

I would like to conclude with a little comment on academic freedom. Academic freedom has been a term that has been much abused lately to take advantage of freedom, to destroy the colleges. I do not think academic freedom includes the right to burn down Wheeler Auditorium [a recently gutted building at Berkeley] —nowadays, amnesty for all wrong-doers, etc., etc. I want to emphasize right now the idea that academic freedom should put its emphasis on the academic. It doesn't mean total freedom for action, but it does mean total freedom of ideas.

I would like San Francisco State College (and I am sure Dr. Hitch [President of the University of California] agrees with me) and the University of California to be places where all kinds of ideas can be energetically debated, argued about back and forth, struggled over, as ideas. But the University is not a staging area for revolution. The University is not itself an organization to induce social change except through education itself, but it is a place where social change can be contemplated, so that when we go out of the University into labor unions, into churches, into businesses, into government and so on, we can produce the social changes we dreamed about and argued about in the Universities. That is what academic freedom is all about.

So when I think about academic freedom every now and then I have a day dream in which I have a seminar with Joan Baez and David Harris, her husband, at one end of the table with General Westmoreland at the other, talking about non-violence and exposing all the students who thought they might be interested in the subject.

In other words, the College stands ready for change, experimentation, searching into the future, preparing our students if possible not for the careers of yesterday, but for the careers of tomorrow. With your help, Gentlemen, I hope we can do it.

Thank you very much.

*Questions from Members of the
Commonwealth Club to
Dr. S.I. Hayakawa after His Speech*

QUESTION: How many students are involved in the disruptive movement; about what percentage of the SFSC registrants are participants?

ANSWER: That's rather hard to answer. Supposing we say that we have 18,000 students. If you said 10% were involved, that would be 1,800, wouldn't it? Well, that's pretty high. I would say about 5% at most. We arrested an awful lot of them yesterday—it amounted to 483—and that took care of a lot of them.

QUESTION: We have a number of questions on the proposal for a black studies department. Assume that the black studies department were established, what is the availability of scholars qualified to administer such a department and teach its courses at college and University levels?

ANSWER: To what degree are there scholars available to teach black studies at college and University levels? I think that the supply is adequate for our modest program. I saw a preliminary outline—at least one of the Deans looked over a preliminary outline—of the availability of people in this area and he said that he was satisfied that the people were competent and able to do this. Now if every college in the country started to give a black studies program, the supply might run out, but we're fairly ahead of the parade on this.

QUESTION: Why should a college offer black culture courses at all? Now there are none in Japanese and Italian and we are all Americans. Isn't American history and culture good enough?

ANSWER: This leads to the heart of the problem. Those of us who are of descent other than African come from intact cultures; that is, the French, the Swedes, the English, the Irish, the Japanese and the Chinese have a historical background and they also have societies here like the Hibernian Society, the Chinese Family Associations, the German choirs, and all sorts of things to keep alive some sense of the culture they came from. So the child may rebel against this culture, but he knows he comes from a culture, whereas, the American Negro, with his immediate heritage of slavery, had his background culture completely destroyed and his memory of it erased through the experience of 300 years of the brainwashing of slavery. He was told he was inferior, meant only to be a slave, until finally many of them really believed it.

One of the great results of the civil rights revolution is the black man's acceptance of himself as a full human being. He is getting over his concept that he is inferior and intended by God to be a slave. And therefore, he wants to know what his roots are, what he has contributed to the building of this country. You will notice that our ordinary textbooks do not make any great thing of how much the Negros have contributed to the building of this country. They also want to know something about their ancestral backgrounds. In fact, what the American Negro wants is a sense of cultural identity, of racial identity, which all the rest of us have but of which, through historical circumstance, the black man was deprived. And I think it will make him a better citizen to have this kind of background because the African culture and the American Negro culture are far richer than most of us know. The knowledge of this will enable the Black man to hold his head up in pride along with the rest of us, and this will make him a better citizen. So I feel very much that there should be some kind of Black Studies program.

QUESTION: Please itemize the demands that the BSU has made that have been met and comment on your attitude regarding these demands.

ANSWER: I am not going to itemize the demands. Some of them have to do with simple matters of personnel which are so petty that we don't need to go into them, and some demands are simply redundant. When you knock out some of the redundant ones, I think the number of demands are reduced down to eleven or twelve. But there are certain things that have not been met, and one I should like to comment on is the indiscriminate admission of all members of minority groups [a comment on one of the BSU demands] that may apply for admission into the College. This I shall resist.

Before I became President, under an experimental program, 428 under-qualified students were authorized to be admitted. Three hundred were actually admitted and 128 more can therefore be admitted. This is, frankly, an experimental program. We do not know yet the results of that experiment. It may be disastrous, or it may be a very good thing. But, every time we admit an under-qualified student with the limited space we have, we have to keep out someone who really worked hard through high school to qualify himself for admission at San Francisco State, and it is totally unfair to keep out those who have tried very hard to get into San Francisco State and to keep them out in favor of those who didn't make the grade.

Now there is, however, an entire community college or junior college system in which admission standards are deliberately kept low so that anyone can get a chance to prove himself able to take on college work. The junior colleges are all more experienced and better staffed than we are to take on the work of preparing the under-qualified student for upper level college work. Therefore, if there should be pressure for unlimited enrollment at all, more opportunities for this should be generated in the junior colleges, and I think more money and the necessary resources should be allotted to the junior colleges if this demand continues. That's where the pressure should be.

QUESTION: How long ago was the request for Afro-American courses first made? I have been told that requests were made three years ago and present problems are the result of no action taken on the original requests. I would like to have your comments.

ANSWER: I don't know, since I was not in the Administration, exactly how long ago the requests were first made. I do know that college bureaucracies, like other bureaucracies, are not very prompt to act. I also know something else, that not only the colleges are slow to change, but that when a whole new body of studies is proposed, a good deal of arguing and discussion and exploration is necessary. Notice, as I have said earlier in my remarks, that there were twenty-two courses in Black studies that were already in operation this fall. These are all partial answers to this question. Instead of having the whole Black Studies Department right away, as soon as it was asked for, we tried out these courses in various departments to see if they were viable, to see if they had enough intellectual content to justify themselves and a separate department. Now that they have been going for some time, maybe we can unite all these separate courses in psychology, literature, sociology, etc., and put them all together in one department. It seems to me that the progress that has been made has been quite remarkably fast, all things considered.

You see, I came to San Francisco State College in 1955; they wanted me to set up a Semantics curriculum, and twelve years later it still doesn't exist.

QUESTION: How about a break in the serious aspect of your talk? I am quite interested in your personal welfare. Do you have a rating in Judo?

ANSWER: I don't know any of the Japanese martial arts except the use of chopsticks.

QUESTION: How do Governor Reagan and the Trustees justify their refusal to negotiate with the teachers and students?

ANSWER: The questioner ought to ask *them*. Well, there is a tricky thing about the word "negotiate," to start with. Actually, discussions have been going on with various teachers, when you say the teachers, you know, there are many, many groups of teachers. There is the American Federation of Teachers which is on strike, but there is also the Association of California State College Professors, the Association of University Professors, the California State Employees Association, and so on. Then when you say negotiate with students, well you try very hard to negotiate with the students. I have tried. All sorts of discussions have been going on in all sorts of directions. And I think that one of the things we are running up against is, when you say "Why don't we negotiate with them?"—what do you do when they come to you and say, "These are non-negotiable demands."? What I have tried to do myself is state a position about the non-negotiable demands, and then to stand back and wait for a response. What can you do when they say they're "non-negotiable"? So some of the time I have been standing pat and waiting for a response from others, and sometimes intermediators have induced some response here and there, but the log jam isn't quite broken yet.

QUESTION: What is the future for Professor Hare after his arrest yesterday?

ANSWER: I don't know. That is in the hands of the courts now, isn't it?

QUESTION: Will you enforce the law according to which a five day absence of teachers means resignation?

ANSWER: There is not a question of enforcing it. We are in the middle of discussing this. We are in the middle of negotiations about this, and in the middle of explanations about it from the State Comptrollers' Office, and so on. You know, I better not comment on this at the moment. We are also in the middle of fact-finding as to whom these rules apply. So I am just not prepared to comment. Except to say this much: That when you have people as free in their movements as college professors are—many of them with classes only on Tuesday and Thursday, or Monday, Wednesday, Friday, some of them with field-trips arranged to various places or to museums or social service agencies or schools—and so on, and with the assumption of professionalism so that there is no time clock to punch to see that they have done their work regularly, we assume that they all do it. With that kind of relaxed situation, with some people in ordinary times holding their evening creative writing sessions, for example in their own homes, we have no ready way of quickly gathering the data to say that A, B, and C were absent for five days, and D, E, and F were not. And so just the sheer mechanism of finding out who was working and who was not, is simply terribly complicated, and we are still in the middle of it.

QUESTION: Would you favor amnesty for those arrested for campus violence if this were the sole remaining issue, to resolve the existing dispute?

ANSWER: I doubt it. I would like to comment on this point because it involves, for me, a very important moral issue. I think that we all have the right to dissent. I think that if we find a law morally objectionable enough so that we want to disobey it—in protest against that law, in order to test it in the courts or something—I think that we all have a moral obligation to disobey that law, and to test it in the courts. But if we do, we must expect to be punished under the law as it now exists, and if we are punished, we suffer martyrdom, and that martyrdom itself is communication to the rest of the community that this is an unjust law—because a nice guy like me is going to jail. This is the technique used by Martin Luther King, Gandhi and other great moralists.

Now to flout a regulation or a law in order to make a moral assertion, and then to say "I am not to be punished because I was being so moral,"—this is martyrdom on the cheap, and I despise it. That is why I say: Let's pay the consequences, let's face up to the consequences of what we do; this is the essence of moral responsibility. Furthermore, amnesty is not consistent with the other demands so often made by the student strikers: "due process, due process." If you have due process, you can't have amnesty.

QUESTION: I have heard it said that the real purpose of the strikers and those causing the disruption is insurrection, so that even if all of their demands are met, there will be more. Who is behind what appears to be a conspiratorial plan? Will you please comment?

ANSWER: As I said at the beginning, I believe there is a conspiratorial plan. I don't know who is behind it. I am not about to attribute it to a foreign power or anything as melodramatic as that. But I do believe that there is a wide-spread wave of serious disenchantment with all our institutions that actuates a small but very vehement minority of our young people. Berkeley has had a lot of trouble with them. We have had a lot of trouble with them. In some way or other they are really determined to destroy things. I cannot otherwise account for American boys and girls carrying Viet Cong flags in the streets. I cannot otherwise account for their marching down California Street not too long ago crying: "Ho, Ho, Ho Chi Minh!" Why? And the little picture of Che Guevara that they carry and treasure to their bosoms? What's going on? I don't understand. I am not at all sure that they are inspired from abroad. The fact that these young people exist and the fact that they feel this way may be due to some very serious oversights in the way you and I, as the older generation, have structured this culture. Maybe there is something we omitted that should have been there. So therefore, we have to look into ourselves, among other things. But still, the fact does exist that there is a significant number of very vocal, sometimes quite bright young people, who really are hostile to the whole culture as such. And I still don't understand.

QUESTION: Do you believe that your status as acting president will be changed to permanent president? And will you accept this honor?

ANSWER: Sir, I will cross that bridge when I come to it.

Campus Violence: A Fascist Conspiracy

Max Rafferty

Conspiracy, n. A combination of persons for an evil or unlawful purpose.—*The New Century Dictionary*

Yes, we conservatives believe the so-called student activism is a conspiracy. Everything we've read which emanates from the Chicago headquarters of the S.D.S. confirms us in our belief that the ugly violence at San Francisco State is directed and organized by a combination of persons which also directs and organizes such skull-cracking and arson at Berkeley, Northwestern, Columbia, and a score of convulsed campuses in between. As I write this, I have before me an S.D.S. handbook detailing methods of subversion for the faithful, and a letter signed by one Michael Klonsky, National Secretary for the Students for a Democratic Society, in which he describes his national organization as an "enemy of the state."

As for the Black Students Union, the Panthers, the Muslims, and their ilk, everyone who has really paid any attention to these groups puts them in exactly the same category as the Mafia in modern times and the infamous Molly Maguires of my own Irish ancestors prior to the turn of the last century. They thrive on terror, they batten upon fear, and they live by threats and intimidation. I regard them with the same mingling of reprobation and contempt which before their advent I reserved for the Ku Klux Klan, a racist gang which they resemble more than somewhat, incidentally.

What, then, makes student activism worth commenting upon? To me, it is one question, which was asked me the other day by a sober and highly puzzled university student, and which rang all the alarm bells as far as I was concerned:

"How can we really tell just which laws should be obeyed today?"

As the French say, this gave me furiously to think, and put the whole sorry farrago of campus lootings, burnings, and assaults in a much more serious light, at least insofar as I was concerned. Maybe it's because a conservative just naturally respects government by laws and distrusts government by groups or individuals.

What we're confronted with is a mutation of the do-it-yourself craze which began back in the Fifties with carpentry and linoleum-laying. The fad escalated to home-building around the start of the present decade, and now in the Sick Sixties it has spread at last to legislation and policy-making. I sympathize with the fellow who enjoys baking his own bricks down in the cellar, or who installs a fancy bird bath in his own front yard, but I'm beginning to wonder about this "every-man-his-own-Supreme-Court" syndrome exemplified by my innocent campus questioner.

Every time our college students open a newspaper they are regaled not only with four-letter words but also with dime-novel anecdotes of starry-eyed, unwashed Galahads who are currently demonstrating their invincible idealism by smashing windows, assaulting deans, and setting fire to ivied halls of learning, all in the holy name of deeply held personal convictions.

The laws are no good, you see. They're irrelevant. Or the Regents' regulations are oppressive. So we'll make our own personal laws and rules. We'll do it ourselves. So goes the refrain, from San Francisco to Columbia.

I used to tell my classes in American Government that a democratic society can exist only on the premise that the majority is usually right, and that the minority which disagrees has its only recourse in trying to change the majority's mind through logic, reasoning, and persuasion.

In individual instances, of course, this is a gross oversimplification. The majority has been wrong a lot of times in our history. We Americans were domestically wrong a few years back when we overwhelmingly elected Warren G. Harding president. We were internationally wrong a little later when we confused Charles DeGaulle with Joan of Arc. We were meteorologically wrong when we poisoned our air and polluted our water supply.

But still my thesis holds up. Over the long haul, a democratic society simply has to operate on the principle that the majority is right, if only because the alternative principle is that the majority is wrong. And this is precisely the premise which every Fascist elite in history has adopted in justifying its rise to power.

Almost weekly, different student delegations visit me in my Sacramento office. Oddly enough, they seem little concerned with curriculum changes, racial discrimination, absentee professors, impersonal administrators, and the like. Oh, these may be the headline issues of the moment, but they're actually just flotsam and jetsam on the underlying sea of student discontent. What the activists really want is power. Power to control policy. Power to spend tax money. Power to hire and fire professors.

So I ask them two pertinent questions:

(1) "In any tax-supported institution belonging to the people, who should set policy for that institution?"

The immediate unthinking answer I always get is: "Those who attend the institution."

But this thesis will withstand only about thirty seconds of logical analysis. If a public institution should indeed be turned over to its inmates, then the orphans should operate the orphanage, the insane should set policy for the asylum, the convicts should run the penitentiary, and the patients should govern the hospital.

A tax-supported institution must be controlled by those who pay the taxes. Who else could possibly control it? And this means *ALL* the people of the state, not just a microscopically small minority of students and professors. If certain groups of students want to set up a college of their own, then by all means they should do so. It's a free country. But they should do it with their own money, not with their neighbors' money.

(2) "If the people's institutions should indeed be controlled by the people who support and populate them, then under what circumstances should these institutions have their policies determined by anyone except the representatives of the people themselves?"

And the answer to Question Number 2 just has to be: "None." Under no conceivable concatenation of circumstances can a democratic society permit the policies of its institutions to be determined by anyone except its own legally selected servants, responsible to all the people. Most assuredly, democratic institutions cannot be run by stray groups of students and professors who are responsible to nobody on God's earth except themselves alone.

Certainly students and professors should have an important voice in policy making. After all, they are the ones most directly affected by the policies. But to say that they should be consulted is a far cry from saying that we should turn over the whole shebang to them, lock, stock, and barrel, as the more rabid among them are currently demanding.

These are my two questions. Quite often they are met with blank looks and puzzled head-shakings, mute indictments of the failure of these youngsters' professors to teach them the most important things any citizen needs to know. Then, as punishment, I usually launch into a brief if unsolicited lecture on life in a democratic republic, which goes this way:

"The only glue that holds a society like ours together is mutual respect for the democratically enacted laws which alone stand between us and anarchy. When any one of us unilaterally defies the will of the majority as embodied in the laws and regulations which the representatives of all of us have enacted, then what that individual is really doing is demonstrating his disbelief in and his contempt for the democratic process. And this is Fascism.

"It is widely agreed that the individual's rights must be protected, and I agree. This is the whole reason for the Constitution and the courts. But when it is argued that because a man sincerely believes himself to be right and everyone else is wrong, including the courts, this gives him the right to defy the law, then I must disagree profoundly. Yet this is precisely the claim of the campus activist, black or white. Because he doesn't agree with the will of the people as expressed through their representatives, he has the right to bring the orderly machinery of the institution to a grinding halt, or even to burn the place down.

"Twaddle. In fact, pernicious poppycock.

"This is the argument of some moronic arsonist or a twitchy-eyed bomb-thrower. It is not the argument of a rational adult, or even of a reasonably thoughtful child. It is, however, the argument of a Hitler, as some of us ruefully recall.

"Take the campus draft-card burner, for instance. He may not like the Vietnam War. With my only son on active duty in Vietnam, neither do I, I do assure you. However, I don't happen to like paying my taxes, either. Does the fact that a given law or enacted regulation excites my dislike, my mistrust, even my uncontrollable loathing entitle me to disobey it? Does my conscientious objection to several of the features of the graduated income tax give me the right to refuse to pay it?

"It does not.

"It gives me the right to change it, if I can persuade the majority of my fellow citizens that I am right and the law wrong. It gives me the immemorial right to petition, to remonstrate, to demonstrate peaceably and legally. It emphatically does not give me the right to set my own convictions, no matter how passionately or belligerently held, above the law of the land or the rules of the institution which I am attending as the guest of the taxpayers.

"Remember this: When any man places himself above the law, to that extent exactly he weakens the protection of the law for all his fellow citizens. To that extent also he throws open the gates to wholesale defiance of laws in general, and to the eventual rampancy of crime triumphant.

"And this, students, is where we all came in. About 1,000,000 B.C."

End of lecture.

Lawlessness, collegiate or otherwise, is as old as the human race. Yet today's collegiate activists and their more mature apologists act as if lawlessness were something breathlessly mod. They are equally confused about the true purposes of higher education. Columnist James Reston chortled a few months ago: "Columbia University will never be the same. It went on for a long time operating like a medieval university, concerned primarily with the history of man through the ages, but indifferent to man in the slum outside its gates."

Now just a minute, Mr. R. Let's define our terms, as John Stuart Mill used to say. What is a university, anyway?

My dictionary defines it as "an institution of higher learning of the highest grade, having various schools or faculties concerned with instruction in all or many of the highest branches of learning."

Odd, isn't it? Not one word about the university as a disseminator of black or white power propaganda. Nothing to the effect that a university exists to revolutionize singlehandedly the nation's social, political, or economic order. Not even a hint that a university is supposed to clean up the slums, burn down the Pentagon, or even repeal the Selective Service Act.

No, my dictionary apparently doesn't believe that a university is set up to make young people either contented or rebellious, liberal or conservative, affluent or poverty-stricken.

It's set up to make men learned. Period.

Insofar as the black student is concerned, the university affords him access to the tools of learning, so that in later life he will be equipped to solve his own problems. It enables him to compete successfully with men of other colors. It offers him a way out of the ghetto and the slum. It opens for him all the gates which have been closed to him for so long. So great a promise does it hold for the black student that it is both heart-rending and grimly hilarious to see him smashing and burning down the very institution which alone offers him salvation.

But to Mr. Reston, the university is a cross between urban development and a Che Guevara rally, preoccupied always with the "man in the slum outside the gates."

It isn't, you know. In this country, we have Offices of Economic Opportunity and Job Corps and Urban Redevelopment Boards coming out of our ears. Their mission in life is the "man outside the gates."

The university, on the other hand, concerns itself quite rightly with the man *INSIDE* the gates, with the would-be scholar—black or white, rich or poor—who has come to it for learning. All it should ask of him is that he maintain scholarship standards, permit the institution to meet the intellectual needs of others, and emerge from its halls after four years a more learned man than when he entered them.

This implies, of course, that (a) the university must not be used for any purpose except to provide the individual with the intellectual tools he needs in order to pursue the truth, and (b) in order to do this, the university cannot forever be charging madly off in all directions like Stephen Leacock's famous horseman to solve vast socioeconomic problems which it was never designed to deal with in the first place.

After a man becomes truly educated, he then possesses the mental lumber he needs in order to build either a conservative temple or a liberal pad, wherein he can dwell more or less contentedly all his life long. He is equipped then to become a reformer or a revolutionist or even a Republican, if that is where his informed bent takes him.

But while he is still in school—in other words, while he is still accumulating the relevant data for his next fifty years or so—he should be exposed with beautiful impartiality to all possible points of view on every controversial subject from Keynesian socialism to the origin of the ancient Etruscans.

A university is simply too important to each individual who so often sacrifices to attend it to be turned into a slum clearance project, as Mr. Reston would apparently like it to be. This nation already knows how to eliminate its slums and can do so whenever it really feels like spending the money.

What we don't know very much about is the truth in regard to life and the universe, and how to equip ourselves in order to pursue that elusive Grail. Only higher education can supply the greatly prized and highly specialized equipment needed in the search.

The proper menu of the university, then, is not Mr. Reston's proposed hash and slumgullion. It's nothing less than nectar and ambrosia, the food which alone can make men like gods.

This being so, why all the rioting and the revolting, the burning and the barnyard rhetoric which are turning our campuses into a cross between a boiler factory and a gladiatorial arena? Where is the academic leadership which we have nurtured so long and so expensively, and of which we have a right now to expect much better things than we have been getting of late?

This question leads us gently but inevitably on to the core of the whole mess which is American higher education today: not the activist students at all, but the minority of college professors who have traded their academic birthright for a mess of Maoist pottage, and who are only now beginning to look nervously over their shoulders, the prey to belated and handsomely deserved second thoughts.

If that same higher education mess were not so truly messy, I would be grimly savoring the exquisite dilemma in which the leftist professors find themselves these days. The classic Jacobin dictum that every revolution winds up devouring its own children like old Saturn is being borne out yet once again, this time in the hallowed halls of academe.

Last year's lurch-ins, smash-ups, and lock-outs on so many distracted campuses had several elements in common. One was the abject spinelessness of most of the college presidents. Another was the Neanderthal ferocity of some of the student storm troopers who brought Nazi-type terrorism into our colleges for the first time. But the real common denominator was the covert encouragement given the neo-Nazis by certain professors. It amounted to a surreptitious, lip-smacking, "Go-ahead-and-bust-things-up-and-we'll-stand-behind-you" prodding which some critics have charitably described as irresponsible but which I prefer to call evil. Any teacher who abets violence and lawbreaking on the part of his students is a Pied Piper of destruction, and a coward to boot.

Why a coward? Because his own future isn't in danger. He can always fall back upon academic freedom, his local faculty senate, or the American Association of University Professors if anyone dares to question his role as a corrupter of the young. His students, however, have no protection against the lifelong police records which they acquire as a result of listening to their professor's advice to loot, riot, and trespass.

Recently, I'm happy to say, the professorial chickens have begun coming home to roost. One economics prof last year found himself the target of resignation demands because one of the militant groups didn't appreciate one of his lectures on existing Federal aid programs. His harried superiors duly receipted for the usual veiled threats, bullying bluster, and dictatorial demands for his immediate ouster on penalty of unspeakable consequences. In California quite recently, one dean was actually so intimidated physically that he handed in his enforced resignation. Another was firebombed out of his home with Molotov cocktails. Several professors are under attack by student groups because of their color—in this case, white.

What price academic freedom now, professor?

The cream of the jest is that the beleaguered instructor today is almost certainly a flaming liberal. After all, a conservative economics professor is hard to come by these days. So here we have an academic Dr. Frankenstein who has undoubtedly spent his professional life nurturing and pampering and coddling the fevered ego of a little monster named Student Activism, only to find himself chivvied from pillar to post today by a gruesome grownup golem who makes Boris Karloff look like Harold Stassen by comparison.

The consternation among the professors is growing daily and is pathetic to behold. Or at least it would be if some of us didn't remember how these mixed-up mentors encouraged their present hecklers to rebel for the sake of rebelling, to demonstrate for the sake of demonstrating, to flout authority for the sake of chaos.

A teacher's job is to get enough logic, learning, and factual data into the immature heads of his students so that in later life if they still want to protest they will at least know what they are protesting about. And all the academic senates in Christendom notwithstanding, his job is definitely not to use his students as surrogate sluggers, sit-inners, and saboteurs for his own tweedy, pipe-puffing, comfortable, Olympian self.

Your bully-boys are like all the rest, professor. They strike first at the target closest at hand. And you're it. Better cool 'em, or find yourself at trail's end teaching only what the activists will let you teach.

On the students' part, activism stems from three causes: affluence in the form of parental largesse, exhibitionism on the part of the activist, and permissiveness by the college authorities. Take away any one of these three legs, and the activist stool falls to the ground. Many of the unwashed and hairy rioters, exuding a visible aura of unwashed disinhibition and looking remarkably like so many unmade beds, are present-day counterparts of the old English remittance man. Their families can no longer stand to have them around, so they get monthly allowances on condition that they stay as far away from home as possible.

Most of them are hypocrites. They hanker wistfully and vocally after public martyrdom, but they take care to go first class. Who ever heard of a genuine, 14-karat martyr demanding amnesty, for example? Or flying sobbing to the motherly apron of the ACLU every time a sit-in fails or a slugging victim fights back unexpectedly? Shades of St. Joan!

This hypocrisy was first brought home to me when the Russian rape of Czechoslovakia evoked nothing but thunderous silence from the collegiate champions of peace, love, and egalitarianism. When the Soviet tanks rolled into Prague and splashed the curbs of that suffering city with the blood of its innocent citizens, I waited with baited breath for the Russian embassy to be stoned, the picket lines to march, the placards to sprout. Surely those who had been so frantic in their protests against America's involvement in Vietnam would howl their rage to the four winds and write their indignation on the very heavens in letters of fire at this cynical and brutal act of Russian aggression. At least we Americans were invited into Vietnam by a recognized government. But who the devil invited the Russians into Prague?

As I said, I waited. And I waited. I'm still waiting. But at least in California, nothing at all happened. No demonstrations. No picket lines. Nary a placard. The silence was positively tumultuous. And it was total.

What made the difference? Why, because in the one instance it was poor old Uncle Sam who was involved, and it's the "in" thing for the protesters to foul-mouth their own country. But when holy Communist Mother Russia decides to invade and enslave and torture and kill her defenseless neighbors, then the campus bleeding-hearts piously avert their gaze, cross over gingerly to the other side of the street, and walk rapidly in the other direction, whistling hurriedly as they go.

What damnable hypocrites they are, to be sure!

This is why, as I said in the beginning, I refuse to take this particular sort of white activism seriously. It is made possible only by the jelly-like supineness of college presidents and boards of trustees. If the latter really wanted to blow the whistle on this sort of nonsense, all they need do is instruct their administrators to prepare a list of students who advocate or practice campus violence, and then expel them. Every one of them. Permanently. There is no place in higher education for the incendiary or the plug-ugly. And if necessary, get court orders keeping them from returning to the scene of their crimes.

The same treatment should be meted out to the professors who abet the junior-grade Fascists. Fire them. If some classes have to be closed until some positive-minded instructors can be recruited to take their place, close them. And if a strike is called as a protest, announce that the institution is in business for those who want to use its facilities, and that anyone who doesn't want to attend it will be permanently accommodated.

The sincere student who is honestly confused is another matter, and most of my remarks herein have been aimed at him. So, in another way, is the Black Power activist. He has apparently decided to visit upon the rest of us the sins of our slave-holding great-grandparents, and to make our universities battlegrounds in his current war against men long dead. As a monument to this tour-de-force in futility, the Black Power student is trying to destroy the only institution which can really help him, and which only now has come to be open to him in large numbers for the first time in history.

The Panthers and the Muslims, then, are self-declared enemies of the state. They add nothing to the American dream; they only subtract from it, and try to muck it up. Therefore every effort must be made to subtract them in turn from our campuses, if only to safeguard the lives and safety of the serious students and professors of all races. It would be as stupid to allow such advocates of racist mass murder to infiltrate our student bodies today as it would have been to permit the bundsters of the Third Reich to do so in 1939.

It may be argued that my solutions are negative. So they are, just as a cancer operation is negative, and of necessity. Before the patient's diet and muscle tone can be improved, the tumor must be excised. After the operation, then we can talk about physical therapy and mental reconditioning. So also in our colleges we can devise means of improving communication, opening up new courses of study, and improving curriculum, all badly needed, incidentally.

But first things first.

The activists do not want to improve our institutions. They want to burn them down. The proof is there for all to see, on every writhing, smoking, agonizing campus which the anarchists have hit so far.

Concessions are useless. Amnesties generate more terror. Appeasement escalates violence. Fawning breeds contempt.

The time has come for the decent to act. In a democratic society, the minority which attempts forcibly to subvert the will of the majority does so at its own peril. We conservatives understand the proper role of a minority group, for we are one ourselves. And never do we threaten or blaspheme or smash. This is why the groups now trying to restore dignity and peace to our afflicted campuses are mostly conservative in nature. The liberals, as usual, spilled the milk in the first place. Also as usual, we conservatives are having to mop it up.

Activists—subverters—bullyboys—look to yourselves. The people are fed up.

Observations on Race and Class at San Francisco State

Robert Chrisman

The BSU launched its strike against the Administration of San Francisco State College on November 6, 1968. Exactly two months later, AFT local 1352 at that college began its strike, with full labor sanction. Now San Francisco State College is confronted with two strikes, both strong, both effective, that have moved into statewide and national prominence.

They are twin strikes and they are of historical significance, for they are the first time students and teachers have coordinated their strikes against an institution, with maximum effect. They further represent a strike of both labor and race against racism and labor oppression. Though technically open, the campus is in no condition to operate under anything resembling "normal" circumstances. Since the AFT struck, all union services have stopped at the college: the delivery of food, books and other supplies, the collection of garbage. Many staff personnel are also on strike honoring the picket lines. In January, the college was 20% operative.

The strikes have, each, an independent identity, a unique nature, with completely different methods and tactics and with quite different constituencies. But they are the same. For both students and teachers are striking against the same "boss," the Trustees who administer the State college system.

To use a simile, they are like those astronomical configurations, twin stars. Each has a different orbit, both revolve around the same gravitational point, each is affected by the gravitational field of the other, but seen from a distance, they seem to be one. Using an earthier example, one labor official observed, "Each one says I'm not related to the other guy, one says negotiable, the other says non-negotiable, but they're Siamese twins, joined at the tailbone."

Now entering their fourth month, the strikes have impressive support and a remarkable spirit and resilience. Students have endured hundreds of arrests and beatings, the arrests now totalling over 700, including the largest mass arrest in San Francisco history, 483 on January 23. AFT strikers have continued in the face of a restraining order and a temporary injunction, appearing in a massive picket line of 247 at the campus the morning after the restraining order was issued, having voted by unanimous acclamation to defy the order.

The context of the San Francisco State College strike is a familiar one. An urban college with an enrollment of 18,000, San Francisco State is one of two public colleges in a city of 747,500 people. It is the only four-year college, the other public college being City College of San Francisco, a junior college that has reached maximum enrollment with no plans for expansion. Almost half the population of San Francisco is non-white, this term including black, Latin-American and Oriental groups. The last frontier of class mobility is college. The two public colleges at San Francisco are not sufficient to meet the demands of the citizens affected.

The situation is further strained by California's Master Plan for Higher Education, begun under the Donahoe Act of 1960. The Master Plan sets admission standards for all public colleges in California. At present, the top 12-1/2 percent of high school graduates are eligible for the University of California and its branches. The next 37-1/2 percent are eligible for the State college system; the bottom 50 percent must attend junior college. Flexibility of entrance is minimum.

The net result of the Master Plan has been the enforcement of de facto segregation in higher education in California. And, by not allowing local administration of state colleges a sufficient budget and curricular leeway, the Chancellor and the Trustees have perpetuated a traditional college structure, not flexible institutions which provide meaningful alternatives to that structure, as is relevant to their local communities.

The typical college structure has been consistently geared to middle-class and upper-middle-class white students in its entrance requirements, standards and curriculum. Non-white students and the children of blue-collar workers have minimum access to the State and UC systems. College, instead of being the frontier of class mobility, has become the barrier to it. Institutional race and class distinctions are enforced by college, not dissolved.

Such, in brief, was the context of San Francisco State College as of fall 1968. The Black Students Union, formed in 1964, has been the voice of black criticism at San Francisco State. As early as 1965, it had demanded some form of Black Studies, some change of entrance requirements at San Francisco State, to permit black participation in the college. Similar criticism has been voiced by the Third World Liberation Front (TWLF), a more recent group, which represents all non-white students on campus. Within a day or so after the BSU strike TWLF added five demands of its own and joined the strike.

The BSU strike did not occur in a vacuum on November 6. It emerged as a final act, from a familiar pattern of urgent black demand and token white response. The decision-making machinery of the college, its evaluation standards, its criteria for making changes—in short, its whole bureaucratic apparatus—was too slow, ponderous and deliberately resistant to do the necessary thing at the right time, which was to make sweeping institutional changes, institute a Black Studies program, and a black student recruitment program, and provide the black personnel needed for making the changes effective. For the first time, the white power structure of San Francisco State was having significant demands made upon it, a legitimate black demand for *real* black power, and it resisted. It resisted from motives of personal racism; it resisted because its ethnocentrism became racism under stress; it resisted because it did not have the fire and imagination necessary to meet a revolutionary situation with a revolutionary solution. It chose instead to offer compromise and token solution: that there would be Black Studies, but *experimental* Black Studies, under the aegis of the Experimental College.

Each proposed black course was to be approved by the department it affected and, depending upon the department, be taught either by a white instructor or a black instructor or, most frequently, be sponsored by a white instructor with a black graduate student doing the actual teaching. Under the latter system, the sponsor would get three units of pay, the black TA would get student assistant funds, with monthly salaries ranging from $50 to $200 per month. Further, the courses would be designated as Experimental and have only elective credit. It was a sharecropper concept of Black Studies. There was no Department of Black Studies, no Chairman of Black Studies, no departmental autonomy, and no control by black students or black faculty of curriculum, course content or personnel. All were subject to the judgment of the very departments which had been criticized for not meeting the needs of black students in the first place. The "solution" was intolerable.

In February, 1968, BSU recruited and the Administration hired Dr. Nathan Hare, the distinguished sociologist and consultant for Black Studies, to come to San Francisco State College and design and chair a Black Studies Department. Dr. Hare's proposal called for an upper-division Black Studies major of 36 units, with 9 elective units. Built into the proposal were machineries for developing student involvement with the black community, through internships and service projects, to assure black community support for the Black Studies major once he was graduated from San Francisco State and returned to the community to earn his living in it.

The program met with various forms of institutional resistance, from individual racism to bureaucratic stalling, to the final plea of, "We don't have any money or power, we'll have to study it for a while and try to get it started in fall 1969 with three black teachers."

On November 6, 1968, BSU struck.

The BSU strike began at 12 noon; by 1:20 the campus was officially closed under orders from President Robert Smith. It was not a strike in any conventional sense; few picket lines were posted or sanctions requested. BSU simply closed the campus. BSU strategy and tactics were clear and simple: 1) it anticipated a long struggle; 2) it recognized that it had only its own resources to draw upon during the first phase of the strike; 3) it recognized that it could not fight the establishment with its own weapons, force and bureaucracy. What it had at its disposal was mobility, purpose, organization, initiative and high morale. It therefore chose to make the campus uncomfortable for anyone who did not honor its strike, with tactics which ranged from discussions and arguments, to solicited and unsolicited "teach-ins" of classes in session. Mass occupation of buildings, mass confrontations with police, and mass arrests were discouraged. Discomfort was the order of the day, the same kind of discomfort as that a flea inflicts upon a dog. Though no physical match for the dog, a flea or numbers of fleas can make a dog move and make ease of existence impossible for him.

The violence of students has been exaggerated. There were skirmishes of an individual nature: several "John Wayne" fistfights between white and black, one broken window, due to a typewriter having been thrown through it, and some personal invective. But there was no deliberate, wide-scale mass violence, despite claims of Administration and the general press.

What did occur was something quite different: white faculty and Administration confused the violence of their reactions with real violence. Feeling violent, white personnel claimed BSU was violent. "Violence" became the password in faculty discussions, and the index to press coverage. The unwillingness of white faculty to distinguish violence from demonstration and harassment was critical; tension, fear and hatred mounted because of that failure, the bulk of those negative emotions generated by whites toward blacks. Ancestral memories of murder, rape and theft haunted white faculty—Nat

Turner had risen again to claim his bloody vengeance and they, minions of the white establishment, were to be his victims.

The accumulated guilt and paranoia of white America surfaced, sent subliminal ripples of reaction throughout the white faculty; rationalization and defensiveness leapt into the breach to defend the individual's psyche, and sayings such as these became common: "Well, I don't know what they've got against me, I've done my best but the system just doesn't . . . ." Or, "I agree with the basic ideas of BSU but the means they're using are wrong." Or, "A college should not be political." Or, "They're violating my academic freedom." Or, "They'd better watch out, they're going to polarize the white reactionaries and we'll lose what progress we've made." Or, "I'm willing to sit down and discuss the issues, but I don't like threats and violence."

These various quotes all expressed one thing: a deep resentment at having illusions of bourgeois power and privilege threatened or destroyed. Though no one avowed he was a racist, most did not like BSU's strike. Though everyone agreed with BSU's fight against racism, very few moved for immediate implementation of the ten BSU demands. Though no one hated Negroes, very few enjoyed or liked a group of angry black faces and words, and all faculty mutually agreed they were not racist. Hovering in the background as a ransom against racism was a check to CORE or having given a black student a good break or having felt grief for Martin Luther King, or having a personal friendship with a black. All served as shields for the naked confrontation of white racism within one's self and one's institutions.

The cornerstone of such mechanisms was the ideal of maintaining bourgeois privilege. Bourgeois privilege is the idea that the man of moderate means has full sanction under law, has full and unequivocal civil rights, has significance in the political fortune of his country, has the respect and esteem of his fellowman because he is living a productive and morally righteous life, and that his voice is heard, will be heard and shall be obeyed, when it is collective, by all the power structures that obtain. Such is the illusion of bourgeois privilege—that the existence of man is ordered and reasonable and can be regulated through non-aggressive and articulate discussion, with full respect accorded each discussant, and the appropriate action to follow. No, no, it was not racist, it had nothing to do with having a white skin; no, no, it did not discriminate against color or class; though I am proud of my professionalism, I *am* democratic. White faculty and administrators did not realize that BSU had taken such protestations at their word for 5 years and having assessed them, then moved to strike against the system that makes such illusions tenable for its employees at the same time that it violates those illusions constantly. Faculty further did not realize that they had no real power, which is the basis of any kind of privilege. The only real power or privilege they had was a white skin. So that, like it or not, the line between privileged and oppressed was white skin.

The appearance of police was inevitable. President Smith had stated at his first address to San Francisco State faculty that he had no "ideological block against calling police on campus." The police were called on campus, the City of San Francisco's notorious Tactical Squad, a group of police organized recently as a result of mass anti-Vietnam and peace demonstrations and in anticipation of black uprisings in San Francisco. They are not police officers in the conventional sense. They are more like urban commandos, with different training and different duties from those of the typical police officer. They are trained for "crowd control" and equipped accordingly. They are organized around "squad" concepts, each squad with an officer and a photographer. They are equipped with blue helmets and blue plastic face masks, four-foot riot sticks, gas masks, tear gas guns and Mace, use of the last two authorized at the officer level.

The Tac Squad had been on campus for several days, in the gymnasiums and the basements of various campus buildings; from time to time they had marched through the campus as a show of strength and as a deterrent to action that might result from the daily rallies being held.

On November 13, they moved and the first of innumerable clashes between police and students began. A squad of ten or eleven officers marched down the campus and stood in formation 50 or 60 feet from the temporary building that housed BSU and where BSU had just completed a televised press conference. A large crowd of students gathered around the Squad once it had appeared. Jeering and insults began. The Tac Squad charged the crowd and the exact cause of the charge has not been determined.

According to their commanding officer, the police had appeared following a complaint by a television cameraman that he had been attacked and his camera broken by a student. Within the hour, a student claimed that he had been assaulted by a television cameraman. In any case the crowd was chased away, some were injured and some arrested *as a consequence of the dispersal action*, not for previous offenses.

The police phase of the campus strike had begun. The pattern of student and police encounters which shaped the rest of the fall semester had been started. The cries, "On strike, shut it down," and "Pigs off campus," gained a substance that was sustained throughout the semester. Active student support for the strike intensified and broadened and exceeded 5000 and many more students provided passive support, attending rallies and refusing to actively cooperate with an Administration that relied on police and bureaucracy to meet an emergency and not on decisive, positive leadership. The die had been cast, for the BSU-TWLF strike.

The more liberal faculty members were alarmed at the events that had been occurring prior to the BSU strike of November 6: all basic faculty prerogatives regarding due process and personnel policy had been encroached, and the Trustees were removing more and more autonomy from the campus, by directly giving the President orders and limiting his maneuvering room. Two ex officio members of the Trustees are Governor Reagan and Max Rafferty, State Superintendent of Schools, both elected to their offices by promises to the conservative element to restore "law and order on California campuses," which meant, in context, to stop black militants, white radicals and liberal teachers, their protests and their programs.

The BSU strike of November 6 and the appearance of police on campus made it urgent that faculty come up with some action that would resolve student, faculty, Administration and Trustee differences. General faculty meetings were held, Department meetings were held, Academic Senate meetings were held, there were innumerable cocktail confabs of various cliques for the next week. Produced were countless hundreds of resolutions, recommendations, and petitions which had no binding power upon anybody and which, in general, interested nobody but the author, and that but briefly. Faculty response took the form of elaborate parliamentary maneuvering, carefully worded amendments to the motion, substitute motions, points of order, of information, of personal privilege, the whole faculty converted into one vast revolving, resolving ditto machine. As in a nightmare of prehistory, one had the image of watching an embattled dinosaur, ordained for extinction, move through its pitiful and scant tropisms, inadequate in the face of the threat, the two feeble brains in head and tail sluggish in operation and unable to coordinate, enmeshed in the tar pit of its own rigidity. Finally, faculty decisions were not binding on the President anyway; the President could overrule without faculty reprisal.

The final hope for the faculty came with the Convocation of November 20-21 and November 26, in which faculty, students and administrators agreed to panel discussion of the issues, with closed circuit telecast of the Convocation. President Smith's agreement to the Convocation was reluctant. He had express orders from the Trustees to keep classes open and maintain a routine schedule, even though the faculty had voted, 487-15, for the Convocation of November 26. Though he had won a vote of confidence from the faculty, he did not wish to rigidify his position by acting in such a way as to force a confrontation with the Trustees. The Convocation was the nearest he would come to any discussion, mediation or negotiation of the issues with BSU, the Trustees' mandate having been "no negotiations, no discussions." The Convocation was a form of compromise by students, teachers and Administration on the unbearable tension of "open campus" versus "closed campus," and it could allow striking students and Administration room in which to maneuver.

But the Trustees confronted Smith and on November 26, he resigned. The Trustees appointed Dr. S. I. Hayakawa the same day, as acting President. Hayakawa cancelled the Convocation, dismissing it as a "bull session," and began his regime on December 2 with the Declaration of a state of emergency, which forbade teaching anywhere but in the assigned classroom, which forbade rallies or use of the Speaker's Platform, which forbade the use of any amplifying equipment on the campus, which limited picketing, and which provided for summary suspension of all violators of this dictum, students and teachers alike. Dr. Hayakawa had forced the final confrontation.

On January 6, 1969, AFT Local 1352 struck.

Dr. Hayakawa's regime is the most oppressive in San Francisco State College history. During the first 30 working days of his regime, he has been responsible for the arrests of more than 600 persons. From December 2 through January 25, approximately 600 police were deployed daily, when "classes" were in session. Anyone who violated his decrees was punished immediately. All illusions were stripped away: teachers and students were indeed powerless, for the democratic apparatus of the college had no binding power. Hayakawa was boss. Period.

The AFT's decision to strike was deliberate and considered. To many it seemed tardy, in view of the daily decimation of the campus. One faculty group of 50 or 60 had already begun picketing against the repressive measures of the Administration and its reliance on police power to solve its problems. In their protests against racism and repression they are reminiscent of Abolitionists and they express an important element of AFT's moral resolve—the John Brown motif. Called the Ad Hoc Committee and the Fac Squad, they were not demonstrating for wages or personnel policies, but against a clear violation of human rights. They further recognized an opportunity to cleanse the college of racism, once and for all.

However, AFT 1352 could not secure labor sanction on a human-rights issue, and its own labor grievances were long festering. In the model afforded by the college, it became clear that the sources of race and class oppression were the same. In this respect, the twin strikes at San Francisco State promised perhaps the first resolution of the labor-race stalemate that has existed throughout the history of the United States and which focused during the Civil War and afterward.

AFT 1352 took a strike vote the first week in December, on the 4th. It attempted mediation of the issues with the Trustees during Christmas holidays, to no avail. The San Francisco Labor Council granted strike sanction, on December 9, to be effective the day the union began its strike. On January 6, 1969, AFT Local 1352 struck.

The general conditions of San Francisco and San Francisco State made such a strike possible. The BSU and TWLF had been sufficiently pressured and politicized by the College's system to strike. So had a liberal portion of the faculty in AFT Local 1352.

The question remains: how can the actions of a student club mobilize a faculty organization, which in turn mobilizes the liberal establishment of the community? Involved in such a sequential mobilization is the jumping of class and interest barriers. A student is not, functionally, a bourgeois, though he might have middle-class aspirations and values. Functionally a student is of the masses, of the lower-salaried, who have little economic or political leverage on the system. Further, they necessarily struggle through college to get middle-class leverage. In the classic sense of the term, they are the modern proletariat. Their interests then can come into conflict with teachers, who have achieved bourgeois standing. The proverbial conflict between the radical student and his reserved, conservative teacher might well reflect their difference of class investment. The waves of student uprisings across the United States—the world for that matter—might reflect this class reality, particularly in the case of the French and Chinese rebellions, where students made explicit identification with the working classes.

However, *teachers and students both work for the same employer*. That is the most important realized fact of the entire struggle at San Francisco State. Previous mores and regulations at colleges had all ignored this fact. Indeed, the protocol of colleges seems designed to conceal it totally, to smother it under a screen of traditions, manners and rules. The unwritten rule against "fraternization with students," the separation of dining facilities, the separation of social facilities, all served to conceal the fact that teachers and students have vital interests in common. Instead, a benevolent paternalism was encouraged as the official relationship between student and teacher, with the promise that if the student were a "good boy" he would inherit the bourgeois privilege the professor held, might indeed taste of it prematurely, through a supper, a round of drinks, or several sets of tennis together.

Such a paternalism had several effects. It "brainwashed" students into believing that their interests were best served by each of them making individual contracts with their various instructors. Collective action by students for an improved college was co-opted by the whole perceptual set of the institution itself. It did not occur to students that their interests were best served through a collective approach until recently. That same realization has been even slower in coming to teachers, who have regarded themselves as professionals and sole bargaining agents for their own individual skills. The concept of collective action has been an alien one and collective bargaining, a totally foreign idea. The teacher assumed that his privileges and power as a bourgeois were unassailable, and that he therefore had no need for the instruments of the weaker and the more oppressed, which were boycott, strike, collective action and collective bargaining.

The confrontations at San Francisco State College relieved many teachers of that idea. Through their painful catechism, teachers learned that they had only illusions of bourgeois privilege and power, not the thing itself, and that the instruments of collective action were essential if that power were to be even obtained, not to mention being defended.

A Postscript

On March 3, 1969, AFT Local 1352 returned to work at San Francisco State College, ending the longest teacher's strike in California history. The settlement package was satisfactory to the AFT as a labor force and to the San Francisco Labor Council which supported the AFT Local. Indeed, it was a victory, for the package laid a strategic base for further militant labor action. It was in writing; there were no reprisals against strikers; the Trustees had negotiated and the grievance procedure was improved.

But the AFT settlement did not include a settlement of the BSU strike, though such a settlement was part of AFT's strike demands and the most important issue to the Local, aside from its own survival. At present, the BSU strike is still not settled. The class dispute is settled, but not the race dispute.

Hope would have had a joint settlement of the strikes. The bitter facts of institutionalized racism and the manipulation of labor against race which prevail in this society did not allow for such a settlement. The labor establishment had made it very clear that it did not support the student strike officially or, in the great majority, unofficially. In its public relations, the AFT followed the same tack, stressing its independence of the BSU strike, not only to broaden its base of support among whites hostile to the student strike, but to assuage its own ambivalences.

Though victorious in the labor sense, AFT became the victim of its own propaganda with respect to the BSU strike. The labor establishment demanded that it divorce itself from the BSU strike, to receive labor's support; AFT officially divorced itself from that strike, though the intimate cooperation of students and teachers created a daily picket line 1000 to 2000 strong, at that campus. The Trustees said, in effect, since you are a distinctly different strike, here is *your* settlement. And so, the settlement was effected.

There is a melancholy echo of the Civil War in this resolution. The moral and economic inflammation of that war was slavery, was racism. But the rationale that Lincoln had to adopt was the preservation of the Union. For the Northern white masses believed that their labor interests were best served through racism, not equality, for the enslavement of a black eliminated him from being a competitor on the open job market. The North would not rally behind a war to end racism, as Lincoln well knew, but it could be persuaded to fight slavery when that fight was presented as a means to the end of preserving the Union and the economic interests of the Northern masses. Though in substance focal to the Civil War and the key issue, racism was in the war's procedure regarded as incidental. Consequently, in the post-Civil War period, black freedom was not given primary attention, but regarded as something to be eventually taken care of as the victorious North went about its business of expansion, and left the black American to the devices of the defeated racists.

In its war against racism, the North became the victim of its own propaganda, that propaganda maintaining that the War was not to end racism. As a result, when the war ended, Northern leadership got no mandate to end racism, once and for all. The original assumption prevailed: that race interests were not class interests. And so, the United States continued about its business, its deepest questions unresolved.

Thus, 105 years later, the same pattern can recur, as in the crisis at San Francisco State College. There may be a growing hope, however, that blacks and whites, students and teachers, may realize that they are all subject to the same establishment and form an enduring alliance, with the recognition that if one man is not free, then no man is free. Or, as Frederick Douglass said, "The man who is right is a majority."

The Case for Separatism: *"Black Perspective"*

Nathan Hare

"Appalling" is the only word I know that begins to describe the sneaky way in which critics like Roy Wilkins accuse us of "separatism." Our cries for more black professors and black students have padded white colleges with more blacks in two years than decades of whimpering for "integration" ever did.

We blacks at white colleges remain associated with racists physically, although we seek social and psychological independence from their oppression. The Amos 'n' Andy administrators at Negro colleges, by contrast, are physically separated but accommodated to their dependence on white racism as well as the establishment's remote control of their black destiny.

Blacks who teach at white colleges have argued long and bitterly over course content and instructor assignments with white departmental chairmen of various shades of racist persuasions. They would rather have a white moderate professor with a Ph.D. teaching a history sequence starkly barren of blackness than a black man without a degree who has spent long hours in research on the subject. They hold up the white Ph.D.'s publications in learned journals, unmindful of the fact that a black man doing research, for example, on the slavery era in "learned journals" is obliged to footnote slave-master historians or historians acceptable to a society which then condoned black slavery. Second-rate colleges require black persons with functionally white minds, using the Ph.D. as one tested means of policing that policy, yet at the same time, first-class universities think nothing of hiring an unschooled Eric Hoffer, who now holds forth at Berkeley.

With regard to source content, the white aim is mainly to black out the black perspective. White professors at universities such as Yale will dust off old courses in race relations and African tribalism for what might be called a polka-dot studies program, while Negro professors will trot out their old courses in Negro history and Negro music for Negro-studies courses which they cynically call black. If all a black-studies program needs is a professor with a black skin to prattle about Negro subject matter, then our Negro schools would never have failed so painfully as they have.

In the search for educational relevance, black today is revolutionary and nationalistic. A black-studies program which is not revolutionary and nationalistic is, accordingly, quite profoundly irrelevant. The black revolutionary nationalist, aware and proud of his blackness, demands the right to exist as a distinct category, to be elevated as such by any means necessary. The Negro, contrarily, would just as soon be white. He longs to escape his blackness and, in the search for integration achieves disintegration.

Thus, the key to the difference between a black-studies program and a Negro-studies program is a black perspective. Black students are descendants of a people cut off from their attachment to land, culture and nation (or peoplehood). This condition is aggravated further by a whitewashed education. The expressive phase of the black-studies program is designed to regenerate the mortified ego of the black child. For instance, a proud black history can restore and construct a sense of pastness, of collective destiny, as a springboard to the quest for a new collective future. For black children crippled by defeatist attitudes, hardened by generations of exclusion, this is potentially therapeutic.

Pragmatic Component

At the same time, we must resist the white perspective which seeks to restrict black studies to the stereotyped study of art and religion predominantly. Black studies should comprise a comprehensive, integrated body of interdisciplinary courses just as in the case of long-established departments of social science and American studies. There is a desperate need for a pragmatic component which focuses on the applied fields of knowledge such as economics.

Many will argue that science and mathematics are "pure" subjects; though that may be true in a sense, the uses of science may be directed toward atomic weapons of destruction or, in the case of a community-oriented black studies, devoted to such matters as rat control.

I can visualize, for instance, a reading problem in "black" mathematics that would not be saturated with middle-class referents such as stocks and bonds. Rather, the teacher might ask in order to whet the ghetto child's appetite for math: "If you loot one store and burn two, how many do you have left?" The example might be improved; but there is no substitute for a black perspective based on the principle of self-control.

The Case Against Separatism: *"Black Jim Crow"*

Roy Wilkins

In the 1920s in Kansas City, Mo., I learned a lesson that I never forgot. It has come home to me forcibly these past twelve months in the demands of 1968-69 Negro college students for autonomous black units on some of their campuses. A Kansas City school-bond issue for the then racially segregated town provided $985,000 to build an athletic plant and field for a junior high school for white students—and $27,500 to convert a factory building into an elementary school for black children.

This was the ugly face of segregated education. The system must not be revived. It must not be invited back at the request, nay, the ultimatum of black students themselves.

No person who has watched the halting march of Negro civil rights through the years can fail to sympathize with the frustrations and anger of today's black students. In their hurt pride in themselves and in their outrage, they have called retreat from the tough and trying battle of a minority for dignity and equality. They don't call it a retreat, of course. They have all sorts of fancy rationalizations for their course. They renounce "white middle-class values" so they can refuse logically to be judged by the standards of the times and of the place they live in. Every black dissenter is an Uncle Tom and every white one a racist. Vituperation, not reason, is invoked.

Racial Breast-Beating

They say they need to get together in their own dormitories to build a common strength. After they are strong and sure of themselves they will be able to meet other groups as true equals.

Who can declare them completely wrong? Certainly they are right about the strength that comes from being with their brothers. Certainly they are right about the usefulness of a study of Afro-American history and culture. They are right, also, in calling for increased enrollment of Negro students and in requesting more black faculty members. But in demanding a black Jim Crow studies building within a campus and exclusively black dormitories or wings of dormitories, they are opening the door to a dungeon. They do not see that no black history becomes significant and meaningful unless it is taught in the context of world and national history. In its sealed-off, black-studies centers, it will be simply another exercise in racial breast-beating.

Abdication

To oppose black academic separatism is not to ignore black youth or to be unmindful of the spirit displayed by so many of them. They must be heard and they are heard; I have talked on numerous occasions with student groups, some members of which were not Wilkins cheerleaders. But it would be an abdication of responsibility, to them and to those who will follow us both, to acquiesce in a course which we know to be wrong, solely to avoid their criticism.

The key word in the current spate of similarly worded demands of black students is "autonomous." No university administration faithful to its trust can grant this. There is substantial informed opinion that tax money cannot be used to set up racial enclaves within campuses. I am sure that sooner or later a court test would arise. And all this is apart from the practical difficulty that it costs more money to establish real studies centers than most colleges can afford and that the qualified personnel—black or white—is simply not available at this time.

The demanding students might well find themselves saddled with a poor substitute for a center, foisted on them by an administration ready to buy peace at any price. Thus would segregated education once more run true to form.

An alternative with good chances of success would be to concentrate as a beginning on two centers of genuine stature, one on the East Coast and one on the West. The financing and staffing of two such university-based institutes would not be an impossible task, and they would draw not only on their own resident scholars but on exchange and visiting personnel as well. Meanwhile, valid courses in Afro-American history and culture should be established at all good colleges and universities to the extent that qualified faculty, black or white, can be found. Also, it should be the immediate task of every school claiming to be a school to provide an extensive library on the Negro past and present, in Africa, and in the New World.

Incidentally, the familiar "reading course" should not be disdained: after all, my generation had no "black-studies" curriculum—but we found ways to learn about ourselves and our past.

Black Power:
Its Need and Substance

Stokeley Carmichael and
Charles V. Hamilton

"To carve out a place for itself in the politico-social order," V. O. Key, Jr. wrote in *Politics, Parties and Pressure Groups*, "a new group may have to fight for reorientation of many of the values of the old order" (p. 57). This is especially true when that group is composed of black people in the American society—a society that has for centuries deliberately and systematically excluded them from political participation. Black people in the United States must raise hard questions, questions which challenge the very nature of the society itself: its long-standing values, beliefs and institutions.

To do this, we must first redefine ourselves. Our basic need is to reclaim our history and our identity from what must be called cultural terrorism, from the depredation of self-justifying white guilt. We shall have to struggle for the right to create our own terms through which to define ourselves and our relationship to the society, and to have these terms recognized. This is the first necessity of a free people, and the first right that any oppressor must suspend.

In *Politics Among Nations*, Hans Morgenthau defined political power as "the psychological control over the minds of men" (p. 29). This control includes the attempt by the oppressor to have *his* definitions, *his* historical descriptions, *accepted* by the oppressed. This was true in Africa no less than in the United States. To black Africans, the word "Uhuru" means "freedom," but they had to fight the white colonizers for the right to use the term. The recorded history of this country's dealings with red and black men offers other examples. In the wars between the white settlers and the "Indians," a battle won by the Cavalry was described as a "victory." The "Indians'" triumphs, however, were "massacres." (The American colonists were not unaware of the need to define their acts in their own terms. They labeled their fight against England a "revolution"; the English attempted to demean it by calling it "insubordination" or "riotous.")

The historical period following Reconstruction in the South after the Civil War has been called by many historians the period of Redemption, implying that the bigoted southern slave societies were "redeemed" from the hands of "reckless and irresponsible" black rulers. Professor John Hope Franklin's *Reconstruction* or Dr. W. E. B. Dubois' *Black Reconstruction* should be sufficient to dispel inaccurate historical notions, but the larger society persists in its own self-serving accounts. Thus black people came to be depicted as "lazy," "apathetic," "dumb," "shiftless," "good-timers." Just as red men had to be recorded as "savages" to justify the white man's theft of their land, so black men had to be vilified in order to justify their continued oppression. Those who have the right to define are the masters of the situation. Lewis Carroll understood this:

"When I use a word," Humpty Dumpty said in a rather scornful tone, "it means just what I choose it to mean—neither more nor less."

"The question is," said Alice, "whether you *can* make words mean so many different things."

"The question is," said Humpty Dumpty, "which is to be master—that's all."*

---

*Lewis Carroll, *Through the Looking Glass*. New York: Doubleday Books, Inc., p. 196.

Today, the American educational system continues to reinforce the entrenched values of the society through the use of words. Few people in this country question that this is "the land of the free and the home of the brave." They have had these words drummed into them from childhood. Few people question that this is the "Great Society" or that this country is fighting "Communist aggression" around the world. We mouth these things over and over, and they become truisms not to be questioned. In a similar way, black people have been saddled with epithets.

"Integration" is another current example of a word which has been defined according to the way white Americans see it. To many of them, it means black men wanting to marry white daughters; it means "race mixing"—implying bed or dance partners. To black people, it has meant a way to improve their lives—economically and politically. But the predominant white definition has stuck in the minds of too many people.

Black people must redefine themselves, and only *they* can do that. Throughout this country, vast segments of the black communities are beginning to recognize the need to assert their own definitions, to reclaim their history, their culture; to create their own sense of community and togetherness. There is a growing resentment of the word "Negro," for example, because this term is the invention of our oppressor; it is *his* image of us that he describes. Many blacks are now calling themselves African-Americans, Afro-Americans or black people because that is *our* image of ourselves. When we begin to define our own image, the stereotypes—that is, lies—that our oppressor has developed will begin in the white community and end there. The black community will have a positive image of itself that *it* has created. This means we will no longer call ourselves lazy, apathetic, dumb, good-timers, shiftless, etc. Those are words used by white America to define us. If we accept these adjectives, as some of us have in the past, then we see ourselves only in a negative way, precisely the way white America wants us to see ourselves. Our incentive is broken and our will to fight is surrendered. From now on we shall view ourselves as African-Americans and as black people who are in fact energetic, determined, intelligent, beautiful and peace-loving.

There is a terminology and ethos peculiar to the black community of which black people are beginning to be no longer ashamed. Black communities are the only large segments of this society where people refer to each other as brother—soul-brother, soul-sister. Some people may look upon this as *ersatz*, as make-believe, but it is not that. It is real. It is a growing sense of community. It is a growing realization that black Americans have a common bond not only among themselves, but with their African brothers. In *Black Man's Burden* John O. Killens described his trip to ten African countries as follows:

> Everywhere I went people called me brother . . . "Welcome, American brother." It was a good feeling for me, to be in Africa. To walk in a land for the first time in your entire life knowing within yourself that your color would not be held against you. No black man ever knows this in America [p. 160].

More and more black Americans are developing this feeling. They are becoming aware that they have a history which pre-dates their forced introduction to this country. African-American history means a long history beginning on the continent of Africa, a history not taught in the standard textbooks of this country. It is absolutely essential that black people know this history, that they know their roots, that they develop an awareness of their cultural heritage. Too long have they been kept in submission by being told that they had no culture, no manifest heritage, before they landed on the slave auction blocks in this country. If black people are to know themselves as a vibrant, valiant people, they must know their roots. And they will soon learn that the Hollywood image of man-eating cannibals waiting for, and waiting on, the Great White Hunter is a lie.

With redefinition will come a clearer notion of the role black Americans can play in this world. This role will emerge clearly out of the unique, common experiences of Afro-Asians. Killens concludes:

> I believe furthermore that the American Negro can be the bridge between the West and Africa-Asia. We black Americans can serve as a bridge to mutual understanding. The one thing we black Americans have in common with the other colored peoples of the world is that we have all felt the cruel and ruthless heel of white supremacy. We have all been "niggerized" on one level or another. And all of us are determined to "deniggerize" the earth. To rid the world of "niggers" is the Black Man's Burden, human reconstruction is the grand objective [p. 176].

Only when black people fully develop this sense of community, of themselves, can they begin to deal effectively with the problems of racism in *this* country. This is what we mean by a new consciousness; this is the vital first step.

The next step is what we shall call the process of political modernization—a process which must take place if the society is to be rid of racism. "Political modernization" includes many things, but we mean by it three major concepts: (1) questioning old values and institutions of the society; (2) searching for new and different forms of political structure to solve political and economic problems; and (3) broadening the base of political participation to include more people in the decision-making process. These notions (we shall take up each in turn) are central to our thinking throughout this book and to contemporary American history as a whole. As David Apter wrote in *The Politics of Modernization*, " . . . the struggle to modernize is what has given meaning to our generation. It tests our cherished institutions and our beliefs. . . . So compelling a force has it become that we are forced to ask new questions of our own institutions. Each country, whether modernized or modernizing, stands in both judgment and fear of the results. Our own society is no exception" (p. 2).

The values of this society support a racist system; we find it incongruous to ask black people to adopt and support most of those values. We also reject the assumption that the basic institutions of this society must be preserved. The goal of black people must *not* be to assimilate into middle-class America, for that class—as a whole—is without a viable conscience as regards humanity. The values of the middle class permit the perpetuation of the ravages of the black community. The values of that class are based on material aggrandizement, not the expansion of humanity. The values of that class ultimately support cloistered little closed societies tucked away neatly in tree-lined suburbia. The values of that class do *not* lead to the creation of an open society. That class *mouths* its preference for a free, competitive society, while at the same time forcefully and even viciously denying to black people as a group the opportunity to compete.

We are not unmindful of other descriptions of the social utility of the middle class. Banfield and Wilson, in *City Politics*, concluded:

> The departure of the middle class from the central city is important in other ways. . . . The middle class supplies a social and political leavening in the life of a city. Middle-class people demand good schools and integrity in government. They support churches, lodges, parent-teacher associations, scout troops, better-housing committees, art galleries, and operas. It is the middle class, in short, that asserts a conception of the public interest. Now its activity is increasingly concentrated in the suburbs [p. 14].

But this same middle class manifests a sense of superior group position in regard to race. This class wants "good government" for *themselves*; it wants good schools *for its children*. At the same time, many of its members sneak into the black community by day, exploit it, and take the money home to their middle-class communities at night to support their operas and art galleries and comfortable homes. When not actually robbing, they will fight off the handful of more affluent black people who seek to move in; when they approve or even seek token integration, it applies only to black people like themselves—as "white" as possible. *This class is the backbone of institutional racism in this country.*

Thus we reject the goal of assimilation into middle-class America because the values of that class are in themselves anti-humanist and because that class as a social force perpetuates racism. We must face the fact that, in the past, what we have called the movement has not really questioned the middle-class values and institutions of this country. If anything, it has accepted those values and institutions without fully realizing their racist nature. Reorientation means an emphasis on the dignity of man, not on the sanctity of property. It means the creation of a society where human misery and poverty are repugnant to that society, not an indication of laziness or lack of initiative. The creation of new values means the establishment of a society based, as Killens expresses it in *Black Man's Burden*, on "free people," not "free enterprise" (p. 167). To do this means to modernize—*indeed, to civilize*—this country.

Supporting the old values are old political and economic structures; these must also be "modernized." We should at this point distinguish between "structures" and "system." By system, we have in mind the entire American complex of basic institutions, values, beliefs, etc. By structures, we mean the specific institutions (political parties, interest groups, bureaucratic administrations) which exist to conduct the business of that system. Obviously, the first is broader than the second. Also, the second assumes the legitimacy of the first. Our view is that, given the illegitimacy of the system, we cannot then proceed to transform that system with existing structures.

The two major political parties in this country have become non-viable entities for the legitimate representation of the real needs of masses—especially blacks—in this country. Walter Lippmann raised the same point in his syndicated column of December 8, 1966. He pointed out that the party system in the United States developed before our society became as technologically complex as it is now. He says that the ways in which men live and define themselves are changing radically. Old ideological issues, once the subject of passionate controversy, Lippmann argues, are of little interest today. He asks whether the great urban complexes—which are rapidly becoming the centers of black population in the U.S.—can be run with the same systems and ideas that derive from a time when America was a country of small villages and farms. While not addressing himself directly to the question of race, Lippmann raises a major question about our political institutions; and the crisis of race in America may be its major symptom.

Black people have seen the city planning commissions, the urban renewal commissions, the boards of education and the police departments fail to speak to their needs in a meaningful way. We must devise new structures, new institutions to replace those forms or to make them responsive. There is nothing sacred or inevitable about old institutions; the focus must be on people, not forms.

Existing structures and established ways of doing things have a way of perpetuating themselves and for this reason, the modernizing process will be difficult. Therefore, timidity in calling into question the boards of education or the police departments will not do. They must be challenged forcefully and clearly. If this means the creation of parallel community institutions, then that must be the solution. If this means that black parents must gain control over the operation of the schools in the black community, then that must be the solution. The search for new forms means the search for institutions that will, for once, make decisions in the interest of black people. It means, for example, a building inspection department that neither winks at violations of building codes by absentee slumlords nor imposes meaningless fines which permit them to continue their exploitation of the black community.

Essential to the modernization of structures is a broadened base of political participation. More and more people must become politically sensitive and active (we have already seen this happening in some areas of the South). People must no longer be tied, by small incentives or handouts, to a corrupting and corruptible white machine. Black people will choose their own leaders and hold those leaders responsible to *them*. A broadened base means an end to the condition described by James Wilson in *Negro Politics*, whereby "Negroes tended to be the objects rather than the subjects of civic action. Things are often done for, or about, or to, or because of Negroes, but they are less frequently done *by* Negroes" (p. 133). Broadening the base of political participation, then, has as much to do with the quality of black participation as with the quantity. We are fully aware that the black vote, expecially in the North, has been pulled out of white pockets and "delivered" whenever it was in the interest of white politicians to do so. That vote must no longer be controllable by those who have neither the interests nor the demonstrated concern of black people in mind.

As the base broadens, as more and more black people become activated, they will perceive more clearly the special disadvantages heaped upon them as a group. They will perceive that the larger society is growing more affluent while the black society is retrogressing, as daily life and mounting statistics clearly show. . . . V. O. Key describes what often happens next in *Politics, Parties and Pressure Groups:* "A factor of great significance in the setting off of political movements is an abrupt change for the worse in the status of one group relative to that of other groups in society. . . . A rapid change for the worse . . . in the relative status of any group . . . is likely to precipitate political action" (p. 24). Black people will become increasingly active as they notice that their retrogressive status exists in large measure because of values and institutions arraigned against them. They will begin to stress and strain and call the entire system into question. Political modernization will be in motion. We believe that it is now in motion. One form of that motion is Black Power.

The adoption of the concept of Black Power is one of the most legitimate and healthy developments in American politics and race relations in our time. The concept of Black Power speaks to all the needs mentioned in this chapter. It is a call for black people in this country to unite, to recognize their heritage, to build a sense of community. It is a call for black people to begin to define their own goals, to lead their own organizations and to support those organizations. It is a call to reject the racist institutions and values of this society.

The concept of Black Power rests on a fundamental premise: *Before a group can enter the open society, it must first close ranks.* By this we mean that group solidarity is necessary before a group can operate effectively from a bargaining position of strength in a pluralistic society. Traditionally, each new ethnic group in this society has found the route to social and political viability through the organization of its own institutions with which to represent its needs within the larger society. Studies in voting behavior specifically, and political behavior generally, have made it clear that politically the American pot has not melted. Italians vote for Rubino over O'Brien; Irish for Murphy over Goldberg, etc. This phenomenon may seem distasteful to some, but it has been and remains today a central fact of the American political system. There are other examples of ways in which groups in the society have remembered their roots and used this effectively in the political arena. Theodore Sorensen describes the politics of foreign aid during the Kennedy Administration in his book *Kennedy*:

> No powerful constituencies or interest groups backed foreign aid. The Marshall Plan at least had appealed to Americans who traced their roots to the Western European nations aided. But there were few voters who identified with India, Colombia or Tanganyika [p. 351].

The extent to which black Americans can and do "trace their roots" to Africa, to that extent will they be able to be more effective on the political scene.

A white reporter set forth this point in other terms when he made the following observation about white Mississippi's manipulation of the anti-poverty program:

> The war on poverty has been predicated on the notion that there is such a thing as a community which can be defined geographically and mobilized for a collective effort to help the poor. This theory has no relationship to reality in the deep South. In every Mississippi county there are two communities. Despite all the pious platitudes of the moderates on both sides, these two communities habitually see their interests in terms of conflict rather than cooperation. Only when the Negro community can muster enough political, economic and professional strength to compete on somewhat equal terms, will Negroes believe in the possibility of true cooperation and whites accept its necessity. En route to integration, the Negro community needs to develop a greater independence—a chance to run its own affairs and not cave in whenever "the man" barks—or so it seems to me, and to most of the knowledgeable people with whom I talked in Mississippi. To OEO, this judgment may sound like black nationalism. . . .[1]

The point is obvious: black people must lead and run their own organizations. Only black people can convey the revolutionary idea—and it is a revolutionary idea—that black people are able to do things themselves. Only they can help create in the community an aroused and continuing black consciousness that will provide the basis for political strength. In the past, white allies have often furthered white supremacy without the whites involved realizing it, or even wanting to do so. Black people must come together and do things for themselves. They must achieve self-identity and self-determination in order to have their daily needs met.

Black Power means, for example, that in Lowndes County, Alabama, a black sheriff can end police brutality. A black tax assessor and tax collector and county board of revenue can lay, collect, and channel tax monies for the building of better roads and schools serving black people. In such areas as Lowndes, where black people have a majority, they will attempt to use power to exercise control. This is what they seek: control. When black people lack a majority, Black Power means proper representation and sharing of control. It means the creation of power bases, of strength, from which black people can press to change local or nation-wide patterns of oppression—instead of from weakness.

It does not mean *merely* putting black faces into office. Black visibility is not Black Power. Most of the black politicians around the country today are not examples of Black Power. The power must be that of a community, and emanate from there. The black politicians must start from there. The black politicians must stop being representatives of "downtown" machines, whatever the cost might be in terms of lost patronage and holiday handouts.

Black Power recognizes—it must recognize—the ethnic basis of American politics as well as the power-oriented nature of American politics. Black Power therefore calls for black people to consolidate behind their own, so that they can bargain from a position of strength. But while we endorse the *procedure* of group solidarity and identity for the purpose of attaining certain goals in the body politic, this does not mean that black people should strive for the same kind of rewards (i.e., end results) obtained by the white society. The ultimate values and goals are not domination or exploitation of other groups, but rather an effective share in the total power of the society.

Nevertheless, some observers have labeled those who advocate Black Power as racists; they have said that the call for self-identification and self-determination is "racism in reverse" or "black supremacy." This is a deliberate and absurd lie. There is no analogy—by any stretch of definition or imagination—between the advocates of Black Power and white racists. Racism is not merely exclusion on the basis of race but exclusion for the purpose of subjugating or maintaining subjugation. The goal of the racists is to keep black people on the bottom, arbitrarily and dictatorially, as they have done in this country for over three hundred years. The goal of black self-determination and black self-identity—Black Power—is full participation in the decision-making processes affecting the lives of black people, and recognition of the virtues in themselves as black people. The black people of this country have not lynched whites, bombed their churches, murdered their children and manipulated laws and institutions to maintain oppression. White racists have. Congressional laws, one after the other, have not been necessary to stop black people from oppressing others and denying others the full enjoyment of their rights. White racists have made such laws necessary. The goal of Black Power is positive and functional to a free and viable society. No white racist can make this claim.

A great deal of public attention and press space was devoted to the hysterical accusation of "black racism" when the call for Black Power was first sounded. A national committee of influential black churchmen affiliated with the National Council of Churches, despite their obvious respectability and responsibility, had to resort to a paid advertisement to articulate their position, while anyone yapping "black racism" made front-page news. In their statement, published in the *New York Times* of July 31, 1966, the churchmen said:

We, an informal group of Negro churchmen in America, are deeply disturbed about the crisis brought upon our country by historic distortions of important human realities in the controversy about "black power." What we see shining through the variety of rhetoric is not anything new but the same old problem of power and race which has faced our beloved country since 1619.

. . . The conscience of black men is corrupted because having no power to implement the demands of conscience, the concern for justice in the absence of justice becomes a chaotic self-surrender. Powerlessness breeds a race of beggars. We are faced with a situation where powerless conscience meets conscienceless power, threatening the very foundations of our Nation.

We deplore the overt violence of riots, but we feel it is more important to focus on the real sources of these eruptions. These sources may be abetted inside the Ghetto, but their basic cause lies in the silent and covert violence which white middle class America inflicts upon the victims of the inner city.

. . . In short, the failure of American leaders to use American power to create equal opportunity *in life* as well as *law*, this is the real problem and not the anguished cry for black power.

. . . Without the capacity to participate with power, i.e., to have some organized political and economic strength to really influence people with whom one interacts, integration is not meaningful.

. . . America has asked its Negro citizens to fight for opportunity *as individuals* whereas at certain points in our history what we have needed most has been opportunity for the *whole group*, not just for selected and approved Negroes.

. . . We must not apologize for the existence of this form of group power, for we have been oppressed as a group and not as individuals. We will not find our way out of that oppression until both we and America accept the need for Negro Americans, as well as for Jews, Italians, Poles, and white Anglo-Saxon Protestants, among others, to have and to wield group power.

It is a commentary on the fundamentally racist nature of this society that the concept of group strength for black people must be articulated—not to mention defended. No other group would submit to being led by others. Italians do not run the Anti-Defamation League of B'nai B'rith. Irish do not chair Christopher Columbus Societies. Yet when black people call for black-run and all-black organizations, they are immediately classed in a category with the Ku Klux Klan. This is interesting and ironic, but by no means surprising: the society does not expect black people to be able to take care of their business, and there are many who prefer it precisely that way.

In the end, we cannot and shall not offer any guarantees that Black Power, if achieved, would be non-racist. No one can predict human behavior. Social change always has unanticipated consequences. If black racism is what the larger society fears, we cannot help them. We can only state what we hope will be the result, given the fact that the present situation is unacceptable and that we have no real alternative but to work for Black Power. The final truth is that the white society is not entitled to reassurances, even if it were possible to offer them.

We have outlined the meaning and goals of Black Power; we have also discussed one major thing which it is not. There are others of greater importance. The advocates of Black Power reject the old slogans and meaningless rhetoric of previous years in the civil rights struggle. The language of yesterday is indeed irrelevant: progress, non-violence, integration, fear of "white backlash," coalition. Let us look at the rhetoric and see why these terms must be set aside or redefined.

One of the tragedies of the struggle against racism is that up to this point there has been no national organization which could speak to the growing militancy of young black people in the urban ghettos and the black-belt South. There has been only a "civil rights" movement, whose tone of voice was adapted to an audience of middle-class whites. It served as a sort of buffer zone between that audience and angry young blacks. It claimed to speak for the needs of a community, but it did not speak in the tone of that community. None of its so-called leaders could go into a rioting community and be listened to. In a sense, the blame must be shared—along with the mass media—by those leaders for what happened in Watts, Harlem, Chicago, Cleveland and other places. Each time the black people in those cities saw Dr. Martin Luther King get slapped they became angry. When they saw little black girls bombed to death *in a church* and civil rights workers ambushed and murdered, they were angrier; and when nothing happened, they were steaming mad. We had nothing to offer that they could see, except to go out and be beaten again. We helped to build their frustration.

We had only the old language of love and suffering. And in most places—that is, from the liberals and middle class—we got back the old language of patience and progress. The civil rights leaders were saying to the country: "Look, you guys are supposed to be nice guys, and we are only going to do what we are supposed to do. Why do you beat us up? Why don't you give us what we ask? Why don't you straighten yourselves out?" For the masses of black people, this language resulted in virtually nothing. In fact, their objective day-to-day condition worsened. The unemployment rate among black people increased while that among whites declined. Housing conditions in the black communities deteriorated. Schools in the black ghettos continued to plod along on outmoded techniques, inadequate curricula, and with all too many tired and indifferent teachers. Meanwhile, the President picked up the refrain of "We Shall Overcome" while the Congress passed civil rights law after civil rights law, only to have them effectively nullified by deliberately weak enforcement. "Progress is being made," we were told.

Such language, along with admonitions to remain nonviolent and fear the white backlash, convinced some that that course was the *only* course to follow. It misled some into believing that a black minority could bow its head and get whipped into a meaningful position of power. The very notion is absurd. The white society devised the language, adopted the rules and had the black community narcotized into believing that that language and those rules were, in fact, relevant. The black community was told time and again how *other* immigrants finally won *acceptance*: that is, by following the Protestant Ethic of Work and Achievement. They worked hard; therefore, they achieved. We were not told that it was by building Irish Power, Italian Power, Polish Power or Jewish Power that these groups got themselves together and operated from positions of strength. We were not told that "the American dream" wasn't designed for black people. That while today, to whites, the dream may *seem* to include black people, it cannot do so by the very nature of this nation's political and economic system, which imposes institutional racism on the black masses if not upon every individual black. A notable comment on that "dream" was made by Dr. Percy Julian, the black scientist and director of the Julian Research Institute in Chicago, a man for whom the dream seems to have come true. While not subscribing to "black power" as he understood it, Dr. Julian clearly understood the basis for it: "The false concept of basic Negro inferiority is one of the curses that still lingers. It is a problem created by the white man. Our children just no longer are going to accept the patience we were taught by our generation. We were taught a pretty little lie—excel and the whole world lies open before you. *I obeyed the injunction and found it to be wishful thinking.*" (Authors' italics)[2]

A key phrase in our buffer-zone days was non-violence. For years it has been thought that black people would not literally fight for their lives. Why this has been so is not entirely clear; neither the larger society nor black people are noted for passivity. The notion apparently stems from the years of marches and demonstrations and sit-ins where black people did not strike back and the violence always came from white mobs. There are many who still sincerely believe in that approach. From our viewpoint, rampaging white mobs and white night-riders must be made to understand that their days of free head-whipping are over. Black people should and must fight back. Nothing more quickly repels someone bent on destroying you than the unequivocal message: "O.K., fool, make your move, and run the same risk I run—of dying."

When the concept of Black Power is set forth, many people immediately conjure up notions of violence. The country's reaction to the Deacons for Defense and Justice, which originated in

Louisiana, is instructive. Here is a group which realized that the "law" and law enforcement agencies would not protect people, so they had to do it themselves. If a nation fails to protect its citizens, then that nation cannot condemn those who take up the task themselves. The deacons and all other blacks who resort to self-defense represent a simple answer to a simple question: what man would not defend his family and home from attack?

But this frightened some white people, because they knew that black people would now fight back. They knew that this was precisely what *they* would have long since done if *they* were subjected to the injustices and oppression heaped on blacks. Those of us who advocate Black Power are quite clear in our own minds that a "non-violent" approach to civil rights is an approach black people cannot afford and a luxury white people do not deserve. It is crystal clear to us—and it must become so with the white society—*that there can be no social order without social justice*. White people must be made to understand that they must stop messing with black people, or the blacks *will* fight back!

Next, we must deal with the term "integration." According to its advocates, social justice will be accomplished by "integrating the Negro into the mainstream institutions of the society from which he has been traditionally excluded." This concept is based on the assumption that there is nothing of value in the black community and that little of value could be created among black people. The thing to do is siphon off the "acceptable" black people into the surrounding middle-class white community.

The goals of integrationists are middle-class goals, articulated primarily by a small group of Negroes with middle-class aspirations or status. Their kind of integration has meant that a few blacks "make it," leaving the black community, sapping it of leadership potential and know-how. As we noted in Chapter I, those token Negroes—absorbed into a white mass—are of no value to the remaining black masses. They become meaningless show-pieces for a conscience-soothed white society. Such people will state that they would prefer to be treated "only as individuals, not as Negroes"; that they "are not and should not be preoccupied with race." This is a totally unrealistic position. In the first place, black people have not suffered as individuals but as members of a group; therefore, their liberation lies in group action. This is why SNCC—and the concept of Black Power—affirms that helping *individual* black people to solve their problems on an *individual* basis does little to alleviate the mass of black people. Secondly, while color blindness *may* be a sound goal ultimately, we must realize that race is an overwhelming fact of life in this historical period. There is no black man in this country who can live "simply as a man." His blackness is an ever-present fact of this racist society, whether he recognizes it or not. It is unlikely that this or the next generation will witness the time when race will no longer be relevant in the conduct of public affairs and in public policy decision-making. To realize this and to attempt to deal with it does not make one a racist or overly preoccupied with race; it puts one in the forefront of a significant *struggle*. If there is no intense struggle today, there will be no meaningful results tommorrow.

"Integration" as a goal today speaks to the problem of blackness not only in an unrealistic way but also in a despicable way. It is based on complete acceptance of the fact that in order to have a decent house or education, black people must move into a white neighborhood or send their children to a white school. This reinforces, among both black and white, the idea that "white" is automatically superior and "black" is by definition inferior. For this reason, "integration" is a subterfuge for the maintenance of white supremacy. It allows the nation to focus on a handful of Southern black children who get into white schools at a great price, and to ignore the ninety-four percent who are left in unimproved all-black schools. Such situations will not change until black people become equal in a way that means something, and integration ceases to be a one-way street. Then integration does not mean draining skills and energies from the black ghetto into white neighborhoods. To sprinkle black children among white pupils in outlying schools is at best a stop-gap measure. The goal is not to take black children out of the black community and expose them to white middle-class values; the goal is to build and strengthen the black community.

"Integration" also means that black people must give up their identity, deny their heritage. We recall the conclusion of Killian and Grigg: "At the present time, integration as a solution to the race problem demands that the Negro foreswear his identity as a Negro." The fact is that integration, as traditionally articulated, would abolish the black community. The fact is that what must be abolished is not the black community, but the dependent colonial status that has been inflicted upon it.

The racial and cultural personality of the black community must be preserved and that community must win its freedom while preserving its cultural integrity. Integrity includes a pride—in the sense of self-acceptance, not chauvinism—in being black, in the historical attainments and contributions of black people. No person can be healthy, complete and mature if he must deny a part of himself; this is what "integration" has required thus far. This is the essential difference between integration as it is currently practiced and the concept of Black Power.

The idea of cultural integrity is so obvious that it seems almost simple-minded to spell things out at this length. Yet millions of

Americans resist such truths when they are applied to black people. Again, that resistance is a comment on the fundamental racism in the society. Irish Catholics took care of their own first without a lot of apology for doing so, without any dubious language from timid leadership about guarding against "backlash." Everyone understood it to be a perfectly legitimate procedure. Of course, there would be "backlash." Organization begets counterorganization, but this was no reason to defer.

The so-called white backlash against black people is something else: the embedded traditions of institutional racism being brought into the open and calling forth overt manifestations of individual racism. In the summer of 1966, when the protest marches into Cicero, Illinois, began, the black people knew they were not allowed to live in Cicero and the white people knew it. When blacks began to demand the right to live in homes in that town, the whites simply reminded them of the status quo. Some people called this "backlash." It was, in fact, racism defending itself. In the black community, this is called "White folks showing their color." It is ludicrous to blame black people for what is simply an overt manifestation of white racism. Dr. Martin Luther King stated clearly that the protest marches were not the cause of the racism but merely exposed a long-term cancerous condition in the society.

Footnotes

[1]Christopher Jencks, "Accommodating Whites: A New Look at Mississippi," *The New Republic* (April 16, 1966).

[2]*The New York Times* (April 30, 1967), p. 30.

Toward a More Meaningful Revolution: Ideology in Transition

Melvin H. Posey

Introduction

This paper is an attempt to analyze those forces which are presently operating in the Black communities to help issue in social change. Moreover, it is an attempt to analyze and evaluate the relevance of the current "Black Power" Movement and its leadership to the future of American politics.

The significance of the "Black Power" Movement is that it has the potential for mobilizing the Black masses into a very cohesive politically-oriented pressure group, which would be able not only to influence the outcome of decisions made on the local, state, and national levels, but which would also be able to place into positions of power those who would be responsive to the needs of the Black people. It is also my feeling that the Black leadership of the various civil rights organizations could begin to set up within the confines of various Black communities political organizations which would create a new style of life for those who reside within the ghettos. These organizations would be able to award those whose efforts had sided in the creation of a politically conscious Black community, and eventually help bring about a total reorganization of the political, economic, and social structure in the United States.

Black Power as a Political Ideology

The key to the political future of Black people in America rests with the direction which the Black Power Movement takes. If its leadership pursues a political course of action, then Black Power as a political ideology would provide them with a *modus operandi* for securing the support of the Black "masses," and the respect of both Blacks and whites—the latter being outside of the Black community. On the other hand, if it fails to bring about unity among Blacks, the "Revolution" will be in grave danger.

Up until 1966, the Black "protest" organizations were utilizing all of their resources without an ideology that could win the confidence and the trust of an alienated, impoverished Black community. These organizations were very dependent upon the white majority financially and politically. The white majority only conceded to the demands of the "protest" groups when it chose to do so. Consequently, most of the Black leaders were not able to win concessions without diluting their resources to a point where their influence was limited. In short, most of the Black leaders were, and still are, powerless.

In 1966, the "rhetoric" of Stokeley Carmichael and the Black leadership of CORE and SNCC heightened the "consciousness" of the Black masses to such an extent that the disintegrating Black protest organizations experienced a rebirth of purpose. Sometimes there develops within an oppressed group, individuals who either by virtue of their talents, intellect, charisma, or leadership ability begin to urge that group to pursue a different direction in the pursuit of group goals. The groups may or may not respond to the appeals of this individual, but when he begins to echo the sentiment of the group and begins to work with the group toward group goals, then he becomes in effect the leader of the group. During this time of crisis, this leader attempts to establish an ideology that will win the support of competing partisans so as to present a united front. Carmichael came into a position of leadership mainly as a result of his promise to stop the majority group from exploiting Black people by any means necessary. In 1965 he had worked in Mississippi as an effective organizer and had encouraged the political participation of Blacks as a means for ending the social, economic, and political discrimination that has prohibited the Black community from becoming self-sufficient. He somehow got distracted, stopped organizing, and became "mediarized." Apparently the task of organization was bigger than the stature of the man. Robert A. Dahl says that "those who want to influence the electorate must first go through the mass media."[1] Carmichael bought the line and got smashed by those authorities who were threatened by the new ideology of Black

Power. As the most articulate advocate of Black Power, he was in fact the civil rights movement, and was beginning to win the trust of the Black masses, whose language he knew so very well. However, the "rhetoric" of revolution is not valuable to the Black masses when there are no economic benefits forthcoming. "Rhetoric" must soon be replaced by the fulfillment of promises and commitments, and this requires an intelligence network which can effectively get information into the masses who are being organized. A leader of an "ego trip" cannot spend very much time organizing, building up a political organization, or taking care of business in the Black communities where he is most needed. The most effective exercise that Carmichael performed was stressing the need for Blacks to control their own destinies. The mounting discontent experienced by other Black leaders as they attempted to obtain economic and political concessions from both good white "liberals" and "die hard," resistant conservatives, made it necessary for Black leaders to cut their ties with the white majority until such time as Blacks could build up and utilize a reservoir of resources; i.e., their numbers, intelligence network, finances, political influence, as well as cultural and intellectual traditions. Black leaders began to articulate the necessity for Blacks to control their own organizations and institutions; the result was the purging of whites from positions of leadership within civil rights organizations, and the emergence of Stokeley Carmichael and the "Black Power" philosophy.

The utility of the concept of "Black Power" lies in the fact that as an ideology, it still means different things to many different people within and outside of Black communities and is therefore subject to refinement. Not only that, but within the Black communities there has been an ideological vacuum—one which was created with the death of the American architect of nonviolence: Dr. Martin Luther King.

The ideology of nonviolence, with all of its ramifications, was an appeal to the moral "conscience" of Blacks and whites in American society. But it was not an ideology that could be embraced by the Black masses.

Dr. King was considered by many to be a national leader and a great religious leader, yet he was very ineffective in organizing the Black masses in *both* the North and the South. King's inability to influence those in the positions of power to concede to the demands of the Black protest groups was due to the fact that he was not able to promise that a certain mode of action would not be taken by other Black protest organizations. He therefore could not make commitments which were binding. Not only was Dr. King unable to keep other civil rights organizations under control, but he was also unable to convince the leadership of many of these groups that nonviolence was the ideology that was to secure the promise of "life, liberty, and the pursuit of happiness" for the Black masses.

The ideology of nonviolence was valid only if those within the Black community recognized and supported the program of Dr. King. If the Black leaders did not, could not, support Dr. King, and if the demands presented to those in positions of power were not met, then nonviolence was a useless concept. When the rioting broke out in the Black ghettos and King was not able to control the more militant groups, the ideology of nonviolence was on its deathbed; and when Dr. King was assassinated in April, 1968, nonviolence in America died with him.

As a minority group, and a very economically impoverished minority group, the only weapons which Black people have had to fight with have included the righteousness of "the cause," the moral strength of its group members, and its large numbers; all of which are important, but they do not necessarily bring about changes in the distribution of resources.

The effectiveness of any protest movement based on non-violence as an ideology, assumes that those against whom you are conducting the protest will recognize their "wrongs" and get right with God. Although the ideology of nonviolence may win the sympathy of some of those in the oppressing group, it cannot be an ideology that wins respect with the oppressed group. Nor does it influence those in power to release the oppressed group from economic slavery and social inequalities.

America is a nation of politicians and economic "interest" groups. And any group which does not have economic resources within its confines cannot bargain with a more organized, better led group—especially when that group happens to be in the majority, and controls the instruments and means of production.

The concept of Black Power as a political ideology offers a different direction for protest groups. It is not a concept that espouses love and forgiveness, but race pride and Black identity. Plus it advocates that Black masses begin to push for unconditional participation in the American society. Besides that, it offers Blacks an opportunity to protest directly against the object of protest: the white man.

Although the leaders of the Black Power Movement have very few resources, are not economically independent, and have not been able to win the support of the masses, they do have a new ideology—one that is not based on the promise of "rights" by moral persuasion, but on the promise of "rights" by political persuasion, and any other means necessary.

The morality of "power" is that it concedes nothing without demand and direct confrontation. A nation that has been built by the labor of an oppressed minority is not to be respected by the oppressed; nor can the oppressor be "reasoned with"—he must be persuaded to concede to just demands.

The discontent of the Black "masses" made them very vulnerable to the new ideology of "Black Power"; and Black youth especially has been moving with the ideology. Nothing is more evident of the impact that the "Black Power" concept has had than is the emergence of Black Student Unions on college campuses, Black Student Associations, Black Social Work Associations, Black Business Associations, and Black political parties. Most of these groups are now the strongest supporters of Black Power. The problem seems to be that few leaders can convince partisans as to which ideological path should be pursued, and which path will bring about meaningful gains to the masses of Blacks.

Many of the Black Power advocate groups seem to be doing their own thing. Yet most Black leaders are apparently confident of at least one fact: Black people will have to direct their own protest organizations, their own political organizations, and their own institutions.

Nathan Glazer and Daniel Moynihan wrote in 1963 that

> It is probable that no investment of public and private agencies on delinquency and crime prevention programs will equal the return from an investment by Negro-led and Negro-financed agencies. It is probable that no offensive on the public school system to improve the educational results among Negroes will equal what may be gained from an equivalent investment by Negro-led and Negro-financed groups and an increase in the number of Negro teachers and principals. It is possible that no effort to change the patterns of the Negro lower class family will be effective when the white family is in disorder, when strong families of whatever kind, native and ethnic, show signs of disintegration; but if anything can be done, it is likely that Negro agencies will be far more effective than public agencies and those of white Protestants.[2]

In 1966, many Black leaders were able to voice an "Amen" to Glazer's and Moynihan's observations. (The only thing that Moynihan and Glazer failed to mention was where the money or the other resources were coming from to bring about a change in the social, economic, and political situation of Blacks in America.)

The concept of "Black Power" as an ideology set the stage for the kinds of sentiments, values, and attitudes that would bring about group solidarity within Black communities. But the language for social change within the Black communities somehow has been confused with other languages which have nothing to do with revolutionary analysis, strategy, or programming.

One explanation for this confusion is that sometimes those who echo ideas are least able to carry them out.

In 1967, the National Conference on New Politics stressed the need to organize Blacks on the local levels, and the need to expend time, energies, and money in Black neighborhoods to concert Blacks in these neighborhoods into a Black power structure.[3]

The importance of transforming the Black communities into independent self-sufficient political units has much validity since power concedes nothing except by demand; and, in order to demand, any group must have the support of interest groups within that community. When a community is without "resources," it becomes even more important to be able to influence the decisions.

Fletcher Knebel says that "In a pluralistic society such as the American, power is a compound item—part political, part social, and part economic. The last is by far the most pervasive; for in a thousand and one blunt and subtle ways the dollar works it influence.[4] Black people do not have too many dollars these days, nor very many other resources to control their destinies; but within the ghettos is a reservoir of human "resources" that has never experienced any real sense of power.

A successful politically oriented Black Power Movement with functioning political organizations on the state and local levels would help to utilize this "resource." Such organizations rest upon the development of a sense of political "consciousness" among the masses.

It would seem that the emphasis of the Black leadership of the Black Power Movement should be on political organization as a means of achieving economic power and social equality.

The "issues" upon which the Black leadership could pursue the group's interests would have to be such as to come directly into conflict with the salient economic and political interests of those within the social structure who already control the instruments and means of production, and who are not now responsive to the needs of the Black communities. It is obvious, and it should be obvious to all, that those in positions of power find it to their advantage to not press for concessions for those who are economically powerless, especially when they see how economically prosperous they can become by dealing with the "powerless" as consumers only.

Many Black "protest" organizations are now very mobile, unpredictable, and unable to make commitments which are binding. Members often get frustrated and alienated while fighting against discrimination when there are no tangible results or rewards. When a group "protests" against discrimination, the leaders must be able to control the members of that group. In short, there is a need for organizational structures which can both reward and discipline members.

The Panther Party

In some cities where Black leaders have attempted to organize Blacks into a political structure, the problems seem to have outnumbered the processes. For example, the Black Panther Party in Oakland, California had two very articulate spokesmen in Huey P. Newton and Eldridge Cleaver. The former is now in jail, and the latter is a fugutive from the law. Both had uttered the rhetoric of revolution, both had charisma, and both had stated the need for organizing the masses. Yet, they too seem to have been "mediarized," and ineffective in organizing Blacks in Oakland and in nearby San Francisco.

In attempting to push the ideology of Black Power, these two men found that the one way of winning recruits was to create and support a "rhetoric revolution." "Black Power" now was interpreted as "coming from the barrel of a gun," and it was to be achieved by "pig-calling" and putting "mother- - - -" up against the wall. The Black Panther leaders seemed to assume that Black people were going to be involved in "revolution" every single day. Yet the Black masses that these leaders had hoped to recruit into the Panther Party did not come forth; mainly because there were no rewards offered to members other than guns. Consequently, the Black Panther Party organization formed a coalition with the Peace and Freedom Party during the last political election. Such a coalition was bound to fail for several reasons: First, the Panther Party did not have the support of the Black masses. It entered into a premature coalition. To quote Stokeley Carmichael and Charles V. Hamilton, authors of *Black Power: The Politics of Liberation*: "It is eventually hoped there will be a coalition of poor Blacks and poor whites. This is the only coalition which seems acceptable to us and we see such a coalition as the major internal instrument of change in the American society."[5]

Carmichael and Hamilton further state the "viable coalitions therefore stem from four pre-conditions:

a. The recognition by the parties involved of their respective self interests.
b. The mutual belief that each party stands to benefit in terms of that self interest from allying with the other or others.
c. The acceptance of the fact that each party has its own independent bases of power and does not depend for ultimate decision making on a force outside itself.
d. The realization that the coalition deals with specific and identifiable as opposed to general and vague goals.[6]

It is difficult to understand how the Panther Party was able to form a coalition with whites before it had mobilized and organized the community in which it was functioning. It was necessary to form a coalition with Black partisan supporters in the Black community before forming any other coalition.

Second, the "issue" that the Peace and Freedom Party was interested in was the war in Vietnam. On the one hand I think that Black people are concerned about the war in Vietnam, but on the other hand I don't think that they are now or ever have been interested in joining third party movements. As Joseph Loftus says, "The political landscape is littered with the tombstones of burned out third party ambitions."[7] The issues that Black people are interested in have much to do with their economic and social status in the American society. Jobs, housing, and education are salient "issues" with which many Blacks identify.

Third, the acquisition of guns is not sufficient to secure the support of a community that has few tangible resources. Fourth, the Panther Party did not know how to organize or work within a political party organization.

Furthermore, the Panther Party failed to organize Black people into a political force because it utilized all of its resources in attempting to win a spot in the mass media. Apparently it was necessary for the Black leadership to get on television to tell white people how "Black" and "powerful" they were. The only problem was that the masses, although they could sympathize with the Panthers, could not "dig the action" *in toto*; while the Black leadership of the Panther Party was telling white people how "Black" they were, the white leadership and its organizations went about the business of "taking care of" more compromising Blacks.

The Panther Party, because it has depleted most of its resources, has very few rewards to give to those within its organization. The image portrayed by the Black Panther Party is that of being a "revolutionary type" of organization. Yet the party has achieved very few concessions for the masses through its revolutionary actions. The leadership seems to think that guns, rocks, and rhetoric can be more effective in bringing about changes in the situation of Black people than the maintenance of a strong, well-defined, viable political organization. Such thinking may win recruits, but it does not win powerful Black allies.

Today the Panther Party suffers from a lack of leadership, the type of leadership that can make commitments and use its resources to influence those who make the decisions. Because of its "revolutionary" outlook, the Panther Party cannot secure the necessary resources to make its operations successful. At this point, the Black masses cannot support "revolutionaries" who cannot deliver some goodies. There is a difference between a strategy for winning concessions and a strategy for the sake of a strategy. The Black Panther Party continues to shout about revolution when the salient interests of Black people, such as jobs, housing, better schools, and social equality, hang in the balance. The "revolution" would be complete in Oakland if the Black Panther Party would concentrate on these issues.

The Black Panther Party in Oakland, as well as other so-called "revolutionary" groups, seems to lack a proper analysis of the social, economic, and political situation of Black people in the United States. But if they do understand the situation, then what is perhaps lacking is a basic understanding of the concept of "power" in its relative and absolute senses.

During the past month the internal and external problems of the Panther Party seem to stem from a lack of leadership. Those who could push the ideology of Black Power as a concept which could lead to political power are not now in a position of authority within the organization. Thus, there is a sense of a lack of direction on the part of those who are left to carry on in the absence of leaders who could arouse mass support.

Talcott Parsons says that "Power . . . is the generalized capacity to secure the performance of binding obligations by units in a system of collective organization when the obligations are legitimized with reference to their bearing on collective goals, and where, in case of recalcitrance, there is a presumption of reinforcement by negative situational sanctions—whatever the actual agency of enforcement."[8] In the "Parsonian" language of "power," the Panther Party in Oakland is bankrupt. It does not seem to be able to make any types of commitments to partisan supporters, nor does it have any way of constraining its members except through the use of guns and threats.

To mobilize the Black masses, the Panther Party will have to develop a new revolutionary strategy. The philosophy of those who organize the masses must appeal to the latter's salient interests.

Black Economics

A community without economic resources is a powerless community, and consequently, any Black leader who emerges from that community has a powerless base from which to get into a position of power. As I have suggested earlier, Black leaders have been protest leaders, revolutionary leaders, religious leaders, and many other types—but seldom have successful business leaders emerged. Part of the explanation for this rests with the fact that the economic resources of the Black community have always been outside of the Black community in the hands of the white majority group.

Some Black business leaders have recently embraced an idea called "Black Capitalism"—an idea advanced by Richard Nixon during his presidential campaign. One of the most vocal Black leaders to support this idea has been the Reverend Leon Sullivan, whose church is one of the largest in Philadelphia. The Reverend Sullivan has used his base of power—the church—to attempt to get Blacks into business enterprises. Since he is the founder of Philadelphia's Opportunities Industrialization Centers, he is in a position to exert political influence, but the reality of the situation is that because of his dependency on whites for support, his political position cannot be very useful to advancing the interests of the Black masses. He does have a large following, yet he is not very respected by the masses who feel that he has "sold out."[9]

As necessary as I think that an economic structure is, I do not believe that it can be built up by the use of loans from white "capitalists"—whose primary "interest" is as always in the making of profits. In fact, the idea of becoming a "Black capitalist" should be insulting to Black businessmen. For over three hundred and fifty years "white capitalists" have drained the Black communities of all of their economic wealth! And now, when their power bases within the Black communities are in danger of being destroyed by discontent Blacks, they begin to talk about making Blacks "capitalists."

Black leaders need to become aware of the fact that the Black masses do not want or need "Black capitalists." They need Black leaders—men who are concerned about the conditions under which Black people live. The need is for jobs and education. Black people can then build their own economic bases with the use of their own Black hands.

The National Observer in its November 25, 1968, issue stated:

> Black capitalism is no panacea for the problems of America's non-white poor. Many, perhaps most of the unemployed and underemployed who want to better their lot are probably more interested in a well paying job than they are in owning businesses. On the other hand, equal economic opportunity is an empty phrase if vital capital and technical resources are denied arbitrarily on the basis of race or place of residence . . . For the Negro, the new capital, whether in the form of white supported loans or community based investment companies, is Uncle Louie.[10]

Neither jobs nor vital capital nor technical assistance will be forthcoming unless Black leaders can make commitments which will be honored by Black people. However, an economically impoverished Black community cannot support a powerless leader who has no program, no strategy, and no politically oriented organization.

A. H. Raskin, in his analysis of the American economy, states that

The national economy has been moving uphill for seven years, the longest period of sustained peace time prosperity on record. Americans have been cutting up their individual slices of this economic melon in two contradictory ways. They have deposited $55 billion in savings banks (in New York alone, the growth in deposits was $3.3 billion in a single year); at the same time they have built up $92 billion of installment debt for automobiles, washing machines, and other enrichers of existence, on which they pay almost as much interest as the Government does on its $330 billion mountain of national debt. Tax consumer income after taxes—and with adjustment to neutralize the impact of higher wages has risen 40% since the start of the long boom. Ten million more persons have jobs and unemployment hovers around 4%, the lowest level in this decade.

The left-out in much of this progress, unfortunately, is the man who started at the bottom—the Negro. He and his family now make up 11% of the American population, and there remains more bleakness than cheer in his economic situation. The Negro unemployment rate is still double that for whites. Four Negroes out of ten live below the poverty lines, more than triple the ratio among whites. One in seven is dependent on public welfare. Those with jobs are moving into middle class income ranges much more rapidly than whites, but that is principally because, in relative terms, there are so many more to move. The median income of Negro families remains only 58% of the white level."[11]

Black leaders must therefore begin to utilize an ideology which will be able to mobilize the large number of Blacks into a cohesive self-perpetuating political community. It is my thesis that the best way of achieving this end is "Black Power."

The Need for a New Political Orientation

C. W. Mills says that "changes in the American structure of power have come about by institutional shifts in the relative positions of the political, economic, and military orders."[12] Thus, if Blacks are going to be the initiators of political reorientation, they must begin to get into those positions which would permit them to utilize their resources to influence the outcome of decisions as such decisions bear directly upon the lives of 23 million Black people. As James Q. Wilson has written, "Groups not in position to know in time cannot act in time; protest as a strategy is better suited to blocking change than to initiating it and this requires a good intelligence network."[13] I have always been somewhat sympathetic to those within the Black communities who point out that even "qualified" Black men like Ralph Bunche, Robert Weaver, Thurgood

Marshall, and other Blacks in government don't seem to have access to the "inner circle" of those who are responsible for making decisions in America related to domestic and foreign policy. Such exclusion of these men offers ample evidence of the fact that somehow Blacks were never supposed to lead or control their own destinies. What is necessary is a Black intelligence network through which Black leaders will be able to know how to utilize themselves more effectively in the political arena.

William Kornhauser advances the thesis that social pluralism supports liberal democracy.[14] What does a group in a caste system do when the concept of social pluralism embraces everyone but them? What does it do when the "liberal democracy" is, in fact, a racist society which does not want to relinquish any of its power? Kornhauser states that "the major guarantee against the aggrandizement of power by elites is the existence of a plurality of groups that are equal enough in power to generate genuine competition for leadership on the several levels of political society. A danger of bureaucratization is that it will undermine the bases for a plurality of group interests and organizations."[15] What does a group do when it has always been counted out of the competition before the game starts? What does it do when it has no viable organizations which it can use to directly affect the power elites? And what does it do when it has few group interests which conflict with those in the class structure?

The answers to most of these questions will come from Black leaders who recognize that those who own nothing in American society control nothing, and consequently are perceived as representing nothing.

Politics, Ethnic Groups, and Assimilation

Black leaders must begin to devise ways of breaking out of a *caste* system in which there are few marketable resources. They must begin to break into the class structure by any means necessary, but mainly through the political structure.

The inaccessibility of Black leadership to those who make the decisions can, in the long run, create a situation for Black people that is not only undesirable, but contrary to the group's vested interests.

The caste system created in the American society by those who control the instruments and means of production will not be changed without direct pressure from a highly organized, highly trained Black community.

Ralf Dahrendorf says that "Groups are masses of people in regular contact or communication, and possessing a recognizable structure."[16] And he further notes that "Interest groups are groups in the strict sense of the sociological term; and they are the real agents of group conflict. They have a structure, a form of organization, a program or goal, and a personnel of members."17

I think that it is time that Blacks, be they revolutionaries or Uncle Toms, begin to recognize that America is a nation of many interest groups, and that although it might be gratifying to some Blacks to say that "political power comes through the barrel of a gun," such rhetoric has nothing to do with a real analysis of the use of power. When a group lives in a society where the dominant economic class is also the majority group, it must learn to play the games of that group in power.

An examination of how other ethnic groups have "made it" in America should provide some information which would be of benefit to those who are interested in changing the social, economic, and political situation of Black people.

Whereas, the history of Black people for the past three hundred and fifty years has been *a history of protest* against overt and subtle forms of discriminatory practices which have been carried on by the host society, the history of other ethnic groups, including the Italians, the Germans, the Jews, the Russians, the Japanese, the Chinese, and now even the Puerto Ricans, has been *a history of class conflicts*. These groups have made it in American society because from their initial contact with the WASP group they sought economic status.

Robert Dahl, in his analysis of ethnic politics in New Haven, relies on the hypothesis that "an ethnic group passes through three stages on the way to political assimilation."18

In the first stage the members of the ethnic groups are almost proletarian. They work with their hands for wages in shops and factories. In some socioeconomic characteristics they are highly homogeneous. They are low in status, income, and influence. For leadership, they depend on highly influential politicians who have come from previously assimilated ethnic groups. Members of the new group serve sometimes as intermediaries between the group and the older leaders, acquiring in the process moderate influence and experience as sub-leaders. Some of these ethnic sub-leaders eventually receive nominations for minor offices, such as alderman, where the constituency is drawn predominantly from the sub-leader's ethnic group . . . Political homogeneity, then, is a function of socioeconomic homogeneity. . . .19

In the second stage,

. . . an increasing and by now significant proportion of the group have white collar jobs and other social characteristics of the middling strata. High status, income, and self-confidence allow some to gain considerable political influence. They begin to challenge and overthrow the incumbent leaders on whom they hitherto have been dependent; amidst charges of betrayal and ingratitude they now move into positions of leadership. Depending on the size of his ethnic group and local attitudes, an ethnic leader may even receive a major party nomination for a leading city-wide office, such as the mayoralty . . . Consequently, an ethnic candidate who can avoid the diverse socio-economic issues is still able to activate strong sentiments of ethnic solidarity in all strata of his ethnic group; he can command a significantly higher proportion of the votes of his group than can a candidate without the ethnic tie.[20]

In the third stage, according to Dahl,

Large segments are assimilated into the middling and upper strata; they have middle class jobs, accept middle class neighborhoods, and look to others in the middling strata for friends, associates, and marriage partners. To these people, ethnic politics is often embarrassing or meaningless. Political attitudes and loyalties have become a function of socioeconomic characteristics. Members of the group display little political homogeneity. Although sentimental and traditional attachments to a particular party may persist, they are easily ruptured. The political effectiveness of a purely ethnic appeal is now negligible among the middling and upper strata. A middle class or upper class candidate who happens to be drawn from an ethnic group may use this tie to awaken sentiments of pride; he may win votes, but to do so he must also emphasize socioeconomic issues.[21]

The majority of Black people are still in the "stage one" phase of being assimilated. This fact stems from the initial experience of Black people in America.

The history of Black people in America for the past three hundred and fifty years has been a history of organized protest against discriminatory practices. The institution of slavery was such as to deny to Black people an organizational apparatus for the development of leadership that could, in fact, deal with those issues which were relevant to Black people as a group. The Black people in America *were* the issues. Black people were not brought to this country to become a part of a class structure. They were to be the *commodities* upon which that class structure was to be made viable and lucrative.

When a human group is the "economic interest" over which social classes compete, then there is no precedent for that group to build its own social structure.

The Emancipation Proclamation which was signed by the "white racist" Abraham Lincoln in 1863 freed the slaves as an "economic interest" of competing social classes, but kept the

Negroes in a caste system. This system was to never participate in the social, economic, and political life of the American society. The attitude of those in the power structure during the time of slavery and even today is that "Blacks will have only what we choose to give them." Or as Chief Justice Taney said in 1857, Black people have no rights that white people have to respect.[22]

Such an attitude made it necessary during the time of slavery to conduct protest movements, and since the protests were leveled against the majority group, it is quite obvious that it was not going to pursue "interests" which were subject to undermine the existing state of power relations.

The fact remains that although these protest groups and organizations were important because of the nature of the conflict between Blacks and whites throughout the United States, they played a very small role in changing the economic and political structures. It is only when the economic interests of the dominant class are threatened that it begins to make room in the social structure for members of ethnic groups, or even becomes responsive to the demands of the ethnic groups. Groups in power are primarily concerned with continuity and stability. They seldom give up power, if they give it up at all.

In a sense, any form of social protest by a group has its effect on the total social structure, but when a group for three hundred and fifty years is not able to leave the "protest" stage because of prohibitions imposed by the majority group and dominant economic class, its chances for social mobility are quite slim—especially when the group in question is a "visible" minority. It is one thing to have to spend a lifetime protesting for the right to use the bathroom, to ride on a bus, or to eat in a restaurant; none of these interests in fact threaten the salient economic and political interests of those in positions of power. It is quite another thing to push for jobs, housing, better educations, and political representation. All of the latter conflict directly with the interests of the existing social classes.

The other ethnic groups managed to move through their initial stages of being assimilated fairly rapidly; they did not have to prove themselves to the dominant economic class. Their ability to be absorbed into the white society, because their physical characteristics resembled more the host society's standard of beauty, etc., made it unnecessary for them to remain in a caste position. In short, the main thing that these groups had to do was to melt into "whiteness."

A second factor that permitted these other ethnic groups to assimilate is that the dominant economic class did not prohibit them from setting up their own political machinery. As a matter of fact, it was ethnic politics which enabled many members of the power elite to maintain the positions they hold now. The white leadership could make promises to these groups which it later was able to keep; but when it came to the point of dealing with Black people, the politicians knew exactly how to exploit the Black vote without even going into the Black communities. Why should a politician pay attention to a community that has no economic interest groups, no business community, and no political organizations through which to command the loyalties of its group members? And why should politicians pay attention to a community where there is a lack of leadership?

It's very strange that in 1964, a book had to be written with such a title as *Who Speaks for the Negro?*—especially since Black people had been in the United States for over three hundred years!

Still a third important factor in permitting other ethnic groups to assimilate is the fact that labor unions such as the American Federation of Labor, the United Mine Workers, and the CIO played an important role in the early history of the American industrial development. These unions were able to speak for the ethnic groups. The unions were highly organized, well financed, and very well managed by men like Samuel Gompers, George Meany, and John Mitchell.[23]

The most important thing about these unions, though, is the fact that when they began to press for higher wages for the laborers, they were able to win tangible economic, political, and social concessions; consequently, the members of the ethnic groups felt as though they were a part of the social structure. The unions provided the medium through which these groups could express their grievances. There was no need for them to develop a group of protest leaders or to conduct long protest campaigns: the unions helped them get better paying jobs, housing, and educational opportunities. Apprenticeship programs were set up in local communities which permitted the new immigrant groups to develop a marketable skill in their own community; consequently, these groups were also able to develop business structures within the local communities. During the early 1900s, it took very little capital to set up small business enterprises, and to expand when the volume of sales increased.

In short, there were precedents set for the new immigrant groups by those "WASPs" who had initially set the style for all other groups to follow. The WASPs were racists, so it was quite natural for the new immigrants to become racists too.

It should now be clear that I am suggesting that the reason for the social situation of Black people in the United States is that the conflict which Blacks have had with whites has never, until recently, been a direct threat to the economic interests of the latter. When Black Power advocates push an ideology which has as its basic tenets social and economic issues, the shell of caste is smashed and the class conflicts begin. Such is the state of affairs in America. The riots of the past four years have been the result of the competition between Black and white laborers for blue and white collar jobs. A second level of competition has been between Blacks who have now decided to push for administrative jobs in areas which have heretofore been considered the white man's.

It is my feeling that the real class conflicts will now begin, and that the Black people in America can, as a group operating through political organizations, move toward political power.

The Politics of Large Numbers

Karl Marx wrote that

The possessing class and the proletarian class express the same human alienation. But the former is satisfied with its situation, feels itself well-established in it, recognizes this self-alienation as its own power, and thus has the appearance of a human existence. The latter feels itself crushed by this self-alienation, sees in it its own impotence, and the reality of an inhumane situation. It is, to use an expression of Hegel's, 'in the midst of degradation the revolt against degradation,' a revolt to which it is forced by the contradiction between its humanity and its situation, which is an open, clear and absolute negation of its humanity. Within the framework of alienation, therefore, the property owners are the conservatives, and the proletarians the destructive party.[24]

No statement points more clearly to the nature of the Black revolution in America. Indeed, not only have Blacks been alienated from the human family, but they have been alienated from access to the social class structure.

Marx further writes that

The more developed and universal is the political thought of a people, the more the proletariat—at least in the beginning of the movement—wastes its forces on foolish and futile uprisings which are drowned in blood. Because the proletariat thinks politically, it sees the sources of bad conditions in will, and all the means of improvement in force and the overthrow of a particular form of State.... The social life from which the worker is shut out is a social life very different in kind and extent from that of his political sphere. The social life from which his own labor excludes him, is life itself, physical and cultural life, human morality, human activity, human enjoyments, real human existence. Human life is the true social life of man. As the irremediable exclusion from this life is much more complete, more unbearable and contradictory than the exclusion from political life, so is the ending of this exclusion, and even a limited reaction, a revolt against it, more fundamental, as man is more fundamental than the citizen, human life more than political life. The industrial revolt may thus be limited, but it has a universal significance; the political revolt may be universal, but it conceals under a gigantic form a narrow spirit.[25]

According to Marx,

A social revolution has thus a universal aspect, because though it may occur in only one manufacturing district, it is a human protest against an unhuman life, because it begins from the single real individual, and because the social life against this exclusion from which the individual reacts, is the real social life of man, a really human life. The political aspect of a revolution consists of the movement of the politically uninfluential classes to end their exclusion from political life and power. Its standpoint is that of the State, an abstract whole, which only exists by virtue of its separation from real life, and which is unthinkable without the organized opposition between the universal idea and the individual existence of man. A revolution of a political kind also organizes, therefore, in accordance with this narrow and discordant outlook, a ruling group in society at the expense of society

... Or else a 'social revolution with a political aspect' is simply a paraphrase of what used to be called simply a 'political revolution' or 'revolution' *tout court*. Every revolution breaks up the old society; to this extent, it is social. Every revolution overthrows the existing ruling power; to this extent, it is political.[26]

The Negro revolution thus far has been a social revolt against the old order. It is time for the revolt to take on a more political image. Since the oppressed group in the American society is also the minority group, the tactics of the revolutionary process must be channeled to fit the circumstances.

A successful revolution in America must win allies, and it must not alienate those in the proletarian class who at some point would possibly form some sort of tentative coalition for the purpose of wielding political influence. Since many of the other immigrant groups or ethnic groups that have come to America have been white, their interests are presently similar to those within the power hierarchy. Therefore, those Black leaders who seek to win white recruits must first of all exercise influence over those who live within the Black communities. The essence of exercising influence over partisan groups within the Black communities is that the direction toward operational unity is established. Most oppressed groups become prisoners to their environment. It becomes a necessity for those who seek to be "free" to change the circumstances of such imprisonment. To be able to "free" itself from an economically and socially impoverished environment, a group must find ways of changing the existing socio-economic structure. And in America this structure can be changed only by large numbers operating against those who are in the seats of power. Black leadership must begin to develop the concept of Black power by making use of the political resources now available within the Black communities.

This means that short and long range objectives must be planned and a reorientation of purpose must be such as to win recruits. Blacks must be convinced of the trustfulness of those who lead, and those whites who are recruited must be recruited for the purpose of pursuing issues which are of interest to both groups.

Such a strategy might be called the politics of large numbers since those resources most available for mobilization in economically and socially impoverished communities are the people themselves. The organization of large numbers of black and white laborers for political purposes is a first step toward affecting the decision making process which has kept the oppressed groups "in their places."

Harris and Brink (1963) wrote in their book *The Negro Revolution in America* that ". . . the future of the Negro revolution in large part, depends on how Negroes will fight through the impediments to registration, and how many will cast their ballots in every election from now on."[27]

James Q. Wilson stated that

There are very few precedents from which one might infer predictions about political behavior when Negroes are in the majority in the city or county, and vote. (In Washington, D. C. Negroes are in the majority, but there are few issues of substance to decide through the vote.) There are some southern communities which are over 50 percent Negro and in which many (though not all) Negroes vote. Little is known about them except that while the franchise has ended harassment by public officials and law enforcement officers, it has not revolutionized the living conditions of the Negroes. Perhaps the safest prediction is that the vote will have very different effects in different places.[28]

The accuracy of these scholars' observations are born out by the political behavior of Blacks between the years 1963 and 1968.

The Voting Rights Act of 1965 provided the protections necessary for Black voters in the South to overcome the "impediments of registration."[29] The most important fact to note here is that *for the first time the civil rights organizations* were working together to secure the franchise. In 1963 the COFO organization (Council of Federated Organizations) was formed. It was composed of all of the civil rights organizations functioning in Mississippi, including SNCC, CORE, NAACP, SCLC, and a number of other groups such as the Holmes County Voters' League and the Ruleville

Citizenship Organization, to help bring about the franchise for Blacks in the deltas of the South.[30] This organization was the first effective Black political machine to organize the Black masses. Its goal was to register Blacks in order to have political influence. It was successful in that goal; however, the experience of the civil rights struggle in Mississippi has not been repeated successfully in any city where there is a large concentration of Blacks. By the end of 1966, 995,000 Blacks in the South had registered to vote![31]

Although there seems to be a significant increase in the numbers of Blacks registering in the South, there are still over 2,500,000 Blacks who have not registered—for some explainable as well as unexplainable reasons—even though they are eligible.[32]

In the industrial states of the North, there were 3,550,000 Blacks registered to vote by the end of 1967. In the early part of 1968, a total of 50,000 more Blacks registered—bringing the total up to 4,000,000 by the time of the 1968 Presidential election.[33]

Harris and Brink have estimated the potential electoral vote of Blacks in the South to be over 5,184,000. In 1963, the total registered voters in the South was 1,600,000 or 30% of its potential; by 1966, 1,083,000 more Blacks had registered.[34] This number has steadily increased during 1969.

In 1964, the Black vote helped to elect Lyndon Johnson to the office of President.[35] In 1965, John Lindsay became the Mayor of the City of New York after receiving some 44% of the Black vote.[36] In 1965, Carl B. Stokes came within one percentage point of becoming the Mayor of Cleveland.[37] In 1966, Ernest "Fritz" Hollings of South Carolina won election to the United States Senate with the help of 89% of the Black vote.[38] In 1967, Blacks helped to elect a Black man to the office of sheriff in Macon County, a county made up of 84% Blacks.[39] The significance of his election was that he won in a county where twice as many whites are registered as Blacks, a condition which prevails in no less than sixty-seven countries.[40] (It should be noted that Carl Stokes in 1967 became the Mayor of Cleveland by a thin 1,700 votes, and Robert Hatcher became the Mayor of Gary, Indiana by an even smaller percentage.)[41] In 1968, the Black vote helped to elect Alan Cranston to the United States Senate.[42]

The impetus for change in the political behavior of Blacks stems from the fact that there were issues which were of interest to the Black people in many communities. The issues—namely, "law and order," jobs, open occupancy, police brutality, welfare, de facto segregation in most of the major cities' school systems, the death of Dr. Martin Luther King, and voting rights in the South—were transformed into political currency by both white and Black leaders. Add to this list the controversy over the concept of Black Power and it becomes clear that the political behavior of Blacks in many cities was indeed taking on a different style.

Presently Black people in America number about 23 million, or about 10% of the total population. Most of these 23 million are concentrated in the South and the big industrial states—namely, Mississippi, Alabama, Texas, Florida, Georgia, Louisiana, Arkansas, Virginia, Tennessee, North Carolina, South Carolina, New York, Illinois, Michigan, California, New Jersey, Ohio, and Pennsylvania.[43]

By the end of 1970, six million Black babies will be born; and, by the end of 1970 too, there will be some 14.5 million Blacks living in central cities.[44] By 1975, the Black population in 23 major cities is expected to reach the critical level of 40 percent or more of the electorate.[45]

Thus it is possible to see that in "numbers," Blacks are their own greatest asset or resource. It now remains for Black leaders to develop the political machinery through which the masses will be able to become a strong political pressure group.

It will be necessary for Black leaders to use every means necessary to unite Black people. In the absence of resources within the Black communities, Black leaders will have to depend mostly on their own styles of leadership to gain the support of the masses. People will not sacrifice the small comforts they have unless they know that they can trust those who represent them to win larger concessions.

The concept of Black Power does offer Black people an opportunity to redefine their political priorities. Yet a minority group cannot effect changes without strong political machinery. As members of a caste system, and as members of a minority group, the future of Black people is somewhat dependent upon the political process. Coalitions may have to be formed, but such coalitions must have the support of a large segment of Black people as well as Black leaders. As Black leaders become skilled in the art of political organization, discipline will become much easier to maintain among all partisan groups within the communities.

Summary and Conclusions

This paper has been an attempt to show that the Black Power movement is not an "extremist" movement, but that the ideology of Black Power is a necessary prerequisite for the survival of Black people in the American society. The following conclusions can be drawn from this analysis of the concept of Black Power as an ideology, and the Black Power movement as a unifying force:

1. The concept of Black Power provides the most useful ideology for unifying Black people into a political community

that is conscious of its obligations, commitments, loyalties, and group goals.

2. The concept of Black Power as an ideology for realizing political goals is not an end in and of itself, but offers a beginning for accomplishing new ends with a new ideology.

3. The economic and social situation of Black people in America is such that the most powerful issues for focusing upon group objectives, for obtaining political victories, include jobs, housing, rat control, police brutality, higher education, and "white racism."

4. The Black Power Movement has great political relevance to the future of Black people in America as it directs the resources of protest toward the object of protest—the white society.

5. The concept of Black Power as an ideology can provide the strategy necessary for the development of political structures within Black communities on local and county levels.

6. Politics or political warfare has never been the opium of Black leaders, but in the future as they become more experienced in the political area, they will become more effective with and outside of the Black communities.

7. The chief "resource" which must be converted into political currency is the large numbers of Blacks who now live in urban communities. Therefore Black leaders must appeal to Black supporters with an ideology which will insure them that their time, energies, sacrifices, and loyalties will in both the long and short run bring about meaningful concessions in the form of greater redistribution of economic and political rewards.

8. As increasing numbers of Blacks register to vote, the political structure in the United States will be completely restructured.

9. The Black communities must develop an economic base within their confines while at the same time moving away from dependency upon white leadership, white domination, and white control.

10. Coalitions with white groups should not be formed until coalitions with Black partisan supporters are so secure as to bring about greater benefit to Black people, and not just to Black leaders and Black organizations.

11. There is a need for a reevaluation of "revolutionary" tactics and strategies.

12. Nonviolent protest should be utilized according to the benefits that can be gained by the Black community. As Black people have advanced "the cause" they have found that nonviolence as an ideology is a way of curing some of the ills of

the souls, but not for changing the deplorable living conditions and economic exploitations of which they have been the constant victims.

The current ideologies of the various civil rights organizations are sometimes conflicting, though not necessarily diametrically opposing. The discontent between these organizations has come about because of the differences as related to strategy and methodology as well as the fact that Black leaders could not ever commit themselves to achieve limited objectives. Many of the Black protest leaders claim that they have the support of the Black masses, when in fact their base of power lies outside of the Black community, and not within.

A degree of trust is now developing between Black leaders and the Black masses, but this trust has not generated into mutual sharing of group objectives and loyalty.

Thus, the sense of powerlessness of Black people in America is reflected in the absence of influence that Black leaders have over those in positions of power. Control of the political and economic power domains of Black communities is still held directly and indirectly by whites. In dealing with those in positions of authority, or their agents, Black leaders have not been able to make any commitments that are binding; and the majority group has never conceded to the demands of Black communities because the leaders have not been able to make commitments, plus the simple fact that it has not wanted to. America is a land of economic and political interest groups. Consequently, in dealing with Black leaders, those in positions of authority have not had to concede to the demands of Blacks primarily because whites are in the majority, and secondly because there are few economic resources within the Black communities.

Most ethnic groups that have come to this country have become socially mobile because they were immediately in conflict with the salient economic interests of the majority group, plus they were immediately a part of the class structure by virtue of their ability to assimilate into or melt into "whiteness." The visibility of the Black masses has been a major factor in prohibiting Blacks from securing a foothold in the economic and political life of America. With the rise of the Black Power Movement, Blacks no longer have to be preoccupied with whether or not they are going to be accepted by the majority group, by melting into whiteness. The new medium of participation is Black Power, which speaks not to acceptance, but to vested interests, and the utilization of the political machinery to protect the vested interests of 23 million Black Americans.

Footnotes

[1] Robert A. Dahl, *Who Governs?* (New Haven, 1961), p. 256.

[2] Nathan Glazer and Daniel Moynihan, *Beyond the Melting Pot* (Cambridge, 1964), p. 84.

[3] Nathan Wright, *Black Power and Urban Unrest* (New York, 1967).

[4] Fletcher Knebel, reported in *Look* magazine, July 26, 1968, p. 70.

[5] Stokeley Carmichael and Charles V. Hamilton, *Black Power, the Politics of Liberation* (New York, 1967), p. 82.

[6] *Ibid.*, p. 79.

[7] Joseph A. Loftus, "Third Parties," *New York Times Election Handbook* (New York, 1968), p. 121.

[8] Reinhard Bendix and Seymour Martin Lipset, *Class, Status and Power* (New York, 1966), p. 244.

[9] "Black Capitalism," *National Observer*, Nov. 25, 1968, pp. 1-10.

[10] *Ibid.*, p. 10.

[11] A. H. Raskin, "Profile of the Voter," *New York Times Election Handbook*, p. 153.

[12] C. W. Mills, *The Power Elite* (New York, 1956).

[13] James Q. Wilson, "Negro Politics," *Daedalus: Journal of the American Arts and Sciences*, p. 966.

[14] William Kornhauser, *The Politics of Mass Society*, (New York, 1959), p. 13.

[15] *Ibid.*, p. 236.

[16] Ralf Dahrendorf, *Class and Class Conflict in Industrial Society* (Stanford, 1959), p. 180.

[17] *Ibid.*, p. 180.

[18] Robert A. Dahl, *Who Governs?* p. 34.

[19] *Ibid.*, p. 34.

[20] *Ibid.*, p. 35.

[21] *Ibid.*, p. 35.

[22] Albert P. Blaustein and Robert Zangrando, *Civil Rights and the American Negro* (New York, 1968), p. 162.

[23] Julius Jacobson, ed., *The Negro and the American Labor Movement* (New York, 1968), p. 49 ff.

[24] T. B. Bottomore, *Karl Marx, Selected Writings and Social Philosophy* (New York, 1956), p. 231.

[25] *Ibid.*, p. 236 ff.

[26] *Ibid.*, p. 25 ff.

[27] William Brink and Louis Harris, *The Negro Revolution* (New York, 1963), p. 95.

[28] James Q. Wilson, *The Negro In Politics* (New York, 1965), p. 949.

[29] Len Holt, *The Summer that Didn't End* (New York, 1965), p. 31.

[30]William Brink and Louis Harris, *Black and White,* p. 87.

[31]*Ibid.,* p. 87.

[32]A. H. Raskin, *op. cit.,* p. 82.

[33]Brink and Harris, *The Negro Revolution,* p. 82.

[34]Brink and Harris, *op. cit.*

[35]*Ibid.,* p. 79.

[36]*Ibid.,* p. 81.

[37]*Ibid.,* p. 87.

[38]*Ibid.,* p. 83.

[39]*Ibid.,* p. 83.

[40]A. H. Raskin, *op. cit.,* p. 58.

[41]*Sacramento Bee,* November 8, 1968, p. 7 ff.

[42]Brink and Harris, *op. cit.,* p. 80.

[43]U.S. Riot Commission, "Report of the National Advisory Committee on Civil Disorders," p. 409.

[44]*Ibid.*

[45]Brink and Harris, *op. cit.* p. 80.

The Stuggle for San Francisco State

Bill Barlow and Peter Shapiro

On February 2, 1969, over five hundred people gathered at the San Francisco Labor Temple to demonstrate their support for the striking students and faculty at San Francisco State College. The rally marked the transition of the strike into its second semester; but more important, it was the first time that a broad cross section of Bay Area labor leaders had publicly announced their support for the students as well as the striking faculty of the American Federation of

Teachers. Representatives of the strikers were joined on the rostrum by delegates from the black community, the Latin community, the Chinese and Japanese community; and by spokesmen for the teamsters, the longshoremen, the oil workers, the farm workers, the hospital employees and the painters. The rally did not represent any significant turning point in the strike, but it did tend to reflect its magnitude and its importance to the San Francisco community. Statistical data alone bear out the contention that the S. F. State strike is without precedent in the string of campus rebellions which have occurred since the FSM at Berkeley in 1964. Now three months old, it is already the longest sustained student strike in American history, and the AFT walkout represents the first faculty strike in the history of California higher education. Since the first week of the strike, up to 600 police, some of them from outside the City, have occupied the campus on a daily basis. Over 700 people have been arrested, 456 on a single day for participating in an "illegal" on-campus rally. Classroom attendance hovered around 50% before the AFT went out, and plunged down to about 20% during the final months of the fall semester. Overall, the campus has been effectively paralyzed for most of the semester, and there are no indications that a let-up will occur in the spring.

The strike was initially called in the last week of October by the Black Students Union around a series of grievances involving a proposed Black Studies Department, admission policies, financial aid and personnel disputes. But before it even began, the situation was compounded by the suspension of English instructor George Murray, a member of the BSU central committee and Minister of Education of the Black Panther Party. Murray's suspension came on the heels of a growing number of attacks on the Black Panthers by public officials, coupled with an intensified degree of police harrassment; it was carried out without even the pretense of due process. By the time the strike was launched on November 6th, it had gained the support of several hundred white students and had broadened to include five other third world student organizations on campus. These groups included the Mexican-American Student Confederation (MASC), the Asian–American Political Alliance (AAPA), the Latin American Student Organization (LASO), the Philippine-American Collegiate Endeavor (PACE), and the Intercollegiate Chinese for Social Action (ICSA); they had allied together with the BSU under the umbrella organization, Third World Liberation Front (TWLF). Together, they issued a set of 15 demands which projected the needs of the third-world students on campus, and took the position that the strike would not end until all the demands had been met.

The administration's response was both frantic and equivocal: President Robert Smith called for negotiations, called in the cops, and closed down the campus whenever a large student-police clash occurred. The faculty went into special session and emerged calling for a campus-wide convocation to discuss the issues—convocations having been used in the past to co-opt student activism on campus. But history was not to repeat itself this time around; the TWLF effectively utilized the convocation to broaden the campus' understanding of their grievances, and to expose the procrastination of the administration. The continued vacillation of President Smith succeeded in completely undercutting his position, and by the end of November, under pressure from Governor Reagan and the State College Trustees, he had resigned. The Trustees then appointed S. I. Hayakawa to take Smith's place.

Hayakawa, a self-styled "liberal Democrat" with a fervid distaste for student activism, became the executor of Reagan's "hard line" strategy. He declared a "state of emergency," banned all free speech and assembly, and vowed to keep the campus open by any means necessary. The first two weeks of December were marked by a pattern of daily violence and confrontations between students and police. The escalation of the struggle brought the black and other minority communities out to the campus to declare their support for the strike, and to deplore the use of massive police force against the students. In addition, the AFT began to lay the groundwork for a strike of its own, drawing up a list of grievances and requesting strike sanctions from the San Francisco Labor Council. With public support for the strike growing, Hayakawa closed the campus a week early for the Christmas holidays. During the vacation a rash of "citizens committees" and outside mediators attempted to arbitrate the strike, but the Trustees refused to enter into any kind of formal negotiations, and all mediation efforts fell through. The Labor Council gave the AFT strike sanctions, and January 6th found students and faculty jointly manning picket lines at all the entrances to the campus. Hayakawa maintained his posture of open-campus-with-police-occupation, but attendance was way off and the strain was beginning to show.

Despite the threats of mass firings of professors and court injunctions against both student and faculty picketing, the month of January saw the school effectively closed down by persistent picketing. The only serious skirmishes took place when the cops would raid the picket lines to selectively "bust" student strike leaders. But this intimidation did not deter the strikers, and the semester ground to a close with class attendance fixed at around 20% and final exams hopelessly disrupted.

Meanwhile, the impact of the strike was being felt on other campuses in California. The AFT locals at a number of other State Colleges staged a one-day sympathy strike, and at San Jose State, where the local AFT had gone out in conjunction with the S. F. State chapter, twenty-eight professors were fired. San Fernando Valley State College reached a state of crisis over a similar series of student demands in mid-December. The College of San Mateo erupted on December 13th, after which it was literally turned into an armed camp. And at U. C. Berkeley, a TWLF had formed, drawn up their own set of demands, and begun a strike that was slowly gaining momentum. What had started at S. F. State as an isolated student action had mushroomed into a statewide educational crisis.

Education: a Race and
Class Privilege

The rapid spread of the S. F. state strike suggests a set of issues which cannot be confined to one campus. In point of fact, the strike marks the culmination of a process which began ten years ago. Prior to 1959, California was fond of advertising the fact that it had one of the most inclusive, tuition-free, publicly-supported higher-education systems in the United States. Its state colleges were supposedly prepared to accommodate any student in the top 70% of his graduation class, percentile rating being determined by grade point average; for the top 33%, there was also the University of California, rapidly achieving a national reputation as one of the leading new "multiversities." In accordance with industry's increasing needs for skilled, college-trained personnel and California's exploding population, both these institutions were expanding at an impressive rate.

A progressive educational system, however, can't be supported with a regressive tax structure, and the California tax structure is highly regressive. Business and industry bear only 20% of the state's general tax burden; personal income tax, the only truly progressive tax in the state, accounts for no more than 20% of the total state tax, and even here, the taxable income of a person making $500,000 a year tends to be no more than $20,000. Taking into account the shift to the consumer with sales taxes, the state's largest single source of tax revenue, and the shift to the tenant with property taxes, it is, in the words of one expert, "not unreasonable to assume for public policy purposes that household units in California bear at least 80% of the tax burden." Standard Oil of California pays no state taxes at all, and the biggest firms of the agri-business industry, one of the state's two or three largest, pay no more than $50,000 a year. Thus, despite the fact that it has potentially one of the richest tax bases in the nation, California was able to spend only $10.79 per $1000 of personal income on higher education in 1965, as compared with $17.89 for the other 25 western states.

As a direct result of such conditions, 1959 found the state higher-education system in the throes of a fiscal crisis. Enrollments had been increasing steadily since the period immediately following the Korean war, and, the war babies having come of age, the educational system was due for an explosion. In the period between 1960 and 1975, full-time enrollment figures were expected to triple, the increase being felt most acutely at the lower-division level. As it turned out, the state colleges and the university were to add, on the average, one new campus every year between 1958 and the present, to say nothing of expansion of existing institutions. Plans for several of these new campuses were already before the state legislature at the beginning of its 1959 session. The legislators knew very well that, barring a drastic revision of the state tax structure or a drastic redistribution of the state's wealth, it would be impossible for California to continue to underwrite mass public higher education—unless its commitment to do so were modified in some crucial way. To come to grips with the problem, they authorized the Liaison Committee of the University of California Board of Regents and the State Board of Education to draw up a Master Plan for Higher Education in California. Ten years later, the fruits of that document have become a major issue of the student strike, not only at San Francisco State, but at U C. Berkeley, the College of San Mateo, and literally dozens of other campuses where the grievances of third-world students are erupting or have threatened to erupt.

The authors of the Master Plan faced a perplexing dilemma. The pauperization of the state demanded that public higher education be trimmed down to size, or at least made more "efficient." Their charge from the state legislature was to eliminate "duplication of efforts" on the part of the state colleges and the university, between which there was an increasingly bitter competition, not simply for state funds, but for the federal research grants upon which the prestige and the fiscal well-being of American academic institutions were coming increasingly to depend. At the same time, the Master Plan was expected to somehow maintain the facade of state-supported college education available to all who needed it; thus, it simply would not do to deal with exploding enrollments by placing an absolute ceiling on the number of students the state was willing to educate. Hopes that the private colleges might relieve some of the burden were to no avail, since the private colleges, too, were having financial difficulties, owing to the decreasing purchasing power of endowment income, the shortage of federal funds, and an already prohibitive tuition level which effectively excluded most of the state's population.

A worse problem was the failure of the higher education system as a whole to stay in tune with the job market. Too many students were being trained for the wrong kind of jobs; not enough were being maneuvered into the technical courses and vocational training out of which the bulk of the work force was supposed to emerge. Somehow, within the framework of the public subsidy, the functions of the various institutions had to be made more specialized; some way had to be found to exert a greater degree of control over the number of students who were channeled toward the various levels of the employment pyramid.

Out of this set of seeming contradictions, the Master Plan evolved a unique and unsettling solution. As a way of quantitatively limiting the maximum enrollments of the various institutions on the basis of what the state was able to afford, it altered the institutions qualitatively by jacking up their academic admissions standards, reducing the number of college-eligible students, and channeling the rest into two-year "junior colleges" financed chiefly by local rather than state taxes. In terms of their students, the junior colleges served functionally to prolong high school by two years. As for the four-year schools, admission to the University of California was now restricted to the top 12-1/2% of the high school graduation classes, while admission to the state colleges was permitted for the top 33%. The junior colleges were theoretically "open to everybody"; hence, the boast that the higher education system as a whole was being made more inclusive than ever. The claim is true in the most limited sense only, for even as the system was made more "inclusive," an elaborate and incredibly rigid class structure was built into it.

To determine which of the "segments"—junior college, state college, or university—a particular student would attend, the Master Plan made liberal use of the "tracking system," which quickly became a fixture in the California public schools. Students are "tracked" as early as second grade, the purpose being to separate the "college material" from the "less academically inclined." While the former are groomed for the social role the state expects them to assume ten years later, the latter's education is an exercise in social control at its crudest, with only halfhearted attempts at remedial coursework and, later, vocational training. Tracking is done on the basis of IQ test scores; ultimately, a student's eligibility for admission to the four-year colleges—previously dependent on grade point average alone—is determined in no small part by his scores on the College Board exams. Both of these are standardized tests which are generally acknowledged to promulgate a conventional, white-middle-class bias; they penalize the black or third-world student, the poor student, and often the creative student. The reason for this is fairly obvious: implicit in the notion that all students can be evaluated according to a uniform national standard is a total disregard for social, ethnic or cultural differences, to say nothing of those of individual temperament. Moreover, the inherent inflexibility of such standards renders them incapable of taking into account a student's special experiences or educational needs. Rather, his academic worth is determined by a set of social functions which have nothing to do with either him or his education—save, of course, for the limitations they impose on both. Under the Master Plan, these academic standards were invoked for the purpose of rationalizing certain inconsistencies in the California tax structure, though the stated rationale was strictly educational.

Such conditions are part of a nation-wide educational malaise. But it is particularly striking to see the way they affected the California public colleges. It might have been expected that the effective exclusion of minorities would continue at the University of California, which had always tended to be a lily-white school. But the drop in minority enrollment in the state colleges was more drastic. At San Francisco State alone, the implementation of the Master Plan was immediately followed by the decline in black enrollment from 12% to 3%—this in a city whose public schools were rapidly approaching 70% nonwhite.

Income distribution throughout the three levels of the public higher-education system suggests that there is a class bias, as well as race bias, built into the Master Plan. Nearly two-thirds of the students in the junior colleges have parents whose yearly income is less than $10,000. For the state colleges, the figure is precisely one-half. And for the University of California, two-thirds of the students come from family income brackets of OVER $10,000 a year, and for a majority, the figure is closer to $12,000. The significance of this lies in the fact that the income brackets under $10,000 a year pay over half the state's taxes. At least half these taxpayers are third world, among them 3 1/2 million chicanos, 1 1/2 million blacks, as well as Chinese, Japanese, Filipinos and American Indians. Yet the state spends twice as much money on the average university student as on the average state-college student, and three times as much on the average state college student as on the average junior-college student. In effect, the working people and the ethnic minorities of California are forced to subsidize the quality education of the children of the rich, while their own children are lucky to get two years of schooling in the sparsely-financed junior colleges.

This last set of statistics points up one of the supreme inconsistencies in the Master Plan. Theoretically, the three "segments" were created not simply on the basis of entrance requirements or academic standards; rather, they sought to comply with the state legislature's directive that there be no "duplication of efforts." Each segment was given a different "function" and expected to "strive for excellence in its own sphere." To the university fell the responsibility for graduate instruction and research; conveniently, this also gave it a monopoly on federal grants. The state colleges were supposed to be the major institutions of undergraduate education. And the junior colleges were designed to siphon off students from the four-year colleges and thereby reduce the operating costs of the system as a whole; confined to lower-division work, they were supposed to salvage "late bloomers" and redirect them into the four-year schools when they were better equipped to cope with the difficulties of college-level work. But this "differentiation of functions" does not show up in the budgeting of the respective institutions, which actually makes the dictum "excellence in your own sphere" an impossibility. Though undergraduate education is supposedly the province of the state colleges, more is spent both in teaching salaries and in total instructional expenditure on undergraduate education at the university. And though the junior colleges are supposed to specialize in lower-division education, the state colleges get more money, both in teaching salaries and total instructional expenditure, for their own lower divisions. University libraries are far better funded and better supplied; the university receives far more in capital outlays. But the worst discrepancies show up in the area of faculty workload, salaries, and fringe benefits. Average salaries at the university exceed those at state colleges by over $1000; for full professors, the gap is nearly $3000. The state college faculty have one of the heaviest workloads in the nation. They have less time for sabbatical leaves, less opportunities to do research (even without federal grants), fewer paid assistants. And they have no formal contract rights whatsoever, a situation which became painfully obvious when an across-the-board pay cut for state college faculty, which happened to violate the terms under which most of them had been hired, was upheld by the courts on the grounds that none of those terms had been in writing. Claims to "excellence in their sphere" notwithstanding, the state colleges have clearly been relegated to the status of second-class institutions.

For the junior colleges, the situation is even more transparent. For most students the junior colleges are essentially a dead end; while those who graduate and go on to continue their education do well academically once they are enrolled in four-year colleges, they constitute only 10% of the total junior college population. The rest either drop out or else are waylaid by the institution's mammoth counseling and testing operations, which carry over the tracking system to the collegiate level. The proportion of transfer students to dropouts or vocational trainees varies somewhat from district to district, depending on the kind of tax base the district has . . . and the extent to which its taxpayers are willing to pay a second tax for higher education. Where the tax base falters, private industry usually steps in to lend its support to what amounts to a public subsidy for its job training and recruitment costs. Naturally, such support is always for services rendered. As with the high schools, the junior colleges tend to cultivate an elite of "successful" students while their fellow students fall by the wayside. If is, of course, specious to say that these "late bloomers" are being magnanimously given a "second chance" by the Master Plan, since it was the Master Plan which originally deprived them of their first.

The whole invidious process is presided over by the Coordinating Council on Higher Education, one of the least discussed but most ominously significant aspects of the Master Plan. The function of the CCHE, according to the Master Plan, is to review budget and capital outlay requests for the public colleges, interpret their "functional differentiation," and generally develop plans for the "orderly growth of higher education in California." Its membership comprises three representatives apiece from the respective administrations of the junior colleges, the state colleges, the private colleges, and the university, and six representatives from the "general public." (For "general public" read corporate elite; as with the U. C. Regents and the State College Trustees, these gubernatorially-appointed "common men" are invariably scions of agri-business, the big utilities, banking and real estate, oil and corporate law. Needless to say, their attitude toward both education and the nonwhite and working class communities usually reflects this background.) The neo-class structure of the Master Plan having failed to resolve the fiscal difficulties of the California public colleges, there are now indications that the CCHE is preparing to abandon the idea of a broadly-based, inclusive higher-education system altogether. A recent report prepared for the CCHE suggests that the survival of the colleges may well depend on their ability to bind themselves, totally and inextricably, to the biggest and most dynamic of the new "growth industries," eliminate all of their functions which do not pertain directly to the needs of those industries, and abandon any pretense of attempting to meet the educational needs of either the individual student or the community. The authors of the report undoubtedly had Stanford University in mind when they put forth this new concept of an academic institution. Stanford grew from an "underprivileged" institution into the second-largest research and development complex in the United States by nurturing and being nurtured by the booming defense industries in the Palo Alto area. The university leases its land, through the Stanford Industrial Park, to electronics and aerospace corporations, and hires out its facilities, through the Stanford Research Institute, to the CIA and the Defense Department for counter-insurgency and germ warfare work. Accessible as it is to the military-industrial complex, however, Stanford is one of the costliest (in terms of tuition), most exclusive schools in the United States. While the University of California was one of the first of the big "multiversities," and therefore came to be accepted as something of a model for "jet-age education," Stanford suggests the same concept at a more advanced stage. U. C. Berkeley built itself up on federal grants, which accounted for nearly half its total budget, and relatively minor alliances with agri-business. But agri-business is quickly being supplanted by defense as California's biggest industry, and where U. C.'s defense contracts were made through the federal government, Stanford hires itself out directly to Litton, Lockheed, and Hewlett-Packard, whose purse-strings are far less tight. Its status as a private institution makes possible the kind of collusion with private industry which would be illegal for a public university. Moreover, unencumbered by state or federal bureaucracy, blessed with a high tuition rate and an exclusive academic character, Stanford is both more efficient and more capable of intense specialization than public institutions, which retain certain obligations to the taxpayer. Yet it is still eligible for public subsidies and public support, and the increasing orientation of the CCHE is to provide it with precisely that kind of support—at the expense of the state colleges.

There is good reason to believe that this may be the wave of the future in California education: shift the burden from the public to the private sector; abandon the educational welfare state; maximize the output of the intellectual resources upon which the "growth industries" depend by trimming away frills and cultivating an educational elite. Governor Reagan put it all very neatly in a recent state of the state message: "Publicly-supported higher education is not a right; it is a privilege." That sentence may well be the final epitaph of mass public higher education in California, the Master Plan having been the first. It certainly precludes any kind of educational system which is responsible to the community, or responsive to the community's needs.

The Quiet Revolution

Striking students at S. F. State are only now becoming aware of the significance of the Master Plan and the operations of the CCHE. As early as 1962, however, when the Master Plan was just beginning to shape education in California along class lines, some S. F. State students were developing their own concept of the college's relationship to the surrounding community. With the traditional "rah-rah" student activities on campus in a state of decline, some students became interested in the idea of making the campus a base for community organizing and civil-rights agitation. Their first target was the student government, which held nominal control over $300,000 in compulsory student body fees; to gain control of it, they evolved a style and continuity with respect to campus politics which allowed a hard core of student activists to win every student-body election except one between 1963 and the present. This secured a financial base from which a series of educational-reform and community-action programs were launched.

Dominated in their early stages by white students, these programs developed along two lines. The first, spearheaded by those students who had been primarily responsible for wresting control of the student government, was geared toward involvement in the political processes of the campus and the community. The initial project to grow out of it was the Tutorial Program, one of the first of its kind in the nation, which sought to help ghetto children and other rejects of the public school system on an each-one-teach-one basis. It was within this program that students set the precedent of utilizing student body funds for the renting of off-campus facilities and for paying students to do work in the community. By 1965, the Tutorial Program had become institutionalized as an ongoing student activity, and the Community Involvement Program (CIP) was set up. The CIP developed out of a project to send students to Mississippi in the summer of 1964. $10,000 was allocated by the student legislature to pay their expenses, but the Chancellor of the State College tied the money up all summer in the first of a long series of disputes over the right of students to handle their own funds. In any event, the money for the Mississippi Summer Project eventually went into the creation of the CIP, which became engaged in such activities in the local community as tenants-union organizing, welfare-rights agitation, the Delano grape strike, and some tentative forays into white middle-class neighborhoods. On campus, the CIP was primarily responsible for establishing the Work-Study Program, which gave students academic credit for their community work, and the student-run "underground" weekly, Open Process. Both these activities became separate programs, annually funded by the Associated Students.

The second trend in the student programs was represented by the creation of the Experimental College (EC) in the spring of 1966. The students associated with it were convinced that, education being the primary instrument of social indoctrination, educational reform would lead necessarily to social reform. They set up their own courses and even hired their own professors, among them Paul Goodman and LeRoi Jones; and after lengthy discussion with faculty and administration succeeded in getting the college to set up a "special studies" series through which Experimental College offerings could be officially accredited. The EC was the only white student program that directly involved large numbers of students. Anyone could teach a course, any subject was acceptable, and liberal credit arrangements could be provided through the special studies loophole. But while the EC was able to launch a few satellite programs of its own, including Draft Help and MAX (a professor-evaluation booklet based on student surveys), it was never able to adequately reconcile the divergencies in its overall program.

The nature of this internal conflict was familiar enough: the original founders of EC had envisioned it as a vehicle for reforming the standard curriculum and teaching methods at S. F. State, which required a political perspective and a structured plan of development. But the open-to-everybody principle attracted a flood of visionaries from San Francisco's then-flourishing hip community, who wanted a non-political, unstructured environment in which to do their own thing. Given these tendencies, the EC was never able to develop a coherent approach to educational reform, and when the Haight-Ashbury scene collapsed in late 1967, the smorgasbord offerings of the Experimental College became less and less relevant to the educational issues on campus.

The rise of the white student programs was accompanied by the emergence of black students as a potent political force. Prior to 1965, S. F. State's black students were mainly organized into the Negro Students Association (NSA). Primarily a social club, the NSA had some black nationalist leanings, but seldom if ever involved itself in campus politics. Times were changing, however; the civil-rights movement had given way to Black Power, and the Watts rebellion tore away the facade of peaceful progress. At S. F. State, a new core of black activists were beginning to develop their own political perspective for black students. They adopted the model of the student programs and the student government as a potential financial base; and by the spring of 1966 they had inaugurated a black arts and culture series in the Experimental College. Subsequently, they began moving into the Tutorial Program, and their influx brought about a significant change in policy, whereby children were now to be tutored by students who shared their ethnic background and cultural experience. Since most of the children in the program were black, this new policy effectively brought it under control of the black students. By the summer of 1966, the NSA had become the Black Students Union, and Jimmy Garrett, a prime mover in its political redirection, was working to develop a complete black-studies curriculum. Not content with confining black-studies courses to the Experimental College, Garrett pushed initially for their incorporation into the programs of existing academic departments. The ultimate goal, however, was an officially recognized, academically "legitimate" Black Studies Department, funded by the college and created and controlled by black people.

This strategy was soon to lead to direct confrontations with the college administration, and by implication, with the Master Plan. It was one thing to set up an experimental college funded by student money; but it was quite another thing to demand that the college fund new programs and departments within its existing structure. Line-item budgeting left the college with virtually no resources to fund new programs, and not even the Trustees had a great deal of fiscal flexibility. The Master Plan had dictated one set of educational priorities, and now black students were pushing for an entirely different arrangement.

By the fall of 1967 a new mood of student militancy was sweeping the campus, its main sources being the BSU and the Students for a Democratic Society. SDS had set up a chapter on campus the previous fall and had immediately pulled off a successful cafeteria boycott around the issues of lower prices and student control; now it was attempting, with less success, to mobilize students around the war-related issues of class rankings and military recruiters. The former issue was made irrelevant by the 1967 Draft Law before very much could be done about it; the latter was chiefly symbolic, and attracted sympathy, but not much enthusiasm. The BSU, in addition to its tutorial and other community-oriented ventures, continued to push for an autonomous Black Studies Department and a special-admissions program which would waive academic entrance requirements for a certain number of incoming black students. The importance of special admissions was becoming critical, since the tracking system had reduced the college's black enrollment from over a thousand to a few hundred. This sort of institutionalized racism, coupled with the growing anti-BSU line taken by the Journalism Department-controlled campus daily, led to a brawl in the paper's office between black students and white staff members, as a result of which nine black students were suspended. The BSU countered by calling a demonstration, marked by fistfights and a few broken windows, which succeeded in closing down the campus for a day and eventually getting the eight suspended students reinstated. From that point on, racism became a central issue at S. F. State.

The situation escalated in the spring of 1968. Supported by a student referendum, SDS mounted a campaign to get AFROTC off campus; faculty and administration response was equivocal. Meanwhile, the administration had promised the BSU a Black Studies Department, and Nathan Hare, a black sociologist from Howard University, was brought in to head it. A tentative special-admissions program had also been approved. But a new element had entered the campus struggle. In February the History Department had dismissed Juan Martinez, a "troublesome" professor and the only chicano on the faculty. The writings of Fanon and the colonial ideology of the Black Panthers had begun to have their impact, and the general notion of third-world solidarity brought a number of ethnic minorities together to demand his rehiring. TWLF was born, demanding—in addition to the retention of Martinez—that chicanos, Orientals and Filipinos be accorded the same kind of concessions the BSU had wrung from the administration; specifically, more third-world faculty, and an expanded special-admissions quota. The last week of May found them jointly occupying the administration building with SDS, which was still demanding ROTC's ouster. Under pressure from the Mexican community, President John Summerskill granted the three TWLF demands and then departed abruptly for Ethiopia, throwing the campus into a state of chaos. The spring semester ended with the ROTC issue still unresolved, and the participants in the sit-in had to settle for a partial victory.

It soon became clear that it was not even that, however, for in capitulating to the third-world demands, President Summerskill had made a lot of promises that the college was in no position to keep. By now bled virtually dry by the economy squeeze of the Master Plan, S. F. State was over $750,000 in debt. Special admissions could not be adequately funded; the financial-aids office was utterly incapable of dealing with the problems of the special admittees; and the Black Studies Department existed on paper only. Financial resources could have been made available by cutting back on other college programs, of course, but the first tendency of any bureaucracy is to give priority to what is already established. Frustrations mounted; finally the BSU, determined to clear things up once and for all, decided to marshal its own forces and compel the administration to declare its position. The strike was called; a few days later TWLF joined it, and the battle had begun.

The Issues at State

From the strike's inception, TWLF took the position that the fifteen demands were non-negotiable, that the strike would not end until all fifteen were met. This position has baffled many outsiders, including some sympathetic observers who feel that the strike would gain more public support if TWLF expressed a willingness to "sit down and talk." But the nature of the demands and the issues underlying them is such that they cannot be dealt with except as a unit. Taken separately, the demands are all but meaningless in terms of TWLF's ultimate goals; together, they pose the most substantive kind of challenge, not simply to the S. F. State administration, but to the whole direction education in California has taken since the implementation of the Master Plan. The connection here—and this cannot be overstressed—is not merely a symbolic one. The Master Plan and the state's fiscal situation made the institutionalized racism of the California higher education system a matter of economic and political necessity, in the most direct and obvious sense. But posing an alternative to that institutionalized racism also necessitates that students move beyond the symbolic, into the realm of the programmatic—something no previous campus uprising has really done.

The increasing militancy of the black liberation movement, and the official efforts to direct it into "harmless" channels (such as Nixon's "black capitalism"), has given terms like "black studies" an air of legitimacy. But the *concept* of black studies has not yet been clearly defined. Several of America's elite colleges, including Yale and Harvard, have already formulated plans for undergraduate programs in "Afro-American studies." Such programs are, to quote S. F. State's Nathan Hare, "aimed at 'rehabilitating' individual students and potential students by means of pride in culture, racial contributions generally, and regenerated dignity and self-esteem." The crucial phrase, of course, is "individual students." Harvard and Yale may be very enlightened in terms of the kinds of curricula they are willing to offer, but even with an extensive scholarship or special-admissions program for minority students, they are not accessible to the masses of blacks, and it would be ludicrous to suggest that they would in any way be prepared to meet the educational needs of the black community *as a whole*. They are capable, however, of cultivating what one foundation executive calls a "talented tenth." A select group of black students could, without straining the resources of the college or the economy as a whole, be singled out, given special attention, and bombarded with courses with which they could identify. But, as Hare points out, no matter how "relevant" an education the college sought to give these students, its efforts would be basically self-defeating, since they would simply serve to isolate the students that much more from their own communities, thereby lessening the sense of identification with their people which is supposedly the educational and ideological basis for the black-studies curriculum.

For the black student, then, the program would fail. But would it really fail for the college authorities, or for the corporate elite? Robert Hoover, ousted head of the College Readiness Program at the College of San Mateo (one of the few successful experiments in community-based minority education, now effectively killed by the local campus administration), has pointed out that of the ten percent of America's black population which succeeds in getting through college, only two percent return to the black community upon graduation. The rest are "integrated" into white society, contributing whatever skills they may have picked up in college to the economy of white America and lending a shred of legitimacy to the myth of "Negro progress." Meanwhile the black community, robbed of the trained manpower it so desperately needs to overcome its traditional position of dependency, continues to languish, now worse off than ever.

But the proposed cultivation of a "talented tenth," particularly at elite colleges with better financial resources, may produce a new kind of "exploitation-through-education." Conceivably, it could devote itself to turning out not so much the "professional token Negroes" of the immediate past as new black bourgeoisie, the hip black administrators of the immediate future. The latest of the official responses to the threat of civil insurrection in the inner cities is an attempt to build up a sophisticated native bourgeoisie in the black colony, composed of carefully-trained "leaders," with federal or foundation backing, who, it is reasoned, are more capable of "keeping the lid on" than the discredited, distrusted, and despised white administrators. Until this class is built up, there will be plenty of demand for such administrators, though their sinecure will be enjoyed at the expense of the rest of the black community.

TWLF's response to this trend can be seen in the most controversial of the fifteen demands, that which demands that all third-world students seeking to enroll at the college be admitted. Without such a stipulation, TWLF has steadfastly maintained, an ethnic-studies program is effectively useless, since it does not address itself to the needs of the entire community, but to those of a privileged few. And the underlying principle of the S. F. State strike is that it is for the nonwhite community, not the "racist administrators," to decide what kind of educational opportunities their children will recieve; hence, the demand that the ethnic-studies programs be completely autonomous. "We don't want equality," says TWLF leader Roger Alvarado, "we want self-determination"—a simple statement which suggests the complete failure of American education, not simply for third-world students, but for everybody. And needless to say, the educational philosophy behind the demand for an autonomous program is completely irreconcilable with the race-class bias of the Master Plan, corporate control of the university, and the whole notion that the first duty of higher education is to develop a skilled work force for private industry.

Nor should the significance of the distinction between black studies and ethnic studies, between a black students' strike and a third-world strike, be overlooked. The whole notion of an alliance between a number of nonwhite groups, of third-world solidarity, suggests an ideological orientation, drawn from Fanon, which in itself is potentially revolutionary, enveloping as it does a condemnation of American imperialism and its displacement and exploitation of nonwhite races and nations within our borders. The third-world alliance flies in the face of traditional American pluralism, with its traditional adage that the squeaking wheel gets greased. What if all four wheels squeak at the same time?

In California, chicanos outnumber blacks by more than two to one, and their educational needs are, if anything, more acute, but they have never been highly politicized. Similarly, San Francisco's Chinatown is a popular tourist trap whose public image—one of a "self-helping" community of successful businessmen, studious and obedient children, hierarchies made legitimate by quaintness and tradition, and a generally docile, contented, respectable populace— veils an abominable, overcrowded ghetto with one of the highest TB rates in the nation, where people work fourteen hours a day in sweatshops for starvation wages and the average educational level is not even second grade (the city-wide average is 12th grade). Here too are victims of American racism; here too are people with demands to make on the ruling class. A college administration desirous of peace at any price could have tried to accommodate the black students by cannibalizing existing departments and programs to scare up money for black studies. But the demand for an entire School of Ethnic Studies, accessible to the entire nonwhite community, flies in the face of the Master Plan and the whole trend toward elitism in California education.

Like the third-world students, the faculty is also reacting to a *deterioration* of their position within the structure of the colleges. There is the wage differential between themselves and the University faculty; there is the heavy workload; there is the complete absence of contract rights, and the denial of access to the research grants and the academic prestige accorded to University professors. Moreover, there is a complete lack of any real voice in the decision-making processes which ultimately govern the conditions under which they are forced to work—that being the exclusive province of the state legislature, the governor, and his political appointees on the CCHE and the Board of Trustees. The proviso of the Master Plan that the state colleges were to be treated like second-class institutions carried with it the added proviso that the state-college faculty were to be treated like second-class professionals and second-class human beings.

The AFT's response to all this has been far from radical. Their demands are centered mainly around bread-and-butter issues such as salaries, workload, grievance procedures and fringe benefits. The underlying principles the teachers seek to establish are their right to strike and their right to bargain collectively with the Trustees. But if their grievances are plain enough, the way they envision the resolution of the crisis is quite another matter. Certainly collective-bargaining rights for the faculty will upset the present power relationships within the state-college system, but it is difficult to say whether it would lead to fundamental changes in the nature of the system itself. The AFT's present position with respect to the TWLF demands is that the grievances of the third-world students, growing out of the Master Plan or the absence of adequate financial resources to run the state colleges, are primarily the responsibility of a reactionary administration in Sacramento. To rectify this, some AFT leaders have, in conjunction with liberal Democratic politicians in the Bay Area, concocted a bizarre proposal for autonomy and "home rule" for S. F. State—the presumption apparently being that San Francisco, a labor town with a liberal mayor, would make a more beneficent guardian for S. F. State than those madmen in the state capital who stay in office on the votes of Southern California right-wingers.

The "home-rule" proposal may be developing into a slick marriage of convenience: the AFT, taking on the whole state-college system, is in need of allies; and the Democrats, with the 1970 elections just around the corner, are looking for issues to attack Reagan on. But there is one key flaw in this little scheme, at least with respect to the fifteen demands: it was not Reagan who created the Master Plan, but the administration of liberal Democrat Pat Brown. Moreover, for every reactionary Trustee or CCHE member appointed by Reagan, there is at least one other who is just as reactionary and who was appointed by Brown. And as for the fiscal conditions which made the Master Plan an economic necessity, it is unlikely that either the Republicans or the Democrats can revamp the state tax structure, based as it is on the needs of California industry.

The AFT is also courting another ally, in the form of the San Francisco labor establishment. Getting strike sanctions from the Central Labor Council was no easy feat, since labor in general has been hostile toward campus rebellions, especially where they involve racial issues. But the labor establishment faces a crisis of its own: union membership has not been growing and as automation becomes more prevalent it may actually begin to decline. The largely unorganized public-service employees may therefore represent the last and best hope for the continued prestige of the labor movement; and with the nation's educational system showing severe signs of internal strain, teachers may be one of the most promising areas of labor's new frontier. Accordingly, union leaders in San Francisco hesitatingly lent their support to the AFT, stipulating at the same time that they wanted no part of the student side of the strike. Then the continued refusal of the Trustees to negotiate caused labor support for the AFT to grow, particularly after the local courts ruled that the faculty walkout was illegal, public employees not yet having the right to strike.

But the workers themselves only began to show signs of sympathy for the strike at S. F. State after Bay Area cops attacked the picket lines of striking hospital workers and striking oil workers. The students' hatred for the cops then began to make some sense to union members; still, this is hardly a basis for a "worker-student alliance," especially where neither the workers nor the students have found a programmatic way to relate to each other's struggles. While third-world students have been able to mobilize strong support from their own respective communities, white students have found it difficult to reach the white working class. The racial connotations of the student strike leave workers either apathetic or threatened, while the social image and bohemian appearance of many white radicals tend to create a cultural barrier between the two groups.

That this barrier should be so serious a problem is an indication of both the considerable progress of, and a major failing of, the white student movement. On the one hand, the sudden interest on the part of most white radicals in "hooking up with the rank and file"— devoid as it is of any consistent programmatic approach and organizational framework—suggests the ideological development of the movement, which involves both an increasing awareness of the dynamics of American imperialism and an increasingly Marxist critique of American capitalism. Yet the "worker-student alliance" is also rapidly becoming a matter of necessity. The sense of moral commitment and the desire to better the plight of others which marked the early days of the movement are rapidly becoming inadequate to sustain it. When the civil-rights movement was redefined, white "missionaries" were no longer needed—as the white students in the S. F. State Tutorial Program were quick to discover. Now that the opposition to the Vietnam war has been fragmented by the Paris negotiations, the anti-war movement appears to have reached an impasse. Campus revolts, particularly where they fail to involve issues as critical to the community as they are to the students, arc becoming frozen into predictable patterns which shrewd administrators are becoming more and more adept at containing, as the disastrous Moses Hall sit-in at U. C. Berkeley attests. Moreover, campus radicals—particularly at S. F. State, where the college presidency changed hands three times in a period of less than six months—are increasingly beginning to discover that what have been posed as campus issues cannot be confined to the campus: their origins and solutions lie beyond the pale and power of the local administrative autocracy.

Indeed, the astonishing success of the S.,F. State strike—and the freshness and originality of the tactics employed—can be directly attributed to the fact that it was led by third-world students, with white students in a supportive role. Certain characteristics unique to S. F. State were factors in the quality of the third-world leadership. It is, in name if not in fact, a community college in an urban environment, with four different ghetto areas nearby. Its activist students had at least three years of intensive community work behind them, and the fact that white and third-world students had worked together in the past lessened the distrust and fear of manipulation. Most significantly, the tutorial and community work of the third-world students gave them a genuine sense of an off-campus constituency, and a thorough understanding of that constituency's needs . . . which are clearly reflected in the fifteen demands. As a result, there was a total absence of the symbolic issues which have so often marked campus revolts led by white students (such as Columbia, where the whole history of the University's shady real-estate operations in Harlem were capsulized in the Morningside Heights gym).

The nonsymbolic nature of the S. F. State strike was likewise reflected in the tactics, which carefully avoided the usual ritual seizure of buildings and planned confrontation with police. Instead of "living the revolution" inside an occupied building for a brief, apocalyptic period culminating in a Big Bust, and then attempting to prolong things by playing upon the shock of police occupation (which, at many campuses, is becoming less and less of a shock); the TWLF opted for a "protracted struggle," closing the campus and keeping it shut down not by simply impairing normal campus activity, but by making it totally impossible.

The white students have played an important role in keeping the strike going, however. They supplied most of the manpower for the demonstrations, the picket lines, and the clashes with the cops; they turned out an abundance of literature, from the daily leaflets to in-depth analyses in pamphlets, the student paper *Open Process*, and the highly successful *Strike Daily* wall poster. They got strike information out all over the state, put together fund-raising benefits for bail, set up an agit-prop, organized an AFT local for teaching assistants, and formed departmental caucuses around issues raised by the strike. The last three activities should far outlive the strike; indeed, the strike has provided white students with a new educational context. Classes and grades have given way to a readjustment of educational priorities along radical lines. Where the college was once viewed as a sanctuary for young people not knowing what else to do, or a social escalator for students on the make, it is now often likened to a factory or a concentration camp. White students who have been striking for the last four months will find it difficult to resurrect their forgotten academic goals, and, having come to such a point, it is winning the struggle, rather than winning the degree, that counts.

The crucial question—how white students will go beyond the strike—remains, but the strike itself may provide an answer. Recently white strikers, searching for allies, have begun taking a more serious interest in labor disputes, especially in the Bay Area; students now join union picket lines whenever possible and attempt to explain the student strike to white workers. Until now, it has mainly been a one-way street, though the presence of students on their picket lines has given rise to a certain tentative interest in the student struggle on the part of union members. But the students have not as of yet developed a sharp focus on the class issues inherent in the S. F. State strike. The exclusion of working-class students from higher education has gone virtually unmentioned. Students need to find ways of relating not only who controls the college (there has been the usual exposing of the corporate affiliations of the state-college trustees), but also what they utilize the college for and how that functions in a way that deprives the lower economic classes of educational opportunity. Though it is too late for any white demands (such as open enrollment for everybody), the example set by the third-world students should impel white students to begin developing a programmatic approach toward the educational needs of their own communities. This means that white radicals will initially have to come to grips with the broader, more subtle and complex class bias that is built into the educational institutions, just as the TWLF has managed to effectively focus on and attack the race bias of the college. This projection of race bias, in the context of the S. F. State strike, has been central in turning an educational issue into a community issue; and only when class becomes a viable educational issue on campus, will the chances of establishing clear links with a working-class constituency become more than a vague ideological concept for the white student movement.

On the Line at San Francisco State

Todd Gitlin

Ronald Reagan has called the strike at San Francisco State College an "insurrection," and so it is. He has also called it a stunt rigged by a handful of "anarchists," which it is not. Now in its thirteenth week, the strike is the longest in US college history. Unlike others, it is protracted, tactically supple, and a mass movement. It has triggered an unprecedented political teachers' strike. It has splashed over the academic banks into Chinatown, black ghettoes and chicano barrios, labor unions, and other schools. That flood may recede, but the countryside will be permanently changed.

It began, as insurrection does in America, with the blacks. In 1966 the Black Student Union (BSU) was founded by Jimmy Garrett, a former SNCC organizer from Watts, who moved it from black culture (dashikis, naturals, LeRoi Jones-in-residence) through tutorials and into militancy. In December, 1967, nine BSU members were arrested for beating up the editor of the campus paper for his race slurs. With inspiration from the Panthers, the black students discarded their early roles as success models for ghetto youths, and began to think of themselves as active "servants of the community" —political tutors.

Twenty years ago, a black college graduate would "return" to the ghetto from the campus as a doctor or lawyer. Five years ago he might have gone to Mississippi as his community's "proxy." Today, he goes back to his community as revolutionary—or never really leaves. So at colleges like S. F. State, where the blacks are not so far off the streets themselves, the school is seen as an extension of the community. Responding to the demands and needs of the community-campus complex, the BSU began pushing for a Black Studies Department. It was an idea whose time had come at scores of schools around the country, and it made particular sense for the education of the black graduate of the Seventies. The *substance* of Black Studies would be useful in preparing students for their roles as ghetto social activists. But perhaps more important, the *institution* of a black-controlled department within the white-run college provides one way out of the bind imposed on black students by white authorities who cannot even recognize their own dominating system.

But not only blacks were on the move. In California, black people are not even a majority of the minorities; at State, the various hyphenated-Americans "of color" formed the Third World Liberation Front (TWLF), a coalition which at least nominally included blacks. Last spring, TWLF students at State sat-in for three demands: 428 special admissions for minority-group students, 10 faculty positions filled by Third World choices, and the retention of a radical professor, Juan Martinez, who had been fired by the rear-guard history department. The action was accompanied by noisy disruption—startling in those days, but hardly remarkable now.

The Black Student Union was theoretically involved in last year's protest, but most members were not heavily implicated in the action. The leading actors were militant Mexican, Filipino, Latin-American, Chinese and Japanese "minority" students, allied with SDS white radicals. They were strong enough to drive President John Summerskill first to distraction—and then to the use of San Francisco's small but vicious police Tactical Squad. The whites never won their own demand to throw Air Force ROTC off campus, but it was all too much for Summerskill, who one day in May fled to a teaching job at Haile Selassie University in Addis Ababa. Popular with the "silent" white students in the mainstream, Summerskill had become a parable of McCarthyesque liberalism, finding solace finally in flight. A man generous and upstanding for the Fifties cannot hold power in the last Sixties, so fast have the seasons changed: he must choose either the Authorities or the opposition—or the space between the grindstones.

The Third World students at first seemed to have won their points, but in time the victory turned Pyrrhic. Juan Martinez was limited to non-teaching "duties" and only 300 of the allocated special admissions were ever admitted. The Black Students Union discovered what it called institutional racism in the person of the Financial Aids Officer, who refused to give earmarked funds for incoming "minority" students. The 300 who did get in—many of them right off the street—had not been schooled to patience in the face of racial insults and administrative delays.

During the summer and early fall, black and Third World students worked to codify their essential demands, to test the structure's racism. Finding no positive response from the new President, a terrified liberal by the apt name of Robert Smith, they planned to strike Nov. 6.

At first, the "media" highlighted only one dramatic and personalized BSU demand: reinstatement of English teacher and Black Panther Minister of Education George Murray, who had been suspended by the Trustees of the State College system for allegedly inviting black students to carry guns in self-defense. Obsessed by Panther nightmares, the Trustees and the press couldn't grasp the coherence of the 10 (later 15) demands of the blacks and Third World students, with their common thrust against racism and powerlessness. Murray was only one item on the list, but he became a convenient target for the agri-businessmen and Reagan hacks who dominate the Board of Trustees, and who wanted to get them a Panther—just as the University Board of Regents had cracked down on Eldridge Cleaver's right to teach at Berkeley.

In their package of 15 demands, the blacks and Third World students were trying to define the bare requirements of their self-determination. (Their identity was so ill-perceived that non-"white" students had trouble finding a convenient name for themselves; "third world" is the best so far, but still inexact.) Aside from Murray's reinstatement, they called for a School of Ethnic Studies, with 50 teachers and the entire curriculum to be chosen by the TWLF, and with a 20-teacher Black Studies Department under equivalent control of the blacks; elevation of Nathan Hare, a black teacher from Howard chosen to direct Black Studies, to full professorial status; replacement of the ungenerous Financial Aids Officer by a black; admission of all "minority" students who want to attend the college; complete amnesty; and retention of student control over student funds, which the Trustees are trying to grab.

The only point that looked utopian on its face was the demand for blanket admissions; yet how else was the disguised racism of College Boards and high school "achievement" to be plowed under? Test scores and school grades reflect race and class position. The standards for admission which colleges set accept the assumptions of privilege. Over fifty percent of high school students in the Bay Area (where S. F. State draws most of its admissions) are members of black or Third World "minorities," but at the College, only 10 percent are non-"white." If it were true, as officials said, that blanket admissions for minorities would wreck the college system, then by the same token that system proved itself unable to survive except by perpetuation of inequality.

The demands for Black and Ethnic Studies Departments looked fairly reasonable, but they came smack against the State Colleges' bankruptcy. Two years ago, faculty salaries were actually cut 1.8 percent across-the-board by the pauperized state (there is a bare seven percent state tax on corporate profits, but even so, influential companies like Standard Oil get off tax-free). But the bankruptcy is more political than financial. Early in the strike the Trustees did free some money for "minority" admissions, and in December, Acting President S. I. Hayakawa was able to "concede" a Black Studies Department, to be headed by Nathan Hare, as long as the President retained ultimate control. So the real bite in the demands was the TWLF insistance on control—over finances, curriculum, hiring and firing and admissions. It staggered liberals: the TWLF students were demanding more than other departments had, which was thought to be "unfair." That was precisely the point. The BSU's Nesbitt Crutchfield explained:

"The innovative education we're talking about will show black and Third World students what mechanisms and power determine and exploit them, what powers make our fathers castrated automatons. We're going to bring them to that education factory and show them these powers and how and why they must be changed. This is why we're having so much trouble with the demands—because they're talking about self-determination. If we were asking for a 'Negro studies program' that talked about cooperating with the system, then we would have been back in school weeks ago."

Call them revolutionary or reformist, the demands had to be non-negotiable, as the Trustees quickly acknowledged by their own refusal to negotiate. The lines were drawn very clear and very fast, with not much waiting room in the middle, between the black movement and its allies, and the corporate illiberals who people the Board of Trustees. Which education, for whom, and for what? the strikers asked, day after day, and if you feel the sharpness of the question you will understand the sharpness, the implacability of the strike that ensued.

"I'm a friend of labor!" Acting President Hayakawa, the dean of the pseudo-social science of general semantics, told a meeting with labor officials not long ago. "Why, I chose to teach at S. F. State rather than at a more important university because I wanted to keep in touch with the lower classes!"

Semanticists will have no trouble understanding State, if they keep in mind Hayakawa's words. State even looks like a factory. Slapped up in the Damp Belt near the Pacific Ocean, hard by the original ticky-tacky houses and the tickier-tackier shopping centers, the buildings have neither history nor contemporaneity: they are merely functional. When Trustee (and plutocrat-architect) Charles

Luckman rejected Moshe Safdie's brilliant design for a student-financed student union, he said it clashed with prevailing architecture. In a similar vein (although the similarity may not be immediately apparent), Luckman said of the educational system in his Trust, "We are determined to use this power of knowledge, and its effect on the soul, to fight our greatest enemy, Communism." Whatever their function, most of the 18,000 students (at least a third of them part-time) come to school on the trolley, which stops across the street. They must know that they are in training for a life-time of commutation.

Consider California's public higher education system as a sprawling commercial enterprise, pretending to a work ethic—the redeeming value of ideas, presumably—but designed for profitable efficiency and gradated ("tracked") into distinct functional layers. The standard for segregation is high school "achievement," and its mechanism is the 1959 Master Plan for Higher Education—a creation not of Reagan's reactionary regime but of Pat Brown's liberal first term. Whatever else it may be, the system is a master plan of liberal elitism. At the top, the several University campuses draw off the creamy one-eighth of the State's high school graduating classes, and out come high professionals and managers for the great corporations. At the bottom, the two-year junior colleges take on all comers, and process them into clerks, punch-card operators, foremen—the dregs of the white-collar labor force. Squeezed in the middle are the 18 State Colleges, limited by the Master Plan to the upper third of the high school graduates, who at the end of their four years on the educational assembly lines are expected to fill the swelling demand for teachers, social workers and other public functionaries, as well as the lower reaches of the managerial slough.

The junior colleges never pretended to be more than meal-ticket diploma mills, but the State Colleges—S. F. State foremost among them—never eased into their middling station. Lavish Berkeley is only a Bay and an invidious comparison away, and many S. F. State faculty members, with good credentials and a will to craftsmanship, have felt the pinch. State College salaries average $1500 below University levels; class loads in the two systems are over 12 and under nine "hours" a week, respectively; the Colleges have scarcely any funds or facilities for research, few sabbaticals, hardly any graduate teaching assistants: the University has a near-monopoly of doctoral programs. The S. F. State faculty feels proletarianized, deprived even of its prerogatives as a self-perpetuating guild. "The first time I've ever felt like a professional was when I yelled 'scab' at a teacher crossing the picket line," one well-liked teacher said recently. Seeds of union action had fertile fields for growth.

The S. F. State catalogue puts the whole schema in sharp relief: "Course offerings leading to the bachelor's and master's degree are designed to satisfy existing student interests and to serve the technical and professional manpower requirements of the State." Any apparent contradiction in that sentence can easily be resolved: "student interests" cannot differ from "manpower requirements." Students are supposed to be prevented from developing unrequired interests by the pressures of the job market, and the manipulations of job counselors. But the urgency of black insurrection was able to break through the pressure-system to redefine "student interests," and the movement came crashing against the colonial business logic of the State College Trustees, stretching the tension between "interests" and "requirements" to the breaking point; and there lies the rock-bottom explanation for the intensity of the strike, the beatings, the more than 650 arrests.

As I drive back from State every day I pass Moncada Street; the verbal allusion conjures visual images of clubs threshing through crowds, clubs swinging down from horseback like polo sticks, clubs pounding guts. . . . Chicago was an artificial scene, four days with a built-in ending. You knew that somehow, if you could crawl through the Convention days, you would go home to pick up the pieces of your life. But San Francisco State is every day; there is no ending, there are only beginnings, mounting toward some encampment at Moncada.

The BSU declared the strike and the TWLF has steered it, choosing both strategy and tactics; white strikers (led by Progressive Labor and others in SDS, along with students from the new experimental "programs," community organizers and "concerned" types) have never contested for leadership, or tried to form "white" demands. Reagan and Hayakawa have called the BSU "pawns" of SDS; if anything it is the other way 'round, though the whites are willing followers. The implacability of the black/brown/yellow leaders, along with their general tactical finesse, has satisfied most white activists; over the long haul the leaders have explained themselves well enough to the mass of white students to coax the overwhelming majority of them to strike. There is something of radical charity in the white position, but it is tempered by a sense of common interest and common enemy. At delicate moments, when momentum has flagged, the authorities have intervened with nasty and brutish force to drive home the stark impossibility of neutrality. Brute force is not gratuitous: when the Authorities can't buy brains, they bust heads.

The genius of the strike unfolded as early violence—the celebrated typewriter through an office window—but soon yielded to classroom education, still afflicted with a certain harshness but mellowing over the weeks as some white strike supporters discovered they could elicit support by patiently connecting black degradation to the delusion and idiocy of white education. Blacks started talking to whites. Two weeks into the strike, unprovoked, the Tac Squad left its boiler-room bivouac, thundered onto the green, lined up next to the Black Student Union office, and charged a crowd, singling out well-known students for beating. One cop pulled his gun. Some of the fifty faculty members already striking in sympathy interposed themselves.

A few days later President Smith closed the campus. The Trustees were furious. After Thanksgiving, the faculty finessed Smith and set up a three-day "convocation" for the discussion of the issues. TWLF spokesmen explained the demands in lavish detail; thousands of students listened, enthralled. But the TWLF had been promised that classes would be called off during these televised sessions; when Smith refused, striking students stormed out and massed in classroom building hallways. Plainclothes cops—whom the students call "secret police"—tried to make arrests; students freed their brothers and sisters; one cop (a volunteer from posh Piedmont across the Bay) fired in the air, then leveled his gun on the crowd and yelled, "Freeze, this is it!" Then he ran; and so did Smith, who later in the day resigned.

In his place, the Trustees named S. I. Hayakawa, a bizarre self-proclaimed "liberal Democrat" who purported to be expert in matters of black people (he had once written for the *Chicago Defender*), who had recently defended Mayor Daley's police, and who was the driving force behind the right-wing Faculty Renaissance group. With folk tales called "general semantics" he had gained a reputation as the Eric Hoffer of the Academy.

Hayakawa immediately nullified the First Amendment (no assemblies on campus), declared his confidence in the police to solve State's problems, and garnered $100,000 for PR from his Chicago millionaire friend, Positive Mental Attitude insurance magnate W. Clement Stone. Among his new aides was a World Business professor who earned degrees in 1939 and 1942 from the University of Berlin. Hayakawa promised jazz festivals (but couldn't recruit the black jazzmen); flowers (he was lei-ed by Hawaii's Young Americans for Freedom); and a "warm, swinging" atmosphere. The morning that classes resumed, he jumped up on a strike sound-truck off campus and disconnected the wires, firing English Professor Kay Boyle on the spot for calling him "Eichmann" (he later retracted; she didn't). The next morning, Dec. 3, the Tactical Squad crashed a peaceful picket line and terrorized the entire cafeteria in the course of its head-busting chase. That afternoon open warfare broke out, students resorting to sticks and stones against the onslaught of 600 police. More than 30 strikers were arrested, dozens were beaten that "Bloody Tuesday," and from then on it was clear that a majority of students were striking, at least passively with their bodies. Over the next weeks rallies and on-campus marches mustered up to 5,000 at a time. The arrest toll mounted two and three at a time; acknowledged leaders got slapped with felony warrants, but kept coming back. The cops became an occupying army.

On Bloody Tuesday, the 200-member local of the American Federation of Teachers voted to ask S. F. Central Labor Council strike sanction. Not until after Christmas did approval come, but in the meantime Hayakawa had estranged even the academic Bourbons. S. F. State AFT membership more than doubled. Other State College locals threatened to strike, San Jose's actually going out in January, but without much student support. The AFT off-campus picket line, with student support, has kept classroom attendance below 20 percent since Jan. 6. The AFT has its own guild-like demands—from a smaller teaching load to free parking—aside from "resolution of the student demands," but it is no secret that their main impulse is support for the student strike. (The Labor Council pretends otherwise to keep its racist unions in line.) "Hitchhikers," Hayakawa calls the AFT, and some of them are, but the leaders insist they will not sell out the student demands. The Local voted unanimously to violate the State's temporary restraining order against the teacher strike, and the picket line was cooperative until Jan. 23. On that day the TWLF held its first on-campus rally since the teachers had gone out, and 486 (including a few teachers and community supporters) were corralled by the Tac Squad and arrested.

The stakes have steadily escalated: not only self determination for students of color, not only political breathing space and self-esteem for teachers (a few have already been fired "administratively," and all striking for five days are considered to have resigned by State law), but the residual self-respect of the unions—all are hanging fire. In the past month local police have busted up hospital and oil-workers' pickets in the Bay Area; these and other locals have endorsed the strike and lent at least token support, seeing San Francisco's hard-won labor permissiveness in jeopardy. Black, chicano, Japanese, Chinese and white support groups, including some of the ethnic partriarchs, have formed. Not yet a student-worker alliance, largely because of working-class racism and bias against students, it is still the closest we've seen.

State Superintendent of Schools Max Rafferty has said that the school needs "fewer students, fewer teachers, and more order," and all three may be in the cards. Order based on mass expulsions and firings would be precarious indeed, like an education maintained, as Reagan proposes, "at the point of a bayonet, if necessary." A less explosive possibility would be a partial "accommodation" of student demands by the Authorities, with the striking teachers left holding the bag. The Trustees know the implications of collective bargaining in the unorganized education industry, and they may prefer the cheaper deal—if they can get the students to deal. But meanwhile the sundrenched split-level middle class which applauds Hayakawa's hard line can see nothing wrong with a militarized campus, and will not understand what the fuss was about in the first place. They all prefer to believe—with Hayakawa in his wilder moments—that five percent of the student body, "hopped up on drugs," aided by notorious "outsiders, including some from France," have shattered their dreams of salvation and profits via the Master Plan. Hayakawa has been named the Gallup Poll's "Educator of the Year."

Complex as it is, the strike at S. F. State amounts to a battlefield in a class war. Class war is always violent and the outcome is always in doubt until everyone has been forced to choose sides. As the stakes rise and orthodox strike tactics are exhausted, violence tends to be indiscriminate, and class war may even blur into race war. It is impossible now to present a clear scenario for the end of the strike: the Trustees could concede "enough"; there may be truces; Hayakawa may be expended; the teachers and students may be split. This strike may be crushed, but the college cannot now pretend to isolation from the war that burns through America. A new generation is finally getting an education, though the college may have to be destroyed in the process.

Three

The Sources

Who and Why

The articles in this section are based on careful and systematic studies of student attitudes and behavior and give special attention to the institutional, social, and psychological factors which are causally implicated in producing student dissent.

Kenneth Keniston, author of *The Uncommitted,* describes two general types of student dissenters: the alienated and the activists. Steeped in romanticism and nostalgia, the alienated students are really anti-political in the sense that they reject solutions to social problems which do not at the same time involve sweeping reorganization of social values and social morality. The activists—students who have strong political commitments and who lack the rebellious feelings of the alienated students—are described in considerable detail by Matthews and Prothro. They found that although activist black students in the South were opposed to the "system" and actively working to change it, they were also more likely than nonactivists to believe that they had a better chance of achieving change through the system than outside it.

In his paper on activist students at the University of Chicago, Flacks found that among white, middle-class activist students there was a merging of romanticism, intellectualism, humanitarianism, and moralism which they expressed through political action directed both at immediate, pragmatic goals and at long-term social change.

Otten points out the interplay between student aspirations and institutional rigidity over a long period of time and how this has produced an escalation of dissent. Much the same thing is reflected in Robert Somers' empirical studies of Berkeley student opinion, which reveal that students had substantially less trust in the good intentions of the university administration in 1968, during a period of relative calm on campus, than they did in 1964, during the height of the now-famous FSM demonstrations.

One finding that appears in these papers (supported by much other evidence as well) is often very puzzling to critics of the student political movements of the 60's. The evidence clearly points to the conclusion that activist students are intellectually and academically superior to their nonactivist peers and are also rather strongly committed to democratic values and norms. Kenniston points out that dissent (at the time he was writing) was largely concentrated on the most prestigious campuses and that the participants in demonstrations, radical student organizations and other types of political activism were, even when compared with their relatively elite peers, smarter, more attentive to the media and disproportionately drawn from families which were socially and educationally elite. Flacks also finds high social status and high educational attainment among dissidents' families.

The activist black college students studied by Matthews and Prothro were also disproportionately drawn from middle-class families, and, relative to both their college and age peers, were rather high achievers. Negro student activists, like their white counterparts, tend to be concentrated in the humanities and in the social and physical sciences. These disciplines are, of course, largely oriented toward learning per se and mainly attract persons who are not greatly concerned with upward mobility and so do not view their education as primarily preparation for a vocation. An absence of a clear vocational choice itself suggests relatively greater independence from the dominant values of the society, an independence recently dramatized in somewhat extreme form by Dustin Hoffman in his role as Benjamin in "The Graduate."

While conspiracy theories of student rebellions are given wide support in the pronouncements of congressmen and certain educators (see section II) and in public opinion, the best empirical evidence suggests that activist students are not mental slaves of agents of foreign powers, but rather are attempting to implement values which have been transmitted to them by their parents and which are very much a part of the liberal tradition in America. As far as we know, all empirical studies of student activists (including those reprinted here) find that the parents of activists are largely sympathetic with their children's social outlook, tactics, and political goals. Indeed, given the liberal values of their parents, it would be more surprising if student activists did not behave as they do rather than act like little ladies and gentlemen.

Of course, if students clearly move from nonviolent to violent tactics, if national and even international organizations of student radicals continue to form, and if students who are clearly anarchistic and violent begin to play a greater role in student demonstrations, it will be necessary to re-assess the findings we have so far on the political socialization of the student activists. But it is not likely, we believe, that such an assessment will reveal any large body of conspirators. The activist movement still counts the vast majority of its supporters among persons who are committed to democratic procedures and radical social change and who possess the intellectual and political resources to make much of their dream a reality.

The Sources of Student Dissent

Kenneth Keniston

The apparent upsurge of dissent among American college students is one of the more puzzling phenomena in recent American history. Less than a decade ago, commencement orators were decrying the "silence" of college students in the face of urgent national and international issues; but in the past two or three years, the same speakers have warned graduating classes across the country against the dangers of unreflective protest, irresponsible action and unselective dissent. Rarely in history has apparent apathy been replaced so rapidly by publicized activism, silence by strident dissent.

This "wave" of dissent among American college students has been much discussed. Especially in the mass media—popular magazines, newspapers and television—articles of interpretation, explanation, deprecation and occasionally applause have appeared in enormous numbers. More important, from the first beginnings of the student civil rights movement, social scientists have been regular participant-observers and investigators of student dissent. There now exists a considerable body of research that deals with the characteristics and settings of student dissent (see Lipset and Altbach, 1966; Block, Haan and Smith, forthcoming; Katz, 1967; Peterson, 1967 for summaries of this research). To be sure, most of these studies are topical (centered around a particular protest or demonstration), and some of the more extensive studies are still in varying stages of incompletion. Yet enough evidence has already been gathered to permit tentative generalizations about the varieties, origins and future of student dissent in the nineteen sixties.

In the remarks to follow, I will attempt to gather together this evidence (along with my own research and informal observations) to provide tentative answers to three questions about student dissent today. First, what is the nature of student dissent in American colleges? Second, what are the sources of the recent "wave of protest" by college students? And third, what can we predict about the future of student dissent?

Two Varieties of Dissent

Dissent is by no means the dominant mood of American college students. Every responsible study or survey shows apathy and privatism far more dominant than dissent (see, for example, *Newsweek,* 1965; Katz, 1965; Reed, 1966; Peterson, 1966; Block, Haan and Smith, forthcoming). On most of our twenty two hundred campuses, student protest, student alienation and student unrest are something that happens elsewhere, or that characterizes a mere handful of "kooks" on the local campus. However we define "dissent", overt dissent is relatively infrequent and tends to be concentrated largely at the more selective, "progressive", and "academic" colleges and universities in America. Thus, Peterson's study of student protests (1966) finds political demonstrations concentrated in the larger universities and institutions of higher academic calibre, and almost totally absent at teachers colleges, technical institutes and non-academic denominational colleges. And even at the colleges that gather together the greatest number of dissenters, the vast majority of students—generally well over 95%—remain interested onlookers or opponents rather than active dissenters. Thus, whatever we say about student dissenters is said about a very small minority of America's six million college students. At most colleges, dissent is not visible at all.

Partly because the vast majority of American students remain largely uncritical of the wider society, fundamentally conformist in behavior and outlook, and basically "adjusted" to the prevailing collegiate, national and international order, the small minority of dissenting students is highly visible to the mass media. As I will argue later, such students are often distinctively talented; they "use" the mass media effectively; and they generally succeed in their goal of making themselves and their causes highly visible. Equally important, student dissenters of all types arouse deep and ambivalent feelings in non-dissenting students and adults—envy, resentment, admiration, repulsion, nostalgia and guilt. Such feelings contribute both to the selective over-attention dissenters receive and to the often distorted perceptions and interpretations of them and their activities. Thus, there has developed through the mass media and the imaginings of adults a more or less stereotyped—and generally incorrect—image of the student dissenter.

The Stereotyped Dissenter. The "stereotypical" dissenter as popularly portrayed is both a Bohemian and political activist. Bearded, be-Levi-ed, long-haired, dirty and unkempt, he is seen as profoundly disaffected from his society, often influenced by "radical" (Marxist, Communist, Maoist, or Castroite) ideas, an experimenter in sex and drugs, unconventional in his daily behavior. Frustrated and unhappy, often deeply maladjusted as a person, he is a "failure" (or as one U.S. Senator put it, a "reject"). Certain academic communities like Berkeley are said to act as "magnets" for dissenters, who selectively attend colleges with a reputation as protest centers. Furthermore, dropouts or "non-students" who have failed in college cluster in large numbers around the fringes of such colleges, actively seeking pretexts for protest, refusing all compromise and impatient with ordinary democratic processes.

According to such popular analyses, the sources of dissent are to be found in the loss of certain traditional American virtues. The "breakdown" of American family life, high rates of divorce, the "softness" of American living, inadequate parents, and, above all, overindulgence and "spoiling" contribute to the prevalence of dissent. Brought up in undisciplined homes by parents unsure of their own values and standards, dissenters channel their frustration and anger against the older generation, against all authority, and against established institutions.

Similar themes are sometimes found in the interpretations of more scholarly commentators. "Generational conflict" is said to underly the motivation to dissent, and a profound "alienation" from American society is seen as a factor of major importance in producing protests. Then, too, such factors as the poor quality and impersonality of American college education, the large size and lack of close student-faculty contact in the "multiversity" are sometimes seen as the latent or precipitating factors in student protests, regardless of the manifest issues around which students are organized. And still other scholarly analysts, usually men now disillusioned by the radicalism of the 1930's, have expressed fear of the dogmatism, rigidity and "authoritarianism of the left" of today's student activists.

Activism and Alienation. These stereotyped views are, I believe, incorrect in a variety of ways. They confuse two distinct varieties of student dissent; equally important, they fuse dissent with maladjustment. There are, of course, as many forms of dissent as there are individual dissenters; and any effort to counter the popular stereotype of the dissenter by pointing to the existence of distinct "types" of dissenters runs the risk of over-simplifying at a lower level of abstraction. Nonetheless, it seems to me useful to suggest that student dissenters generally fall somewhere along a continuum that runs between two ideal types—first, the political activist or protester, and second, the withdrawn, culturally alientated student.

The activist. The defining characteristic of the "new" activist is his participation in a student demonstration or group activity that concerns itself with some matter of general political, social or ethical principle. Characteristically, the activist feels that some injustice has been done, and attempts to "take a stand", "demonstrate" or in some fashion express his convictions. The specific issues in question range from protest against a paternalistic college administration's actions to disagreement with American Vietnam policies, from indignation at the exploitation of the poor to anger at the firing of a devoted teacher, from opposition to the Selective Service laws which exempt him but not the poor to—most important—outrage at the deprivation of the civil rights of other Americans.

The initial concern of the protester is almost always immediate, ad hoc and local. To be sure, the student who protests about one issue is likely to feel inclined or obliged to demonstrate his convictions on other issues as well (Heist, 1966). But whatever the issue, the protester rarely demonstrates because his *own* interests are jeopardized, but rather because he perceives injustices being done to *others* less fortunate than himself. For example, one of the apparent paradoxes about protests against current draft policies is that the protesting students are selectively drawn from the subgroup *most* likely to receive student deferments for graduate work. The basis of protest is a general sense that the selective service rules and the war in Vietnam are unjust to others with whom the student is identified, but whose fate he does not share. If one runs down the list of "causes" taken up by student activists, in rare cases are demonstrations directed at improving the lot of the protesters themselves; identification with the oppressed is a more important motivating factor than an actual sense of immediate personal oppression.

The anti-ideological stance of today's activists has been noted by many commentators. This distrust of formal ideologies (and at times of articulate thought) makes it difficult to pinpoint the positive social and political values of student protesters. Clearly, many current American political institutions like de facto segregation are opposed; clearly, too, most students of the New Left reject careerism and familism as personal values. In this sense, we might think of the activist as (politically) "alienated". But this label seems to me more misleading than illuminating, for it overlooks the more basic *commitment* of most student activists to other ancient, traditional and credal American values like free speech, citizen's participating in decision-making, equal opportunity and justice. In so far as the activist rejects all or part of "the power structure", it is because current political realities fall so far short of the ideals he sees as central to the American creed. And in so far as he repudiates careerism and familism, it is because of his implicit allegiance to other human goals he sees, once again, as more crucial to American life. Thus, to emphasize the "alienation" of activists is to neglect their more basic allegiance to credal American ideals.

One of these ideals is, of course, a belief in the desirability of political and social action. Sustained in good measure by the successes of the student civil rights movement, the protester is usually convinced that demonstrations are effective in mobilizing public opinion, bringing moral or political pressure to bear, demonstrating the existence of his opinions, or, at times, in "bringing the machine to a halt". In this sense, then, despite his criticisms of existing political practices and social institutions, he is a political optimist. Moreover, the protester must believe in at least minimal organization and group activity; otherwise, he would find it impossible to take part, as he does, in any organized demonstrations or activities. Despite their search for more truly "democratic" forms of organization and action (e. g., participatory democracy), activists agree that group action is more effective than purely individual acts. To be sure, a belief in the value and efficacy of political action is not equivalent to endorsement of prevalent political institutions or forms of action. Thus, one characteristic of activists is their search for new forms of social action, protest and political organization (community organization, sit-ins, participatory democracy) that will be more effective and less oppressive than traditional political institutions.

The culturally alienated. In contrast to the politically optimistic, active, and socially-concerned protester, the culturally alienated student is far too pessimistic and too firmly opposed to "the System" to wish to demonstrate his disapproval in any organized public way.[1] His demonstrations of dissent are private: though nonconformity of behavior, ideology and dress, through

---

[1]The following paragraphs are based on the study of culturally alienated students described in *The Uncommitted* (1965). For a more extensive discussion of the overwhelmingly anti-political stance of these students, see Keniston (1966) and also Rigney and Smith (1961), Allen and Silverstein (1967), Watts and Wittaker (1967), and Wittaker and Watts (1967).

personal experimentation and above all through efforts to intensify his own subjective experience, he shows his distaste and disinterest in politics and society. The activist attempts to change the world around him, but the alienated student is convinced that meaningful change of the social and political world is impossible; instead, he considers "dropping out" the only real option.

Alienated students tend to be drawn from the same general social strata and colleges as protesters. But psychologically and ideologically, their backgrounds are often very different. Alienated students are more likely to be disturbed psychologically; and although they are often highly talented and artistically gifted, they are less committed to academic values and intellectual achievement than are protesters. The alienated student's real campus is the school of the absurd, and he has more affinity for pessimistic existentialist ontology than for traditional American activism. Furthermore, such students usually find it psychologically and ideologically impossible to take part in organized group activities for any length of time, particularly when they are expected to assume responsibilities for leadership. Thus, on the rare occasions when they become involved in demonstrations, they usually prefer peripheral roles, avoid responsibilities and are considered a nuisance by serious activists (Draper, 1965).

Whereas the protesting student is likely to accept the basic political and social values of his parents, the alienated student almost always rejects his parents' values. In particular, he is likely to see his father as a man who has "sold out" to the pressures for success and status in American society: he is determined to avoid the fate that overtook his father. Toward their mothers, however, alienated students usually express a very special sympathy and identification. These mothers, far from encouraging their sons towards independence and achievement, generally seem to have been over-solicitous and limiting. The most common family environment of the alienated-student-to-be consists of a parental schism supplemented by a special mother-son alliance of mutual understanding and maternal control and depreciation of the father (Keniston, 1965a).

In many colleges, alienated students often constitute a kind of hidden underground, disorganized and shifting in membership, in which students can temporarily or permanently withdraw from the ordinary pressures of college life. The alienated are especially attracted to the hallucinogenic drugs like marijuana, mescalin and LSD, precisely because these agents combine withdrawal from ordinary social life with the promise of greatly intensified subjectivity and perception. To the confirmed "acid head", what matters is intense, drug-assisted perception; the rest—including politics, social action and student demonstrations—is usually seen as "role-playing".[2]

The recent and much-publicized emergence of "hippie" subcultures in several major cities and increasingly on the campuses of many selective and progressive colleges illustrates the overwhelmingly apolitical stance of alienated youth. For although hippies oppose war and believe in inter-racial living, few have been willing or able to engage in anything beyond occasional peace marches or apolitical "human be-ins". Indeed, the hippies' emphasis on immediacy, "love" and "turning-on", together with his basic rejection of the traditional values of American life, innoculates him against involvement in long-range activist endeavors, like education or community organization, and even against the sustained effort needed to plan and execute demonstrations or marches. For the alienated hippie, American society is beyond redemption (or not worth trying to redeem); but the activist, no matter how intense his rejection of specific American policies and practices, retains a conviction that his society can and should be changed. Thus, despite occasional agreement in principle between the alienated and the activists, cooperation in practice has been rare, and usually ends with activists accusing the alienated of "irresponsibility", while the alienated are confirmed in their view of activists as moralistic, "up-tight", and "un-cool".

[2]The presence among student dissenters of a group of "nonstudents"—that is, drop-outs from college or graduate school who congregate or remain near some academic center—has been much noted. In fact, however, student protesters seem somewhat *less* likely to drop out of college than do nonparticipants in demonstrations (Heist, 1966), and there is no evidence that dropping out of college is in any way related to dissent from American society (Keniston and Helmreich, 1965). On the contrary, several studies suggest that the academically gifted and psychologically intact student who drops out of college voluntarily has few distinctive discontents about his college or about American society (Suczek and Alfort, 1966; Pervin et al, 1966; Wright, 1966). If he is dissatisfied at all, it is with himself, usually for failing to take advantage of the "rich educational opportunities" he sees in his college. The motivations of students dropping out of college are complex and varied, but such motivations more often seem related to personal questions of self definition and parental identification or to a desire to escape relentless academic pressures, than to any explicit dissent from the Great Society. Thus, although a handful of students have chosen to drop out of college for a period in order to devote themselves to political and societal protest activities, there seems little reason in general to associate the drop-out with the dissenter, whether he be a protester or an alienated student. The opposite is nearer the truth.

Obviously, no description of a type ever fits an individual perfectly. But by this rough typology, I mean to suggest that popular stereotypes which present a unified portrait of student dissent are gravely oversimplified. More specifically, they confuse the politically pessimistic and socially uncommitted alienated student with the politically hopeful and socially committed activist. To be sure, there are many students who fall between these two extremes, and some of them alternate between passionate search for intensified subjectivity and equally passionate efforts to remedy social and political injustices. And as I will later suggest, even within the student movement, one of the central tensions is between political activism and cultural alienation. Nonetheless, even to understand this tension we must first distinguish between the varieties of dissent apparent on American campuses.

Furthermore, the distinction between activist and alienated students as psychological types suggests the imcompleteness of scholarly analyses that see social and historical factors as the only forces that "push" a student toward one or the other of these forms of dissent. To be sure, social and cultural factors are of immense importance in providing channels for the expression (or suppression) of dissent, and in determining *which* kinds of dissenters receive publicity, censure, support or ostracism in any historical period. But these factors cannot, in general, change a hippie into a committed activist, nor a SNCC field worker into a full-time "acid-head". Thus, the prototypical activist of 1966 is not the "same" student as the prototypical student bohemian of 1956, but is rather the politically aware but frustrated, academically oriented "privatist" of that era. Similarly, as I will argue below, the most compelling alternative to most activists is not the search for kicks or sentience but the quest for scholarly competence. And if culturally-sanctioned opportunities for the expression of alienation were to disappear, most alienated students would turn to private psychopathology rather than to public activism.

Stated more generally, historical forces do not ordinarily transform radically the character, values and inclinations of an adult in later life. Rather, they thrust certain groups forward in some eras and discourage or suppress other groups. The recent alternation in styles of student dissent in America is therefore not to be explained so much by the malleability of individual character as by the power of society to bring activists into the limelight, providing them with the intellectual and moral instruments for action. Only a minority of potential dissenters fall close enough to the midpoint between alienation and activism so that they can constitute a "swing vote" acutely responsive to social and cultural pressures and styles.

The rest, the majority, are characterologically committed to one or another style of dissent.

The Sources of Activism

What I have termed "alienated" students are by no means a new phenomenon in American life, or for that matter in industrialized societies. Bohemians, "beatniks" and artistically-inclined under-graduates who rejected middle-class values have been a part of the American student scene, especially at more selective colleges; they constituted the most visible form of dissent during the relative political "silence" of American students in the 1950's. What is distinctive about student dissent in recent years is the unexpected emergence of a vocal minority of politically and socially active students.[3] Much is now known about the characteristics of such students, and the circumstances under which protests are likely to be mounted. At the same time, many areas of ignorance remain. In the account to follow, I will attempt to formulate a series of general hypotheses concerning the sources of student activism.[4]

It is abundantly clear that no single factor will suffice to explain the increase of politically-motivated activities and protests on American campuses. Even if we define an activist narrowly, as a student who (a) acts together with others in a group, (b) is concerned with some ethical, social, ideological or political issue, and (c) holds liberal or "radical" views, the sources of student activism and protest are complex and inter-related. At least four kinds of factors seem

[3]Student activisim, albeit of a rather different nature, was also found in the nineteen thirties. For a discussion and contrast of student protest today and after the Depression, see Lipset (1966a).

[4]Throughout the following, I will use the terms "protester" and "activist" interchangeably, although I am aware that some activists are not involved in protests. Furthermore, the category of "activist" is an embracing one, comprising at least three sub-classes. First, those who might be termed *reformers,* that is, students involved in community organization work, the Peace Corps, tutoring programs, Vista, etc., but not generally affiliated with any of the "New Left" organizations. Second, the group of *activists proper,* most of whom are or have been affiliated with organizations like the Free Speech Movement at Berkeley, Students for a Democratic Society, the Student Non-violent Coordinating Committee or the Congress on Racial Equality or the Vietnam Summer Project. Finally, there is a much publicized handful of students who might be considered *extremists,* who belong to doctrinaire Marxist and Trotskyite organizations like the now-defunct May Second Movement. No empirical study with which I am acquainted has investigated the differences between students in these three sub-groups. Most studies have concentrated on the "activist proper", and my remarks will be based on a reading of their data.

involved in any given protest. First, the individuals involved must be suitably predisposed by their personal backgrounds, values and motivations. Second, the likelihood of protest is far greater in certain kinds of educational and social settings. Third, socially-directed protests require a special cultural climate, that is, certain distinctive values and views about the effectiveness and meaning of demonstrations, and about the wider society. And finally, some historical situations are especially conducive to protests.

The Protest-Prone Personality

A large and still-growing number of studies, conducted under different auspices, at different times and about different students, presents a remarkably consistent picture of the protest-prone individual (Aiken, Demerath and Marwell, 1966; Flacks, this issue; Gastwirth, 1965; Heist, 1965, 1966; Lyonns, 1965; Somers, 1965; Watts and Whittaker, 1966; Westby and Baungart, 1966; Katz, 1967; and Paulus, 1967). For one, student protesters are generally outstanding students; the higher the student's grade average, the more outstanding his academic achievements, the more likely it is that he will become involved in any given political demonstration. Similarly, student activists come from families with liberal political values; a disporportionate number report that their parents hold views essentially similar to their own, and accept or support their activities. Thus, among the parents of protesters we find large numbers of liberal Democrats, plus an unusually large scattering of pacifists, socialists, etc. A disproportionate number of protesters come from Jewish families; and if the parents of activists are religious, they tend to be concentrated in the more liberal denominations—Reform Judaism, Unitarianism, the Society of Friends, etc. Such parents are reported to have high ethical and political standards, regardless of their actual religious convictions.

As might be expected of a group of politically liberal and academically talented students, a disproportionate number are drawn from professional and intellectual families of upper middle-class status. For example, compared with active student conservatives, members of protest groups tend to have higher parental incomes, more parental education, and less anxiety about social status (Westby and Braungart, 1966). Another study finds that high levels of education distinguish the activist's family even in the grandparental generation (Flacks, this issue). In brief, activists are not drawn from disadvantaged, status-anxious, underprivileged or uneducated groups; on the contrary, they are selectively recruited from among those young Americans who have had the most socially fortunate upbringings.

Basic Value Commitments of Activists. The basic value commitments of the activist tend to be academic and non-vocational. Such students are rarely found among engineers, future teachers at teachers colleges, or students of business administration (see Trent and Craise's article in this issue). Their over-all educational goals are those of a liberal education for its own sake, rather than specifically technical, vocational or professional preparation. Rejecting careerist and familist goals, activists espouse humanitarian, expressive and self-actualizing values. Perhaps because of these values, they delay career choice longer than their classmates (Flacks, this issue). Nor are such students distinctively dogmatic, rigid or authoritarian. Quite the contrary, the substance and style of their beliefs and activities tends to be open, flexible and highly liberal. Their fields of academic specialization are nonvocational—the social sciences and the humanities. Once in college, they not only do well academically, but tend to persist in their academic commitments, dropping out *less* frequently than most of their classmates. As might be expected, a disproportionate number receive a B.A. within four years and continue on to graduate school, preparing themselves for academic careers.

Survey data also suggest that the activist is not distinctively dissatisfied with his college education. As will be noted below, activists generally attend colleges which provide the best, rather than the worst, undergraduate education available today. Objectively then, activists probably have less to complain about in their undergraduate educations than most other students. And subjectively as well, surveys show most activists, like most other American undergraduates, to be relatively well satisfied with their undergraduate educations (Somers, 1965; Kornhauser, 1967). Thus, disatisfaction with educational failings of the "impersonal multiversity", however important as a rallying cry, does not appear to be a distinctive cause of activism.

In contrast to their relative satisfaction with the quality of their educations, however, activists *are* distinctively dissatisfied with what might be termed the "civil-libertarian" defects of their college administrations. While no doubt a great many American undergraduates distrust "University Hall", this distrust is especially pronounced amongst student protesters (Kornhauser, 1967; Paulus, 1967). Furthermore, activists tend to be more responsive than other students to deprivations of civil rights on campus as well as off campus, particularly when political pressures seem to motivate on campus policies they consider unjust. The same responsiveness increasingly extends to issues of "student power": i.e., student participation and decisions affecting campus life. Thus, bans on controversial speakers, censorship of student publications, and limitations on off-campus political or social action are likely to incense the activist, as is arbitrary "administration without the consent of the administered". But it is primarily perceived injustice or the denial of student rights by the Administration—rather than poor educational quality, neglect by the faculty, or the impersonality of the multiversity—that agitates the activist.

Most studies of activists have concentrated on variables that are relatively easy to measure: social class, academic achievements, explicit values and satisfaction with college. But these factors alone will not explain activism: more students possess the demographic and attitudinal characteristics of the protest-prone personality than are actually involved in protests and social action programs. Situational, institutional, cultural and historical factors (discussed below), obviously contribute to "catalysing" a protest-prone personality into an actual activist. But it also seems that, within the broad demographic group so far defined, more specific psychodynamic factors contribute to activism.

Activists . . . Not in Rebellion. In speculating about such factors, we leave the ground of established fact and enter the terrain of speculation, for only a few studies have explored the personality dynamics and family constellation of the activist, and most of these studies are impressionistic and clinical (e.g. Coles, 1967; Ehle, 1965; Draper, 1965; Fishman and Solomon n.d., 1964; Gastwirth, 1965; Newfield, 1966; Schneider, 1966; Solomon and Fishman, 1963, 1964; Zinn 1965). But certain facts are clear. As noted, activists are *not*, on the whole, repudiating or rebelling against explicit parental values and ideologies. On the contrary, there is some evidence that such students are living out their parents' values in practice; and one study suggests that activists may be somewhat *closer* to their parents' values than nonactivists (Flacks, this issue). Thus, any simple concept of "generational conflict" or "rebellion against authority" is clearly oversimplified as applied to the motivations of most protesters.

Activists . . . Living Out Parental Values. It does seem probable, however, that many activists are concerned with *living out expressed but unimplemented parental values.* Solomon and Fishman (1963), studying civil rights activists and peace marchers, argue that many demonstrators are "acting out" in their demonstrations the values which their parents explicitly believed, but did not have the courage or opportunity to practice or fight for. Similarly, when protesters criticize their fathers, it is usually over their fathers' failure to practice what they have preached to their children throughout their lives. Thus, in the personal background of the protester there is occasionally a suggestion that his father is less-than-"sincere" (and even at times "hypocritical") in his professions of political liberalism. In particular, both careerism and familism in parents are the objects of activist criticisms, the more so because these implicit goals often conflict with explicit parental values. And it may be that protesters receive both covert and overt support from their parents because the latter are secretly proud of their children's eagerness to implement the ideals they as parents have only given lip-service to. But whatever the ambivalences that bind parents with their activist children, it would be wrong to over-emphasize them: what is most impressive is the solidarity of older and younger generations.

Activists ... Family Structure. While no empirical study has tested this hypothesis, it seems probable that in many activist-producing families, the mother will have a dominant psychological influence on her son's development. I have already noted that the protester's cause is rarely himself, but rather alleviating the oppression of others. As a group, activists seem to possess an unusual *capacity for nurturant identification*—that is, for empathy and sympathy with the underdog, the oppressed and the needy. Such a capacity can have many origins, but its most likely source in upper-middle class professional families is identification with an active mother whose own work embodies nurturant concern for others. Flacks' finding that the mothers of activists are likely to be employed, often in professional or service roles like teaching and social work, is consistent with this hypothesis. In general in American society, middle-class women have greater social and financial freedom to work in jobs that are idealistically "fulfilling" as opposed to merely lucrative or prestigious. As a rule, then, in middle-class families, it is the mother who actively embodies in her life and work the humanitarian, social and political ideals that the father may share in principle but does not or cannot implement in his career.

Given what we know about the general characteristics of the families of protest-prone students, it also seems probable that the dominant ethos of their families is unusually equalitarian, permissive, "democratic", and highly individuated. More specifically, we might expect that these will be families where children talk back to their parents at the dinner table, where free dialogue and discussion of feelings is encouraged, and where "rational" solutions are sought to everyday family problems and conflicts. We would also expect that such families would place a high premium on self-expression and intellectual independence, encouraging their children to make up their own minds and to stand firm against group pressures. Once again, the mother seems the most likely carrier and epitome of these values, given her relative freedom from professional and financial pressures.

The contrast between such protest-prompting families and alienating families should be underlined. In both, the son's deepest emotional ties are often to his mother. But in the alienating family, the mother-son relationship is characterized by maternal control and intrusiveness, whereas in the protest-prompting family, the mother is a highly individuating force in her son's life, pushing him to independence and autonomy. Furthermore, the alienated student is determined to avoid the fate that befell his father, whereas the protesting student wants merely to live out the values that his father has not always worked hard enough to practice. Finally, the egalitarian, permissive, democratic and individuating environment of the entire family of the protester contrasts with the overcontrolling, over-solicitous attitude of the mother in the alienating family, where the father is usually excluded from major emotional life within the family.

These hypotheses about the family background and psycho-dynamics of the protester are speculative, and future research may prove their invalidity. But regardless of whether *these* particular speculations are correct, it seems clear that in addition to the general social, demographic and attitudinal factors mentioned in most research, more specific familial and psychodynamic influences contribute to protest-proneness.

The Protest-Promoting Institution

However we define his characteristics, one activist alone cannot make a protest: the characteristics of the college or university he attends have much to do with whether his protest-proneness will ever be mobilized into actual activism. Politically, socially and ideologically motivated demonstrations and activities are most likely to occur at certain types of colleges; they are almost unknown at a majority of campuses. The effects of institutional characteristics on protests have been studied by Cowan (1966) and Peterson (1966), and by Sampson and by Brown in this issue.

In order for an organized protest or related activities to occur, there must obviously be sufficient *numbers* of protest-prone students to form a group, these students must have an opportunity for *interaction* with each other, and there must be *leaders* to initiate and mount the protest. Thus, we might expect—and we indeed find—that protest is associated with institutional size, and particularly with the congregation of large numbers of protest-prone students in close proximity to each other. More important than sheer size alone, however, is the "image" of the institution: certain institutions selectively recruit students with protest-prone characteristics. Specifically, a reputation for academic excellence and freedom, coupled with highly selective admissions policies, will tend to congregate large numbers of potentially protesting students on one campus. Thus, certain institutions do act as "magnets" for potential activists, but not so much because of their reputations for political radicalism as because they are noted for their academic excellence. Among such institutions are some of the most selective and "progressive" private liberal arts colleges, major state universities (like Michigan, California at Berkeley and Wisconsin) which have long traditions of vivid undergraduate teaching and high admissions standards (Lipset and Altbach, 1966) and many of the more prestigious private universities.

Once protest-prone students are on campus, they must have an opportunity to interact, to support one another, to develop common outlooks and shared policies—in short, to form an *activist subculture* with sufficient mass and potency to generate a demonstration or action program. Establishing "honors colleges" for talented and academically-motivated students is one particularly effective way of creating a "critical mass" of protest-prone students. Similarly, inadequate on-campus housing indirectly results in the development of off-campus protest-prone sub-cultures (e.g., co-op houses) in residences where student activists can develop a high degree of ideological solidarity and organizational cohesion.

But even the presence of a critical mass of protest-prone undergraduates in an activist sub-culture is not enough to make a protest without leaders and issues. And in general, the most effective protest leaders have not been undergraduates, but teaching assistants. The presence of large numbers of exploited, underpaid, disgruntled and frustrated teacher assistants (or other equivalent graduate students and younger faculty members) is almost essential for organized and persistent protest. For one, advanced students tend to be more liberal politically and more sensitive to political issues than are most undergraduates—partly because education seems to have a liberalizing effect, and partly because students who persist into graduate school tend to be more liberal to start than those who drop out or go elsewhere. Furthermore, the frustrations of graduate students, especially at very large public universities, make them particularly sensitive to general problems of injustice, exploitation and oppression. Teaching assistants, graduate students and young faculty members also tend to be in daily and prolonged contact with students, are close enough to them in age to sense their mood, and are therefore in an excellent position to lead and organize student protests. Particularly at institutions which command little institutional allegiance from large numbers of highly capable graduate students (Lipset and Altbach, 1966) will such students be found among the leaders of the protest movement.

The Issues of Protest. Finally, issues are a necessity. In many cases, these issues are provided by historical developments on the national or international scene, a point to which I will return. But in some instances, as at Berkeley, "on-campus" issues are the focus of protest. And in other cases, off-campus and on-campus issues are fused, as in the recent protests at institutional cooperation with draft board policies considered unjust by demonstrating students. In providing such on-campus issues, the attitude of the university administration is central. Skillful handling of student complaints, the maintenance of open channels of communication between student leaders and faculty members, and administrative willingness to resist public and political pressures in order to protect the rights of students—all minimize the likelihood of organized protest. Conversely, a university administration that shows itself unduly sensitive to political, legislative or public pressures, that treats students arrogantly, ineptly, condescending, hypocritically or above all dishonestly, is asking for a demonstration.

Thus one reason for the relative absence of on-campus student protests and demonstrations on the campuses of private, non-denominational "academic" colleges and universities (which recruit many protest-prone students) probably lies in the liberal policies of the administrations. As Cowan (1966) notes, liberal students generally attend non-restrictive and "libertarian" colleges. Given an administration and faculty that supports or tolerates activism and student rights, student activists must generally find their issues off-campus. The same students, confronting an administration unduly sensitive to political pressures from a conservative board of regents or State legislature, might engage in active on-campus protests. There is also some evidence that clever administrative manipulation of student complaints even in the absence of genuine concern with student rights, can serve to dissipate the potentialities of protest (Keene, 1966).

Among the institutional factors often cited as motivating student protest is the largeness, impersonality, atomization, "multi-versitification" etc., of the university. I have already noted that student protesters do not seem distinctively dissatisfied with their educations. Furthermore, the outstanding academic achievements and intellectual motivations of activists concentrate them, within any college, in the courses and programs that provide the most "personal" attention: honors programs, individual instruction, advanced seminars, and so on. Thus, they probably receive relatively *more* individual attention and a *higher* calibre of instruction than do non-protestors. Furthermore, protests generally tend to occur at the best, rather than the worst colleges, judged from the point of view of the quality of undergraduate instruction. Thus, despite the popularity of student slogans dealing with the impersonality and irrelevance of the multiversity, the absolute level of educational opportunities seems, if anything, positively related to the occurrence of protest: the better the institution, the more likely demonstrations are.

Nor can today's student activism be attributed in any direct way to mounting academic presures. To be sure, activism is most manifest at those selective colleges where the "pressure to perform" (Keniston, 1965b) is greatest, where standards are highest, and where anxieties about being admitted to a "good" graduate or professional school are most pronounced. But, contrary to the argument of Lipset and Altbach (1966), the impact of academic pressure on activism seems negative rather than positive. Protest-prone students, with their superior academic attainments and strong intellectual commitments, seem especially vulnerable to a kind of academic professionalism that, because of the enormous demands it makes upon the student's energies, serves to cancel or preclude activism. Student demonstrations rarely take place during exam periods, and protests concerned with educational quality almost invariably seek an improvement of quality, rather than a lessening of pressure. Thus, though the pressure to perform doubtless affects *all* American students, it probably acts as a deterrent rather than a stimulus to student activism.

Deprivation of Expectations. What probably does matter, however, is the *relative* deprivation of student expectations (see Brown, this issue). A college that recruits large numbers of academically motivated and capable students into a less-than-first-rate education program, one that oversells entering freshmen on the virtues of the college, or one that reneges on implicit or explicit promises about the quality and freedom of education may well produce an "academic backlash" that will take the form of student protests over the quality of education. Even more important is the gap between expectations and actualities regarding freedom of student expression. Stern (1967) has demonstrated that most entering freshmen have extremely high hopes regarding the freedom of speech and action they will be able to exercise during college: most learn the real facts quickly, and graduate thoroughly disabused of their illusions. But since activists, as I have argued above, are particularly responsive to these issues, they are apt to tolerate disillusion less lightly, and to take up arms to concretize their dashed hopes. Compared to the frustration engendered by disillusionment regarding educational quality, the relative deprivation of civil libertarian hopes seems a more potent source of protests. And with regard to both issues, it must be recalled that protests have been *fewest* at institutions of low educational quality and little freedom for student expression. Thus, it is not the absolute level either of educational quality or of student freedom that matters, but the gap between student hopes and institutional facts.

The Protest-Prompting Cultural Climate

Even if a critical mass of interacting protest-prone students forms in an institution that provides leadership and issues, student protests are by no means inevitable, as the quiescence of American students during the nineteen fifties suggests. For protests to occur, other more broadly cultural factors, attitudes and values must be present. Protest activities must be seen as meaningful acts, either in an instrumental or an expressive sense; and activists must be convinced that the consequences of activism and protest will not be overwhelmingly damaging to them. During the 1950's, one much-discussed factor that may have militated against student activism was the conviction that the consequences of protest (blacklisting, F.B.I. investigations, problems in obtaining security clearance, difficulties in getting jobs) were both harmful to the individual and yet extremely likely. Even more important was the sense on the part of many politically-conscious students that participation in leftwing causes would merely show their naivete, gullibility and political innocence without furthering any worthy cause. The prevailing climate was such that protest was rarely seen as an act of any meaning or usefulness.

Academic Support. . . . Today, in contrast, student protesters are not only criticized and excoriated by a large segment of the general public, but—more crucial—actively defended, encouraged, lionized, praised, publicized, photographed, interviewed and studied by a portion of the academic community. Since the primary reference group of most activists is not the general public, but rather that liberal segment of the academic world most sympathetic to protest, academic support has a disproportionate impact on protest-prone students' perception of their own activities. In addition, the active participation of admired faculty members in protests, teach-ins and peace marches, acts as a further incentive to students (Kelman, 1966). Thus, in a minority of American colleges, sub-cultures have arisen where protest is felt to be both an important existential act—a dignified way of "standing up to be counted"—and an effective way of "bringing the machine to a halt", sometimes by disruptive acts (sit-ins, strikes, etc.), more often by calling public attention to injustice.

Universalism . . . . An equally important, if less tangible "cultural" factor is the broad climate of social criticism in American society. As Parsons (1951, 1960), White (1961), and others have noted, one of the enduring themes of American society is the pressure toward "universalism," that is, an increasing extension of principles like equality, equal opportunity, and fair protection of the law to all groups within the society (and in recent years, to all groups in the world). As affluence has increased in American society impatience at the slow "progress" of non-affluent minority groups has also increased, not only among students, but among other segments of the population. Even before the advent of the student civil rights movement, support for racial segregation was diminishing. Similarly, the current student concern for the "forgotten fifth" was not so much initiated by student activists as it was taken up by them. In this regard, student activists are both caught up in and in the vanguard of a new wave of extension of universalism in American society. Although the demands of student activists usually go far beyond the national consensus, they nonetheless reflect (at the same time that they have helped advance) one of the continuing trends in American social change.

A contrasting but equally enduring theme in American social criticism is a more fundamental revulsion against the premises of industrial—and now technological—society. Universalistic-liberal criticism blames our society because it has not yet extended its principles, privileges and benefits to all: the complaint is injustice and the goal is to complete our unfinished business. But alienated-romantic criticism questions the validity and importance of these same principles, privileges and benefits—the complaint is materialism and the goal is spiritual, aesthetic or expressive fulfillment. The tradition of revulsion against conformist, anti-aesthetic, materialistic, ugly, middle-class America runs through American writing from Melville through the "lost generation" to the "beat generation" and has been expressed concretely in the bohemian sub-cultures that have flourished in a few large American cities since the turn of the century. But today, the power of the romantic-alienated position has increased: one response to prosperity has been a more searching examination of the technological assumptions upon which prosperity has been based. Especially for the children of the upper middle-class, affluence is simply taken for granted, and the drive "to get ahead in the world" no longer makes sense for students who start out ahead.

The meanings of life must be sought elsewhere, in art, sentience, philosophy, love, service to others, intensified experience, adventure—in short, in the broadly aesthetic or expressive realm.

Deviant Views. . . . Since neither the universalistic nor the romantic critique of modern society is new, these critiques affect the current student generation not only directly but indirectly, in that they have influenced the way many of today's college students were raised. Thus, a few of today's activists are children of the "radicals of the 1930's" (Lipset and Altbach, 1966); and Flacks comments on the growing number of intellectual, professional upper middle-class families who have adopted "deviant" views of traditional American life and embodied these views in the practices by which they brought up their children. Thus, some of today's activists are the children of bohemians, college professors, etc. But in general, the explanation from parental "deviance" does not seem fully convincing. To be sure, the backgrounds of activists are "atypical" in a statistical sense, and thus might be termed empirically "deviant". It may indeed turn out that the parents of activists are distinguished by their emphasis on humanitarianism, intellectualism and romanticism, and by their lack of stress on moralism (Flacks, this issue). But it is not obvious that such parental values can be termed "deviant" in any but a statistical sense. "Concern with the plight of others", "desire to realize intellectual capacities", and "lack of concern about the importance of strictly controlling personal impulses"—all these values might be thought of as more normative than deviant in upper middle-class suburban American society in 1966. Even "sensitivity to beauty and art" is becoming increasingly acceptable. Nor can the socio-economic facts of affluence, freedom from status anxiety, high educational levels, permissiveness with children, training for independence, etc. be considered normatively deviant in middle-class America. Thus, the sense in which activists are the deviant offspring of sub-culturally deviant parents remains to be clarified.

Psychological Flexibility . . . . Another explanation seems equally plausible, at least as applied to some student activists—namely that their activism is closely related to the social and cultural conditions that promote high levels of psychological flexibility, complexity and integration. As Bay (1966) has argued, social scientists may be too reluctant to entertain the possibility that some political and social outlooks or activities are symptomatic of psychological "health", while others indicate "disturbance". In fact, many of the personal characteristics of activists—empathy, superior intellectual attainments, capacity for group involvement, strong humanitarian values, emphasis on self-realization, etc.—are consistent with the hypothesis that, as a group, they are unusually "healthy" psychologically. (See also Heist, 1966 and Trent and Craise in this issue). Similarly, the personal antecedents of activists—economic security, committed parents, humanitarian, liberal and permissive home environments, good education, etc.—are those that would seem to promote unusually high levels of psychological functioning. If this be correct, then former SDS president Tom Hayden's words (1966) may be a valid commentary on the cultural setting of activism:

Most of the active student radicals today come from middle to upper middle-class professional homes. They were born with status and affluence as facts of life, not goals to be striven for. In their upbringing, their parents stressed the right of children to question and make judgments, producing perhaps the first generation of young people both affluent and independent of mind.

In agreeing with Bay (this issue) that activists may be more psychologically "healthy" as a group than nonactivists, I am aware of the many difficulties entailed by this hypothesis. First, complexity, flexibility, integration, high levels of functioning, etc. are by no means easy to define, and the criteria for "positive mental health" remain vague and elusive. (See Jahoda, 1958). Second, there are obviously many individuals with these same "healthy" characteristics who are not activists; and within the group of activists, there are many individuals with definite psychopathologies. In any social movement, a variety of individuals of highly diverse talents and motivations are bound to be involved, and global descriptions are certain to be oversimplified. Third, the explanation from "psychological health" and the explanation from "parental deviance" are not necessarily opposed. On the contrary, these two arguments become identical if we assume that the preconditions for high levels of psychological functioning are both statistically and normatively deviant in modern American society. This assumption seems quite plausible.

Whatever the most plausible explanation of the socio-cultural sources of activism, the importance of prevailing attitudes toward student protest and of the climate of social criticism in American seems clear. In the past five years a conviction has arisen, at least among a minority of American college students, that protest and social action are effective and honorable. Furthermore, changes in American society, especially in middle-class child rearing practices, mean that American students are increasingly responsible to both the universalistic and romantic critique of our society. Both strands of social criticism have been picked up by student activists in a rhetoric of protest that combines a major theme of impatience at the slow fulfillment of the credal ideals of American society with a more muted minor theme of aesthetic revulsion at technological society itself. By and large, activists respond most affirmatively to the first theme and alienated students to the second; but even within the student protest movement, these two themes coexist in uneasy tension.

The Protest-Producing
Historical Situation

To separate what I have called the "cultural climate" from the "historical situation" is largely arbitrary. But by this latter term I hope to point to the special sensitivity of today's student activists to historical events and trends that do not immediately impinge upon their own lives. In other nations, and in the past, student protest movements seem to have been more closely related to immediate student frustrations than they are in America today. The "transformationist" (utopian, Marxist, universalistic or democratic) aspirations of activist youth in rapidly developing nations often seem closely related to their personal frustrations under oppressive regimes or at "feudal" practices in their societies; the "restorationist" (romantic, alienated) youth movements that have appeared in later stages of industrialization seem closely connected to a personal sense of the loss of a feudal, maternal, and "organic" past. (See Lifton, 1960, 1963, 1964). Furthermore, both universalistic and romantic youth movements in other nations have traditionally been highly ideological, committed either to concepts of universal democracy and economic justice or to particularistic values of brotherhood, loyalty, feeling and nation.

Anti-ideological .... Today's activists, in contrast, are rarely concerned with improving their own conditions and are highly motivated by identification with the oppressions of others. The anti-ideological bias of today's student activists has been underlined by virtually every commentator. Furthermore, as Flacks notes, the historical conditions that have produced protest elsewhere are largely absent in modern America; and the student "movement" in this country differs in important ways from student movements elsewhere. In many respects, then, today's American activists have no historical precedent, and only time will tell to what extent the appearance of organized student dissent in the 1960's is a product of locally American conditions, of the psychosocial effects of a technological affluence that will soon characterize other advanced nations, or of widespread changes in identity and style produced by psycho-historical factors that affect youth of all nations (thermonuclear warfare, increased culture contact, rapid communications, etc.).

Sensitivity to World Events. But whatever the historical roots of protest, today's student protester seems uniquely sensitive to historical trends and events. In interviewing student activists I have been impressed with how often they mention some world-historical event as the catalyst for their activism—in some cases, witnessing via television of the Little Rock demonstrations over school integration, in another case, watching rioting Zengakuren students in Japan protesting the arrival of President Eisenhower, in other cases, particularly among Negro students, a strong identification with the rising black nationalism of recently independent African nations.

Several factors help explain this sensitivity to world events. For one, modern means of communication make the historical world more psychologically "available" to youth. Students today are exposed to world events and world trends with a speed and intensity that has no historical precedent. Revolutions, trends, fashions and fads are now world wide; it takes but two or three years for fashions to spread from Carnaby Street to New York, New Delhi, Tokyo, Warsaw, Lagos and Lima. In particular, students who have been brought up in a tradition that makes them unusually empathic, humanitarian and universalistic in values may react more intensely to exposure via television to student demonstrations in Japan than to social pressures from their fellow seniors in Centerville High. Finally, this broadening of empathy is, I believe, part of a general modern trend toward the *internationalization of identity*. Hastened by modern communications and consolidated by the world-wide threat of nuclear warfare, this trend involves, in vanguard groups in many nations, a loosening of parochial and national allegiances in favor of a more inclusive sense of affinity with one's peers (and non-peers) from all nations. In this respect, American student activists are both participants and leaders in the reorganization of psychosocial identity and ideology that is gradually emerging from the unique historical conditions of the twentieth century (Lifton, 1965).

A small but growing number of American students, then, exhibit a peculiar responsiveness to world-historical events—a responsiveness based partly on their own broad identification with others like them throughout the world, and partly on the availability of information about world events via the mass media. The impact of historical events, be they the world-wide revolution for human dignity and esteem, the rising aspirations of the developing nations, or the war in Vietnam, is greatly magnified upon such students; their primary identification is not their unreflective national identity, but their sense of affinity for Vietnamese peasants, Negro sharecroppers, demonstrating Zengakuren activists, exploited migrant workers, and the oppressed everywhere. One of the consequences of security, affluence and education is growing sense of personal involvement with those who are insecure, non-affluent and uneducated.

The Future of Student Activism

I have argued that no single factor can explain or help us predict the future of the student protest movement in America: active expressions of dissent have become more prevalent because of an *interaction* of individual, institutional, cultural and historical factors. Affluence and education have changed the environment within which middle-class children are raised, in turn producing a minority of students with special sensitivity to the oppressed and the dissenting everywhere. At the same time, technological innovations like television have made available to these students abundant imagery of oppression and dissent in America and in other nations. And each of these factors exerts a potentiating influence on the others.

Given some understanding of the interaction of these factors, general questions about the probable future of student activism in America can now be broken down into four more specific questions: Are we likely to produce (a) more protest-prone personalities? (b) more institutional settings in which protests are likely? (c) a cultural climate that sanctions and encourages activism? and (d) a historical situation that facilitates activism? To three of the questions (a, b and d), I think the answer is a qualified yes; I would therefore expect that in the future, if the cultural climate remains the same, student activism and protest would continue to be visible features on the American social landscape.

Consider first the factors that promote protest-prone personalities. In the coming generation there will be more and more students who come from the upper middle-class, highly educated, politically liberal professional backgrounds from which protesters are selectively recruited (Michael, 1965). Furthermore, we can expect that a significant and perhaps growing proportion of these families will have the universalistic, humanitarian, equalitarian and individualistic values found in the families of protesters. Finally, the expressive, permissive, democratic and autonomy-promoting atmosphere of these families seems to be the emerging trend of middle-class America: older patterns of "entrepreneurial-authoritarian" control are slowly giving way to more "bureaucratic-democratic" techniques of socialization (Miller and Swanson, 1958). Such secular changes in the American family would produce a growing proportion of students with protest-prone personalities.

Institutional factors, I have argued, are of primary importance in so far as they bring together a critical mass of suitable protest-predisposed students in an atmosphere where they can interact, create their own subculture, develop leadership and find issues. The growing size of major American universities, their increasing academic and intellectual selectivity, and the emphasis on "quality" education (honors programs, individual instruction, greater student freedom)—all seem to promote the continuing development of activist sub-cultures in a minority of American institutions. The increasing use of graduate student teaching assistants in major universities points to the growing availability of large numbers of potential "leaders" for student protests. Admittedly, a sudden increase in the administrative wisdom in college Deans and Presidents could reduce the number of available "on-campus" issues; but such a growth in wisdom does not seem imminent.

Cultural Climate May Change. In sharp contrast, a maintenance of the cultural climate required for continuation of activism during the coming years seems far more problematical. Much depends on the future course of the war in Vietnam. Continuing escalation of the war in Southeast Asia will convince many student activists that their efforts are doomed to ineffectuality. For as of mid-1967, anti-war activism has become the primary common cause of student protesters. The increasing militancy and exclusivity of the Negro student civil rights movement, its emphasis on "Black Power" and on grass-roots community organization work (to be done by Negroes) is rapidly pushing white activists out of civil rights work, thus depriving them of the issue upon which the current mood of student activism was built. This fact, coupled with the downgrading of the war on poverty, the decline of public enthusiasm for civil rights, and the increasing scarcity of public and private financing for work with the underprivileged sectors of American society, has already begun to turn activists away from domestic issues toward an increasingly singleminded focus on the war in Vietnam. Yet at the same time, increasing numbers of activists overtly or covertly despair of the efficacy of student attempts to mobilize public opinion against the war, much less to influence directly American foreign policies. Continuing escalation in Southeast Asia has also begun to create a more repressive atmosphere towards student (and other) protesters of the war, exemplified by the question, "Dissent or Treason"? Already the movement of activists back to full-time academic work is apparent.

Thus, the war in Vietnam, coupled by the "rejection" of white middleclass students by the vestigial black Civil Rights Movement is producing a crisis among activists, manifest by a "search for issues" and intense disagreement over strategy and tactics. At the same time, the diminution of support for student activism tends to exert a "radicalizing" effect upon those who remain committed activists— partly because frustration itself tends to radicalize the frustrated, and partly because many of the less dedicated and committed activists have dropped away from the movement. At the same time, most activists find it difficult to turn from civil rights or peace work toward "organizing the middle-class" along lines suggested by alienated-romantic criticisms of technological society. On the whole, activists remain more responsive to universalistic issues like peace and civil rights than to primarily expressive or esthetic criticisms of American society. Furthermore, the practical and organizational problems of "organizing the middle-class" are overwhelming. Were the student movement to be forced to turn away from universalistic issues like civil rights and peace to a romantic critique of the "quality of middle-class life", my argument here implies that its following and efficacy would diminish considerably. Were this to happen, observations based on student activism of a more "universalistic" variety would have to be modified to take account of a more radical and yet more alienated membership. Thus, escalation or even continuation of the war in Vietnam, particularly over a long period, will reduce the likelihood of student activism.

Yet there are other, hopefully more permanent, trends in American culture that argue for a continuation of protests. The further extension of affluence in America will probably mean growing impatience over our society's failure to include the "forgotten fifth" in its prosperity: as the excluded and under-privileged become fewer in number, pressures to include them in American society will grow. Similarly, as more young Americans are brought up in affluent homes and subcultures, many will undoubtedly turn to question the value of monetary, familistic and careerist goals, looking instead toward expressive, romantic, experi-ential, humanitarian and self-actualizing pursuits to give their lives meaning. Thus, in the next decades, barring a major world conflagration, criticisms of American society will probably continue and intensify on two grounds: first, that it has excluded a significant minority from its prosperity, and second, that affluence alone is empty without humanitarian, aesthetic or expressive fulfillment. Both of these trends would strengthen the climate conducive to continuing activism.

World Wide Protest-Promoting Pressures . . . . Finally, protest-promoting pressures from the rest of the world will doubtless increase in the coming years. The esteem revolution in developing nations, the rise of aspirations in the impoverished two-thirds of the world, and the spread of universalistic principles to other nations—all of these trends portend a growing international unrest, especially in the developing nations. If young Americans continue to be unusually responsive to the unfulfilled aspirations of those abroad, international trends will touch a minority of them deeply, inspiring them to overseas activities like the Peace Corps, to efforts to "internationalize" American foreign policies, and to an acute sensitivity to the frustrated aspirations of other Americans. Similarly, continuation of current American policies of supporting anti-communist but often repressive regimes in developing nations (particularly regimes anathema to student activists abroad) will tend to agitate American students as well. Thus, pressures from the probable world situation will support the continuance of student protests in American society.

In the next decades, then, I believe we can forsee the continuation, with short-range ebbs and falls, of activism in American society. Only if activists were to become convinced that protests were ineffectual or social action impossible is this trend likely to be fundamentally reversed. None of this will mean that protesters will become a majority among American students; but we can anticipate a slowly-growing minority of the most talented, empathic, and intellectually independent of our students who will take up arms against injustice both here and abroad.

In Summary . . . Throughout this discussion, I have emphasized the contrast between two types of students, two types of family backgrounds, and two sets of values that inspire dissent from the Great Society. On the one hand, I have discussed students I have termed alienated, whose values are apolitical, romantic, and aesthetic. These students are most responsive to "romantic" themes of social criticism; that is, they reject our society because of its dehumanizing effects, its lack of aesthetic quality and its failure to provide "spiritual" fulfillment to its members. And they are relatively impervious to appeals to social, economic or political justice. On the other hand, I have discussed activists, who are politically involved, humanitarian and universalistic in values. These students object to our society not because they oppose its basic principles, but because it fails to implement these principles fully at home and abroad.

In the future, the tension between the romantic-alienated and the universalistic-activist styles of dissent will probably increase. I would anticipate a growing polarization between those students and student groups who turn to highly personal and experiential pursuits like drugs, sex, art and intimacy, and those students who redouble their efforts to change American society. In the past five years, activists have been in the ascendant, and the alienated have been little involved in organized political protests. But a variety of possible events could reverse this ascendency. A sense of ineffectuality, especially if coupled with repression of organized dissent, would obviously dishearten many activists. More important, the inability of the student protest movement to define its own long-range objectives, coupled with its intransigent hostility to ideology and efficient organization, means that *ad hoc* protests are too rarely linked to the explicit intellectual, political and social goals that alone can sustain prolonged efforts to change society. Without some shared sustaining vision of the society and world they are working to promote, and frustrated by the enormous obstacles that beset any social reformer, student activists would be likely to return to the library.

How and whether this tension between alienation and activism is resolved seems to me of the greatest importance. If a growing number of activists, frustrated by political ineffectuality or a mounting war in Southeast Asia, withdraw from active social concern into a narrowly academic quest for professional competence, then a considerable reservoir of the most talented young Americans will have been lost to our society and the world. The field of dissent would be left to the alienated, whose intense quest for *personal* salvation, meaning, creativity and revelation dulls their perception of the public world and inhibits attempts to better the lot of others. If, in contrast, tomorrow's potential activists can feel that their demonstrations and actions are effective in molding public opinion and, more important, in effecting needed social change, then the possibilities for constructive change in post-industrial American society are virtually without limit.

References

Aiken, M., Demerath, N. J., and Marwell, G. Conscience and confrontation: some preliminary findings on summer civil rights volunteers. University of Wisconsin, 1966 (mimeo).

Allen, M., and Silverstein H. Progress report: creative arts—alienated youth project. New York: March, 1967.

Bay, Christian. Political and apolitical students: facts in search of theory. *Journal of Social Issues*, 1967, 23, (3).

Bernreuter, Robert G. The college student: he is thinking, talking, acting. *Penn State Alumni News*, July, 1966.

Block, J., Haan, N., and Smith, M. B. Activism and apathy in contemporary adolescents. In J. F. Adams (Ed.), *Contributions to the understanding of adolescence*. New York: Allyn and Bacon, forthcoming.

Coles, Robert. Serpents and doves: non-violent youth in the South. In Erik Erikson (Ed.), *The challenge of youth*. New York: Basic Books, 1963.

Coles, Robert. *Children of crisis*. Boston: Little, Brown, 1967.

Cowan, John Lewis. Academic freedom, protest and university environments. Paper read at APA, New York, 1966.

Draper, Hal. *Berkeley, the new student revolt*. New York: Grove, 1965.

Ehle, John. *The free men*. New York: Harper and Row, 1965.

Erikson, Erik H. (Ed.) *The challenge of youth*. New York: Basic Books, 1963.

Fishman, Jacob R., and Solomon, Frederic. Psychological observations on the student sit-in movement. *Proceedings of the Third World Congress of Psychiatry*. Toronto: University of Toronto/McGill, n.d.

Fishman, Jacob R., and Solomon, Frederic. Youth and social action. *The Journal of Social Issues*, 1964, 20, (4), 1-28.

Flacks, Richard E. The liberated generation: an exploration of the roots of student protest. *Journal of Social Issues*, 1967, 23, (3).

Gastwirth, D. Why students protest. Unpublished paper, Yale University, 1965.

Hayden, T. Quoted in *Comparative Education Review*, 1966, 10, 187.

Heist, Paul. Intellect and commitment: the faces of discontent. *Order and freedom on the campus*. Western Interstate Commission for Higher Education and the Center for the Study of Higher Education, 1965.

Heist, Paul. The dynamics of student discontent and protest. Paper read at APA, New York, 1966.

Jahoda, Marie. *Current concepts of positive mental health*. New York: Basic Books, 1958.

Katz, J. The learning environment: social expectations and influences. Paper presented at American Council of Education, Washington, D. C., 1965.

Katz, J. The student activists: rights, needs and powers of undergraduates. Stanford: Institute for the Study of Human Problems, 1967.

Keene, S. How one big university laid unrest to rest. *The American Student*, 1966, 1, 18-21.

Kelman, H. D. Notes on faculty activism. *Letter to Michigan Alumni*, 1966.

Keniston, Kenneth. American students and the 'political revival.' *The American Scholar*, 1962, 32, 40-64.

Keniston, Kenneth. *The uncommitted*. New York: Harcourt, Brace and World, 1965a.

Keniston, Kenneth. The pressure to perform. *The Intercollegian*. September, 1965b.

Keniston, Kenneth. The faces in the lecture room. In R. S. Morison (Ed.), *The American university*. Boston: Houghton Mifflin, 1966a.

Keniston, Kenneth. The psychology of alienated students. Paper read at APA, New York, 1966b.

Keniston, Kenneth, and Helmreich, R. An exploratory study of discontent and potential drop-outs at Yale. Yale University, 1965. (mimeo)

Kornhauser, W. Alienation and participation in the mass university. Paper read at American Ortho-Psychiatric Association, Washington, D. C., 1967.

Lifton, Robert Jay. Japanese youth: the search for the new and the pure. *The American Scholar*, 1960, 30, 332-344.

Lifton, Robert Jay. Youth and history: individual change in post-war Japan. In E. Erikson (Ed.), *The challenge of youth*. New York: Harper and Row, 1963.

Lifton, Robert Jay. Individual patterns in historical change. *Comparative Studies in Society and History*. 1964, 6, 369-383.

Lifton, Robert Jay. Protean man. Yale University, 1965. (mimeo)

Lipset, Seymour M. Student opposition in the United States. *Government and Opposition,* 1966a, 1, 351-374.

Lipset, Seymour M. University students and politics in underdeveloped countries. *Comparative Education Review*, 1966b, 10, 132-162.

Lipset, Seymour M., and Altbach, P. G. Student politics and higher education in the United States. *Comparative Education Review*, 1966, 10, 320-349.

Lipset, Seymour M., and Wolin, S. S. (Eds.), *The Berkeley student revolt.* Garden City, New York: Doubleday, 1965.

Lyonns, G. The police car demonstration: a survey of participants. In S. Lipset and S. Wolin (Eds.), *The Berkeley student revolt*. Garden City, New York: Doubleday, 1965.

Michael, Donald Nelson. *The next generation. the prospects ahead for the youth of today and tomorrow.* New York: Vintage, 1965.

Miller, Michael, and Gilmore, Susan. (Eds.), *Revolution at Berkeley*. New York: Dell, 1965.

Miller, Daniel R. and Swanson, Guy E. *The changing American parent.* New York: Wiley, 1958.

Newfield, Jack. *A prophetic minority*. New York: New American Library, 1966.

Newsweek. Campus, 1965. March 22, 1965.

Parsons, Talcott. *The social system.* Glencoe, Ill.: Free Press, 1951.

Parsons, Talcott. *Structure and process in modern societies*. Glencoe, Ill.: Free Press, 1960.

Paulus, G. *A multivariate analysis study of student activist leaders, student government leaders, and non-activists.* Cited in Richard E. Peterson, *The student Left in American higher education*. Draft for Puerto Rico Conference on Students and Politics, 1967.

Pervin, Lawrence A., Reik, L. E. and Dalrymple, W. (Eds.), *The college drop-out and the utilization of talent*. Princeton: Princeton University, 1966.

Peterson, Richard E. *The scope of organized student protest in 1964-65.* Princeton: Educational Testing Service, 1966.

Peterson, Richard E. The student Left in American higher education. Draft for Puerto Rico Conference on Students and Politics, 1967.

Reed, M. Student non-politics, or how to make irrelevancy a virtue. *The American Student*, 1966, 1, (3), 7-10.

Rigney, Francis J., and Smith, L. D. *The real bohemia*. New York: Basic Books, 1961.

Schneider, Patricia. A study of members of SDS and YD at Harvard. Unpublished B. A. thesis, Wellesley College, 1966.

Solomon, Frederic, and Fishman, Jacob R. Perspectives on the student sit-in movement. *American Journal of Ortho-Psychiatry*, 1963, 33, 873-874.

Solomon, Frederic, and Fishman, Jacob R. Youth and peace: a psycho-social study of student peace demonstrators in Washington, D. C. *The Journal of Social Issues*, 1964, 20, (4), 54-73.

Somers, R. H. The mainsprings of the rebellion: a survey of Berkeley students in November, 1964. In S. Lipset and S. Wolin (Eds.), *The Berkeley student revolt*. Garden City, New York: Doubleday, 1965.

Stern, G. Myth and reality in the American college. *AAUP Bulletin*, Winter, 1966, 408-414.

Suczek, Robert Francis, and Alfert, E. Personality characteristic of college dropouts. University of California, 1966. (mimeo)

Trow, Martin. Some lessons from Berkeley. Paper presented to American Council of Education, Washington, D. C. 1965.

Watts, William Arther, and Whittaker, D. Some socio-psychological differences between highly committed members of the Free Speech Movement and the student population at Berkeley. *Applied Behavioral Science*, 1966, 2, 41-62.

Watts, William Arther, and Whittaker, D. Socio-psychological characteristics of intellectually oriented, alienated youth: a study of the Berkeley nonstudent. University of California, Berkeley, 1967. (mimeo)

Westby, D., and Braungart, R. Class and politics in the family backgrounds of student political activists. *American Social Review*, 1966, 31, 690-692.

White, Winston. *Beyond conformity*. Glencoe, Ill.: Free Press, 1961.

Whittaker, D., and Watts, W. A. Personality and value attitudes of intellectually disposed, alienated youth. Paper presented at APA, New York, 1966.

Wright, E. O. Student leaves of absence from Harvard College: A personality and social system approach. Unpublished paper, Harvard University, 1966.

Zinn, Howard. *SNCC, the new abolitionists*. Boston: Beacon, 1965.

Ruling Out Paternalism: Students and Admininstrators at Berkeley*

C. Michael Otten

The present well-publicized crisis of campus authority has been attributed to the civil rights movement, the Vietnam war, a small band of militant agitators, the generation gap, and even to television. The following pages offer another interpretation, one which may go further in explaining the past and clarifying the present. I shall suggest that the earlier basis of authority in the university, that which produced consent and legitimated administrative action, was the loyalty of students to the institution—fond affection for the campus community, devotion to its traditions, and self-sacrificing commitment to its welfare. This basis for authority, which has been declining since the 1920's, has now largely disappeared. The sources of decline are several, and some will be mentioned. Of particular interest, however, will be one source, administrative responses to the decline itself. These, I shall assert, have hastened the decline of loyalty. More important, they have contributed to the establishment of a new basis for authority, though one that remains ambiguous in its implications for freedom and stability in the university.

*Many people have contributed to the general ideas and the historical content of the dissertation from which this paper is derived. Professors Philip Selznick and Philippe Nonet have aided me in the general research for order in the often chaotic history of the university, while Sheldon L. Messinger has been especially helpful with this particular paper. Also, the work would not have been possible without financial support from the Russell Sage Foundation, administered by the Center for the Study of Law and Society, University of California, Berkeley.

The paper begins with a brief discussion of the phenomenon of loyalty and then turns to an examination of student loyalty to the university, and administrative responses to its decline in particular. Materials are drawn largely from the history of the University of California, as is perhaps only fitting at this time, given this topic. I have little doubt that the forces discussed also are found elsewhere.

I

"Loyalty" is a personal commitment that binds a person to something outside of himself. This commitment can have powerful consequences for action, for it may transcend, and even contradict, narrow self-interest. Loyalty is also an effective, subtle, and powerful form of control. As John Schaar has noted:

Loyalty is felt to impose obligations which must be fulfilled if one is to please others and be judged in their eyes. There are few explicit and formal sanctions against a breach of loyalty; the controls . . . are worked into the very fabric of the group life. . . . [Loyalty is a] cement that binds men together in an harmonious union. Through shared commitments individuals break the shell isolating them from other persons.[1]

Loyalty to the university, then, is a commitment to the good of the institution over and above other interests, a source of control and a "cement that binds." It binds not only equals to equals but also subordinates to superordinates. Where there is loyalty, alienation is minimized, order prevails, and compliance is nearly automatic.[2] This is the ideal, and under Benjamin Ide Wheeler's presidency (1899-1919) the University of California approximated that ideal.

Nowhere are the bonds of loyalty more fully realized than in the family, and it is especially significant that Wheeler stressed family imagery when talking about the university. His first official speech to students contained the following exhortation, which remained a dominant theme during his twenty-year reign: "This University shall be the family's *Glorious Old Mother . . . Love her.*"[3] Referring to the university as "the family's Glorious Old Mother" proved to be more than a rhetorical device. Wheeler, himself, acted like a father to the students and even addressed them as "my children." The infusion of familial imagery in the structures of authority was exemplified by the President's Report to the Governor, in which he called the powerful student judicial body the "household tribunal."

Loyalty was not just an emotional byproduct of a gathered group of undergraduates; it was consciously defined, carefully nurtured, and deliberately sustained by Wheeler himself.[4] From about 1900 to World War I, honor societies, student self-government, and classroom honor systems swept through higher education, bringing with them institutional allegiances which remain strong even today.[5] Within the university the honor societies, composed of outstanding young men, embodied the highest aspirations of the community. President Wheeler encouraged and used the societies; indeed, his whole system of "student self-government" rested upon the prominent senior men who belonged to the "Royal Order of the Golden Bear." The "Golden Bear" contained within itself the leaders of nearly all the "command posts" of student life—major fraternities, student newspaper, judicial committee, team athletics, etc. Wheeler also attended most of the important rallies and student meetings; he went to the football practice sessions and led the collegians in the bimonthly "senior singings." His presence and availability[6] personified the university, and affectionate identification with the President was easily transferred to the institution.

Student leaders seem to have shared Wheeler's intense institutional commitment. For example, the editor of the student newspaper urged everyone to attend the freshman rally, declaring:

> ... for at this first rally of the year the freshman realizes that there are some things bigger than books. The last doubt is wiped out, it is no longer a question of California or somewhere else. *It is California or nothing ... a torrent of unselfish devotion and love. ... Allegiance* sworn at the freshman rally is not a great mistake.[7]

At the same rally, the president of the student body spoke of the event as a great "religious festival." Indeed, it was a religious happening, in Durkheim's sense of a community rite intensifying loyal devotion to the group.

Loyalty did not terminate with graduation. The alumni attended the rallies, made generous contributions, occasionally attended honor society meetings, and gave advice to students. In a letter to the student newspaper, one alumnus expressed his own hierarchy of commitments, a hierarchy that a beleaguered modern administrator might well envy. Hearing that students were involved in politics, the alumnus raised a "serious complaint" against student members of the California League of Republicans (Progressives). He urged every student "... who places allegiance to his alma mater *above* his political aspirations to unite in putting an end to ... political exploitation," i.e., club meetings in the fraternities.[8] Thus even political loyalty was subordinated to the "family's Glorious Old Mother."

Loyalty had its uses for university authorities, as well as for students basking in communal fellowship. First, devotion to the university operated as a self-imposed check against those activities which might harm the institution. It is no accident that most disciplinary cases involved freshmen. By the time the student reached the exalted and responsible heights of the upper classes, he knew of, and was committed to, the conduct standards of this homogeneous community.

Secondly, and this was quite conscious, students could be trusted with authority because they were "responsible." Students, administrators, and prominent faculty worked side by side, sharing the same goals, the same standards, and the same loyalties. A college man who contributed to the myriad of collegiate activities, student offices, and the honor societies, developed close relations with the permanent members of the community, and he shared their devotion to "Cal."

During this golden age of collegiate loyalty, a philosophy of student government emerged that was to last for nearly half a century. Little was formalized; student government was, to quote President Robert Gordon Sproul,[9] a "gift" that was based upon friendly cooperation between members of the "university family."

Third, and in sharp contrast to the present-day situation, devotion to the "family's Glorious Old Mother" legitimized authorities submitting to outside pressures. No loyal son of California wanted to see the reputation of his revered institution dragged through the mud of public disgrace. Even before Wheeler's time, students had expressed concern for the university's reputation:

> Its [the university's] life is a public one. It lives only upon the esteem in which it is held and can increase only by extending that esteem. . . . It is this consideration that ought to be constantly in the minds of all students and govern them in all their actions.[10]

The difficulties of the modern university administrator, caught between student activists and outside pressure, were unknown in the more tranquil days when submission to "the better classes" was a justified principle of governance. Discipline was uncomplicated by elaborate procedures designed to protect student rights standing above loyalty to the alma mater.

Loyalty further made for tranquility, because the system of authority based upon diffuse devotion was profoundly apolitical. Conflicting interests and potential power struggles were submerged in cooperative devotion to the over-all good of the community. Cooperation, not conflict; unity, not diversity; shared goals, not competing group interests—these were the ideals and, to a large extent, the actuality.

II

In the recurring campaigns to raise "school spirit," loyalty remained a popular undergraduate theme; but as academic standards were improved, and as students became more cosmopolitan and politicized, the old ties weakened. The decline cannot be attributed to any single cause, but rather was the outcome of numerous interacting events. Wheeler's two immediate successors, General David Barrows (1919-1923) and William Campbell (1923-1930), did not have the same personal appeal, the leisure, nor the inclination to befriend the students. And although Sproul apparently had appeal (if less time than Wheeler), by the time he took over in 1930, the depression had radically changed the entire situation. But the causes of change lie deeper than presidential personalities.

In 1920, the faculty "revolted" and gained significant powers over promotion, academic standards, and administration; with this came greater emphasis on scholarship. A new era of intellectual seriousness was unequivocally announced in the 1922-1923 Report of the President to the Governor of the State:

Much of the mediocre scholarship of our undergraduate student body is due to the actual conditions permeating the institution. The *excessive attention given to undergraduate activities and social affairs* among student organizations, and the *relegation of scholarship to a secondary place* by many students, are the chief causes of the conditions (of mediocre scholarship) to which I refer.[11]

Raising educational standards allowed less time for fun; it also implied less prestige for the extracurricular activities which supported student government. Without the blessing of a popular university president, being a student leader had far less appeal.

At the same time, it appears that students themselves became more intellectually serious. A small, sophisticated group, centering around the literary journals, were downright cynical about the old way of life. They were at least as committed to literary standards as they were to the institution. As an editor of one student journal put it, "The dark days of rah-rah are over . . . many of the [students] drink, neck, and steal fire axes. But all of them think a little. College administrators are beginning to get worried."[12] Dissent was literary, not political, inspired by Mencken, not Marx;

but it was real dissent, nevertheless. And although the number of dissenters was small, their voice was loud and public. The transfer of loyalty from the community to literary standards induced problems of control. A powerful segment of the public, ranging from mothers and ministers to the governor of California, was outraged by the "filth" pouring from student pens. But students refused to compromise their "art" to please the philistines and to protect the university's reputation, and despite the support of a few younger faculty members, they were either expelled or their publications banned.

At the same time, World War I dramatically demonstrated that the university was part of the larger world. The Army mobilized the campus, planted tents on the playing fields, and led the boys off to war; returning veterans did not think Cal's winning football team was the most important thing in life. In response to, and also promoting, the growing concern with the larger world, the *Daily Californian* hooked into the national news services. The student newspaper carried front page headlines about major events and included editorials, letters, and articles on important news items.

Size was another factor breaking down the old ties. From 1910 to 1920 the student population grew from 3,700 to over 10,000. During Wheeler's early days, probably every student personally knew at least one student leader. Overlapping networks of friendship helped to transmit traditions, insure knowledge of standards, and serve as a source of social control. Later presidents had less time to spend with students; and they established intermediaries between themselves and the student body. The institution had become impersonal and less easy to identify with. Furthermore, the dominance of the undergraduate was receding as the proportion of graduate students rose from 1 per cent in 1920 to 22 per cent in 1930.

All the above-mentioned trends—emphasis on scholarship, de-emphasis on extracurricular activities, growing student sophistication, decreasing isolation, and increasing impersonality—began in the 1920's and carried through to the modern university. In 1932 another extremely important element was added to the decline of loyalty. That was radical politics, and its coming spelled the end of an era in American education.

Young, well-educated, articulate Norman Thomas had special appeal to the "college men" when he ran against Roosevelt and Hoover. He was the first socialist to make a dent at conservative "Cal." Socialism, and later communism, provided an alternative focus for student commitment. Eventually the new political commitment gave rise to the accusation that the "family's Glorious

Old Mother" had taken up a new female role, catering to the desires of big business. The "militant minority," as politically active students were sometimes called, developed political skills, which they put to use off and on the campus. Their activities upset the conservative powers which controlled the state of California. These powers, in turn, expressed disapproval of student political activities. The administration could not legally prevent individual students from political involvement and expression, but it could ban political activities from campus. This the administration proceeded to do. As a consequence of administrative actions, activist students increasingly came to view the administration as an agent of suppression for reactionaries. In brief, the response of university administrators to students active in politics furthered the decline of loyalty; student activists, in particular, found it increasingly difficult to feel affection for their "alma mater" or for the officials who ruled her.

III

The administration could not fall back upon ties of sentiment to control dissident students. They turned, instead, to elaboration of formal rules.

From the administration's point of view, the most extreme dissidents were "disloyal." They were not concerned with the "welfare of the entire university" but sought to "exploit their university connections." In view of the former uses of devotion to the "family's Glorious Old Mother," the situation had far-reaching consequences. Self-control and subtle social pressure to protect the university's reputation were rendered ineffective. Radicals had developed a social system of their own, and they shunned the old ideals and norms of behavior embedded in collegiate culture. Furthermore, it was no longer legitimate for the administration to submit to outside pressures, for these pressure groups were the "enemy" of the radicals.

Finally, the radicals gained control of student government and it became "irresponsible."[13] Yet the whole system of student government was founded upon "responsibility," trust, and friendly cooperation. It did not rest upon power and rights but upon cooperation and privilege. Sproul never hesitated to pronounce that his idea of student government was a direct descendant of Wheeler's, that the structure was ". . . subject always to the approval of the President as head of the *University family*" and that ". . . such a relationship can be maintained only upon the basis of *mutual goodwill and cooperation* between *all members of the family*, with the interests of the university as a whole always in mind."[14] The activists, on the other hand, rejected the family imagery, and they sharply dissented from the administration's definition of the "good of the whole." They argued that student government was a "right," not a "privilege"; that the good of the whole was not furthered by banning political activity from the campus, but only the good of the conservatives.

As goodwill, trust, and "responsibility" ebbed, administrative control moved in to fill the void. The less personal pattern of authority clearly started in the 1930's, when the administration established formal regulations which were to govern student activists. Little if any consultation with students preceded the promulgation of these rules. The general policy was to keep the university ". . . entirely independent of all political and sectarian influence" by banning all partisan activity from the campus.[15] Written regulations specified the policy, and they also unequivocally placed the administration in charge of interpreting and implementing the regulations.[16]

Other instances of formalization during this period may be listed. In the early 1930's students officially lost control of discipline; in 1936 university regulations explicitly gave the President final decision-making power over the use of student facilities; in 1938 the ban on political events was extended to "spontaneous rallies"; in 1941 the American Student Union, which had gained control of the student government, lost its campus privileges; in the early 1950's student government lost control of athletics and its own finances. However, as long as amiable and persuasive President Sproul reigned, there were limits to the reliance on rules. President Sproul thoroughly enjoyed, and made time for, face-to-face meetings with all kinds of student leaders, whether they were radicals, reactionaries, or moderates. With his famous booming voice, incredible memory for names, and easy laugh, he was uniquely capable of personalizing the hard edge of bureaucratic rules.

The movement toward governance by rules accelerated with the appointment of Clark Kerr as president in 1958. Although President Sproul had elaborated rules aimed at controlling student activities, particularly activities with political repercussions, he was able to temper the rules with personal appeals, persuasive arguments, and "man-to-man" talks. Further, Sproul, operating under less politicized conditions, had taken a "hard line," as his fellow administrators called it, against all political activity on the campus. And the "hard line," whatever else might be said of it, had the virtues of simplicity and clarity and, therefore, defensibility against charges that the administration was being inconsistent with its own proclaimed policies. President Kerr, on the other hand, because of temperament and circumstances, did not temper the rules with personal appeals. Even more important, he liberalized the rules to permit more political discussion on the campus itself. But in the activist 1960's[17] the lines between permitted discussion and banned advocacy, between action and partisanship, became extremely complicated. To protect the political non-alignment of the university, rules had to be elaborated and procedures spelled out. Ironically, if understandably, it was the elaboration of rules— "bureaucratization"—not liberalization, that became the focus of attention for the activist students. A myth developed about the "whittling away" of student "rights" when, in reality, they had never existed.

IV

Long before the Free Speech Movement (FSM) of 1964, the emergent pattern of rule-based authority was attacked by a growing number of student activists and concerned faculty. Criticism began with attacks on specific rules; but, as the conflict revealed the inner workings of the administrative process, the issues became more general. Eventually, the very basis of consent eroded to the point where the entire pattern of authority seemed illegitimate to sectors of the student body.[18] These criticisms are worth examining, because they highlight the inherent strains in the style of authority adopted by the university administration, and they suggest possible future trends.

First, the policy of "neutrality" came to be regarded as unduly restrictive in that it banned all political activity from campus. Such anomalous incidents as Presidential candidate Adlai E. Stevenson having to speak in the city streets bordering the campus during 1956 raised questions about the right of university authorities to deny students permission to engage in activities which were open to other citizens. Second, it was argued that administrative application of the policy was biased, favoring the "power structure." Critics pointed to such decisions as allowing Episcopal Bishop Pike to speak on the campus but denying Malcolm X the same privilege two days later because he was a "religious leader." Third, with an increase in student political activity, administrative interpretation and implementation of the rules appeared increasingly "bureaucratic," in the pejorative sense of that term. A plethora of detailed rules were created to specify general regulations. At the same time, there often seemed to be no rules to guide difficult decisions. A maze of administrators with unclear and overlapping jurisdictions developed, creating confusion. A decision could, and sometimes did, go to the secretaries in the dean's office, to a vice-chancellor, to the chancellor, to the president, and even to the regents. Confronted with vague rules and undefined channels of authority, rumors would spread about "behind-the-scenes maneuvering" and "submission to outside pressures." Finally, in cases of rule violation, disciplinary proceedings centered around the office of the dean of students. Students argued that the administration was acting as legislature, prosecutor, judge, and jury, and that the whole system lacked the most minimum standards of due process.

Over the years, attacks on the restrictiveness of the policy of neutrality, administrative bias, inconsistency, and the lack of due process added up to a full-scale challenge to the legitimacy of university authority. The only elements missing were a demand for formal participation of students in the formulation and implementation of the rules, and the mobilization of students to press that demand. These came in 1964.

Thus in the area of student political activities, an area which came to have central importance, the administration moved from reliance on personal appeals and persuasions to a constitutionally justified principle of neutrality. This led to a necessity for written rules in order to specify the general principle; and, as these rules were challenged, even more elaboration was required.

Retrospectively we may interpret these events to mean that a pattern of "legal-rational" authority has come to characterize the university, to replace the "traditional" and "paternalistic" pattern that existed earlier. Such a pattern, abstractly considered, is legitimated by an appeal to rules and to the principles such rules are purported to express, rather than to sentiments of loyalty or devotion. Legal-rational authority, it has been said,

assumes the existence of a formally established body of social norms designed to organize conduct for the rational pursuit of specified goals. In such a system obedience is owed not to a person—but to a set of impersonal principles.[19]

Now the criticisms enumerated above suggest that it was less the general pattern of legal-rational authority that came under attack than the specific style in which this authority was exercised. In fact, despite occasional grumblings about impersonality, criticism largely called for an increasing, not a lessening, of the legal-rational pattern. But it also calls for a new style of control, one more along the lines of what may be called "private government" rather than "managerialism." Such a style of legal-rational authority would be more deeply concerned with the consent and the rights of the governed; concretely, the governed would participate in the formulation of general principles and policies, as well as in the writing of the rules which define the exercise and limits of authoritative power. Further, the structure of internal government would be viewed as a *private legal system*, and thus attention would be directed to incorporation of standards of due process.[20]

The difference between the "managerial" and the "private government" models of legal-rational authority can be further clarified by a brief comparison. "Governance" explicitly deals with ultimate community values, the purposes of the institution; in theory, though not necessarily in fact, "management," or administration, accepts the general values as given.[21] Governance promotes open debate and open decisions based upon community participation; management decides on the basis of expertise and legal responsibilities. Governing decisions are guided by standards of freedom, justice, and participation; management decisions are judged by standards of efficiency and technical results.

V

To put the matter another way, "managerialism" is rule by the administration, whose authority rests upon their legally charged and defined responsibilities combined with their special skills. In "private government," authority would also rest upon legal delegation and specialized skills; however, it would be further conditioned by careful acknowledgment of the consent and the rights of the governed.

Although the legal-rational pattern has been distinctly "managerial," elements of the "private government" pattern have weakly begun to manifest themselves. Considerable analysis of, and agitation for, a system which increases participation and insures due process has already been made.[22] Such a system of control would have far-reaching consequences. Participation in the formulation of policies and rules implies debate and open decisions. Such publicly exposed actions could go a long way toward guaranteeing decisions which are defensible in light of the general policies, student "rights," and mutually acceptable rules. Without participation, the administration leaves itself open to the charge of submitting to outside pressures which operate behind the scenes. Probably no other accusation has been more detrimental to establishing relationships of trust.

Another implication of conceiving administration as a form of private government is that the exercise of authority is then expected to restrain itself: to honor due process standards providing clear rules and fair trial procedures. Due process has particular salience in the modern situation because the issues raised by the activist students are considerably more complicated than those of their panty-raiding predecessors. Why should an essentially constitutional question, such as the advocacy of civil disobedience, be handled in the same manner and by the same office that previously dealt with the old collegiate-type problems? Education has become too important to the individual, the issues have become too complicated, and students are too mature for either the old informal style of the friendly dean or the recent "managerial" manner.[23]

Yet neither criticism of the "managerial" style nor the weak trends toward "private government" mean that radical change is necessarily forthcoming. "Managerialism," backed by force, has been used in the past and there are powerful reasons for believing the pattern may continue. The militant critics of "managerialism" are relatively few in number; and to many, they seem like cranks, malcontents, and hippie dropouts. Furthermore, open debate prior to decision and elaborate procedures of due process are cumbersome and potentially embarassing. (Imagine the veracity of the chancellor being questioned by a student lawyer, or the time it would take to cross-examine busy administrative officials.) But perhaps the biggest difficulty is that meaningful participation probably requires radical decentralization of the university. For participation to be more than play-acting, students and local campus officials, not the statewide administrators and the board of regents, would have to possess the authority to make real decisions and fundamental policies.[24] Yet decentralization would probably mean liberalization and "mistakes," and this could lead to serious public relations problems. In the past, the administration has sought to maintain academic freedom in the classroom and the inflow of resources by using the policies and rules to regulate student activities and to publicly justify various actions. From the administration's point of view, relinquishing final authority over matters of internal governance would be a risky enterprise. Furthermore, the administration sees itself as legally and morally responsible for all those matters which pertain to the use of university facilities.

The remnants of authority based upon self-sacrificing devotion to the "old alma mater" are fading out. "Managerialism" has replaced this style, but it, too, is being challenged. Perhaps a system of "private government" based upon participation and formally constrained power will be the pattern of the future. And perhaps it will not.

Footnotes

[1]John Schaar, *Loyalty in America* (Berkeley, Calif.: University of California Press, 1957), p. 6.

2Of course, there is another side of the loyalty syndrome. In the university marked by students loyal in this sense, conformity to the simple ideals of the collegiate culture was mandatory. Dissenters were hardly tolerated. The faculty was frequently appalled by the stress on loyalty at the expense of scholarship, and social criticism was nearly nonexistent.

3Benjamin Ide Wheeler, *Abundant Life* (Berkeley, Calif.: University of California Press, 1926). The quote is from a speech delivered October 30, 1899, pp. 23-29. Emphasis added.

4Strong emphasis on loyalty fitted into the contemporary philosophy of education. Colleges still had their obligation to develop the full character of the student. They no longer demanded chapel, nor did they uphold the "Christian gentleman" ideal; but educators still adhered to a secularized version of education being a moral, as well as an intellectual, endeavor. Furthermore, the object of training good citizens was an important part of the Progressive Republican philosophy that Wheeler, and many other college presidents, adhered to. (See Rudolph, Fl., *The American College and University* [New York: Vintage Books, 1965], pp. 355-373.)

5Incidentally, the movement was closely allied to the Progressive Republican Party that emphasized the salutary political role of the good, honest, well-educated college graduate.

6President Wheeler's daily rides around campus on his white horse are legendary today.

7These quotes are from the student newspaper, *The Daily Californian*, September 5, 1912. Emphasis added.

8*The Daily Californian*, August 30, 1912. Emphasis added.

9Sproul, President of the University of California from 1930 to 1958, was involved in the Progressive Republican movement during his undergraduate days (1909-1913). He introduced the basic regulations which governed the university until 1964.

10*Occident*, May 28, 1886, editorial. Although beyond the scope of this paper, it is highly interesting that major reference groups were the rich and respectable. Labor unions were practically nonexistent, and, until about 1910, the state was dominated by the Southern Pacific railroad, commonly known as the "octopus."

11*Presidential Reports to the Governor*, 1922-1923, p. 28. The statement was made by Thomas Putnam, Dean of the Undergraduate Division at Berkeley.

12*Occident*, September, 1926, editorial.

13In the late 1930's, the left formed a coalition through the American Student Union (ASU) and won important elections. At various times, the left controlled the student newspaper, the literary magazine, and the student humor publication. Perhaps the most telling indicator of fundamental change took place when the humor magazine turned from obscenity to political satire, thus ending a half-century tradition.

14Sproul to editors of the "Daily Bruin," quoted in George Pettitt, *Twenty-Eight Years in the Life of a University President* (Berkeley, Calif.: University of California Press, 1966), p. 102. Emphasis added.

15The quoted phrase is taken from Section 9, Article 9, of the California State Constitution. A policy of "neutrality," which was claimed to be a specification of the State Constitution, became university "law" on February 15, 1935. Nearly all controversy raised by students has flowed from this policy. It aimed to keep the university, as an institution, politically nonaligned by banning all political activity from the campus. Logically, *this* goal could have been accomplished by allowing, not banning, all such activity from the campuses. It seems obvious that other, unstated, goals were also being implemented through this interpretation of the policy of "neutrality," but this is a topic that cannot be developed here.

16Only once were the students carefully consulted on rule modifications, and that consultation was initiated by the students. In 1957 a group of established student leaders led a major effort to revise the twenty-year-old Regulation 17, which governed the use of facilities. With the support of Chancellor Kerr, the policy was liberalized to allow political candidates to appear on campus and to allow "off-campus" student groups to meet on the campus. Permission had to be obtained from the administration, however, and their approval was not automatic. Since about 1959, when a major revision occurred, rule-making has received increased attention from the highest formal source of university authority, namely, the board of regents. From time to time, the regents discussed proposed revisions, and even implementations, of the regulations. After 1964 they were deeply and publically involved in student affairs.

17There is little doubt that students were increasingly politicized in the late 1950's and 1960's. Everything points to this fact—the number of student political groups, the number of political speakers, demonstrations, pickets, newspaper commentaries, and personal recollections of students, faculty, and administration. The same kind of evidence overwhelmingly suggests that the 1960's were also more politically active than the 1930's.

18Judging from the student support of the Free Speech Movement (FSM), criticisms of the administration had fairly wide appeal. At least one study has suggested that support for the FSM was positively related to academic achievement, as measured by the grade-point average. (See Kathleen Gales, "A Campus Revolution," *British Journal of Sociology*, XVII, No. 1 [March, 1966], pp. 1-19.)

19Peter Blau and Richard Scott, *Formal Organizations: A Comparative Approach* (San Francisco: Chandler, 1962), p. 31. Blau and Scott are, of course, paraphrasing Max Weber.

20Many of these general notions about "private government" have been derived from Philip Selznick. His forthcoming book, *Law, Society and Industrial Justice*, will develop these ideas at length. Also see Arthur Miller, *Private Governments and the Constitution, An Occasional Paper on the Role of the Corporation in the Free Society* (Santa Barbara, Calif.: Center for the Study of Democratic Institutions, 1959).

21Robert Michels, *Political Parties* (New York: Free Press, 1949); and Philip Selznick, *TVA and the Grass Roots* (Berkeley, Calif.: University of California Press, 1949). Both authors give examples of management goal-setting. At the University of California, it was actually the president, with the local campus administrators, who outlined the original policies governing the use of facilities and, in effect, the uses of the university. The evidence further suggests that the regents did not establish earlier policies.

22By far the most significant effort along these lines has been "The Culture of the University: Governance and Education," *Report of the Study Commission on University Governance*, University of California, Berkeley, January 15, 1968. This report was prepared by an eminently qualified staff, jointly sponsored by the academic senate and the student government. To my knowledge, it is the most thorough study yet to appear on the contemporary problems of governance in large state universities.

23William Van Alstyne has spoken of the importance of education as a reason for changing court attitudes toward the student in "Student Academic Freedom and Rule Making Powers of Public Universities: Some Constitutional Considerations," *Law and Society in Transition*, II (Winter, 1965), p. 7.

24The need for decentralization before participation is emphasized by the Study Commission on University Governance (see above, footnote 22). Still another report initiated by the regents themselves said, "The regents have not in fact chosen to delegate most of their enormous power." (See Jerome C. Byrne, "Report on the University of California and Recommendations to the Special Committee of the Regents of the University of California," May 7, 1965; reprinted in *Los Angeles Times*, May 12, 1965). The quote is from the second section of the report.

The Liberated Generation: An Exploration of the Roots of Student Protest *

Richard Flacks

As all of us are by now aware, there has emerged, during the past five years, an increasingly self-conscious student movement in

*The research reported here stemmed from a coalescence of interests of the author and of Professor Bernice Neugarten of the Committee on Human Development of the University

the United States. This movement began primarily as a response to the efforts by southern Negro students to break the barriers of legal segregation in public accommodations − scores of northern white students engaged in sympathy demonstrations and related activities as early as 1960. But as we all know, the scope of the student concern expanded rapidly to include such issues as nuclear testing and the arms race, attacks on civil liberties, the problems of the poor in urban slum ghettoes, democracy and educational quality in universities, the war in Vietnam, conscription.

This movement represents a social phenomenon of considerable significance. In the first place, it is having an important direct and indirect impact on the larger society. But secondly it is significant because it is a phenomenon which was unexpected−unexpected, in particular, by those social scientists who are professionally responsible for locating and understanding such phenomena. Because it is an unanticipated event, the attempt to understand and explain the sources of the student movement may lead to fresh interpretations of some important trends in our society.

Radicalism and the Young Intelligentsia

In one sense, the existence of a radical student movement should not be unexpected. After all, the young intelligentsia seem almost always to be in revolt. Yet if we examine the case a bit more closely I think we will find that movements of active disaffection among intellectuals and students tend to be concentrated at particular moments in history. Not every generation produces an organized oppositional movement.

In particular, students and young intellectuals seem to have become active agents of opposition and change under two sets of inter-related conditions:

When they have been marginal in the labor market because their numbers exceed the opportunities for employment commensurate with their abilities and training. This has most typically been the case in colonial or underdeveloped societies; it also seems to account, in part, for the radicalization of European

of Chicago. The author's interests were primarily in the student movement and the families and social backgrounds of student activists. Professor Neugarten's interests have been primarily in the relations between age groups in American society. The plan to gather parallel data from students and their parents accordingly provided a welcome opportunity for collaboration. The research has been supported in part by grant MH 08062, National Institute of Mental Health; in part by grants from the Carnegie Fund for the Advancement of Teaching and the Survey Research Center of The University of Michigan. I wish to thank Professor Neugarten, Charles Derber and Patricia Schedler for their help in preparing this manuscript; its flaws are entirely my own responsibility.

Jewish intellectuals and American college-educated women at the turn of the century (Coser, 1965; Shils, 1960; Veblen, 1963).

When they found that the values with which they were closely connected by virtue of their upbringing no longer were appropriate to the developing social reality. This has been the case most typically at the point where traditional authority has broken down due to the impact of Westernization, industrialization, modernization. Under these conditions, the intellectuals, and particularly the youth, felt called upon to assert new values, new modes of legitimation, new styles of life. Although the case of breakdown of traditional authority is most typically the point at which youth movements have emerged, there seems, historically, to have been a second point in time—in Western Europe and the United States—when intellectuals were radicalized. This was, roughly, at the turn of the century, when values such as gentility, laissez faire, naive optimism, naive rationalism and naive nationalism seemed increasingly inappropriate due to the impact of large scale industrial organization, intensifying class conflict, economic crisis and the emergence of total war. Variants of radicalism waxed and waned in their influence among American intellectuals and students during the first four decades of the twentieth century (Aaron, 1965; Eisenstadt, 1956; Lasch, 1965).

If these conditions have historically been those which produced revolts among the young intelligentsia, then I think it is easy to understand why a relatively superficial observer would find the new wave of radicalism on the campus fairly mysterious.

In the first place, the current student generation can look forward, not to occupational insecurity or marginality, but to an unexampled opening up to opportunity for occupational advance in situations in which their skills will be maximally demanded and the prestige of their roles unprecedentedly high.

In the second place, there is no evident erosion of the legitimacy of established authority; we do not seem, at least on the surface, to be in a period of rapid disintegration of traditional values—at least no more so than a decade ago when sociologists were observing the *exhaustion* of opportunity for radical social movements in America (Bell, 1962; Lipset, 1960).

In fact, during the Fifties sociologists and social psychologists emphasized the decline in political commitment, particularly among the young, and the rise of a bland, security-oriented conformism throughout the population, but most particularly among college students. The variety of studies conducted then reported students as overwhelmingly unconcerned with value questions, highly complacent, status-oriented, privatized, uncommitted (Jacob, 1957; Goldsen, *et al*, 1960). Most of us interpreted this situation as one to be expected given the opportunities newly opened to educated youth, and given the emergence of liberal pluralism and affluence as the characteristic features of postwar America. Several observers predicted an intensification of the pattern of middle class conformism, declining individualism, and growing "other-directedness" based on the changing styles of childrearing prevalent in the middle class. The democratic and "permissive" family would produce young men who knew how to cooperate in bureaucratic settings, but who lacked a strongly rooted ego-ideal and inner control (Miller and Swanson, 1958; Bronfenbrenner, 1961; Erickson, 1963). Although some observers reported that some students were searching for "meaning" and "self-expression," and others reported the existence of "subcultures" of alienation and bohemianism on some campuses (Keniston, 1965a; Trow, 1962; Newcomb and Flacks, 1963), not a single observer of the campus scene as late as 1959 anticipated the emergence of the organized disaffection, protest and activism which was to take shape early in the Sixties.

In short, the very occurrence of a student movement in the present American context is surprising because it seems to contradict our prior understanding of the determinants of disaffection among the young intelligentsia.

A Revolt of the Advantaged

The student movement is, I think, surprising for another set of reasons. These have to do with its social composition and the kinds of ideological themes which characterize it.

The current group of student activists is predominantly upper middle class, and frequently these students are of elite origins. This fact is evident as soon as one begins to learn the personal histories of activist leaders. Consider the following scene at a convention of Students for a Democratic Society a few years ago. Toward the end of several days of deliberation, someone decided that a quick way of raising funds for the organization would be to appeal to the several hundred students assembled at the convention to dig down deep into their pockets on the spot. To this end, one of the leadership, skilled at mimicry, stood on a chair, and in the style of a Southern Baptist preacher, appealed to the students to come forward, confess their sins and be saved by contributing to SDS. The students did come forward, and in each case the sin confessed was the social class or occupation of their fathers. "My father is the editor of a Hearst newspaper, I give $25"! My father is Assistant Director of the_____Bureau, I give $40". "My father is dean of a law school, here's $50"!

These impressions of the social composition of the student movement are supported and refined by more systematic sources of data. For example, when a random sample of students who participated in the anti-Selective Service sit-in at the University of Chicago Administration Building was compared with a sample composed of non-protesters and students hostile to the protest, the protesters disproportionately reported their social class to be "upper middle", their family incomes to be disproportionately high, their parents' education to be disproportionately advanced. In addition, the protesters' fathers' occupations were primarily upper professional (doctors, college faculty, lawyers) rather than business, white collar, or working class. These findings parallel those of other investigators (Braungart, 1966). Thus, the student movement represents the disaffection not of an underprivileged stratum of the student population but of *the most advantaged* sector of the students.

One hypothesis to explain disaffection among socially advantaged youth would suggest that, although such students come from advantaged backgrounds, their academic performance leads them to anticipate downward mobility or failure. Stinchcombe, for example, found high rates of quasi-delinquent rebelliousness among middle class high school youth with poor academic records (Stinchcombe, 1964). This hypothesis is not tenable with respect to college student protest, however. Our own data with respect to the anti-draft protest at Chicago indicate that the grade point average of the protesters averaged around B-B+ (with 75% of them reporting a B- or better average). This was slightly higher than the grade point average of our sample of nonprotesters. Other data from our own research indicate that student activists tend to be at the top of their high school class; in general, data from our own and other studies support the view that many activists are academically superior, and that very few activists are recruited from among low academic achievers. Thus, in terms of *both* the status of their families of origins *and* their own scholastic performance, student protest movements are predominantly composed of students who have been born to high social advantage and who are in a position to experience the career and status opportunities of the society without significant limitations.

Themes of the Protest

The positive correlation between disaffection and status among college students suggested by these observations is, I think, made even more paradoxical when one examines closely the main value themes which characterize the student movement. I want to describe these in an impressionistic way here; a more systematic depiction awaits further analysis of our data.

Romanticism: There is a strong stress among many Movement participants on a quest for self-expression, often articulated in terms of leading a "free" life—i.e., one not bound by conventional restraints on feeling, experience, communication, expression. This is often coupled with aesthetic interests and a strong rejection of scientific and other highly rational pursuits. Students often express the classic romantic aspiration of "knowing" or "experiencing" "everything."

Anti-authoritarianism: A strong antipathy toward arbitrary rule, centralized decision-making, "manipulation". The anti-authoritarian sentiment is fundamental to the widespread campus protests during the past few years; in most cases, the protests were precipitated by an administrative act which was interpreted as arbitrary, and received impetus when college administrators continued to act unilaterally, coercively or secretively. Anti-authoritarianism is manifested further by the styles and internal processes within activist organizations; for example, both SDS and SNCC have attempted to decentralize their operations quite radically and members are strongly critical of leadership within the organization when it is too assertive.

Egalitarianism, populism: A belief that all men are capable of political participation, that political power should be widely dispersed, that the locus of value in society lies with the people and not elites. This is a stress on something more than equality of opportunity or equal legal treatment; the students stress instead the notion of "participatory democracy"—direct participation in the making of decisions by those affected by them. Two common slogans—"One man, one vote"; "Let the people decide".

Anti-dogmatism: A strong reaction against doctrinaire ideological interpretations of events. Many of the students are quite restless when presented with formulated models of the social order, and specific programs for social change. This underlies much of their antagonism to the varieties of "old left" politics, and is one meaning of the oft-quoted (if not seriously used) phrase: "you can't trust anyone over thirty".

Moral purity: A strong antipathy to self-interested behavior, particularly when overlaid by claims of disinterestedness. A major criticism of the society is that it is "hypocritical". Another meaning of the criticism of the older generation has to do with the perception that (a) the older generation "sold out" the values it espouses; (b) to assume conventional adult roles usually leads to increasing self-interestedness, hence selling-out, or "phoniness". A particularly important criticism students make of the university is that it fails to live up to its professed ideals; there is an expectation that the institution ought to be *moral*—that is, not compromise its official values for the sake of institutional survival or aggrandizement.

Community: A strong emphasis on a desire for "human" relationships, for a full expression of emotions, for the breaking down of interpersonal barriers and the refusal to accept conventional norms concerning interpersonal contact (e.g., norms respecting sex, status, race, age, etc.) A central positive theme in the campus revolts has been the expression of the desire for a campus "community", for the breaking down of aspects of impersonality on the campus, for more direct contact between students and faculty. There is a frequent counterposing of bureaucratic norms to communal norms; a testing of the former against the latter. Many of the students involved in slum projects have experimented with attempts to achieve a "kibbutz"-like community amongst themselves entailing communal living and a strong stress on achieving intimacy and resolving tensions within the group.

Anti-institutionalism: A strong distrust of involvement with conventional institutional roles. This is most importantly expressed in the almost universal desire among the highly involved to avoid institutionalized careers. Our data suggest that few student activists look toward careers in the professions, the sciences, industry or politics. Many of the most committed expect to continue to work full-time in the "movement" or, alternatively, to become free-lance writers, artists, intellectuals. A high proportion are oriented toward academic careers—at least so far the academic career seems still to have a reputation among many student activists for permitting "freedom".

Several of these themes, it should be noted, are not unique to student activists. In particular, the value we have described as "romanticism"—a quest for self-expression—has been found by observers, for example Kenneth Keniston (1965b), to be a central feature of the ideology of "alienated" or "bohemian" students (see also Keniston's article in this issue). Perhaps more important, the disaffection of student activists with conventional careers, their low valuation of careers as important in their personal aspirations, their quest for careers outside the institutionalized sphere—these attitudes toward careers seem to be characteristic of other groups of students as well. It is certainly typical of youth involved in "bohemian" and aesthetic subcultures; it also characterizes students who volunteer for participation in such programs as the Peach Corps, Vista and other full-time commitments oriented toward service. In fact, it is our view that the dissatisfaction of socially advantaged youth with conventional career opportunities is a significant social trend, the most important single indicator of restlessness among sectors of the youth population. One expression of this restlessness is the student movement, but it is not the only one. One reason why it seems important to investigate the student movement in detail, despite the fact that it represents a small minority of the student population, is that it is a symptom of social and psychological strains experienced by a larger segment of the youth—strains not well understood or anticipated heretofore by social science.

If some of the themes listed above are not unique to student activists, several of them may characterize only a portion of the activist group itself. In particular, some of the more explicitly political values are likely to be articulated mainly by activists who are involved in radical organizations, particularly Students for a Democratic Society, and the Student Non-violent Coordinating Committee. This would be true particularly for such notions as "participatory democracy" and deep commitments to populist-like orientations. These orientations have been formulated within SDS and SNCC as these organizations have sought to develop a coherent strategy and a framework for establishing priorities. It is an empirical question whether students not directly involved in such organizations articulate similar attitudes. The impressions we have from a preliminary examination of our data suggest that they frequently do not. It is more likely that the student movement is very heterogeneous politically at this point. Most participants share a set of broad orientations, but differ greatly in the degree to which they are oriented toward ideology in general or to particular political positions. The degree of politicization of student activists is probably very much a function of the kinds of peer group and organizational relationships they have had; the underlying disaffection and tendency toward activism, however, is perhaps best understood as being based on more enduring, pre-established values, attitudes and needs.

Social-Psychological Roots of Student Protest: Some Hypotheses

How, then, can we account for the emergence of an obviously dynamic and attractive radical movement among American students in this period? Why should this movement be particularly appealing to youth from upper-status, highly educated families? Why should such youth be particularly concerned with problems of authority, of vocation, of equality, of moral consistency? Why should students in the most advantaged sector of the youth population be disaffected with their own privilege?

It should be stressed that the privileged status of the student protesters and the themes they express in their protest are not *in themselves* unique or surprising. Student movements in developing nations—e.g., Russia, Japan and Latin America—typically recruit people of elite background; moreover, many of the themes of the "new left" are reminiscent of similar expressions in other student movements (Lipset, 1966). What is unexpected is that these should emerge in the American context at this time.

Earlier theoretical formulations about the social and psychological sources of strain for youth, for example the work of Parsons

(1965), Eisenstadt (1956), and Erikson (1959), are important for understanding the emergence of self-conscious oppositional youth cultures and movements. At first glance, these theorists, who tend to see American youth as relatively well-integrated into the larger society, would seem to be unhelpful in providing a framework for explaining the emergence of a radical student movement at the present moment. Nevertheless, in developing our own hypotheses we have drawn freely on their work. What I want to do here is to sketch the notions which have guided our research; a more systematic and detailed exposition will be developed in future publications.

What we have done is to accept the main lines of the argument made by Parsons and Eisenstadt about the social functions of youth cultures and movements. The kernel of their argument is that self-conscious subcultures and movements among adolescents tend to develop when there is a sharp disjunction between the values and expectations embodied in the traditional families in a society and the values and expectations prevailing in the occupational sphere. The greater the disjunction, the more self-conscious and oppositional will be the youth culture (as for example in the situation of rapid transition from a traditional-ascriptive to a bureaucratic-achievement social system).

In modern industrial society, such a disjunction exists as a matter of course, since families are, by definition, particularistic, ascriptive, diffuse, and the occupational shpere is universalistic, impersonal, achievement-oriented, functionally specific. But Parsons, and many others, have suggested that over time the American middle class family has developed a structure and style which tends to articulate with the occupational sphere; thus, whatever youth culture does emerge in American society is likely to be fairly well-integrated with conventional values, not particularly self-conscious, not rebellious (Parsons, 1965).

The emergence of the student movement, and other expressions of estrangement among youth, leads us to ask whether, in fact, there may be families in the middle class which embody values and expectations which do *not* articulate with those prevailing in the occupational sphere, to look for previously unremarked incompatibilities between trends in the larger social system and trends in family life and early socialization.

The argument we have developed may be sketched as follows: *First*, on the macro-structural level we assume that two related trends are of importance: one, the increasing rationalization of student life in high schools and universities, symbolized by the "multiversity", which entails a high degree of impersonality, competitiveness and an increasingly explicit and direct relationship between the university and corporate and governmental bureaucracies; two, the increasing unavailability of coherent careers independent of bureaucratic organizations.

Second, these trends converge, in time, with a particular trend in the development of the family; namely, the emergence of a pattern of familial relations, located most typically in upper middle class, professional homes, having the following elements:

(a) a strong emphasis on democratic, egalitarian interpersonal relations
(b) a high degree of permissiveness with respect to self-regulation
(c) an emphasis on values *other than achievement*; in particular, a stress on the intrinsic worth of living up to intellectual, aesthetic, political, or religious ideals.

Third, young people raised in this kind of family setting, contrary to the expectations of some observers, find it difficult to accommodate to institutional expectations requiring submissiveness to adult authority, respect for established status distinctions, a high degree of competition, and firm regulation of sexual and expressive impulses. They are likely to be particularly sensitized to acts of arbitrary authority, to unexamined expressions of allegiance to conventional values, to instances of institutional practices which conflict with professed ideals. Further, the values embodied in their families are likely to be reinforced by other socializing experiences—for example, summer vacations at progressive children's camps, attendance at experimental private schools, growing up in a community with a high proportion of friends from similar backgrounds. Paralleling these experiences of positive reinforcement, there are likely to be experiences which reinforce a sense of estrangement from peers or conventional society. For instance, many of these young people experience a strong sense of being "different" or "isolated" in school; this sense of distance is often based on the relative uniqueness of their interests and values, their inability to accept conventional norms about appropriate sex-role behavior, and the like. An additional source of strain is generated when these young people perceive a fundamental discrepancy between the values espoused by their parents and the style of life actually practiced by them. This discrepancy is experienced as a feeling of "guilt" over "being middle class" and a perception of "hypocrisy" on the part of parents who express liberal or intellectual values while appearing to their children as acquisitive or self-interested.

Fourth, the incentives operative in the occupational sphere are of limited efficacy for these young people—achievement of status or material advantage is relatively ineffective for an individual who already has high status and affluence by virtue of his family origins. This means, on the one hand, that these students are less oriented toward occupational achievement; on the other hand, the operative sanctions within the school and the larger society are less effective in enforcing conformity.

It seems plausible that this is the first generation in which a substantial number of youth have both the impulse to free themselves from conventional status concerns *and can afford to do so*. In this sense they are a "liberated" generation; affluence has freed them, at least for a period of time, from some of the anxieties and preoccupations which have been the defining features of American middle class social character.

Fifth, the emergence of the student movement is to be understood in large part as a consequence of opportunities for prolonged interaction available in the university environment. The kinds of personality structures produced by the socializing experiences outlined above need not necessarily have generated a collective response. In fact, Kenneth Keniston's recently published work on alienated students at Harvard suggests that students with similar characteristics to those described here were identifiable on college campuses in the Fifties. But Keniston makes clear that his highly alienated subjects were rarely involved in extensive peer-relationships, and that few opportunities for collective expressions of alienation were then available. The result was that each of his subjects attempted to work out a value-system and a mode of operation on his own (Keniston, 1965b; and this issue).

What seems to have happened was that during the Fifties, there began to emerge an "alienated" student culture, as students with alienated predispositions became visible to each other and began to interact. There was some tendency for these students to identify with the "Beat" style and related forms of bohemianism. Since this involved a high degree of disaffiliation, "cool" non-commitment and social withdrawal, observers tended to interpret this subculture as but a variant of the prevailing privatism of the Fifties. However, a series of precipitating events, most particularly the southern student sit-ins, the revolutionary successes of students in Cuba, Korea and Turkey, and the suppression of student demonstrations against the House Un-American Activities Committee in San Francisco, suggested to groups of students that direct action was a plausible means for expressing their grievances. These first stirrings out of apathy were soon enmeshed in a variety of organizations and publicized in several student-organized underground journals—thus enabling the movement to grow and become increasingly institutionalized. The story of the emergence and growth of the movement cannot be developed here; my main point now is that many of its characteristics cannot be understood solely as consequences of the structural and personality variables outlined earlier—in addition, a full understanding of the dynamics of the movement requires a "collective behavior" perspective.

Sixth, organized expressions of youth disaffection are likely to be an increasingly visible and established feature of our society. In important ways, the "new radicalism" is *not* new, but rather a more widespread version of certain subcultural phenomena with a considerable history. During the late 19th and early 20th century a considerable number of young people began to move out of their provincial environments as a consequence of university education; many of these people gathered in such locales as Greenwich Village and created the first visible bohemian subculture in the United States. The Village bohemians and associated young intellectuals shared a common concern with radical politics and, influenced by Freud, Dewey, etc., with the reform of the process of socialization in America—i.e., a restructuring of family and educational institutions (Lash, 1965; Coser, 1965). Although many of the reforms advocated by this group were only partially realized in a formal sense, it seems to be the case that the values and style of life which they advocated have become strongly rooted in American life. This has occurred in at least two ways: first, the subcultures created by the early intellectuals took root, have grown and been emulated in various parts of the country. Second, many of the *ideas* of the early twentieth century intellectuals, particularly their critique of the bourgeois family and Victorian sensibility, spread rapidly; it now seems that an important defining characteristic of the college-educated mother is her willingness to adopt child-centered techniques of rearing, and of the college educated couple that they create a family which is democratic and egalitarian in style. In this way, the values that an earlier generation espoused in an abstract way have become embodied as *personality traits* in the new generation. The rootedness of the bohemian and quasi-bohemian subcultures, and the spread of their ideas with the rapid increase in the number of families raising their children with considerable ambivalence about dominant values, incentives and expectations in the society. In this sense, the students who engage in protest or who participate in "alienated" styles of life are often not "converts" to a "deviant" adaptation, but people who have been socialized into a developing cultural tradition. Rising levels of affluence and education are drying up the traditional sources of alienation and radical politics; what we are now becoming aware of, however, is that this same situation is creating new sources of alienation and idealism, and new constituencies for radicalism.

The Youth and Social Change Project

These hypotheses have been the basis for two studies we have undertaken. Study One, begun in the Summer of 1965, involved extensive interviews with samples of student activists and non-activists and their parents. Study Two, conducted in the Spring of 1966, involved interviews with samples of participants, non-participants and opponents of the tumultuous "anti-ranking" sit-in at the University of Chicago.

Study One—The Socialization of Student Activists. For Study One, fifty students were selected from mailing lists of various peace, civil rights, and student movement organizations in the Chicago area. An additional fifty students, matched for sex, neighborhood of parents' residence, and type of college attended, were drawn from student directories of Chicago-area colleges. In each case, an attempt was made to interview both parents of the student respondent, as well as the student himself. We were able to interview both parents of 82 of the students; there were two cases in which no parents were available for the interview, in the remaining 16 cases, one parent was interviewed. The interviews with both students and parents averaged about three hours in length, were closely parallel in content, and covered such matters as: political attitudes and participation; attitudes toward the student movement and "youth"; "values", broadly defined; family life, child-rearing, family conflict and other aspects of socialization. Rating scales and "projective" questions were used to assess family members' perceptions of parent-child relationships.

It was clear to us that our sampling procedures were prone to a certain degree of error in the classification of students as "activists" and "nonactivists". Some students who appeared on mailing lists of activist organizations had no substantial involvement in the student movement, while some of our "control" students had a considerable history of such involvement. Thus the data to be reported here are based on an index of Activism constructed from interview responses to questions about participation in seven kinds of activity: attendance at rallies, picketing, canvassing, working on a project to help the disadvantaged, being jailed for civil disobedience, working full-time for a social action organization, serving as an officer in such organizations.

Study Two—The "Anti-Ranking" Sit-in. In May, 1966, about five hundred students sat-in at the Administration Building on the campus of the University of Chicago, barring the building to official use for two and a half days. The focal issue of the protest, emulated on a number of other campuses in the succeeding days, was the demand by the students that the University not cooperate with the

Selective Service System in supplying class standings for the purpose of assigning student deferments. The students who sat-in formed an organization called "Students Against the Rank" (SAR). During the sit-in, another group of students, calling themselves "Students for a Free Choice" (SFC) circulated a petition opposing the sit-in and supporting the University Administration's view that each student had a right to submit (or withhold) his class standings—the University could not withhold the "rank" of students who requested it. This petition was signed by several hundred students.

Beginning about 10 days after the end of the sit-in, we undertook to interview three samples of students: a random sample of 65 supporters of SAR (the protesters); a random sample of 35 signers of the SFC petition (the anti-protesters); approximately 60 students who constituted the total population of two randomly selected floors in the student dormitories. Of about 160 students thus selected, 117 were finally either interviewed or returned mailed questionnaires. The interview schedule was based largely on items used in the original study; it also included some additional items relevant to the sit-in and the "ranking" controversy.

Some Preliminary Findings.   At this writing, our data analysis is at an early stage. In general, however, it is clear that the framework of hypotheses with which we began is substantially supported, and in interesting ways, refined, by the data. Our principal findings thus far include the following:[1]

Activists tend to come from upper status families. As indicated earlier, our study of the Chicago sit-in suggests that such actions attract students predominatly from upper-status backgrounds. When compared with students who did not sit-in, and with students who signed the anti-sit-in petition, the sit-in participants reported higher family incomes, higher levels of education for both fathers and mothers, and overwhelmingly perceived themselves to be "upper-middle class". One illustrative finding: in our dormitory sample, of 24 students reporting family incomes of above $15,000, half participated in the sit-in. Of 23 students reporting family incomes below $15,000, only two sat-in.

Certain kinds of occupations are particularly characteristic of the parents of sit-in participants. In particular, their fathers tend to be professionals (college faculty, lawyers, doctors) rather than businessmen, white collar employees or blue-collar workers. Moreover, somewhat unexpectedly, activists' mothers are likely to be employed, and are more likely to have "career" types of employment, than are the mothers of non-activists.

---

[1]A more detailed report of the procedures and findings of these studies is available in Flacks (1966).

Also of significance, although not particularly surprising, is the fact that activists are more likely to be Jewish than are nonactivists. (For example, 45% of our SAR sample reported that they were Jewish; only about one-fourth of the non-participants were Jewish). Furthermore, a very high proportion of both Jewish and non-Jewish activists report no religious preference for themselves and their parents. Associated with the Jewish ethnicity of a large proportion of our activist samples is the fact the great majority of activists' grandparents were foreign born. Yet, despite this, data from Study One show that the grandparents of activists tended to be relatively highly educated as compared to the grandparents of non-activists. Most of the grandparents of non-activists had not completed high school; nearly half of the grandparents of activists had at least a high school education and fully one-fourth of their maternal grandmothers had attended college. These data suggest that relatively high status characterized the families of activists over several generations; this conclusion is supported by data showing that, unlike non-activist grandfathers, the grandfathers of activists tended to have white collar, professional and entrepreneurial occupations rather than blue collar jobs.

In sum, our data suggest that, at least at major Northern colleges, students involved in protest activity are characteristically from families which are urban, highly educated, Jewish or irreligious, professional and affluent. It is perhaps particularly interesting that many of their mothers are uniquely well-educated and involved in careers, and that high status and education has characterized these families over at least two generations.

Activists are more "radical" than their parents; but activists' parents are decidedly more liberal than others of their status. The demographic data reported above suggests that activists come from high status families, but the occupational, religious and educational characteristics of these families are unique in several important ways. The distinctiveness of these families is especially clear when we examine data from Study One on the political attitudes of students and their parents. In this study, it should be remembered, activist and non-activist families were roughly equivalent in status, income and education because of our sampling procedures. Our data quite clearly demonstrate that the fathers of activists are disproportionately liberal. For example, whereas forty per cent of the non-activists' fathers said that they were Republican, only thirteen per cent of the activists' fathers were Republicans. Only six per cent of non-activists' fathers were willing to describe themselves as "highly liberal" or "socialist", whereas sixty per cent of the activists' fathers accepted such designations. Forty per cent of the non-activists' fathers described themselves as conservative; none of the activists' fathers endorsed that position.[2]

In general, differences in the political preferences of the students paralleled these parental differences. The non-activist sample is only slightly less conservative and Republican than their fathers; all of the activist students with Republican fathers report their own party preferences as either Democrat or independent. Thirty-two per cent of the activists regard themselves as "socialist" as compared with sixteen per cent of their fathers. In general, both non-activists and their fathers are typically "moderate" in their politics; activists and their fathers tend to be at least "liberal", but a substantial proportion of the activists prefer a more "radical" designation.

A somewhat more detailed picture of comparative political positions emerges when we examine responses of students and their fathers to a series of 6-point scales on which respondents rated their attitudes on such issues as: US bombing of North Vietnam, US troops in the Dominican Republic, student participation in protest demonstrations, civil rights protests involving civil disobedience, Lyndon Johnson, Barry Goldwater, congressional investigations of "unAmerican activities", full socialization of all industries, socialization of the medical profession.

Table 1 presents data on activists and non-activists and their fathers with respect to these items. This table suggests, first, wide divergence between the two groups of fathers on most issues, with activist fathers typically critical of current policies. Although activists' fathers are overwhelmingly "liberal" in their responses, for the most part, activist students tend to endorse "left-wing" positions more strongly and consistently than do their fathers. The items showing strongest divergence between activists and their fathers are interesting. Whereas activists overwhelmingly endorse civil disobedience, nearly half of their fathers do not. Whereas fathers of both activists and non-activists tend to approve of Lyndon Johnson, activist students tend to disapprove of him. Whereas activists' fathers tend to disapprove of "full socialization of industry", this item is endorsed by the majority of activists (although fewer gave an extremely radical response on this item than any other); whereas the vast majority of activists approve of socialized medicine, the majority

[2]For the purposes of this report, "activists" are those students who were in the top third of our Activism index; "nonactivists" are those students who were in the bottom third—this latter group reported virtually no participation in any activity associated with the student movement. The "activists" on the other hand had taken part in at least one activity indicating high commitment to the movement (e.g. going to jail, working full-time, serving in a leadership capacity).

TABLE 1
Students' and Fathers' Attitudes on Current Issues

	Activists		*Nonactivists*	
Issue	*Students*	*Fathers*	*Students*	*Fathers*
Per cent who approve:				
Bombing of North Vietnam	9	27	73	80
American troops in Dominican Republic	6	33	65	50
Student participation in protest demonstrations	100	80	61	37
Civil disobedience in civil rights protests	97	57	28	23
Congressional investigations of "un-American activities"	3	7	73	57
Lyndon Johnson	35	77	81	83
Barry Goldwater	0	7	35	20
Full socialization of industry	62	23	5	10
Socialization of the medical profession	94	43	30	27
N	34	30	37	30

of their fathers do not. This table provides further support for the view that activists, though more "radical" than their fathers, come predominantly from very liberal homes. The attitudes of non-activists and their fathers are conventional and supportive of current policies; there is a slight tendency on some items for non-activist students to endorse more conservative positions than their fathers.

It seems fair to conclude, then, that most students who are involved in the movement (at least those one finds in a city like Chicago) are involved in neither "conversion" from nor "rebellion" against the political perspectives of their fathers. A more supportable view suggests that the great majority of these students are attempting to fulfill and renew the political traditions of their families. However, data from our research which have not yet been analyzed as of this writing, will permit a more systematic analysis of the political orientations of the two generations.

Activism is related to a complex of values, not ostensibly political, shared by both the students and their parents. Data which we have just begun to analyze suggest that the political perspectives which differentiate the families of activists from other families at the same socioeconomic level are part of a more general clustering of values and orientations. Our findings and impressions on this point may be briefly summarized by saying that, whereas non-activists and their parents tend to express conventional orientations toward achievement, material success, sexual morality and religion, the activists and their parents tend to place greater stress on involvement in intellectual and esthetic pursuits, humanitarian concerns, opportunity for self-expression, and tend to de-emphasize or positively disvalue personal achievement, conventional morality and conventional religiosity.

When asked to rank order a list of "areas of life", non-activist students and their parents typically indicate that marriage, career and religion are most important. Activists, on the other hand, typically rank these lower than the "world of ideas, art and music" and "work for national and international betterment"—and so, on the whole, do their parents (see also the relevant data presented by Trent and Craise in this issue).

When asked to indicate their vocational aspirations, nonactivist students are typically firmly decided on a career and typically mention orientations toward the professions, science and business. Activists, on the other hand, are very frequently undecided on a career; and most typically those who have decided mention college teaching, the arts or social work as aspirations.

These kinds of responses suggest, somewhat crudely, that student activists identify with life goals which are intellectual and "humanitarian" and that they reject conventional and "privatized" goals more frequently than do nonactivist students.

Four Value Patterns

More detailed analyses which we are just beginning to undertake support the view that the value-patterns expressed by activists are highly correlated with those of their parents. This analysis has involved the isolation of a number of value-patterns which emerged in the interview material, the development of systems of code categories related to each of these patterns, and the blind coding of all the interviews with respect to these categories. The kinds of data we are obtaining in this way may be illustrated by describing four of the value patterns we have observed:

Romanticism: Esthetic and Emotional sensitivity. This variable is defined as: "sensitivity to beauty and art—appreciation of painting, literature and music, creativity in art forms—concern with esthetic experience and the development of capacities for esthetic expression—concern with emotions deriving from perception of beauty—attachment of great significance to esthetic experience. More broadly, it can be conceived of as involving explicit concern with experience as such, with feeling and passion, with immediate and inner experience; a concern for the realm of feeling rather than the rational, technological or instrumental side of life; preference for the realm of experience as against that of activity, doing or achieving". Thirteen items were coded in these terms: for each item a score of zero signified no mention of "romanticist" concerns, a score of one signified that such a concern appeared. Table 2 indicates the relationship between "romanticism" and Activism. Very few Activists received scores on Romanticism which placed them as "low"; conversely, there were very few high "romantics" among the nonactivists.

TABLE 2
Scores on Selected Values by Activism (Percentages)

		Activists	*Nonactivists*
(a)	*Romanticism*		
	High	35	11
	Medium	47	49
	Low	18	40
(b)	*Intellectualism*		
	High	32	3
	Medium	65	57
	Low	3	40
(c)	*Humanitarianism*		
	High	35	0
	Medium	47	22
	Low	18	78
(d)	*Moralism*		
	High	6	54
	Medium	53	35
	Low	41	11
	N	34	37

Intellectualism. This variable is defined as: "Concern with ideas—desire to realize intellectual capacities—high valuation of intellectual creativities—appreciation of theory and knowledge—participation in intellectual activity (e.g., reading, studying, teaching, writing)—broad intellectual concerns". Ten items were scored for "intellectualism". Almost no Activists are low on this variable; almost no nonactivists received a high score.

Humanitarianism. This variable is defined as: "Concern with plight of others in society; desire to help others—value on compassion and sympathy—desire to alleviate suffering; value on egalitarianism in the sense of opposing privilege based on social and economic distinction; particular sensitivity to the deprived position of the disadvantaged". This variable was coded for ten items; an attempt was made to exclude from this index all items referring directly to participation in social action. As might be expected, "humanitarianism" is strongly related to Activism, as evidenced in Table 2.

Moralism and Self Control. This variable is defined as: "Concern about the importance of strictly controlling personal impulses—opposition to impulsive or spontaneous behavior—value on keeping tight control over emotions—adherence to conventional authority; adherence to conventional morality—a high degree of moralism about sex, drugs, alcohol, etc.—reliance on a set of external and inflexible rules to govern moral behavior; emphasis on importance of hard work; concern with determination, "stick-to-itiveness"; antagonism toward idleness—value on diligence, entrepreneurship, task orientation, ambition". Twelve items were scored for this variable. As Table 2 suggests, "moralism" is also strongly related to Activism; very few Activists score high on this variable, while the majority of nonactivists are high scorers.

These values are strongly related to activism. They are also highly intercorrelated, and, most importantly, parent and student scores on these variables are strongly correlated.

These and other value patterns will be used as the basis for studying value transmission in families, generational similarities and differences and several other problems. Our data with respect to them provide further support for the view that the unconventionality of activists flows out of and is supported by their family traditions.

Activists' parents are more "permissive" than parents of nonactivists. We have just begun to get some findings bearing on our hypothesis that parents of Activists will tend to have been more "permissive" in their child-rearing practices than parents of equivalent status whose children are not oriented toward activism.

One measure of parental permissiveness we have been using is a series of rating scales completed by each member of the family. A series of seven-point bipolar scales was presented in a format similar to that of the "Semantic Differential". Students were asked to indicate "how my mother (father) treated me as a child" on such scales as "warm-cold"; "stern-mild"; "hard-soft"—10 scales in all. Each parent, using the same scales, rated "how my child thinks I treated him".

Table 3 presents data on how sons and daughters rated each of their parents on each of four scales: "mild-stern"; "soft-hard"; "lenient-severe"; and "easy-strict". In general, this table shows that Activist sons and daughters tend to rate their parents as "milder", "more lenient", and "less severe" than do nonactivists. Similar data were obtained using the parents' ratings of themselves.

A different measure of permissiveness is based on the parents' response to a series of "hypothetical situations". Parents were asked,

TABLE 3
Sons and Daughters Ratings of Parents by Activism (Percentages)

	Males		Females	
Trait of parent	Hi Act	Lo Act	Hi Act	Lo Act
mild-stern				
per cent rating mother "mild"	63	44	59	47
per cent rating father "mild"	48	33	48	32
soft-hard				
per cent rating mother "soft"	69	61	60	57
per cent rating father "soft"	50	50	62	51
lenient-severe				
per cent rating mother "lenient"	94	61	66	63
per cent rating father "lenient"	60	44	47	42
easy-strict				
per cent rating mother "easy"	75	50	77	52
per cent rating father "easy"	69	44	47	37
N	23	24	27	26

for example, what they would do if their son (daughter) "decided to drop out of school and doesn't know what he really wants to do". Responses to this open-ended question were coded as indicating "high intervention" or "low intervention". Data for fathers on this item are reported in Table 4. Another hypothetical situation presented to the parents was that their child was living with a member of the opposite sex. Responses to this item were coded as "strongly intervene, mildly intervene, not intervene". Data for this item for fathers appears in Table 5. Both tables show that fathers of Activists report themselves to be much less interventionist than fathers of nonactivists. Similar results were obtained with mothers, and for other hypothetical situations.

Clearly both types of measures just reported provide support for our hypothesis about the relationship between parental permissiveness and activism. We expect these relationships to be strengthened if "activism" is combined with certain of the value-patterns described earlier.

A Concluding Note

The data reported here constitute a small but representative sampling of the material we have collected in our studies of the student

TABLE 4
Father's Intervention—"If Child Dropped Out
of School" (Percentages)

Degree of Intervention	Activism of Child	
	High	Low
Low	56	37
High	44	63
N	30	30

TABLE 5
Father's Intervention—"If Child Were Living With Member
of Opposite Sex" (Percentages)

Degree of Intervention	Activism of Child	
	High	Low
None	20	14
Mild	50	28
Strong	30	58
N	30	30

movement. In general, they provide support for the impressions and expectations we had when we undertook this work. Our view of the student movement as an expression of deep discontent felt by certain types of high status youth as they confront the incongruities between the values represented by the authority and occupational structure of the larger society and the values inculcated by their families and peer culture seems to fit well with the data we have obtained.

A variety of questions remain which, we hope, can be answered, at least in part, by further analyses of our data. Although it is clear that value differences between parents of activists and nonactivists are centrally relevant for understanding value, attitudinal and behavioral cleavages among types of students on the campus, it remains to be determined whether differences in family status, on the one hand, and childrearing practices, on the other, make an independent contribution to the variance. A second issue has to do with political ideology. First impressions of our data suggest that activists vary considerably with respect to their degree of politicization and their concern with ideological issues. The problem of isolating the key determinants of this variation is one we will be paying close attention to in further analysis of our interview material. Two factors are likely to be of importance here—first, the degree to which the student participates in radical student organizations; second, the political history of his parents.

At least two major issues are not confronted by the research we have been doing. First, we have not examined in any detail the role of campus conditions as a determinant of student discontent (see the introduction by Sampson and the article by Brown for a further discussion of these institutional factors). The research reported here emphasizes family socialization and other antecedent experiences as determinants of student protest, and leads to the prediction that students experiencing other patterns of early socialization will be unlikely to be in revolt. This view needs to be counterbalanced by recalling instances of active student unrest on campuses where very few students are likely to have the backgrounds suggested here as critical. Is it possible that there are two components to the student protest movement—one generated to a great extent by early socialization; the second by grievances indigenous to the campus? At any rate, the inter-relationships between personal dispositions and campus conditions need further detailed elucidation.

A second set of questions unanswerable by our research has to do with the future—what lies ahead for the movement as a whole and for the individual young people who participate in it? One direction for the student movement is toward institutionalization as an expression of youth discontent. This outcome, very typical of student movements in many countries, would represent a narrowing of the movement's political and social impact, a way of functionally integrating it into an otherwise stable society. Individual participants would be expected to pass through the movement on their way to eventual absorption, often at an elite level, into the established institutional order. An alternative direction would be toward the development of a full-fledged political "left", with the student movement serving, at least initially, as a nucleus. The potential for this latter development is apparent in recent events. It was the student movement which catalyzed professors and other adults into protest with respect to the Vietnam war. Students for a Democratic Society, the main organizational expression of the student movement, has had, for several years, a program for "community organizing", in which students and exstudents work full-time at the mobilization of constituencies for independent radical political and social action. This SDS program began in poverty areas; it is now beginning to spread to "middle class" communities. These efforts and others like them, from Berkeley to New Haven, became particularly visible during the 1966 congressional elections, as a wave of "new left" candidates emerged across the country, often supported by large and sophisticated political organizations. Moreover, in addition to attempts at political organizations, SDS, through its "Radical Education Project" has begun to seek the involvement of faculty members, professionals and other intellectuals for a program of research and education designed to lay the foundations for an intellectually substantial and ideologically developed "new left".

At its convention in September, 1966, SDS approached, but did not finally decide, the question of whether to continue to maintain its character as a campus-based, student organization or to transform itself into a "Movement for a Democratic Society". Characteristically, the young people there assembled amended the organization's constitution so that anyone regardless of status or age could join, while simultaneously they affirmed the student character of the group by projecting a more vigorous program to organize uncommitted students.

The historical significance of the student movement of the Sixties remains to be determined. Its impact on the campus and on the larger society has already been substantial. It is clearly a product of deep discontent in certain significant and rapidly growing segments of the youth population. Whether it becomes an expression of generational discontent, or the forerunner of major political realignments—or simply disintegrates—cannot really be predicted by detached social scientists. The ultimate personal and political meaning of the student movement remains a matter to be determined by those who are involved with it—as participants, as allies, as critics, as enemies.

References

Aaron, Daniel. *Writers on the left.* New York: Avon, 1965.

Bell, Daniel. *The end of ideology.* New York: The Free Press, 1962.

Braungart, R. G. Social stratification and political attitudes. Pennsylvania State University, 1966, (unpublished ms.).

Bronfenbrenner, U. The changing American child: A speculative analysis. *Merrill-Palmer Quarterly,* 1961, 7, 73-85.

Coser, Lewis. *Men of ideas.* New York: The Free Press, 1965.

Erikson, Erik. Identity and the life-cycle. *Psychological Issues,* 1959, 1, 1-171.

Erikson, Erik. *Childhood and society.* New York: Norton, 1963, 306–325.

Eisenstadt, Shmuel N. *From generation to generation.* Glencoe: The Free Press, 1956.

Flacks R. The liberated generation. University of Chicago, 1966. (mimeo)

Goldens, Rose;Rosenberg, Moris; Williams, Robin; and Suchman, Edward. *What college students think,* Princeton: Van Nostrand, 1960.

Jacob, Philip. *Changing values in college.* New York: Harper, 1957.

Keniston, Kenneth. *The uncommitted.* New York: Harcourt Brace, 1965a.

Keniston, Kenneth. Social change and youth in America. In E. Erickson (Ed.), *The challenge of youth.* Garden City: Doubleday Anchor, 1965b.

Lasch, Christopher. *The new radicalism in America.* New York: Knopf, 1965.

Lipset, Seymour. *Political man, the social bases of politics.* Garden City: Doubleday Anchor, 1960.

Lipset, Seymour. University students and politics in underdeveloped countries. *Comparative Education Review,* 1966, 10, 132–162.

Lipset, Seymour and Altbach, P. Student politics and higher education in the United States. *Comparative Education Review,* 1966, 10, 320–349.

Miller, Daniel and Swanson, G. E. *The changing American parent.* New York: Wiley, 1958.

Newcomb, Theodore and Flacks, R. *Deviant subcultures on a college campus.* US Office of Education, 1963.

Parsons, Talcott. Youth in the context of American society. In E. Erikson (Ed.), *The challenge of youth.* Garden City: Doubleday Anchor, 1965.

Shils, Edward, The intellectuals in the political development of new states. *World Politics,* 1960, 12, 329–368.

Stinchcombe, Arthur. *Rebellion in a high school.* Chicago: Quadrangle, 1964.

Trow, Martin. Student cultures and administrative action. In Sutherland, R. *et al.* (Eds.), *Personality factors on the college campus.* Austin: Hogg Foundation for Mental Health, 1962.

Veblen, Thornstein. The intellectual pre-eminence of Jews in modern Europe. In B. Rosenberg (Ed.), *Thorstein Veblen.* New York: Crowell, 1963.

Negro Students and the Protest Movement

Donald Matthews and
James Prothro

On Monday, February 1, 1960, four Negro teen-agers walked into a five-and-ten-cent store in Greensboro, North Carolina, sat down at the lunch counter, and ordered a cup of coffee.[1] When they were refused—local custom permitted Negroes to purchase merchandise in the store but not to eat there—they continued to sit at the counter, silently waiting for service. For a while everyone tried to ignore them. Then the Negro cooks came out of the kitchen and urged the boys to return to their dormitories at North Carolina Agricultural and Technical College, where they were freshmen. The well-dressed youngsters sat on silently until the store closed for the day. Thus began the "sit-ins," a movement that was to plunge the South into turmoil for many months and revolutionize the pace and tactics of Negro civil rights activities in the United States from that day onward.

On Tuesday the four freshmen, joined by about 20 new recruits from A. and T., returned to the same lunch counter. Again they were refused service. Wednesday and Thursday they returned, their numbers swelled by students from Bennett College (a Negro institution near by) and a few white girls from the Woman's College of the University of North Carolina, also located in Greensboro. By Friday, white teen-agers had begun to taunt and heckle the silent demonstrators.

Saturday morning the store was jammed with Negroes and whites, mostly young people. The Negroes continued to sit while

"the white boys waved Confederate flags, chanted, and cursed."[2]
In midafternoon, the manager of the store received an anonymous
bomb threat and police emptied the store. When it opened again
on Monday morning, the lunch counter was closed. Thus ended
—temporarily—the Greensboro demonstration.

But by then Negro students were demonstrating in Winston-
Salem, Durham, Charlotte, and other North Carolina cities. From
this base, the sit-ins rapidly spread into other areas. On
February 11, students from Hampton Institute in Virginia sat in
at the local Woolworth's. The next day student demonstrations
took place in Rock Hill, South Carolina, and Deland, Florida.
Students from Fisk University and Tennessee A. and I. began
demonstrating in Nashville on February 13. Demonstrations broke
out at Montgomery, Alabama, on February 25. By March 5 they
had spread to Houston, Texas. Five days later sit-ins were staged
in Little Rock, Arkansas, and on March 15 in Atlanta, Georgia.
The sit-in movement reached Baton Rouge, Louisiana, on
March 28 and Jackson, Mississippi, on April 11. Within a year
and a half after the initial Greensboro sit-in, demonstrations had
been held in over a hundred cities and towns in every southern
and border state, as well as in Illinois, Nevada, and Ohio. At
least 70,000 Negroes and their white sympathizers had taken part
in them.[3]

Begun as a protest against segregated lunch counters in
variety stores, the movement rapidly expanded its targets to
include all types of public accommodations—parks, swimming
pools, theaters, restaurants, churches, transportation facilities,
museums, art galleries, laundromats, beaches, and courtrooms.
The systematic boycott of segregated business establishments by
the Negro community became the standard—and persuasive—
weapon of the movement. Roused Negro youths demonstrated
even to protest discrimination in employment practices and voter
registration.

All this required organization and liaison with the adult Negro
community and its established leaders. The first Greensboro
demonstrators sought and got assistance from the then little-
known, New York-based Congress on Racial Equality (CORE).
Martin Luther King and the youth leaders of the NAACP were
on the scene in Greensboro before the first week of protest had
ended.[4] These groups continued to provide aid and comfort to
the movement from then on. But the students retained the
initiative. In April the Student Non-violent Coordinating
Committee (SNCC, pronounced "snick") announced that the
students intended to stay free of the control of adult leaders and
organizations.

The reaction of the white South to these developments was overwhelmingly hostile. Most lunchroom proprietors continued to refuse service to Negroes. Public officials warned against participating in the demonstrations, a rash of new anti-trespass laws and ordinances were passed, and older statutes were vigorously enforced. An estimated 3,600 students and their supporters had been arrested by September 1961.[5] A number of Negro students and faculty members—at least 141 students and 58 professors—were dismissed by their colleges and universities for taking part in the movement. Hundreds of students voluntarily withdrew from college to protest these expulsions.

In a number of places, the demonstrators were met with open violence. During the first few weeks of protest, for example, rioting broke out in a Chattanooga store when "whites, mostly students, began throwing flower pots, dishes, bric-a-brac, and other merchandise" at the Negroes sitting at the lunch counter.[6] One white youth found a bullwhip in the store and proceeded to use it on a Negro. In Houston, three masked white men grabbed a young Negro, flogged him with a chain, carved "KKK" on his chest, and hung him by his knees from a nearby tree. Two days after the first Montgomery sit-in, a marauding band of whites attacked a Negro woman with miniature baseball bats concealed in brown paper bags. In several places demonstrating students were barely saved from white mobs by the police, who sometimes had to threaten the use of tear gas and fire hoses. When the police were less alert or less dedicated, the students were beaten.

Throughout all these trials, the students were—with amazingly few exceptions—true to their doctrine of nonviolence. They sat at counters and walked picket lines in silence, neither responding to insults nor expressing outrage at how they were being treated. They neither struck back when assaulted nor resisted arrest. Rarely has this nation seen such a display of courage and self-sacrifice.

Prelude to Protest

Historians will no doubt trace the beginnings of the Negro protest movement to a day earlier than February 1, 1960. The four freshmen at North Carolina A. and T. did not just stumble upon a new approach to desegregation. And their act of "spontaneous rebellion"[7] would not have grown rapidly into a mass movement if conditions had not been ripe.

Most of the Negro youngsters who took part in the protests of 1960 and 1961 were born during the early years of the Second World

War. The war and its aftermath reshaped the world in which they grew up. In the first place, the war had exposed many southern Negroes to nonsegregated societies for the first time. When these veterans returned to the South, many brought home with them a new image of themselves, new hopes and aspirations, and the belief that, having risked their lives in the defense of their country, they deserved nothing less than first-class citizenship. They soon learned that these hopes and dreams were unfounded.

At the same time, the wartime and postwar boom benefited Negroes economically. To be sure, they did not improve their economic position relative to that of whites; rather, they stayed at the bottom of the heap while the entire heap lurched upward. Nonetheless, Negroes began to enjoy goods and services they had never had before; fewer of them lived in abject poverty. Men with empty stomachs rarely rebel; people without purchasing power do not launch economic boycotts of business establishments that do not treat them fairly. Thus the wartime and postwar improvements in the Negro's economic position left him with the same sense of *relative* deprivation as before, but with more economic resources to do something about it.

Finally, the war and postwar boom hastened the Negro flight from the rural South to cities in the South, North, and West, for that is where the jobs were. Life in an urban ghetto is rather different from life on a farm. The informal restraints on aggressiveness toward whites are very largely gone. So, too, are most personal relationships with white people—save the highly impersonal and segmentalized contacts of city dwellers in general. Viewed from the ghetto, whites could easily be thought of as "The Man"—a faceless, collective enemy.

The psychological impact of the Supreme Court's school-desegregation decision on the Negro subculture is hard to overestimate. The Negro journalist Louis Lomax has written:

> It would be impossible for a white person to understand what happened within black breasts on that Monday [May 17, 1954, when *Brown v. Board of Education* was handed down by the Court]. An ardent segregationist has called it "Black Monday." He was so right, but for reasons other than the ones he advances: that was the day we won; the day we took the white man's laws and won our case before an all-white Supreme Court with a Negro lawyer, Thurgood Marshall, as our chief counsel. And we were proud.[8]

The *Brown* decision, hailed as the second Emancipation Proclamation, raised Negro expectations to new heights. But these expectations were to be ground down by the vehemence and ingenuity of southern resistance. The four freshmen at A. and T. had been in grammar school on the day the decision was announced. More than five years later, on the day they began their silent vigil at the Woolworth lunch counter in Greensboro, considerably less than 1 per cent of all Negro students in the South were attending desegregated schools.[9]

This slow progress toward racial equality provoked a growing disillusionment with traditional attacks on segregation and with the established leadership of the Negro community. Until then the battle for civil rights had taken place very largely inside the courtroom. Over the years the NAACP had won an impressive string of legal victories. But how much difference had they made to the average Negro? Seemingly, very little. In local communities the struggle had been led by middle-class Negroes—the only ones with enough status and skill to bargain with what more and more Negroes came to call the "white power structure". At best the results of these endless conferences, committees, and councils were modest. Most Negroes found them imperceptible.

As the Negro masses grew more militant and demanding, the established Negro leaders were caught in a crossfire of conflicting demands. On the one hand, their position as leaders depended on their access to and acceptance by the white community leaders. This, in turn, depended on their having a reputation for "reasonableness" among the whites. On the other hand, if the Negro leaders failed to reflect the growing militancy of their followers, they would lose their influence over the Negro rank and file. Paralyzed by this dilemma, many leaders began to lose the respect and confidence of both Negroes and whites.

The time was ripe for rebellion—rebellion against white domination and segregation, against legalism, against gradual reform through governmental action, against established Negro organizations and leaders.

The first indication of what was to come had occurred in Montgomery, Alabama, in 1955.[10] One day in December, a middle-aged Negro woman named Mrs. Rosa Parks refused to move to the back of a bus. For this insubordination Mrs. Parks was arrested. Within 24 hours a mass boycott of the busses had been organized by an *ad hoc* committee of Negro ministers. One member of this committee was a young Baptist minister named Martin Luther King, Jr. King emerged from the long and bitter boycott as the most eloquent and respected voice that southern Negroes had had for a very long time. King was a militant devotee of direct mass action and civil disobedience. But he also was deeply devoted to a concept of nonviolence that he had learned from Gandhi and from Christian theology. King's ideas—expressed with boldness and emotion—had a profound effect on the Negro community. Undoubtedly they influenced the thinking of the young demonstrators who, a few years later, were to seize the initiative from their elders. The Southern Christian Leadership Conference (SCLC), a loose confederation of ministers organized around King, was another important by-product of the Montgomery boycott.

The next major revolt occurred not in the South but in Wichita, Kansas. In August 1958, what apparently was the first organized "sit-in" was held there.[11] The next week the movement spread to Oklahoma City. Several lunch counters were desegregated, and demonstrations continued to be staged in this border city through 1960 and 1961. Although the sit-ins spread from Oklahoma City to a few other cities in the state—Enid, Tulsa, and Stillwater—they went no farther. A 1959 Miami, Florida, sit-in was a completely unrelated enterprise organized and directed by CORE, which had had experience in direct-action techniques while trying to desegregate housing projects in the North. In any event, the Miami sit-in was brief and abortive.

Thus the four freshmen at North Carolina A. and T. were not the first protesters. But they managed to do something that no one else had been able to do—they drew hundreds and thousands of college students into active protest. They managed to create a region-wide "movement" from what had been scattered and sporadic protests. And they managed to commit this movement to the use of direct, highly provocative tactics in its struggle for freedom and equality. This is more than enough to ensure that February 1, 1960, will go down as a major turning point in the history of the South.

The Extent of Student Participation

Throughout most of the world—Europe, Asia, Latin America, and Africa—university students are a major political force. Strikes, boycotts, rioting, and picketing by students are almost commonplace and have been known to topple governments, force basic changes in public policy, and make and break political careers. By comparison, American college students have been politically passive.

But the four youngsters from North Carolina A. and T. changed all that, at least for Negro students in the South. "If we leave it to the adults," an 18-year-old freshman in Atlanta said, referring to his longing for racial equality, "nothing will become of it." A junior in North Carolina went even further. "You know," he said, "the adults still feel the white man can do no wrong." In Mississippi a freshman girl concluded that "most adults have given up hope or just don't care." Only the young, many Negro students seem to have decided, could bring about a radical change in racial patterns. And they were "tired of sitting back and waiting on the older folks." "Waiting is forever," a sophomore in New Orleans said. "You gotta do something."

During the first year of the protests almost a quarter (24 per cent[12]) of the Negro students in the South took some part in the sit-in movement. From 1 to 2 per cent participated in the more controversial and violent freedom rides. Eighty-five per cent of all Negro students enrolled in predominantly Negro colleges and universities in the South approved of these activities, whereas only 5 percent were opposed to them (See Table 14-1). Student enthusiasm for the protest movement was extraordinary: "It's a new social revolution." "It's the most remarkable movement since the emancipation of the slaves." "This is the day of the *New* Negro." "I think they are just wonderful."

TABLE 14-1.
Feelings of Negro College Students About Sit-ins
and Freedom Rides

Feelings	*Sit-ins*	*Freedom rides*
Strongly approve	53%	49%
Approve	32	35
Neutral	4	5
Disapprove	4	3
Strongly disapprove	1	1
Uncodeable response	2	3
Don't know, no answer, refusal	4	4
TOTAL	100%	100%
N	264	264

The most common form of student participation was sitting-in at counters or waiting rooms, and kneeling-in, lying-in, or standing-in at other public facilities. Sixty-five per cent of the students active in the movement took part in at least one of these activities. This amounts to about 16 per cent of *all* Negro college students in the South—an extraordinarily high percentage of any group to participate in an invariably unpleasant and potentially dangerous activity of dubious legality[13] (See Table 14-2). Twenty-nine per cent of the active students engaged in picketing, and 23 per cent took part in mass demonstrations and marches. Only 3 per cent of the activists claimed that they had taken part in the freedom rides.

The student participants in these protest demonstrations were very matter of fact about them. One sit-inner in Florida said, "There

TABLE 14-2.
What Students Who Participated in the Protest
Movement Did, 1960–1962

Activity	*Percentage of students participating in movement who engaged in activity*	*Percentage of all Negro students who engaged in activity*
Sat in at counter, waiting room, etc.	60%	15%
Picketed	29	7
Took part in mass demonstrations, marches, etc.	23	6
Led or organized Negro protest activities	11	3
Wade-in, kneel-in, stand-in	5	1
Rode on freedom bus, train, etc.	3	1
Donated money	2	a
N	65	264

aGreater than 0, less than 0.5 per cent.
NOTE: Percentages do not total 100 because some students engaged in more than one activity.

were some [whites] who wouldn't eat with us, but they didn't say anything to us; they just quietly left. . . . " Even those who encountered more overt opposition tended to describe their experiences with almost clinical detachment. "Well," a sophomore at Southern University said, "we were at a lunch counter—the Greyhound Bus station in New Orleans—and we just sat in. Then we were thrown out. . . . I was one of the 77 jailed." A freedom rider from Tennessee described his participation in this bloody phase of the protests by saying, "We rode to Alabama. I was put out of the city." Another sit-in participant described his experiences without emotion:

We were met by the police . . . [the] student drivers were given tickets for illegal parking. We were burned on our arms with cigarettes, pushed around, and had doors closed in our faces.

Only rarely do signs of outrage or indignation come through. One freshman from Louisiana complained of the treatment she received at the hands of the police: "I don't think there are any words to describe how dirty the policemen were." Another youngster was shocked by the signs of white hatred:

> Nothing happened except the way the manager acted and the expression of hatred on his face. They placed racks of clothes . . . to block Negroes from seats. I also noticed the expression on the white people's faces. . . . At one store they piled groceries and things on the counter and roped off seats. Nothing happened except the looks we got and the pushing. I don't think I'll ever forget that experience because before I had never conceived of people hating anyone because of his color. Before it was secondhand to me, but this was firsthand experience.

One out of every 6 demonstrators was arrested; one of every 20 was thrown in jail. About 1 in every 10 reported having been pushed, jostled, or spat upon; the same proportion were either clubbed, beaten, gassed, or burned; another 8 per cent were run out of town (See Table 14-3). Only 11 per cent of the protesters reported that nothing untoward had happened to them.

Although student support of the demonstrations was almost unanimous, a majority of the students at predominantly Negro institutions in the South did not actively take part in the protest between 1960 and 1962. The most popular reason given for their failure to participate was their geographical separation from the scene of active protests or a general lack of opportunity (See Table 14-4). "There was no place to go, I suppose," one inactive student in Texas said. "Where I live we had no problem." Smaller numbers pleaded conflicting school or job commitments. "The football coach said not to," one student athlete in Tennessee said. "He didn't want us to get arrested and miss any games or practice. He said we had scholarships to play football, not sit in." A North Carolina student confessed that she ". . . didn't want to have a jail record. One day I'm going to look for a job and this might be held against me." Seven per cent of the reasons volunteered had to do with personal unsuitability, on grounds ranging from "I wouldn't have had the nerve" to "I'm not a non-violent person. I would have found it hard not to go to the aid of someone who was hurt, and this would not help the movement." Very few of the non-participants mentioned opposition from parents ("Mom told me—if I went, try to keep from getting in trouble") or teachers ("They told us we should decide which is more important—education or sit-ins").

But these "explanations" of inactivity, in the face of what must have been substantial social pressure from activist fellow students,

TABLE 14-3.
What Happened to Students Who Participated in
the Protest Movement, 1960–1962

What happened	Percentage of students participating in movement	Percentage of all Negro students
Arrested	15%	4%
Nothing	11	3
Pushed, jostled, spat at	11	3
Called names	8	2
Clubbed, beaten, gassed, burned	8	2
Jailed	6	2
Threatened	6	2
Water or food spilled on	2	a
N	65	264

aGreater than 0, less than 0.5 per cent.

NOTE: Percentages do not total 100 because some students reported more than one of these experiences.

should be interpreted with care. The human ability to rationalize comfortable inaction knows few bounds. So let us examine the participants in the protest movement to see if we can infer, from what we know about their personal characteristics, attitudes, and life situations, why some Negro students in the South actively engaged in protest activities while others did not.

Who Were the Protesters?

The students who poured out of their classrooms into the stores and streets to protest against segregation in 1960 and 1961 were not entirely "typical" Negro college students. Rather, they differed from their schoolmates in a number of identifiable ways. These differences are of some interest in and of themselves. But, more important, they provide clues as to *why* some students were active in the protest movement while others were not. Who, then, were the protesters?

Given the substantial physical risks involved in active protest, one might expect the protesters to be almost entirely young men. In fact, the student protesters were almost as often girls as boys: 48 per

TABLE 14-4.
Reasons Given by Negro Students for Not Participating
in the Protest Movement, 1960–1962

Reasons for nonparticipation	*Percentage of total response*
No special reason, don't know	24%
Geographical separation	21
Lack of opportunity (general)	12
Conflicting school and job commitments	10
Fear of consequences—loss of job, expelled from school, etc.	8
Don't believe in them	8
Personally unsuited for, fear of experience	7
Have not been asked to, didn't know how to	6
Opposition of parents and teachers	4
TOTAL	100%
N	210

cent of the students who personally took part in the sit-ins and freedom rides were female. If the sex ratio in Negro colleges was the same as in white institutions—where female students are almost invariably outnumbered, often two or three to one—this would mean that a larger proportion of the girl students took part in the demonstrations than of the boys. But, in fact, well over half (57 per cent) of the Negro students enrolled in predominantly Negro institutions at the height of the sit-ins were women—a fact that no doubt reflects the special importance of women in the Negro subculture.

If we divide all the students in our sample into three groups according to the extent of their involvement in the protest movement—those who personally took part in the sit-ins and freedom rides (25 per cent), those who belonged to protest organizations but did not themselves take part in the protests and demonstrations (14 per cent), and those who neither belonged to protest organizations nor took part in the protests (61 per cent)—and examine the proportion of each sex at each level of participation, we find 30 per cent of the male students and 21 per cent of the female students at the most active level and 12 per cent of the men and 17 per cent of the women at the second level of involvement. Thus if participation is defined as personal and direct participation in the protests, the male students were a little more likely to be activists than were the female students. If membership in protest organizations is considered an indication of protest activity, the women students were just about as active as the men. Regardless of which view we adopt, we find that the large gap in participation rates between adult Negro males and females reported in Chapter Four just did not exist among the student protesters.

A good deal more important than sex differences in accounting for participation in the protests was the nature of the communities in which the young students were raised (See Table 14-5). The more urban the students' early environment, the more likely they were to have been active in the movement. A third of the students raised in large cities personally took part in the protests, but only 15 per cent of those raised on farms joined the demonstrations and picket lines.

TABLE 14-5.
Home-Community Background of Negro Students and
Their Participation in the Protest Movement

LEVEL OF PARTICIPATION

	Active in protests	*Belong to protest group*	*Neither*	*TOTAL*	*N*
KIND OF COMMUNITY STUDENT GREW UP IN					
Farm	15%	10	75	100%	59
Town	18%	25	57	100%	57
Small City	30%	7	63	100%	81
Large City	33%	18	49	100%	67
PERCENTAGE OF NEGROES IN COUNTY WHERE STUDENT GREW UP					
0–19%	21%	18	61	100%	28
29–39%	32%	12	56	100%	116
40–59%	17%	19	64	100%	81
60% +	19%	10	71	100%	31
SUBREGION OF STUDENT'S HOME					
Deep South	27%	10	63	100%	128
Peripheral South	22%	19	59	100%	134

Three-fourths of the farm boys and girls were completely inactive—that is, they neither took part in the demonstrations nor belonged to a protest group. The active protesters also came, in disproportionate numbers, from areas of moderate concentrations of Negroes. The students raised in areas with very few Negroes (less than 20 per cent of the total population) or large numbers of them (over 40 per cent) were less likely to become involved.

Both of these findings might lead us to assume that the protesters came disproportionately from the Peripheral South. But this would be an error—the students from the Deep South probably were a little more active, personally, than those from the more liberal states on the edge of the region. Almost twice the proportion of students from the Peripheral as from the Deep South joined protest groups and stopped their activity at that point, whereas the students from the Deep South more often tended to be either high-level participants (27 per cent) or totally inactive (63 per cent). But these differences are small indeed. The safer conclusion is that the students in the two subregions took part in the protests at essentially the same rate. Given the greater opposition to the protests in the Deep South, and the far lower levels of adult Negro participation there, this in itself is surprising.

The largest single demographic difference between the students who joined the protest movement and those who did not is their social class (see Table 14-6). The higher the social and economic status of the Negro student, the more likely he was to become an active member of the movement. Over half of the students from families with an annual income of over $6,000 personally participated in the demonstrations or belonged to protest groups, but only 6 per cent of the students from families with an income of less than $2,000 were that active! If we use the occupation of the head of the student's family as an index of status, the same class differences in participation appear.

What, then, does this brief demographic portrait of the Negro protester add up to? *All* Negro college students are extremely fortunate youngsters; very few Negroes have their educational opportunities, and educational achievement is even more highly valued in the Negro subculture than in white America. But even within this select group the protesting students were especially blessed. They tended to come from areas with enough Negroes to create a genuine "Negro problem" but not so many as to result in extreme repression by whites; they tended to come from cities where race relations were, relatively speaking, more benign than in the countryside; and they tended far more often than the average Negro student to come from middle-class homes.

TABLE 14-6.
Social Class of Negro Students and the Extent of Their Participation in the Protest Movement

EXTENT OF PARTICIPATION

	Active personally	*Belonged to protest group*	*Neither*	*TOTAL*	*N*
ANNUAL INCOME OF FAMILY					
Under $1,000	3%	3	94	100%	30
$2,000–$3,999	26%	9	65	100%	69
$4,000–$5,999	19%	21	60	100%	68
$6,000+	34%	19	47	100%	76
OCCUPATIONAL CATEGORY OF HEAD OF STUDENT'S FAMILY					
White-collar	32%	20	48	100%	62
Blue-collar	25%	15	60	100%	146
Farmer	14%	8	78	100%	37
Housewife	18%	0	82	100%	11

"Revolutionary movements seem to originate," Crane Brinton has written in the *Anatomy of Revolution,* "in the discontents of not unprosperous people who feel restraint, cramp, annoyance rather than . . . crushing oppression."[14] A demographic picture of the student protesters suggests that this was the case for the sit-in movement as well. But Brinton's argument is based as much on the psychological attributes of revolutionaries as on their social positions. Let us look at the psychological characteristics of the protesters before we conclude that his analysis holds.

The Psychology of Protest

Negro college students were on the whole much more discontented with race relations in the South of the early 1960's than were the adult Negroes of the region. When asked to rate southern race relations on our self-anchoring "ladder," the average student chose a value of 4.5 as compared to the 5.8 rating made by the average Negro adult a few months earlier (see Figure 14-1). Moreover, the students were much more nearly united in their judgments than were the adults. Almost a third of the adults thought southern race relations were good (rating them 8, 9, or 10), although 15 per cent thought they were as bad as they could imagine (rating them 1). Less than 5 per cent of the students were found at either of these extremes. The overwhelming student view, using their own standards of judgment, was that race relations in the South were bad but could be worse.

FIGURE 14-1.
Ratings of Current Race Relations by Negro
Students and Adults

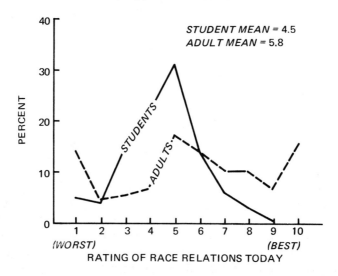

These student evaluations definitely were associated with participation in the protest movement: the students with the greatest sense of discontent tended to be more active in the protest than were the relatively contented (see Table 14-7). Almost a third (32 per cent) of the students who rated the South as either 1 or 2 on the race relations ladder took an active part in the protest. Only 26 per cent of those who rated the region at 3 or 4, 25 per cent who rated it 5 or 6, and only 8 per cent of those who rated it at 7 or 8 were equally involved in demonstrations. Or, to look at the table in a different way, 56 per cent of those students who thought race relations were very bad failed to take any part in the movement, whereas 76 per cent of those who thought race relations were reasonably good neither joined protest groups nor took part in the demonstrations.

These figures by themselves might seem to suggest that the major motivating forces behind the sit-ins and freedom rides were anger, hatred of and hostility toward whites, and alienation from a white-dominated world in which it was the students' misfortune to have been born with a dark skin. This, however, is not the case.

TABLE 14-7.
Extent of Student Participation in the Protest Movement,
by Their Ratings of Race Relations

LEVEL OF PARTICIPATION IN THE PROTEST MOVEMENTS	RATINGS OF CURRENT RACE RELATIONS IN THE SOUTH			
	(Worst) 1 or 2	3 or 4	5 or 6	*(Best)* 7 or 8
Active personally	32%	26%	25%	8%
Belonged to protest group but not active personally	12	11	17	16
Neither active personally nor member of protest organization	56	63	58	76
TOTAL	100%	100%	100%	100%
N	25	96	118	25

Examine Table 14-8. It contains a set of statements about white people in the South and their treatment of Negroes, along with the percentage of the active protesters, inactive members of protest organizations, and nonparticipant students who agreed with each statement. Only 6 per cent of the participants in the sit-ins and freedom rides agreed that "all white people are prejudiced against Negroes," whereas 22 per cent of the inert students believed this statement to be true! Although the difference in attitude between the students with varying degrees of involvement in the protests is smaller for the other statements, the more active students consistently are more tolerant, understanding, and optimistic about white people and segregation than are the inactive students.

The same conclusion is supported when we examine the students' estimates of white opinions on racial questions. Seventy-seven per cent of the Negro students who correctly perceived that "all" or "most" southern whites favored "strict segregation" were totally inactive in the protest movement, whereas those who underestimated the extent of white opposition to Negro demands were far more actively involved (see Table 14-9). The student protesters apparently were not "the children of despair"[15] but of hope and optimism.

The students who actively participated in the protest movement during its early stages felt relatively fortunate when comparing their lot to that of other Negroes in the South. Thus, for example, we find

TABLE 14-8.
Percentage of Negro Students Agreeing With Statements
Indicating Racial Hostility, Pessimism, and Despair, by
Extent of Their Participation in Protest Movement

	LEVEL OF STUDENT PARTICIPATION IN PROTESTS		
STATEMENT	*Active in protests (N = 65)*	*Belong to protest group but not active (N = 38)*	*Neither (N = 161)*
All white people are prejudiced against Negroes.	6%	3%	22%
In spite of what some people say, when Negroes are arrested in the South they do receive fair treatment.	26	39	20
I have seen so much unfairness to Negroes that I don't believe you can ever change the attitudes of white people in the South.	5	8	16
The southern Negro does have a chance to make something of himself.	98	97	96
All white people are alike.	2	0	6

that those students who believed that race relations were better in their home towns than in the South as a whole participated more actively in the protests than those who felt that they had been raised in communities with relatively poor race relations (see Table 14-10). This conclusion presents an apparent paradox. At the beginning of this section we argued that the students who were most discontented with southern race relations tended to participate most heavily in the protest movement. Now we find that the active students felt a greater sense of relative advantage than did the inactive ones! But these attitudes need not be in conflict: quite different standards seem to have been used in arriving at these two judgments. *Compared with other Negroes,* the student protesters felt relatively fortunate. But *judged by absolute standards*—what they felt they deserved as *men*—they felt shabbily treated indeed.

TABLE 14-9.
Negro Student Perceptions of White Support for Strict
Segregation and Extent of Their Participation
in Protest Movement

LEVEL OF PARTICIPATION IN THE PROTEST MOVEMENT	*STUDENTS' PERCEPTIONS OF PROPORTION OF WHITES IN SOUTH FAVORING "STRICT SEGREGATION"*		
	All or most	*About half*	*Less than half*
Active personally	13%	26%	33%
Belonged to protest group but not active personally	10	27	7
Neither active personally not member of protest organization	77	47	60
TOTAL	100%	100%	100%
N	82	85	96

Another psychological characteristic of the active student protesters was their superior factual knowledge of the world outside the South and the Negro ghetto. When we gave the students in our sample a shortened version of the political-information test administered to the adult sample, the protesting students answered more questions correctly (an average of 2.3 out of 4) than the inactive students (1.9). The same protesters read more newspapers (an average of 2.5) than the inactive members of protest groups (2.3) or the totally uninvolved (1.9). The same was true of magazines: the protesters on the average read 3.3 magazines regularly; the nonactive members, 2.8; and the inactive students, 2.7. The protesting students also watched TV and listened to the radio more than the inactive students did. Frequent personal contacts with whites in a variety of circumstances was also positively associated with active participation in the demonstrations. So, too, was travel outside the South. Without a superior acquaintance with the world at large, the Negro youngsters might have remained content with their lot as the most privileged members of a large group of "second-class citizens." But with this knowledge came new standards and reference groups that apparently made this once comfortable status increasingly unbearable.[16]

TABLE 14-10.
Negro Students' Sense of Relative Advantage and Deprivation
and the Extent of Their Participation in
the Protest Movement

LEVEL OF PARTICIPATION IN THE PROTEST MOVEMENT	STUDENT BELIEF ABOUT RACE RELATIONS		
	Better in home community than in South as a whole	*Same in home community as in South as a whole*	*Worse in home community than in South as a whole*
Active personally	33%	23%	15%
Belonged to protest group but not active personally	13	16	15
Neither active personally nor member of protest organization	54	61	70
TOTAL	100%	100%	100%
N	115	62	87

Thus a psychological analysis of the early student protesters does not reveal a portrait of bitter, alienated, and
deprived agitators or "beatniks." Rather, the Negro activists
tended to be unusually optimistic about race relations and
tolerant of whites. They not only *were* better off, objectively
speaking, than other Negroes but *felt* better off. At the same
time, they were far better informed than other Negroes about
the nonsegregated world outside the South. This resulted in a
sense of relative deprivation when they compared their chances
with those of middle-class whites and the values professed by
the white community. Thus the active protesters felt deprived
by "white" or general American standards of judgment at the
same time that they felt relatively advantaged by Negro standards. This distinctive combination of conflicting feelings may
well be, as Brinton argues, a precondition for all rebellions. At
least they seem to have touched off the student protests of
the early 1960's.

*The College Community and Student
Protest Activity*

Despite overwhelming student approval of the objectives and methods of the protest movement, the extent of protest activity varied a great deal from one college campus to another. (See Figure 14-2.) In 20 out of the 30 institutions in which we held interviews, more than 80 per cent of the students approved of the resort to direct action; in all 30 schools a clear majority of the students favored the protest movement. Yet in six colleges, not one student in the sample personally took part in the demonstrations or belonged to a protest organization; in five more institutions, less than 20 per cent of the sample had done either of these things.

FIGURE 14-2.
Variation Between Institutions in Student Approval of an
Involvement in the Protest Movement

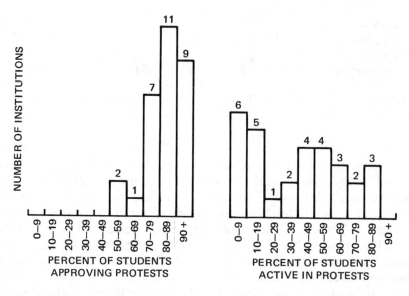

Moral approval is private and cheap; active involvement in a political movement requires a willingness to pay costs and run risks, which for the student protest movement were unusually high. Even so, we would expect to find a positive association between student attitudes at a college and the same students' rate of participation in the protests. The actual Pearsonian coefficient of correlation between student support for and participation in the protests, by college, is +.51. This is a respectably high figure; but it means that only 25 per cent (r^2) of the variation in protest activity from college to college is "explained" by student attitudes. Being a student in some Negro colleges must have made it easy to translate favorable attitudes into action, whereas being a student in other colleges must have made it hard.

Negro colleges differ in a number of ways that may help account for the variations in student protest activity. Eighteen of the colleges in our sample, for example, were state institutions; 12 were private. Although both types of institution depend in large part on white acceptance and financial support, the public colleges are far more vulnerable to pressures from the white community. Financial dependence on private philanthropy (largely northern) differs greatly from financial dependence on a southern state legislature enraged by the "irresponsible" and "revolutionary" activities of "ungrateful" Negro students. The movement threatened more than just the financial support of state schools; many white politicians reacted to the demonstrations by threatening to fire college administrators and professors, to expel students, even to close the Negro schools altogether if the students did not stop forthwith. In some cases these threats were carried out. Understandably, therefore, many administrators of state-supported Negro colleges did everything they could to discourage student participation in the protests. Even without cues from administrators, many students would hesitate to engage in activities that they felt threatened the survival of their *alma mater.*

The Negro colleges vary in size—most are rather small, but a few rival white institutions in size and complexity. Protest activity might be expected to flourish in the larger, more impersonal institutions in which it is harder for administrators to put pressure on individual students. Or we might expect the contrary: the closer personal ties of the small college might make it easier to mobilize student predispositions into group action. In either event, we might reasonably expect the size of the Negro school to affect the rate of student participation in the sit-ins and freedom rides.

Finally, the Negro colleges differ in that elusive attribute called academic "quality." True, no Negro institution in the South rates very well when compared with its white counterparts. Even so, the Negro schools do differ significantly in the quality of education they provide. A superior education—relatively speaking—should lead to the greater knowledge and awareness of alternatives to segregation that we earlier found associated with protest activity. In order to test this speculation, we constructed a scale of academic quality based on such generally accepted indicators as the student-teacher ratio, the proportion of the faculty holding Ph.D. degrees, the number of books in the library, and the dollars spent each year per student.[17]

In Table 14-11, we can see that all three of these characteristics —institutional control, size, and quality—were related to the student

TABLE 14-11.
Characteristics of Negro College and Student Attitudes
Toward and Participation in the Protest Movement

	N	Percentage of students favoring demonstrations	Percentage of students participating in demonstrations[a]	Percentage of students favoring demonstrations who participated[a]
QUALITY OF INSTITUTION				
Type I (best)	37	95%	54%	57%
Type II	53	91	55	60
Type III	61	80	38	48
Type IV (worst)	75	77	21	27
CONTROL OF INSTITUTION				
Private	94	91	53	58
Public	170	79	31	39
NUMBER OF STUDENTS IN INSTITUTION				
Fewer than 1,000	115	87	43	49
1,000–2,499	80	84	36	43
2,500 +	69	77	36	47
NEGRO CONCENTRATION IN COUNTY CONTAINING COLLEGE				
0%–19%	58	95	60	63
20%–39%	104	83	44	53
40% +	102	77	22	29
SIZE OF CITY OR TOWN IN WHICH COLLEGE LOCATED				
100,000 +	109	89	50	56
10,000–99,999	100	78	40	51
Less than 10,000	55	82	17	21

[a] Personally active or belonging to protest organization.

attitudes toward and activity in the protest movement. The proportion of students *favoring* the sit-ins varied from 95 per cent at the best Negro colleges to 77 per cent at the poorest, from 91 per cent in private institutions to 79 per cent in public schools, and from 87 per cent in the smallest colleges to 77 per cent in the largest colleges. These differences in attitudes are relatively small, however, compared to the differences in *participation rates* at these same types of school. Fifty-four per cent of the students at the best colleges either took part in the demonstrations personally or belonged to a protest organization, while only 21 per cent of the students at the poorest institutions were that active. Fifty-three per cent of the students at private colleges were involved in the movement, compared to only 31 per cent at public colleges and universities. The size of the institution seemed to make the least difference in the rate of student participation—43 per cent of the students at the smallest and 36 per cent of the students at the largest colleges either took part in the demonstrations or belonged to one of the protesting organizations.

Finally, note that these same three characteristics of the Negro colleges are related to the proportion of the favorably inclined students who became activists. The mobilization of latent support into active involvement was much more complete at the better, private institutions and slightly more effective in the smaller schools.

The Negro colleges differ not only in their size, quality, and sponsorship but also in the nature of the communities in which they are located. A number are in small, black-belt towns; others are in urban areas with a relatively small Negro population. One would expect more active white hostility to the sit-ins and freedom rides in the first type of setting than in the second. As we can see by referring again to Table 14-11, student protest activities varied according to the size of the place in which the college was located and the proportion of Negroes in its population. Sixty per cent of the students at colleges located in counties with populations containing less than 20 per cent Negroes—and hence characterized by more enlightened white racial attitudes—became protesters; only 22 per cent of the students at colleges in places with populations containing 40 per cent or more Negroes took part. The difference between the most urban and the most rural schools was just about as large.

This entire picture is complicated by the fact that all these characteristics of the colleges and their communities are closely related to one another.[18] Generally speaking, the better colleges tend to be privately controlled, relatively small and located in larger cities with relatively low Negro concentrations compared to the countryside; the poorer institutions tend to be relatively large, public, and rural. When we examine the associations between each of these five characteristics and student protest activity, controlling for all the other factors, two variables emerge with substantial and independent impact on student participation in the protests: the quality of the school, and the degree of Negro concentration in the county in which the school is located (see Table 14-12).

TABLE 14-12.
Quality of College, Negro Concentration in County Containing College, and Student Attitudes Toward and Participation in the Protest Movement

*COLLEGE
CHARACTERISTICS*

Quality	*Percentage Negro in county*	*Percentage of students favoring the demonstrations*	*Percentage of students participating in movement*	*Percentage favoring demonstrations who participated*	*N*
Good	Low	94%	69%	73%	52
Good	High	92	33	36	36
Poor	Low	88	41	47	111
Poor	High	73	14	20	62

NOTE: "Good" quality = types I and II; "poor" quality = types III and IV. Low Negro concentration = 0–39 per cent Negro; high Negro concentration = 40 per cent and above. Participation in movement = personally active or belonging to protest organization.

Can we conclude that variations in student protest among the Negro colleges are largely the result of the quality of education the students received, modified by the varying degrees of white hostility and resistance they faced in their college communities? This certainly is a plausible interpretation of the data introduced so far, but it overlooks one very important factor—the selective recruitment of students. Earlier we found substantial class differences in the level of student protest activity, and the higher-quality schools attract more high-status students than do the inferior schools. These middle-class Negro youngsters may have *come* to college with the attitudes and cognitions that we found to be associated with active protest.

This is true—up to a point. But the kind of school the Negro youths attend still makes a large difference in their participation in the protest movement *after we have controlled for their social class* (see Table 14-13). The low-status students who attended the better

TABLE 14-13.
Family Income and Percentage of Students Participating
in the Protest Movement, Controlling for
Characteristics of College

COLLEGE CHARACTERISTICS		*FAMILY INCOME*	
Quality	Percentage Negro in county	Less than $5,000	More than $5,000
Good	Low	65% (17)	71% (35)
Good	High	35 (17)	32 (19)
Poor	Low	32 (57)	54 (52)
Poor	High	9 (45)	26 (19)

NOTE: See note to Table 14-12.

institutions were just about as active in the protests as were their more fortunate fellow students. In the relatively inferior schools, the high-income students participated much more than the majority of students who were not so well off. But even under these circumstances, the quality of the school and the degree of Negro concentration in the college community were more predictive of student participation in the protests than was the income of the student's family.

The inter-institutional variations in protest activity by students do not, then, appear to be solely the result of selective recruitment. Rather, they seem to flow primarily from the differing quality of the educational experience itself, modified by community differences in white resistance, actual or anticipated.

The Protester as Student

So far we have tried to explain student participation in the protests of 1961 and 1962 without examining our subjects' most central role—that of student. We have found that the active protesters tended to come in disproportionate numbers from middle-class families and urban places where race relations were relatively benign; that they tended to be relatively optimistic, tolerant of whites, and well informed; and that they tended to be students at the better Negro colleges located in communities where white hostility to the protests was likely to be relatively mild. But what kind of *students* were they? And were their characteristics *as students* related to the extent of their activity in the protest movement?

The answer to the last question is definitely "yes." As Table 14-14 shows, the frequency with which Negro students took part in the protests increased moderately from the freshman to the sophomore year. A much sharper increase took place between the second and third year. When we examine the seniors, we find that an impressive 45 per cent of them had personally participated in either the sit-ins or the freedom rides. Four freshmen may have begun the student protest movement, but it was the older, more advanced students who flocked to the movement in disproportionate numbers.

TABLE 14-14.
College Class and Academic Major of Students and the Extent
of Their Participation in the Protest Movement

	Personally active	*Belonged to protest organization*	*Neither*	*TOTAL*	*N*
COLLEGE CLASS					
Freshman	14%	10	76	100%	99
Sophomore	18%	16	66	100%	68
Junior	38%	19	43	100%	47
Senior	45%	11	44	100%	47
ACADEMIC MAJOR					
Humanities	46%	8	46	100%	26
Physical sciences	35%	20	45	100%	49
Social sciences	28%	20	52	100%	50
Vocational (misc.)	19%	12	69	100%	45
Education	12%	11	77	100%	73
Business administration	11%	11	78	100%	18

A tempting conclusion is that the educational efforts of the colleges had something to do with this—that the increase in participation among upperclassmen was the result of their having attended more lectures, read more books, and taken part in more dormitory bull sessions than the younger students—in a word, that they were more fully educated. Americans of all colors have great faith in the power of education to shape opinions and behavior and to "solve" problems, but research on the effects of formal education scarcely justifies such extreme faith.[19] Before we conclude that the college-class differences in participation result from the added education of the upperclassmen, we must dismiss a number of alternative explanations.

First, the underclassmen seemingly had a shorter period of time than the juniors and seniors in which to join the movement; the lower rate of participation among freshmen and sophomores may reflect this fact. But the freshmen could have become active in the movement before going to college—thousands of Negro high-school students did. And the movement had been under way for only about two years at the time of our interviews. Thus the sophomores, juniors, and seniors all had had the same length of time to become active *while in college*, but the frequency with which they did so was very different.

The sharp jump upward in participation between the second and third years suggests still another possibility. The Negro junior colleges all ranked rather low on our scale of academic quality, and students at low quality schools tended to be less active in the movement. The differences in participation between college classes may be merely a reflection of the fact that a disproportionate number of the upperclassmen in our sample were attending high-quality, four-year institutions. This tendency certainly does exist—the students at the poorer schools were rather heavily concentrated in the freshman and sophomore years, while the superior Negro institutions had a better balance among the four college classes. But even after we control for type of college, we find that the upperclassmen participated a great deal more than the freshmen and sophomores (see Table 14-15).

Greater learning apparently does lead to greater participation. And the second academic difference between the protesting and the inactive students substantially reinforces this conclusion: *the subjects that the Negro students were studying in college were strongly related to the extent of their activities in the protest movement* (see Table 14-14). The most active students were majoring in the humanities; 46 per cent of them were personally active in the protests. The physicists, chemists, biologists, and natural scientists generally were just about as active. Students of the social sciences were the third most likely group to become involved. Participation dropped off sharply among the large majority of students engaged in vocational studies, especially education and business administration.

How can we explain these differences in participation? Both the subject matter of these disciplines and the self-selection of students into them are probably relevant. First, the largest group of vocationally oriented students—the education majors—were preparing themselves to enter a highly segregated profession. This aspect of

TABLE 14-15.
College Class, Academic Major, and Student
Participation in the Protest Movement,
Controlling for Type of College Attended

	Good-quality, low percentage Negro	Good-quality, high percentage Negro	Poor-quality, low percentage Negro	Poor-quality high percentage Negro
COLLEGE CLASS				
Juniors and Seniors	85% (26)	67% (9)	55% (38)	29% (24)
Freshmen and sophomores	54% (26)	21% (28)	34% (73)	5% (40)
ACADEMIC MAJOR				
Arts and sciences	76% (33)	50% (18)	60% (48)	8% (24)
Vocational	58% (19)	16% (19)	27% (63)	18% (38)

NOTE: Percentages are of students with the indicated attributes who were personally active or who belonged to protest organizations. Thus the first entry means that 85 per cent of the juniors and seniors at good-quality schools in counties with a relatively low proportion of Negroes were participants.

teaching may discourage the Negro students who are most deeply dedicated to racial integration from majoring in the field, and it may attract those who are most willing to accept segregation. And looking forward to a teaching career—almost always, because of certification requirements, in the state where they are attending college—the education majors may have wanted to avoid an involvement of which their future white employers would not approve. We saw in earlier chapters that once these youths become schoolteachers they will find it difficult, if not impossible, to play a militant role in the racial politics of southern communities. Apparently most education majors accept this restraint while they are still training for the job. Indeed, to follow any strictly vocational line of study in college—such as business administration or nursing—is to prepare oneself to succeed within the confines of the existing social and economic system.

The students who choose to study one of the sciences or the humanities, on the other hand, probably have a greater interest in learning as an end in itself. In the process of their studies—particularly if they are humanists or social scientists—they become thoroughly committed to the universalistic value system of the western world that is so at odds with southern racial realities. To exaggerate a bit, the arts and sciences students are preparing themselves to judge—and perhaps change—the world rather than to rise within it. The vocational student is characterized by less exalted and more materialistic aspirations.

But, again, more mundane factors may account for differences in participation rates. The "impractical" arts and sciences attract higher-status students at all institutions—the poor boy struggling to get through college is more likely to view education as a means of occupational advancement than of acquiring "conspicuous culture." And the academically superior colleges (which tend to be private and expensive) put more stress on education in the arts and sciences than do the poorer, public institutions with their more job-oriented, lower-status clientele. These social class and college biases might account for the differences we have found in participation by field of study—but they do not. When the quality of the college is controlled, the sharp differences in participation by the students' field of study remain little changed (see Table 14-15).

Thus the more and the better the education the Negro college student enjoyed, and the more this education was concerned with the liberal arts and pure sciences, the more likely he was to become an activist in the protest movement. We cannot, of course, "prove" the ultimate "causes" of action. To "control" for all the effects of all other variables is statistically impossible, and to imagine what all these other variables are is intellectually impossible.

But formal education does appear to have played a major role in triggering the student protest movement. The *quantity*, *quality*, and *content* of the Negro youths' education were *all* strongly related to the extent of their protest activities. These relationships cannot easily be explained away on other grounds. Optimism, tolerance, factual knowledge, and rejection of Negro reference groups and values in favor of universalistic and "white" standards characterized the original protesters; these characteristics seem to have resulted, in large part, from their formal schooling. In this case at least, education seems to have played the dynamic role Americans like to assign to it. Whether the action it helped to inspire contributed to a "solution" of a "problem"—another role Americans typically assign to education—is an entirely different matter.

The Impact of the Sit-ins

The concrete results of the sit-ins were impressive—at least by the attenuated standards usually employed in measuring racial progress in the South. By September 1961 the authoritative Southern Regional Council reported that at least one establishment had desegregated its eating facilities in each of 76 cities in the old South. A majority of these successes, however, emerged in three states on the periphery of the region (Florida, North Carolina, and Virginia) and, except in Atlanta and Savannah, Georgia, not one establishment in the Deep South had given in to the protests.[20] Nonetheless, even in some cities in the Deep South people began to realize that the integration of public accommodation was inevitable. "We've been watching these freedom rides and boycotts in other cities," the mayor of Macon, Georgia, is quoted as saying in 1962, "and we're getting the picture. Even Robert E. Lee had to surrender, didn't he?"[21]

But the thousands of students who spearheaded the demonstrations were not really interested in coffee and hamburgers.[22] They were interested in achieving racial equality in the South and in achieving it quickly. It could not be achieved by applying sporadic pressure to a handful of businessmen. But the publicity the demonstrations had generated might turn the trick, and the students knew it. The protests were, in the words of one student in North Carolina, "a way to indicate our dissatisfaction with the way we are treated" and to make "the white people wake up and think about what is happening." The students were well suited to the role. They were, as a Florida sophomore put it,

... sort of "select." They are not the type of Negro that whites usually judge us by. Usually they judge us by the very low class type of Negro, and by the demonstrations they get a chance to see Negroes who are different.

The demonstrations also were a concrete way of proving the urgency and intensity of the young Negroes' demands—"We are striving for equality *and will stop at nothing* to get it!" The demonstrations were, in sum, a classic example of propaganda of the deed. We must judge the efficacy of the sit-ins and the freedom rides primarily by their effect on public opinion.

The Impact on Southern White Opinion

The contrast between the dignity and courage of the young Negro protesters and the ugly and sometimes violent behavior of their white tormentors was not easy to overlook, especially when the same awful scenes were reported day after day on the nation's TV screens and front pages. Even the Virginia *Richmond News Leader*, which prides itself on being the authentic voice of southern traditionalism, was moved to say:

Here were the colored students, in coats, white shirts, ties, and one of them was reading Goethe and one was taking notes from a biology text. And here, on the sidewalk outside, was a gang of white boys come to heckle, a ragtail rabble, slackjawed, black-jacketed, grinning fit to kill, and some of them, God save the mark, were waving the proud and honored flag of the Southern States in the last war fought by gentlemen: Eheu! It gives one pause.[23]

And, after the police in Birmingham and Montgomery failed to protect the freedom riders, the *Atlanta Constitution* wrote:

The point is not to judge the beaten, but to take a look at the beaters. . . . Either a community is going to believe in civilization or it is going to revert to the jungle. . . . To blame the violence on the demonstrators is sophistry of the most hurtful order. These people who go barnstorming across the South in busses are curious. . . .

But this is not the point of what happened in Alabama. Any man in this free country has the right to demonstrate and assemble and make a fool of himself if he pleases without getting hurt. If the police, representing the people, refuse to intervene when a man—any man—is being beaten to the pavement of an American city, then this is not a noble land at all. It is a jungle. But this is a noble land. And it is time for the decent people in it to muzzle the jackals.[24]

Nonetheless, rank-and-file southern whites remained overwhelmingly opposed to the students and their demonstrations. At the time of our interviews with adults—the sit-ins had been under way for about a year, and the freedom rides were just beginning—only 7 per cent of the voting-age whites approved of the demonstrations, and almost all of these had been convinced integrationists before the protests began (see Table 14-16).[25] The sit-ins had the immediate effect of alienating the Negro's friends while solidifying the opposition of his enemies.

Only 17 per cent of the white moderates and 34 per cent of the avowed integrationists approved of the demonstrations early in 1961. Almost 90 per cent of the segregationists clearly opposed them—about a quarter of these, bitterly so. "They think it's time to rule the world," a retired police chief in South Carolina said caustically. "They say the proprietor should close up," an elderly housewife in Montgomery remarked, "but I'd get me a bat and I'd run them out. I

TABLE 14-16.
Attitudes of Southern Whites Toward the Sit-ins,
By Their Racial Attitudes

ATTITUDE TOWARD SIT-INS	*RACIAL ATTITUDES*			
	White segregationists	*White moderates*	*White integrationists*	*All whites*
Strongly approve	a	1%	18%	1%
Approve	1%	16	16	6
Neutral, no attitude toward, uncodeable responses	7	23	34	13
Disapprove	63	53	32	59
Strongly disapprove	24	5	–	17
Have not heard of sit-ins	5	2	–	4
TOTAL	100%	100%	100%	100%
N	443	192	44	694

aGreater than 0, less than 0.5 per cent.
NOTE: "Don't know's" on racial attitude are included in percentages for "all whites."

wouldn't close up." A middle-aged butcher in Crayfish County was even more extreme: "I think white people ought to take them out and horsewhip the black so-and-so's."

Even the vast numbers of white southerners who were repelled by these violent sentiments—and the actions they had triggered—felt that the demonstrators were morally and legally wrong. "Those are privately owned concerns," a college graduate in Capital City said. "They [the Negroes] have no business going in there and making a fuss." A secretary in a south Georgia town felt ". . . they are going about this in the wrong way. They are wrong. Even in a public place you should wait until you are invited. The Negro in the South has never been invited. They are disobeying the ethical code." "After all," a Florida real estate salesman said, ". . . they *do* have facilities where they can eat. It's not a question of their being hungry."

To miss the point of these dramatic events so completely requires powerful psychological defenses. White southerners

—especially the segregationists and the moderates—apparently had such defenses. The major one was the belief that the sit-ins were the result of "outside agitation" rather than of genuine discontent over racial conditions; about half the explanations offered for the sit-ins by white segregationists and moderates and over a third of those offered by white integrationists were along these lines (see Table 14-17).

TABLE 14-17.
Causes of Sit-ins as Seen by Southern Whites,
By Their Racial Attitudes (In Percentage
Of All "Causes" Mentioned)

CAUSES OF SIT-INS	*RACIAL ATTITUDES*			
	White segregationists	*White moderates*	*White integrationists*	*All whites*
"Outside" agitation	53%	47%	37%	50%
"Inside" agitation	19	23	21	20
Agitation, general and unspecified	16	9	7	13
Spontaneous movement	11	18	33	15
Other, unclassifiable	1	3	2	2
TOTAL	100%	100%	100%	100%
N	434	218	54	706

Ironically—in view of the fact that Negro discontent with the NAACP and its legalistic strategy contributed to the demonstrations —the NAACP was seen as the moving force behind the sit-ins. "I think they are paid by this big organization," a clerk in Florida said, "I can't think of it [pause] NAACP—which Nixon is president of." Most other southerners did not confuse the 1960 Republican candidate for president with Roy Wilkins, but over a quarter of them falsely perceived the NAACP as the instigator of the movement. A somewhat smaller number (14 per cent) tended to blame the whole thing on the communists. "Khrushchev is behind all communist action in this country," a housewife in Crayfish County explained. "He says our downfall will have to be from within and this integration [movement] is promoted directly by him."

Next to the NAACP and the communists, northerners were the favorite culprits. The ideas of a semiskilled worker in rural Georgia were fairly typical:

They get started from the North; the Yankees come down here and get them started. They don't want to live with 'em, and they think if they can get us to a' mixing they [the Negroes] will like the climate here and they can send all their niggers down here to live.

"On TV," the wife of a white laborer in Montgomery said, "Negroes can be on and the whites put their arms around them. These Negroes think around here that they can do the same thing." A salesman in Arkansas was convinced that the entire movement was started by Negro entertainers in the North: "You know that tall thin Negro singer with the soft voice? He was the starter of the whole movement. He sponsored the first one and has put in much of the money." White entertainers also got their lumps. "That Dave Garroway," a housewife in Mississippi said, "I used to like him until he talked like he did about the Negroes. [We] ought to put about six in a house with him and let them stay about a week, bet he'd change his mind—after smelling them and really finding out how unclean they are in thoughts and their bodies." Finally, a retired policeman in Florida suggested why so many southern racists could not believe that the sit-ins were a genuine Negro movement. "There's never been a nigger born," he said, "with sense enough to administrate such a thing."

When asked to speculate on the motivation of the demonstrators, most southern whites again displayed their defensiveness by assigning dubious motives to the youngsters who were risking life and limb at the local drugstore (see Table 14-18). Most segregationists and moderates chalked the whole thing off to youthful exuberance ("Well, I think some do it for excitement"), a desire for publicity ("They want their names in the papers and need attention"), or immaturity and ignorance ("They're just crazy and ignorant people"). A sizable minority of white southerners were convinced that the protesters were being paid—"It's the best money for easy work." Still others felt that participation in the protests was merely the result of inborn cussedness: "Some agitators has trouble in their blood. They are just like dope addicts—until they get something started they aren't happy." Only about a fourth of the whites— almost all of them integrationists and moderates—felt that the demonstrating students were motivated by a desire for equality or moral rights.

Thus apparently the sit-ins did not convert many white southerners to the rightness of the Negro cause. Even after five years

TABLE 14-18.
Major Motivation Ascribed to Sit-inners by Whites,
By Their Racial Attitudes

MOTIVATION OF SIT-INNERS	RACIAL ATTITUDES			
	White segregationists	*White moderates*	*White integrationists*	*All whites*
Desire for social equality	12%	21%	37%	16%
Demand for legal rights	7	17	27	11
Youthful exuberance	25	21	11	23
Paid to do it	11	4	–	8
Ignorance, don't know better, duped	25	17	7	22
Communism	5	2	–	4
Love of race, etc.	5	8	9	6
Other, unclassifiable	10	10	9	10
TOTAL	100%	100%	100%	100%
N	353	169	44	576

NOTE: "Don't know's" on racial attitude are included in percentages for "all whites."

of sit-ins most white southerners were unaware of the depth of Negro discontent in the region, as we saw in Chapter Twelve. This frightening ignorance probably would have been even greater had it not been for the protests. But this heightened awareness of Negro discontent was purchased at the price of increased bitterness, tension, and defensiveness among the whites of the South.

The Impact on Southern Negro Opinion

The protests were so dramatic and so well publicized that very few Negroes in the South were untouched by them. After a year of demonstrations, only 14 per cent of the Negro adults in the South had never heard of the sit-ins, and those who had heard of them overwhelmingly approved of them (see Table 14-19). This was true even though many adult Negroes felt—quite accurately—that the "revolt" was almost as much against them and their leadership as against the dominant whites. "My idea is this," a middle-aged laundress in Piedmont County said, "We older people didn't have the guts to do it, but the young people didn't care even if they died." A white-collar worker in North Carolina agreed. "We are too complacent and slow for the young people," he said. "It's the greatest!" a laborer's wife said in Florida. "I tell you, they have courage I never dreamed of."

TABLE 14-19.
Attitudes of Adult Southern Negroes Toward the Sit-ins

Attitude toward sit-ins	*Negro adults*
Strongly approve	30%
Approve	22
Neutral, no attitude toward, uncodeable response	12
Disapprove	19
Strongly disapprove	3
Have not heard of sit-ins	14
TOTAL	100%
N	618

A new mood of impatience and militancy was sparked in Negro adults by the sight of their youngsters being heckled and beaten up by white people. A fifty-ish unemployed porter in Texas said:

I go along with them [the protesters] because I feel if we wait longer it will take longer. So they should make white people wake up to the fact that we are citizens and deserve to be treated that way. Why, all kinds of people can come to this country and receive better treatment than us. You know, even Russians—and whites pretend they hate them. But they can eat in these stores—we can't. Yet we go and die in the war to be treated this way. To hell with America if this is what it gives! White people are fakes. They are selfish and want everything for themselves.

An electrician in Capital City expressed the new mood in less extreme language. "My people have gotten tired of sitting around and waiting for Santa Claus and another Abraham Lincoln," he said in trying to explain the origins of protest activity. "They are coming to the front. And *now* is the time!"

Even the few Negroes who opposed the demonstrations often expressed admiration for the breathtaking boldness of the younger generation. "I don't like that much," a 78-year-old wife of a tenant farmer in Florida said about the tactics of the protesters. "I don't understand it much, I reckon. I don't see why—but you know, I ain't even in the same generation with them children. There is two or three generations 'twixt us, so they don't think like I do. I ain't never been skeered of white peoples, but I sure couldn't do like these children."

And some Negroes opposed the sit-ins only because they wanted something more. A semiliterate painter in Capital City spoke to this point:

We get things. Now just like we got policemans, we get colored bus drivers but they don't drive nowhere but to [slang name of Negro district] and up to the [Negro] school and some of our people is so happy 'til they busting shirt buttons. So the white people do no more cause we is satisfied. It'll be the same way with the sit-ins. They work out something somewhere and some of our folks will just get so glad they can set down by white folks 'til in the end what we got won't be worth the nights them poor people spent in jail.

The solution, as this man saw it, was a more broadly based mass movement:

What I'm driving at is, why should them few little freedom riders and sit-inners be the ones that get pushed around and put in jail and everything while all the rest of us colored folks sit back and wait to enjoy the good part? I think something orta be done but it just don't look like the sit-in is what that is. Look like to me it orta be something all of us work at. Then it would mean more to everybody.

This frustrated activist was soon to have his wish. The sit-ins, by arousing new feelings of racial pride, self-confidence, and impatience with moderation in the Negro population, provided the necessary conditions for the mass protests that followed. This was, perhaps, the most important consequence of the sit-ins.

The Impact on Northern Opinion

The protest movement, when viewed as a propaganda or educational campaign, was not aimed exclusively at a southern audience. The sit-ins, freedom rides, and other forms of mass demonstrations sought to catch the attention of the nation and the

world—and they did. They made "the Negro problem," which
northern whites preferred to forget, the number-one domestic
problem of the country. And certainly the protest movement was far
more favorably received in the North than in the former Confederate
states. Sympathy and support for the protesters poured into the
South—in the form of volunteers, money, and sympathetic treatment
in the mass media. The federal government responded to this new
concern by taking a more aggressive stance in dealing with civil rights
violations in the South. Finally, in the wake of the Birmingham riots
of 1963, President Kennedy proposed a new civil rights act that was
to become law after his death in a far tougher form than he or most
political observers had thought possible. All these developments can
be traced back to the day in Greensboro, North Carolina, when four
young Negroes sat down at the lunch counter in Woolworth's.

But as the mood and tactics of the movement spread northward
and into such areas of interracial contact as housing, employment,
and schools, some whites in the North became concerned and fearful.
Responsible men began talking of a "white backlash." By 1963 a
nationwide survey conducted by Louis Harris for *Newsweek* magazine found that most northern whites favored racial equality in the
abstract but felt strongly that the Negroes were moving too far too
fast. They were also opposed to the direct-action tactics of Negro
protests.[26] The attitudinal gap between southern and nonsouthern
whites on the race problem was still wide, but the gap between black
and white, regardless of section, was beginning to look even wider.

Footnotes

[1] This description is drawn from Daniel H. Pollitt, "Dime Store Demonstrations: Events and Legal Problems of the First Sixty Days," *Duke Law Journal*,
Vol. 1960 (1960), pp. 315-65; and Virgil C. Stroud, *In Quest of Freedom*
(Dallas, Texas: Royal Publishing Co., 1963). Professor Stroud is a member of the
faculty at North Carolina A. and T. College.

[2] Pollitt, *op. cit.*, p. 318.

[3] These estimates were made by the authoritative Southern Regional Council,
"The Student Protest Movement: A Recapitulation," September 1961, p. 3
(mimeo.).

[4] Louis E. Lomax, *The Negro Revolt* (New York: Harper & Brothers, 1962),
pp. 122-23.

[5] Southern Regional Council, *op. cit.*, p. 3.

[6] Pollitt, *op. cit.*, p. 332. The other examples of violence also are drawn from
this article.

[7] Southern Regional Council, *op. cit.*, p. 1.

[8] Lomax, *op. cit.*, pp. 73-74.

[9]*Status of School Segregation-Desegregation in the Southern and Border States* (Nashville, Tenn.: Southern Education Reporting Service, 1960).

[10]Lomax, *op. cit.*, ch. 8.

[11]Southern Regional Council, "The Student Protest Movement, Winter, 1960," February 25, 1960, pp. 2-5 (mimeo.).

[12]This and subsequent figures on the attitudes and behavior of Negro college students are based on interviews with a random sample of southern Negro students enrolled in accredited, predominantly Negro institutions of higher learning in the 11 states of the South. The sample is described in Appendix A.

No doubt students tended to exaggerate the extent of their activity in the protest movement, just as some adults falsely claim they voted in the last election or took part in other praiseworthy activities. The 24 per cent figure is therefore probably a bit high.

[13]At the time these protest activities began, they seemed clearly contrary to prevailing legal concepts of property rights and local ordinances regarding trespassing and disturbing the peace. Subsequent Supreme Court decisions [*Burton* v. *Wilmington Parking Authority*, 365 U.S. 715 (1961); *Lombard* v. *Louisiana*, 373 U.S. 267 (1963)] and the passage of the 1964 Civil Rights Act greatly narrowed the area of racial discrimination permissible by "private" agencies. In *Bell* v. *Maryland*, 378 U.S. 226; *Barr* v. *Columbia*, 378 U.S. 146; *Barrie* v. *Columbia*, 378 U.S. 347; *Robinson* v. *Florida*, 378 U.S. 153; and *Griffin* v. *Maryland*, 378 U.S. 130, all decided on June 22, 1964, the Court reversed convictions for trespass or disturbing the peace without deciding the constitutional issue of whether an individual can practice discrimination in his place of public accommodation with the support of state police and courts to enforce the practice.

[14](Englewood Cliffs, N.J.: Prentice-Hall, 1952), p. 278.

[15]*Ibid.*, p. 278.

[16]Ruth Searles and J. Allen Williams, Jr., in "Negro College Students' Participation in Sit-ins," *Social Forces*, Vol. 40 (1962), pp. 215-19, developed the notion of the shifting reference groups of the Negro protesters. Our analysis has been substantially influenced by their thinking.

[17]See Appendix C for the construction of this scale of academic quality.

[18]The extent of the association between each of these variables can be seen from the matrix of coefficients of association (Q) below:

	Academic quality	Public-private control	Percentage Negro	Size of town
Public-private control	− .75	—	—	—
Percentage Negro in county	0	+ .72	—	—
Size of college town	+ .10	− .68	− .91	—
Size of college	− .29	+ .95	+ .52	− .39

Variables must be dichotomized in computing Q, and the values obtained vary somewhat according to how this is done. The above coefficients should therefore be considered as approximate.

[19]Thus, V. O. Key, Jr., in *Public Opinion and American Democracy* (New York: Alfred A. Knopf, 1961), p. 343, concludes: "In the largest sense the educational system is a great mechanism for conserving the values, the institutions, the practices of the political order. . . . Yet the educational process does not completely embalm the political system. From it there come the political innovators as well as the conservers."

[20]Southern Regional Council, *op. cit.*, pp. 14-15.

[21]*Wall Street Journal*, February 6, 1962.

[22]A professor of the four freshmen at North Carolina A. and T. quotes one of the original protesters as saying, "We didn't want to set the world on fire—all we wanted was to eat." (Stroud, *op. cit.*, p. 18.) This may have been true for the original four protesters, but it certainly was not true for the thousands of other students who later joined the movement.

[23]February 22, 1960.

[24]May 22, 1961. For an analysis of the dubious propaganda value of the freedom rides, see the Southern Regional Council, *The Freedom Ride*, May 1961 (mimeo.).

[25]Only a longitudinal study could demonstrate this point conclusively. Given the evidence on the stability of white racial attitudes presented throughout this book, however, this seems to be a safe assumption to make in analyzing these data.

[26]William Brink and Louis Harris, *The Negro Revolution in America* (New York: Simon and Schuster, 1964), ch. 9, especially pp. 144-45.

The Berkeley Campus in the Twilight of the Free Speech Movement: Hope or Futility?

Robert H. Somers

In the fall of 1964 on the Berkeley campus of the University of California, a student uprising called the Free Speech Movement (FSM) shocked the world of higher education.[1] Since then, stimulated in part by the Berkeley movement, a rash of student disorders have appeared both in this country and abroad.[2] How did Berkeley students view the success of the Free Speech Movement? How did it affect their attitudes toward campus politics, toward the University, and toward future student protests? What was the campus mood by the time the "FSM generation"—those who entered the University in 1964—was preparing to graduate?

Hoping to answer these questions, and hoping also to provide a meaningful educational experience for my class of 120 under-graduates in social research methodology, I initiated an interview survey of a representative sample of the entire student body in February, 1968. Analysis of information from this survey is especially interesting because it can be directly related to two earlier surveys. One of these, which I also conducted as a class project, was made in November, 1964, during the height of the Berkeley rebellion. The second was executed some months later, in the spring of 1965 by Kathleen Gales, then a visitor from the London

School of Economics. Partly at my urging, she replicated many of
the questions that had been asked in my earlier, smaller interview
study.[3]

These earlier studies suggested that the campus protest was
based fundamentally on political grievances of the students rather
than on the nature of quality of education at the University. Students
appeared generally satisfied with their education but felt restricted in
their right to express freely their political opinions.[4] There has been,
since these surveys, a surfeit of proposals for educational reform,
accenting small classes, more active participation of senior professors
in undergraduate teaching, commensurate restriction in the use of
teaching assistants in large lecture courses, more intimate advising, and
so on. I suspected that these proposals were not directed to the major
problem and undertook the new survey to explore this suspicion.

There are those who argue that it is not possible to obtain
adequate and accurate survey information by using student interviewers in a class project. Students, they suggest, will elicit responses
from other students that conform to their own prejudices and may
even cheat on the interviews in response to the pressure of their
other academic and extra-curricular commitments. My experience in
conducting a survey in 1964 challenged this.[5]

In addition, interviewing a student population is a pleasant task
for several reasons: not only do they easily understand fairly
sophisticated questions, but also they have usually formulated
opinions in advance of the questions; the articulate student population is continually discussing common issues in terms shaped in part
by the one community newspaper—on this campus the student-run
Daily California. The selection of a sample of students—we
interviewed 492 in 1968—is easily accomplished according to
statistically valid methods since the whole population of registered
students is available in files assembled by the registrar.

Our interviewing was conducted in late February and early
March of 1968, a short time before the announcement by former
President Lyndon Johnson that he would not seek re-election and
that he would initiate Vietnam peace talks, and also prior to the
assassinations of Martin Luther King, Jr. and Robert Kennedy. Thus
the opinions we collected reflect student political sentiments in the
early months of a momentous year. With major student disorders yet
to occur in New York City and Paris, and the following year in San
Francisco and Berkeley, and elsewhere, opinion from the Berkeley
campus during a period of relative quiescence is of special interest.

In some of the material that is reported here I have made
separate tabulations for students who were on campus during the
Free Speech Movement and for those who were not here at that
time. It should be noted that the students with FSM experience,

remaining on campus in 1968, should not be viewed as a representative sample of all students who were on campus in 1964, as many had graduated and some—perhaps the most alienated—had left school for other reasons.

The Campus Mood in Early 1968

What was the campus mood in early 1968? Asked whether "the campus administration can or cannot *usually* be counted on to give sufficient consideration to the rights and needs of students in setting University policy," 46% of the 1967-1968 student body said it could not, and 23% said they weren't sure. The remainder, a third of the campus, said they thought it could. This is a considerable decrease from 1964, when a majority (56%) agreed that they could count on the administration to protect students' interests. It was my impression from personal observations in 1964 as well as from the survey conducted at that time that students were then generally optimistic about the responsiveness of the University administration to their demands and that many of the demonstrators risked arrest and expulsion by "sitting in" at Sproul Hall—the campus Administration Building—in December, 1964, with great hesitation and timidity. At that time most students manifested a sense of "reluctant desperation" about such provocation, feeling it was their only remaining method to demonstrate the strength of the conviction that they should be able to express their political views. Since that time, the mood appears to have changed. Not only did students in early 1968 place less trust in the Administration as a protector of their interests, but a larger proportion of them (from 51% in the spring of 1965 to 71% three years later) argued that they should have more control over educational policies on campus. To quote a later editorial in the *Daily Californian*[6], there had developed "an atmosphere of mutual disgust and alienation," a mood that pervaded "many of the relationships between students, faculty and the Administration."

A part of this student attitude stemmed from the fact that late in 1967 the Chancellor determined that the student government (ASUC - the Associated Students of the University of California) has illegally permitted graduate students to vote in the student election. He responded to this alleged infraction by removing the ASUC's authorization to collect and appropriate funds and by transferring financial operations of student government to a new "Program and Facilities Board" under his control. In commenting on this move, the student editorial continued,

Student frustration has grown especially desperate this year (1967-8) as a result of Chancellor Heyns' blatant intervention into student affairs through his transfer of ASUC funds to his self-styled Union Program and Facilities Board. [The student government is now discussing with legal counsel the possibility of taking this matter to the courts.] The confused, paralyzed state of student government and the ineffectiveness of its leadership have also compounded the feeling of helplessness students experience in trying to bring change through normal channels. The sterile rhetoric and tactics of evasion employed by the Administration in responding to student initiative continue to denigrate the integrity of students. We are becoming convinced that it will take another cataclysmic protest similar to Columbia's to make this campus receptive to basic change and more consistent with the ideals of education.

Was this searing editorial the rhetoric of a few alienated campus radicals? Such an interpretation would be mistaken, but not unlike views expressed in the early weeks of the Free Speech Movement. Only after the free speech crisis of 1964 did most observers become aware that as many as one-third of the 27,000 students on campus supported not only the goals, but also the tactics of the demonstrators and that another third, while rejecting the tactics, supported the goals. Early commentators argued that a small group of demonstrators who were more loyal to Maoist China than to American principles of democracy and who were perhaps instigated by outside agitators, was the heart of the movement. That was not the case at the time. Nor, apparently, can the vituperativeness of the student editorial writer be shrugged off in 1968.

A review of campus events in 1967-68 should be useful. In mid-October, 1967, students taking part in a nationally-sponsored "Stop the Draft Week" planned an all-night "teach-in" to organize protest against the Vietnam war and support for possibly obstructionist demonstrations at the Oakland Induction Center. Although there was much controversy about the content of such a meeting, Chancellor Heyns agreed to permit the use of campus facilities for the "teach-in" and sought to ensure that illegal actions, such as violation of the Selective Service Law, would not be advocated. Just prior to the teach-in, however, the Alameda County Board of Supervisors obtained an injunction against the University to prohibit the meeting. The Chancellor's office complied with the injunction, and students coming to the planned teach-in found the Student Union locked and dark. The teach-in was held outdoors, with privately owned sound amplification equipment, in violation of campus rules. In part as a response to the violent behavior of the police at a sit-in at the Oakland Induction Center early the next morning, students again assembled in violation of campus rules the following night. Campus authorities subsequently cited 80 students for violation of campus "time, place and manner" rules. A week later the injunction by the County Supervisors was withdrawn, and in the course of later developments, students rallied to the support of the cited students, holding a "mill-in," congregating in and around the Dean's office to protest the suspension of two students. But by the early part of December students sensed the futility of such demonstrations. Realizing support was insufficient, the movement voted, early in December, to suspend further protest activity until the Spring quarter.

Since these developments suggested that a student strike was imminent, (it did not take place) we asked students in our 1968 survey: "If students demonstrating against political suspensions were to call a student strike this spring, do you suppose you would support or oppose them?" Forty-three per cent of our sample claimed they would support such a strike. Seven per cent said they would support it to the extent of risking arrest or expulsion, if necessary. Projecting this 7% into numbers of students in the campus population, and assuming that only half of those would actually take such a drastic step, perhaps 800 students would become so involved. The figure compares well with the 800 persons arrested in the major sit-in of the FSM. Of the remaining students, a quarter felt undecided about supporting such a strike, while a third were opposed.

The FSM in Retrospect

The typical Berkeley student, in other words, seemed as inclined to protest and demonstrate in 1968 as he was in 1964. Yet the expected student strike did not emerge. Was the relative quiescence on campus early in 1968, one legacy of the Free Speech Movement? Some insight into this possibility was obtained by asking students who were here at that time to relate how they felt at the time of interview about the movement and about campus developments since that time.

In considering the attitudes of students toward the FSM, it is useful to make a preliminary ordering of students in terms of the existing political subcultures on campus. For this purpose I have categorized students who claimed that a specific ideological statement was an "accurate reflection" of their views. Four statements were formulated in the interviews:

A. American society is basically unjust, and revolutionary changes are needed.
B. American society is basically unjust, but the needed changes can be made within the system.

C. American society is basically just, but some important changes should be made.

D. American society is basically just, and no changes are needed.

For convenient reference in the following discussion, I shall refer to students acceding to statement A as "radicals;" those to statement B, "reformers;" those to statement C, "moderates;" and those to statement D, "conservatives." There are of course many issues involved in such labeling, and this simple procedure is not intended to imply that the problem of identifying political ideology is not complex. However, this procedure has an advantage over others that are sometimes used in that students are not categorized at all unless they claim a statement is an accurate reflection of their views. Thoughtful students frequently resist such labeling, and indeed, 35% of the student body accepted none of the above statements without qualification. Of the remainder, 14% classified themselves as radicals, 11% as reformers, 39% as moderates, and 1% as conservatives.

Nearly three-fourths of the 1967-68 Berkeley student body was not on campus during the FSM, but many claim to have supported the movement even though they were not here at that time. Forty-nine per cent of the 1968 sample say they supported the FSM (thirteen per cent gave it whole-hearted support) and only 12% say they opposed it; the remainder took no stand. Not surprisingly, radicals were much more inclined to say they supported the FSM; reformers and moderates less so. In our sample, all of the 21 students who were on campus at that time and who in the interview called themselves radicals said they supported the movement, but only 53% of the moderates with direct FSM experience said the same. Reformers took an intermediate position and conservatives were too few to be tabulated.

To what extent did students see the FSM as successful in achieving its goals? We asked students precisely this question, both at the time of the FSM and again in 1968. "Completely successful," replied 13% of the student body in 1965, and 3% in 1968. In retrospect, there was less enthusiasm for the outcome than in those heady days when, particularly because of the ratification by the Academic Senate of the "December 8th" resolutions liberalizing regulations covering "time, place, and manner" of student political activity, it appeared that the movement had achieved significant gains. Eighty-eight per cent of the campus claimed the FSM was at least partly successful in 1965; the figure was down to 67% three years later.

What did students in 1968 who experienced the disorders of 1964-65 mean by a "successful" FSM? It meant various things to various students. Interestingly, some who still acclaimed it as a success expressed themselves primarily in terms of the fact that it mobilized the student body and made them, and others, aware of the problems on the campus. "The FSM was a success because it led to a chain of events so that people started asking questions and became aware of things," remarked a senior in architecture who was politically conservative and opposed to the movement. The more politically radical students were likely to phrase the outcome in terms of heightened political awareness of the student body. A senior in anthropology, a radical and unqualified supporter of the move-ment, remarked that "What the FSM did was not so much to change institutions, but change student attitudes toward radical politics." Other students, especially those who opposed the movement, spoke in different terms, considering the movement a success because the student demonstrators temporarily had the upper hand on campus. A conservative senior in economics, an unqualified opponent of the FSM felt, "The FSM was mostly a success because the students were better organized than their opponents. They temporarily achieved predominance in the balance of power." A common view among conservatives was that the Administration was ineffectively weak.

In spite of the fact that most students considered the FSM a success, they agreed that there have been few lasting gains in terms of changes in the institutional structure of the University. The anthropology major cited above, for instance, went on to say: "But we will have the same problems today in a different form." Another radical supporter of the movement expanded upon this theme:

> I don't think the FSM really achieved its stated goals. The Administration has effectively nullified most of the so-called gains—especially in regard to the time, place and manner rules, as witnessed by the recent suspensions.

Students who viewed the movement as a failure were likely to emphasize a continuing unresponsiveness of the Administration. A qualified supporter of the movement, a history and sociology major, suggested that the FSM was mostly a failure because "the attitudes of the Administration toward students have not changed." Another noted that it was a failure because "It is impossible to change the basic structures of the University from within." And an opponent of the movement spoke in the same terms: "The FSM was mostly a failure because you can't see any tangible results of the movement." Expanding on this, a liberal Republican who opposed the methods employed by the free speech demonstrators but who would in 1968 support a strike, suggested that "the campus is pretty much the same. Students don't have much more to say than they used to have." And another, a history major who was politically moderate and a liberal Democrat, said "the immediate goals of the movement were achieved, but now the campus has returned to the previous state, if not worse." Not surprisingly, the more radical the student, the less likely he was to claim the movement a success. Among all students in the 1968 sample, 82% of the moderates (and an even higher proportion of moderates who supported the movement) considered the FSM a success; 62% of the radicals did.

One expects the memories of a series of campus crises like the FSM to be modified and perhaps distorted in time. There was a tendency for the student body in 1968 to idealize the movement in a sense—students were less likely in 1968 than in 1965 to consider the leaders of the demonstrations "power seekers who have no limits to their demands." Forty-four per cent of the campus agreed with this in the spring of 1965 despite the widespread support for, and apparent success of, the movement. In the present survey, only half as many students took this view of the leadership. On the other hand, they appeared more sophisticated in 1968 than in 1965 about campus politics and recognized that the University administration was not the autonomous power they once thought it to be. Three-fourths of them agreed in 1965, that the University administration was "largely to blame for the whole situation." Only 44% agreed to that statement in 1968. Apparently there was a tendency to shift the blame to outside forces that intruded too heavily on the University. Sixty-three per cent of the 1968 sample viewed the University as "too closely tied to the Establishment;" a statistic that now seems to me to be as significant as any other that has been gathered.

Criticisms of the Educational Process

Among the many continuing responses to the crisis that erupted on this campus in 1964, one of the most prominent is the assumption that the campus is an impersonal and bureaucratic organization, dehumanizing in its impact on students, and in need of drastic reorganization. The Report of the Select Committee on Education of the Academic Senate (the "Muscatine Report")[7] is the most widely circulated of the many reports, critiques, and discussions that have been presented on this topic. It is argued that the campus has grown too large, that students resent being treated in an impersonal way—the IBM card was a pervasive symbol of student discontent during the brief student strike in late 1966—and that consideration should be given to their individuality by advisors and teachers. The University has come to be viewed as a factory, producing skills needed for our technologically advanced society. In 1964, Paul Goodman[8] suggested that:

> At present in the United States, students—middle class youth—are the major exploited class. . . . The labor of intelligent youth is needed, and they are accordingly subjected to tight scheduling, speedup, and other factory exploitative methods. Then it is not surprising if they organize their CIO. It is frivolous to tell them to go elsewhere if they don't like the rules, for they have no choice but to go to college, and one factory is like another.

It is important to consider the extent to which Goodman's analysis of the Free Speech crisis provides an accurate understanding of the basis of the student protest movement. Aware of such criticisms, we asked students in each of the three surveys how satisfied they were with various aspects of the educational institutions on campus. Indeed, it was surprising to find that at about the same time Paul Goodman's remarks appeared in the midst of the campus crisis in the fall of 1964, our survey showed 82% of the campus to be "satisfied with courses, examinations and professors" at the University. Since that time the degree of satisfaction has declined somewhat, to 77% in early 1965 and to 69% in 1968, but it was still relatively high. This suggests that dissatisfaction with *educational* practices was not the principal basis for student unrest on this campus. Students are critical. If they were protesting educational practices, they would not claim to be generally satisfied by them. There were of course, few students who were completely satisfied with the nature of their education at the University. Scathing criticisms of particular professors or particular grading practices could be heard. Yet I think they were not primarily focusing their rebelliousness on the quality of the education they received.

A commonly heard complaint is that the University employs graduate students as teaching assistants in large lecture courses. Students were given an opportunity to criticize this practice when asked whether "the system of using teaching assistants works well at this University." Rather than criticize the system, 56% agreed in 1965 that it worked well, and 58% agreed in 1968.

One would surely expect students to be critical of large classes if they are affronted by the impersonality of the Multiversity. A third of them did agree—the figures in 1965 and 1968 are almost identical—that "some of my classes are so large that it is difficult for me to get much out of them." But one-fifth strongly disagreed. This does not seem to be a sufficient issue to provoke mass protest. Another common criticism of this University is that the faculty, generally renowned, frequently traveling for professional purposes, spend too little time with their students. When students were asked if "most of the professors at Cal are more interested in their research than in their students," 48% disagreed in 1965; 44% in 1968. The major change in response to this question is that students in 1968 were more likely to admit they didn't know the real interests of faculty (22% say "don't know" in 1968 vs. 9% in 1965), perhaps reflecting an increased awareness that, for many faculty, conflicts result from excessive demands on their time. Students are certainly not reluctant to criticize faculty. Nearly three-fifths of the campus maintained in 1968 the view expressed in 1965 that student evaluations should be an important factor in the hiring and firing of faculty members.

In certain respects the campus is an impersonal institution where students may feel lost in the bustle of tens of thousands of students and more than one thousand faculty members, but there are many good opportunities for students to meet each other. A third of the student body said, in 1965, that they often felt lonely on campus. By 1968 the percentage had decreased slightly to 26%. This shift may be a result of the greater freedom that students feel to express themselves now that there is public awareness of problems at the University. Or perhaps the appearance of a "hippie" style of life in the San Francisco Bay area, bringing with it a new receptiveness to strangers, has had some impact. At any rate, the student response to this type of question again fails to reveal widespread sentiments of disaffection and criticism.

On one critical note students agree: the University does sometimes seem to "operate like a factory." There was less conviction about this in 1968 than in 1965 (when 33% of the campus *strongly* indicated agreement compared to 19% in 1968) but overall agreement (moderate or strong) remained at 80%. Thus we return to the imagery of Paul Goodman and finally we come to an area with sufficient agreement and strength of feeling to motivate a rebellion. But there are several different aspects to the notion of a University operating like a factory, and it is useful to consider them separately.

One plausible, factory-like image of the University is that it exists primarily to produce certain kinds of intellectual skills and to foster student development only in areas of direct productive value to the economy. The University, in this view, stands in a kind of colonial relation to the rest of society, providing technical raw materials for the imperial industrial power. Skills and subject-matters that are of no particular value to business, industry and government are not encouraged, while academic subjects of value to these sectors of the Establishment enjoy comfortable support. This conception of the University is one that emphasizes its *external* relations with society and suggests that the close ties between the University and the Establishment distort educational functions.

In some respects, student protests are directed at this image of the University, but it is important to determine in which respects. One does not find students rebelling against the general principle of government or industry support for the University, nor do they level criticism against the manner in which that support is distributed. There is, of course, more support from government and industry for technical and applied fields, but students rarely mention this fact except when such support seems to be oriented to the development of particular institutions and policies to which students are *politically* opposed. As a matter of fact, while financial support to the University does emphasize technical training, nearly all disciplines have enjoyed increased financial aid for students and for faculty research in recent years. To argue that student protests are directed against the general principle of utilization of University resources for societal interests seems too broad and imprecise a claim. Rather, it is the political nature of the interests intruding on the campus that are salient. Student rebellions have been organized against on-campus recruitment by Dow Chemical Company because Dow is the sole producer of napalm.[9] Protests have been directed against recruitment of students for employment in the CIA because of the role played by that organization in Cold War politics.[10] Other specific Establishment-University links have been attacked when students felt the University abetted forces of oppression, racism and imperialism. The Free Speech Movement, after all, traces its origins to the thwarted attempts by students to organize protests against alleged racist policies of the *Oakland Tribune*, the newspaper in an adjacent city. The first large demonstration was in support of an arrested CORE organizer. Rather than view these events as manifestations of purely *educational* problems, it seems more accurate to regard them as *political* problems of the University. They shall be reserved for separate discussion.

Another interpretation may be made of the sense in which the University operates like a factory. Students may view the University with a Chaplin-like imagery where efficiency of product ranks supreme. To economize in the production of knowledge, classes must be large, and faculty few. To substitute for trained faculty, it is necessary to use fledgling faculty, that is, graduate students who assume professorial functions as "teaching assistants." Because an adviser to consider the "whole student" is not necessary to produce a technologically trained intellect, the advising function in the University assumes a very minor and "one-dimensional" role. To make better use of "the plant," classes are held 12 months a year, from eight in the morning until late at night.

This image of the factory is salient in Goodman's remarks. It can be caricatured, but it has some real elements. However, it seems to be more a source of rebelliousness among *faculty* than among students. Faculty have generally resisted the "speed-up" represented by the change-over to a quarter plan from a semester plan and have found it possible to succeed in such resistance only where they represent a sufficiently powerful professional school, such as a School of Law. Teachers find the beginning and ending of a course the most demanding on their time and recognize that by teaching a quarter rather than semester plan this demanding period is increased by as much as 50% a year. Students too, may suffer from the work overload caused by the speed-up, yet many seem willing to tackle lengthy course assignments if they are meaningful. They may resent the impersonality of large lectures, yet recently they raised a clamorous protest on the Berkeley campus regarding the failure of any Department to give a permanent position to a young scholar who amassed a large following in his short stay on campus—in spite of the fact that most students knew him only through very large, indeed, overflowing, lectures.[11] It is commonly acknowledged that some faculty succeed in being provocative and stimulating in a large lecture hall. Students may feel that the content of education is often not worth the competition for high grades but are more inclined to blame themselves than to blame the system if they get into the competitive race for an outstanding record.[12] While these pressures of mass education in the Multiversity may contribute to student restlessness and malaise, apparently they are not sufficient cause for rebellion. Across the country, students are politically active at small colleges as well as at large Universities.

Criticisms of the Political Role of University Students

Students' conception of the University as a factory is not in itself sufficient cause for rebellion; their conception of the University as a conservative force inhibiting and distorting their political visions does seem to be. In reviewing our surveys for evidence of pressure for student political autonomy, it is noteworthy that 60% of our sample is 21 years of age or older—legally, then, adult. In addition, nearly all male students have achieved adulthood in another sense—that of being subject to the draft. Because of high admission standards, students at this University are accustomed to playing an elite role in academic if not other roles. It would be surprising if they did not exert pressure for enfranchisement and for full citizenship.

In the 1964 survey, which took place when there was a great campus debate on what the real issues of the developing Free Speech crisis were, 60% of the sample reported that there was an issue of free speech on campus. They believed that students did have the right to solicit, on the campus grounds, money and support for political movements directed against off-campus institutions. Although then-President Clark Kerr argued convincingly that he had won many new rights for students on a campus that once, in accordance with the rules of the time, denied Adlai Stevenson the right to speak on campus, students have never been content with the degree of progress represented by these changes. With regard to more recent developments, recall that support on campus in 1968 was strong for a student strike "against political suspensions." This, too, is essentially a political matter. Nationally, the student movement has been given credit for some part in the recent faltering of conviction about the efficacy and morality of our policy of escalation in Vietnam. Berkeley students—who generally refer to themselves as liberal Democrats (37%), democratic Socialists (16%), or liberal Republicans (14%)—are politically aware and politically dissenting. They were nearly unanimously (90%) disapproving, in late February and early March of 1968, of the way the Johnson administration was handling the situation in Vietnam. The same unanimity existed on the issue that Negroes did not then "have about all the rights they needed." Recalling now that three-fifths of the student-body felt the university to be too closely tied to the Establishment, these aforestated political sentiments appear to be fundamental in accounting for student unrest.

For purposes of analysis, it is useful to relate student political sentiments to the political role of students and again to recognize two aspects of this role—internal politics and the external relations of the University. Sometimes, as in the hypothetical and non-materializing student strike about which students were questioned in 1968, the two areas overlap. With regard to the political role of students *on* campus, there is continuing and perhaps increasing pressure for "student power." This can mean many different things. For instance: (a) increased student authority in areas of faculty prerogative, including curriculum, faculty selection, teaching and grading practices and the structure of educational institutions. It may also mean (b) increased student authority vis-a-vis the administration in non-political extra-curricular matters including social life, sports, entertainment, and the like. Finally, it can mean (c) an increase in student authority relative to that of the Administration, or even complete student autonomy, in areas of extra-curricular activity that have a direct bearing on politics. Each of these areas is discussed below.

It is important to distinguish between questions of student authority in educational matters—described in the preceding category—and the general question of educational reform. It is possible to restructure the University to make it less factory-like without involving students in the process at all. Perhaps this is a path some would advocate. For two reasons it does not appear that this would reduce the rebelliousness of students. For one, as I argued above, dissatisfaction with educational structures alone is not a sufficient cause of student unrest. Secondly, students feel they should have some say in how the University is restructured. In 1965, 51% of the sample expressed the need for "more control over educational policies," and by 1968 the number had increased to 71%. Clearly there is continuing and increasing pressure by students for authority in this area. Yet this pressure need not and probably will not be manifest in terms of confrontations with faculty authorities. Basic institutions have been changed by the provisions recently made for experimental and student-initiated courses, and many current institutional practices, where criticized, are relatively flexible and modified without mass demonstrations. Students find it relatively easy to initiate a course (faculty time is donated) in an area of special interest to them. There are other unobstrusive adaptive mechanisms within the institution that have come into play in recent years to take the pressure off student protests in this area. Perhaps because some of the most fundamental problems, such as the choice of appropriate content for a liberal education, are recognized by students to be complex and without simple solution, this is not an area that can evoke strong collective sentiment. Thus the role of the student in the determination of educational (as differentiated from political) policies on campus is far from perfect, but it is changing and is not a source of widespread alienation.[12A]

There are some areas of student autonomy on campus that arouse the sentiments of only a small minority of the campus, for example, extra-curricular activities outside of the political realm. Either students are largely uninterested (example: lack of participation in many facets of school athletic activities from cheerleading to football rallies), or they evolve ways of coping with dissatisfactions (manipulation of dormitory rules and other applications of the *in loco parentis* doctrine).

The third area of potentiality for student authority—that of political expression and activity—is the common subject of not only much of the rebellious sentiment manifest in our surveys, but also in the student disorders that have been occurring across the country in recent years. Students are opposed to the war in Vietnam, suspicious of undemocratic tendencies in American foreign policy in various other places, and concerned over blatant as well as subtle instances of racism in many parts of our society. They feel that the University is not playing a progressive role in society and that they are not free to express their critical political views. As evidence of growing distrust of the University Administration on the Berkeley campus since 1964 when there was mass sentiment in favor of the Free Speech Movement is the statistical finding that 56% of the sample agreed in November, 1964, and only 32% agreed in March, 1968, that the Administration could almost always "be counted on to give sufficient consideration to the rights and needs of students in setting University policy." Concerned over what they feel are inadequate safeguards of the rights of students to engage in political protests, troubled by the manner in which the Administration has not given serious consideration to the recent proposals of a Faculty-Student report and proposal on University Governance[13], they had become, by 1968, increasingly willing to strike in support of students suspended from school for their political activities. On this and other campuses, student protests have been directed against restrictions imposed on students for their activities against racism and militarism and against University entanglements in these undemocratic forces, such as cooperation with weapons industries, the CIA, the Department of Defense, and other similar organizations.

Regardless of troubling aspects of the structure of the educational establishment, I think that students would be supportive and perhaps enthusiastic participants in the University community if they considered themselves enfranchised to express their political views and if they felt that the University–through the activities of its faculty, through investment and admission practices, through cooperative arrangements with institutions in the larger society–was playing a critical and progressive role in American society, identifying and opposing sources of racism, inhumanity, and the distortion of American democratic values. It is for this reason that such recent proposals as those of former University President Clark Kerr[14] for an "urban-grant University" that would perform services for the oppressed masses in our cities, analogous to the service orientation of the 19th Century land-grant colleges, are of value and more relevant than proposals emphasizing the need for internal restructuring of the educational process in the form of "cluster colleges" and the like. While only a partial solution, if such proposals were carried out so as convincingly to free the University from close collaboration with the Establishment and place it in the service of the fundamental values of humanity and justice and what Mydral calls the "underclass" in American society, they would provide the basis for an institution of higher education appropriate to the problems and circumstances of 20th Century America.[14A]

Is it not impertinent for students to be this conscious of their political role in society? Perhaps not if they are viewed as a manifestation of a new intellectual class. The place of the intellectual in society and the manner in which scholarly knowledge is shaped by the social position of the intellectual is a dominant theme in the writings of Karl Mannheim, a German sociologist who spent most of his productive life in Britain. In *Ideology and Utopia,*[15] written at a time when fascism was beginning to disrupt the modern world, he reiterated the importance of a class of "socially unattached intellectuals" as a force capable of providing a synthesis of the conflicting strains in modern society and formulating new ideologies more appropriate to the times than those propounded by more parochial interest groups.

It would be foolish to argue that all students, any more than all members of a University faculty, are members of such an intellectual class. There are many students who, remaining in protracted adolescence, do not and may never have the ability, the background, or the will to grapple with the social and political issues of the contemporary world or to propose reflectively formulated and unprejudiced critiques. Yet there are many reasons to suggest that some of the more mature students are even more representative than many faculty of a class of intellectuals straining for a synthesis of contemporary knowledge and ideas and are more capable of suggesting paths of exploration for future generations. With fourteen or more years of formal education added to much extra-curricular reading, discussion and thought, with a modicum of economic security and freedom from family responsibility, having often made no strong career or professional commitments, intensely concerned about the hazards of living and rearing children in the modern world, students have a large measure of the classless social detachment of which Mannheim spoke. The typical faculty member at a prominent University, in contrast, is much less intellectually free, having made commitments to a specialized area of professional study, to a secure and prestigious career for himself and his family, and quite probably to the role of scientific or literary entrepreneur and/or institute administrator. If student demonstrations were viewed as the birth pangs of a new class arising from an emphasis on a higher, liberal education for all in the context of a technologically developing world—including nuclear weapons, electronic communications, mind-expanding drugs and birth control pills—then increasingly constructive suggestions for higher education would ensue.

The Political Culture at Berkeley

Various and sometimes conflicting explanations of the political radicalism of Berkeley students have been offered. An explanation emanating from the "adjustment" school of psychology[16] is that youth are radical because they are, during the college years, experiencing a new-found freedom from conservatively oriented parents. This freedom, combined with immature judgment, accounts for a particularly intense attraction to radical ideology. An alternative and contradictory explanation directed specifically to the Berkeley campus is that Berkeley is particularly attractive to the children of radical parents and that these children maintain the family political tradition by lending a radical emphasis to campus politics.

Both theories have some merit for individual cases. But the political culture on the Berkeley campus cannot be accounted for by explanations that apply to a small minority. With a majority of the students over 21, it would be inappropriate to call them immature. As for the other explanation, only four per cent of the students admit to having socialist fathers. Among the remainder, there is an even division between liberal and conservative fathers and between Democrats and Republicans. The most outstanding characteristics of the political orientations of Berkeley students in relation to those of their fathers are that they are more liberal than their fathers—two-thirds of them have moved at least one step to the left of their father on the political spectrum—and that they are only a little more liberal, not radically so. Only 6% are more conservative than their fathers.

This political mobility to the left from one generation to the next should not be viewed as a descriptive historical fact since it may be that the more liberal children elect to study at Berkeley, while the less liberal children choose other Universities. Nevertheless, it might support the notion that students embrace radicalism in reaction to their parents' views. The data of our 1968 sample do not lend themselves to this interpretation. Students whose fathers are conservative Republicans, for instance, were most likely (39%) to call themselves liberal Republicans. Thirty-seven per cent of the children of liberal Republicans were themselves liberal Democrats. This is also true for those whose fathers are conservative Democrats; 54% were liberal Democrats. Indeed, the attraction of the liberal Democratic label for Berkeley students in 1968 was strong—37% of the students accepted it. It was the most popular choice even for students whose fathers were also liberal Democrats. The few students with socialist fathers did tend to maintain the family politics, but even some democratic socialist fathers spawned liberal Democrats. Radicalism of political label may seem salient at Berkeley because it is openly advertised and espoused, but it in our data was far from the norm. Yet militant opposition to the University administration was the norm.

One can ask if these liberal Democrats on the Berkeley campus were not an unusual breed, espousing revolution while choosing less than revolutionary political labels. Apparently, this was not the case. When asked to select the ideological position that most closely reflected their views, liberal Democrats preferred the "moderate" position: "American society is basically just, but some important changes are needed." This was said to be an "accurate reflection" of their position by 43% of the liberal Democrats and interestingly, was the most popular choice of all political groups on campus, except for the socialists, who generally adhered to the most radical position (with many exceptions among the democratic socialists).

With such widespread campus support, militancy in 1968 was obviously not confined to campus radicals. Of those who identified themselves as liberal Democrats, 41% said they would support a strike against political suspensions, as did 23% of those who identified themselves as liberal Republicans. Twenty to 30% of these groups were undecided about their support for a strike. Stated differently, four-fifths of the strike supporters on campus considered themselves Democrats. Since Democrats are most numerous on campus, this is not surprising. Democratic political views also prevail among opponents of the strike. But it is not true that the 18% of the campus who identified themselves as socialists were the only militants.

The liberal Democrats also happened to be the most widely split on the issue of strike support. While some 60% to 80% of the more conservative political groupings (conservative Democrats, and Republicans whether liberal or conservative) were opposed to a strike, and 60% to 80% of the most leftist groupings (democratic and revolutionary Socialist) would have supported the strike, 41% of the liberal Democratic students would have supported the strike, 30% would have opposed it, and 29% were undecided. The ambivalence of the liberal Democrats is further indicated by the fact that no other political grouping had such a large "undecided" response.

In Conclusion

Why did a Berkeley student strike fail to materialize in the spring of 1968? One can only speculate. It is of course possible to question the validity of responses to our interviewers on support for such a strike, but—as noted below—there is no clear evidence for such skepticism. Perhaps questions about a hypothetical event like a strike are not accurate predictors of behavior, yet the alienation from institutional governing methods manifest in responses to them, certainly is symptomatic of an unhealthy academic community. One might argue that as a result of their experience with the Free Speech Movement, students have a sense of futility about the effectiveness of mass demonstrations. Thus, while students generally viewed the FSM as a success, they also argued that institutions could not be changed from within the University. They may have taken the view that another mass demonstration would have had about the same results as the one in 1964; that is, it would temporarily have achieved some immediate gains. But it would also have disrupted the careers of campus officials, who were not the actual sources of authority, and would again have failed to effect fundamental structural changes. We have some data that pertain to this sense of futility. In November, 1964, students were asked to recall what they felt were the chances, during the early demonstration in September of that year, of the demonstrations succeeding to the extent that students could recruit members and solicit funds for off-campus political activity. Fifty-seven per cent of the sample felt there was a "fair to good" chance of this degree of success. Thirty-four per cent felt there was a similar chance that students would gain full rights of freedom of speech. But only 12% felt there was a chance of students "becoming an autonomous group." When asked about the possible effects of a strike in the 1968 survey, the student body, more politically aware than three years ago, was less optimistic about short run gains. Only 30% felt there was a "fair to good" chance of getting suspended students reinstated, and only 26% believed it likely that students would gain full rights for student political activity. Yet, compared with 1964 percentages, a somewhat larger figure—22% compared to 12%—felt that there was a chance of students becoming an autonomous group. There does appear to be a sense of futility about achieving immediate gains from the Administration, but there is more awareness of the possibility of achieving a fundamental change in the political position of the student in higher education. Part of the explanation for the quiet campus in the spring of 1968 must surely be that students were less likely to blame the University Administration for their grievances and more likely to see the Administration—to the extent that it suppressed their political autonomy—acceding to the demands of more powerful interests outside of the University.

At the same time, it seems unwarranted to argue that the survey data are irrelevant to overt political activity. The 1964 survey revealed percentages—such as the estimate that one-third of the campus agreed not only with the goals but also with the tactics of the FSM—commensurate with estimates of the size of supporting demonstrations in that movement. Another conjecture regarding the

lack of large-scale disorder on the Berkeley campus is that circumstances conducive to mass protest on campus did not materialize.
Such circumstances are of two kinds: relevant issues and effective
leadership. The suspension of students for political activity during
the preceding autumn quarter created the issues. Effective leadership
of the student movement, leadership that would have mobilized
support by articulating grievances, focusing attention on particular
events, and providing a rationale for particular tactics, did not
appear—in part because, without an easy scapegoat (in this case, the
Administration) a rationale was more difficult to provide.

Whatever the reasons for the failure of an organized student
protest movement in the winter and spring of 1968, it is clear that
the Berkeley student body was not satisfied with its role on campus
nor with the place of the University in society. To ignore this
alienation and discontent is to do a disservice to the idealism of
youth and ultimately to many fundamental values in American
society.

Footnotes

[1]For some reports and interpretations see S.M. Lipset and S. Wolin, eds., *The
Berkeley Student Revolt* (Doubleday: New York, 1965); M. Miller and
S. Gilmore, eds., *Revolution at Berkeley* (Dell: New York, 1965); and H. Draper,
Berkeley: The New Student Revolt (Grove: New York, 1965); "News and
comment," *Science*, 148 (1965) pp. 198-202 and 346-349; "A season of
discontent," *California Monthly*, 75 (Feb., 1965) whole issue; and "Chronology
and documents," *California Monthly*, 75 (July-Aug., 1965), pp. 48-63;
S. Warshaw, *The Trouble in Berkeley*, (Diablo Press: Berkeley, 1965); the files of
the *Daily Californian*, the student newspaper at the University of California
(Berkeley); and J. Byrne, "Report on the University of California and
Recommendations to the Special Committee of the Regents of the University of
California," May 7, 1965, unpublished.

[2]See, for example, the Annual Education Reviews of the *New York Times* for
recent years and also H. Bourges, *The French Student Revolt*, (Hill and Wang:
New York, 1968); J. Avron, *Up Against the Ivy Wall: a History of the Columbia
Crisis*, (Atheneum: New York, 1969); "Special Issue: The Universities," *The
Public Interest*, 13 (Fall, 1968) whole issue; "Students and Politics," *Daedalus*,
97 (Winter, 1968) whole issue; "Stirrings out of apathy: student activism and
the decade of protest," *The Journal of Social Issues*, 23 (July, 1967), whole
issue; and *American Behavioral Scientist*, 11, (May-June, 1968), whole issue;
A. Silver, "The University Rebellion," *New York Review of Books*, 12, (30 Jan.
1969), pp. 15-24; H. Aiken, "The Revolting Academy," *New York Review of
Books*, 11 (11 July, 1968), pp. 30-35; F. Dupee, "The Uprising at Columbia,"
New York Review of Books, 11 (26 Sept. 1968), pp. 20-38; H. Arendt,
"Reflections on Violence: A Special Supplement," *New York Review of Books*,
12 (27 Feb. 1969), pp. 19-32; and "Students and Society," Occasional Paper of

the Center for the Study of Democratic Institutions (Santa Barbara, Calif., Dec., 1967).

[3]It is obvious that without the often willing cooperation of students in my large classes in social research methodology in the Fall, 1964 and Winter and Spring, 1967-68, I could not have obtained these data. I am indebted to Professor Gales, London School of Economics, for cooperating in a similar program of research, Spring, 1965. See also K. Gales, "A Campus Revolution," *British Journal of Sociology*, 17 (March, 1966), pp. 1-19.

[4]R. Somers, "The mainsprings of the rebellion: a survey of students at Berkeley, November, 1964," in Lipset and Wolin, eds., *op. cit.*, pp. 530-57.

[5]In the spring of 1965, the staff of the Byrne subcommittee of the Regents of the University of California requested permission to use survey material gathered by my class in 1964 and by Professor Gales's class in 1965. They also asked permission to have the interviews checked for bias by a commercial polling agency. Results of this independent check showed that student interviewers—judging from answers they gave to the same questions—did not bias the results. See "A critique of two surveys of students' attitudes toward the 'Free Speech' demonstrations on the Berkeley campus of the University of California," Field Research Corporation, 14 April, 1965, unpublished.

[6]Editorial, *The Daily Californian*, May 6, 1968, Vol. 198, p. 8.

[7]Report of the Select Committee on Education, *Education at Berkeley* (Academic Senate, University of California, Berkeley, 1966).

[8]P. Goodman, *The New York Review of Books*, 3, January 14, 1965, p. 5.

[9]*Science* 158, pp. 1289-94 (1967).

[10]*New York Times* November 7, 1967, p. 84, *ibid.*, August 25, 1968, p. 52.

[11]*Daily Californian* 193 (March 2, 1967), p. 1.

[12]B. McGuire, *Daily Californian* 198, (May 21, 1968), p. 9. The essay begins, "I have just been informed that I have the highest grade-point average of any graduating senior in the College of Letters and Science (at the University of California, Berkeley). The first thing I would like to say is that it was not worth it."

[12A]Since this was first written in June, 1968, the controversy over whether or not Eldridge Cleaver should be permitted to lecture in a student-sponsored course in the autumn of 1968 led to interference, widely interpreted as political (rather than simply educational), by the Regents of the University (including Governor Reagan) that has led, by the spring of 1969, to a widespread disenchantment from the institutional developments that earlier seemed to be responding to student concerns about curriculum. This is evidence that in many regards the content of education cannot be separated from political concerns, and underlines the extent to which seeming educational problems are in fact of a political nature.

[13]Report of the Study Commission on University Governance, *The Culture of the University: Governance and Education* (The University of California, Berkeley, 1968); see also Dissenting Report, Study Commission on University Governance, *The Challenge to the University* (The University of California, Berkeley, 1968).

[14]Clark Kerr, "Higher Education in the Troubled City," *Lowell Lectures*, Harvard University, April 1, 1968.

[14A]Again, since the paper was written the appearance of a strike on the Berkeley campus led by the Third World Liberation Front has changed somewhat the nature of student protest at Berkeley. Many new issues have been raised in a movement that has not received widespread support from non-Third World students, but one of these issues, that a new institution, such as a College of Third World Studies, should be instituted on the campus and be responsive to the needs of people in Black, Asian and Mexican-American communities in California seems to emphasize the pertinence of such proposals as those recently made by ex-President Kerr.

[15]K. Mannheim, *Ideology and Utopia* (Harcourt, Brace and World, New York, 1964), pp. 153-164.

[16]R. Heyns, *The Psychology of Personal Adjustment* (Dryden, New York, 1958), p. 436. [In addition to other irrational attractions] "Communism usually has the added advantage of representing a belligerent departure from parental beliefs." Such a view, if not placed in proper perspective, could create ill will for the author who is now Chancellor of the University of California at Berkeley.

[17]I am indebted to the Committee on Research and the Office of the Chancellor of the University of California, Berkeley, for financial assistance in collecting the data which form the basis for this report.